SELF, EARTH & SOCIETY

Alienation & Trinitarian Transformation

THOMAS N. FINGER

InterVarsity Press
Downers Grove, Illinois

InterVarsity Press® is the book-publishing division of InterVarsity Christian Fellowship®, a student movement active on campus at hundreds of universities, colleges and schools of nursing in the United States of America, and a member movement of the International Fellowship of Evangelical Students. For information about local and regional activities, write Public Relations Dept., InterVarsity Christian Fellowship, 6400 Schroeder Rd., P.O. Box 7895, Madison, WI 53707-7895.

Scripture quotations, unless otherwise noted, are from the New Revised Standard Version of the Bible, copyright 1989 by the Division of Christian Education of the National Council of the Churches of Christ in the USA. Used by permission. All rights reserved.

ISBN 0-8308-1893-6

Printed in the United States of America ∞

Library of Congress Cataloging-in-Publication Data

Finger, Thomas N.
    Self, earth & society: alienation & trinitarian transformation/
    Thomas N. Finger.
        p.   cm.
    Includes bibliographical references.
    ISBN 0-8308-1893-6 (alk. paper)
        1. Alienation (Theology)   2. Trinity.   I. Title.
    BT731.F56   1997
    233—dc21   97-30739
                                                                                                              CIP

15	14	13	12	11	10	9	8	7	6	5	4	3	2	1
07	06	05	04	03	02	01	00	99	98	97				

Abbreviations

CW   C. G. Jung. *Collected Works.* Edited by Herbert Read, Michael Fordham and Gerhard Adler. 22 vols. New York: Pantheon, 1953-.

TDNT   Gerhard Kittel and Gerhard Friedrich, eds. *Theological Dictionary of the New Testament.* 10 vols. Grand Rapids, Mich.: Eerdmans, 1964-1976.

TDOT   G. Johannes Botterweck and Helmer Ringgren, eds. *Theological Dictionary of the Old Testament.* Grand Rapids, Mich.: Eerdmans, 1974-.

INTRODUCTION

*T*wentieth-century existence has been shaped by rapidly accelerating complexity and change. As the twenty-first century approaches, nothing indicates that this pace is slackening. Whereas home computers, for instance, were relatively rare in 1980, by 1990 computer training had become standard fare in grade-school curricula. Increasingly computer competency, including mastery of repeated software alterations, is becoming mandatory, even for many low-level jobs. In addition, whereas most international communication in 1990 was limited—fast but expensive phone calls or several days by post—e-mail, faxes and videoconferences now connect people with other continents almost instantaneously.

Amid such swiftly shifting complexity, one of our era's most pressing tasks continues to be that of finding and developing a reasonably integrated, stable self. "Indeed, perhaps the most generally accepted characterisation of the modern state of mind is that it is a condition in which the 'struggle to be a self' is nearly impossible" (Frosh 1991:5). Ever faster alterations in technology and business organization make it increasingly difficult for people to discover their vocational identity. (Recent college graduates, it is said, may well make major career changes four times during their working lives.) As breadwinners transition from job site to job site, from school to school and into new careers altogether, they and their families pass through numerous brief, tangential and often superficial relationships.

Such encounters expose them to divergent lifestyles, beliefs and morals, making the task of determining their own guiding values more rudderless and diffuse. Through such processes, families themselves often crack, rendering identifications with new and old parents, siblings and other relatives confused, insecure and shifting. Although such multiple experiences may open up bright possibilities of self-discovery for some, many find it increasingly difficult to align the heterogeneity of relationships, values, demands, attractions and repulsions they experience with any relatively abiding, stable sense of self.

Concern with finding ourselves has occupied our culture throughout this century, and this fixation has increased during the last decade or so. The psychology section of paperback bookstores has expanded into sections on self-help, recovery, addiction and more. Two of every five Americans participates in some variety of small group with self-discovery on its agenda. Despite the threats of managed care to curtail psychotherapy, millions of Americans continue to exhibit a pressing need for it.

This interest in self-discovery has hardly bypassed the churches. Seminary courses and degrees in pastoral counseling proliferate, even while funds for positions in these fields are likely dwindling. Psychological themes and jargon flavor sermons and adult Christian education, and interest in the disciplines of spirituality has expanded far beyond its conventional location within Roman Catholic orders (see chapter five). Church practices, as well as general public experience, attest that finding ourselves keeps getting more difficult as the new century approaches.

The twentieth-century sense of instability, however, has hardly been confined to the inner, psychic world. Social systems and international relations have undergone frequent upheaval while for more than fifty years the nuclear menace has silently but pervasively threatened all life. Continuing pollution of air and water and rapid mineral, agricultural and arboreal exploitation are producing climatological and ecological adversities of global proportions. These plague the continuance of many livelihoods, the health of many communities and the quality of life for just about everyone.

At first glance these psychological and ecological problems seem unrelated. One deals with the inner citadel of the individual but the other with the broadest of earth's biospheric interconnections. One focuses on the personal and the spiritual, the other on the scientific and the physical. One is the concern of individual therapists and small groups, the other of international social, political and economic institutions.

However, as one examines both public and religious literature on these issues, the contrasts begin blurring. Countless environmentalists stress that our treatment of nature will not alter unless we develop a deep inner sensitivity, or spirituality, toward the nonhuman world. This needs to include an increasing contentedness and centeredness within ourselves so that we need not keep exploiting creatures around us to fill inner voids. Psychological and spiritual spokespersons maintain that being cut off from natural environments intensifies our sense of personal rootlessness and that to develop our affective dimensions we need to increase our appreciation of the natural world.

Further, it becomes clear that both psychological and ecological alienation have socioeconomic sides. Environmental problems are more likely to arise, for instance, when economic and social systems are geared to ever-increasing development and consumption. Psychological problems are more likely to emerge when these systems place individuals in relationships of competition or depersonalization. One begins wondering how closely the social processes that disintegrate the self might be related to those that despoil the earth.

Current public conversation, then, hints in various ways that today's quests for finding the self and healing the earth may be interconnected and that both may be shaped by current socioeconomic forces. However, few articles or books explore connections among these dimensions in depth.[1]

Contact points do begin to emerge, though, when one turns to explicitly Christian works. Although writings in pastoral psychology seldom mention our nonhuman environment, the burgeoning spirituality movement often glances in this direction. Also, during the last ten years, works in ecological theology have begun appearing. Although psychology or spirituality seldom supply the central focus of these works, all recognize the importance of this dimension.[2] The time seems ripe, then, for inquiring into how today's concerns for self-formation and for earth healing might be related.

Purpose of This Book

The major purpose of this book is to examine the interconnections among what I will call psychological alienation (of oneself from one's deepest self), ecological alienation (of technological civilization from its nonhuman environment) and social alienation (of individuals and groups from each other, from social institutions and from their social potential). My investigation will be theological in character. The kind of theologizing employed could be called a "critical conversation" with contemporary culture (see Browning 1987:1-17) or perhaps a "public theology."

Though this work will touch on many specific, practical issues, as a theological endeavor it will be chiefly concerned with the most basic intellectual and attitudinal assumptions, frameworks and worldviews with which people approach issues concerning the self, the environment and society. It will be most occupied with those assumptions, frameworks and worldviews which connect with questions of life's deepest meaning and ultimate values—issues which relate to what theologians call God. Theology is a discipline which reflects on these issues explicitly. Yet its considerations carry relevance far beyond debates among academics, for everyone's attitudes and activities are affected by some such general outlook. By means of explicit intellectual considerations, then, theology seeks to inquire into the perspectives which underlie the most widespread forms of current spiritual sensitivity and practical orientation.

By calling my style of theologizing a "critical conversation with culture," I mean that it begins by analyzing ways in which certain issues are being discussed in what we might call "public discourse." It then identifies the major assumptions, worldviews and values operative in these discussions. Finally it brings these into dialogue with *Christian* assumptions, worldviews and values. My approach could also be called "public theology," although it does not share one major assumption of many endeavors that go by this name. Some people argue that to be properly "public" a theology must support its claims on philosophical grounds that every open-minded thinker can affirm. It must not, that is, base its arguments on beliefs unique to Christian tradition (for instance, by appealing to Jesus as authoritative).[3] I reject this contention for two main reasons.

First, it seems to imply that a fairly definite body of assumptions, beliefs and kinds of evidence which "rational" people can accept exists and operates as the criterion for what can and cannot enter public conversation. In actual public conversation, however, many different issues come to the fore, and diverse kinds of arguments often emerge to support them. Some arguments have specific religious premises (such as some used in debates about abortion). It is frequently difficult to determine in advance which kinds of arguments and evidence will be widely accepted and which will not. In other words, a precisely specifiable, unchanging body of standards for public credibility seems not to exist. Novel kinds of claims introduced from unusual perspectives may gain surprisingly large hearings.

Second, what many groups, including the majority of religious groups, consider most important to them are not beliefs they share in common with others but claims distinctive to themselves (such as Christianity's unique beliefs about Jesus). If a theology is restricted to communicating in the public arena only those claims that can be affirmed by a general epistemology, it may be prevented from contributing what is most distinctive to the faith it represents.

When a perspective seems quite foreign to accepted ways of thinking, however, it can come to be more widely accepted in at least two ways. First, the more it can be shown to have a coherent internal logic, a certain inner consistency, the more plausible will it appear. Second, it will seem more persuasive the more that it makes sense out of certain particular issues considered vital on the public scene. Though these two criteria fall short of proving that a given perspective is superior according to one uniform body of standards, they seem to operate, in actual fact, as major reasons some positions receive public hearings.

On the other hand, even though no precise boundaries or standards appear to demarcate the actual, living realm of public *conversation,* it does seem that general distinctions can be made among kinds of *discourse* operating within it. Specifically we may call all argumentation which is clearly grounded in premises distinctive to a particular religion *religious discourse.* All more general kinds of argument designed to appeal to broad spectra of persons we may call *public discourse* (though these do not exhaust the realm of living *public conversation*). Since this distinction can be made, it is normally possible to first focus on the broader ways in which current issues are being discussed *(public discourse),* and then to ask what approach a distinctly Christian theology (a specific *religious discourse*) might make to them.

This is the path that my "critical conversation" with current culture will take. It does not preclude the possibility, however, that theological arguments, or *religious discourse,* might sometimes be operative in *public conversation* or, more important, that theological arguments such as those I will formulate might eventually impact this arena.

Progression of this Book

Since issues of alienation have aroused widespread public concern, I will examine them first (in part one).[4] Many approaches to these themes fall into one of two broad perspectives.

The first I call "conflictive." It assumes that some significant tensions will always exist among whatever phenomena make up the self, ecosystems or human societies. Thus the best possible solution will consist in creating some imperfect measure of balance among these perpetually conflicting components.

The second worldview I call "organismic." It assumes that beneath all conflicting elements a more primordial, virtually ideal harmony exists and that the solution to conflict consists in finding ways to actualize this harmony. The three chapters in part one (chapters two, three and four) will consider, respectively, public discourse on psychological, ecological and social alienation.

Since my main concern is Christian theology, part two will press on to current theological explorations of these three areas. I will consider those theologians whose writings have been most widely read. In dealing with psychological alienation (chapter five), most of the recent spiritual writers I consult will affirm an organismic perspective. Current writers on ecological theology and spirituality (chapter six) will wholly support organicism. A widespread tendency will appear to assume that Christianity's traditional belief in a transcendent God (whose being is distinct from that of human selves and the world) has been a chief source of alienation. A God who is *distinct,* it is apparently assumed, must also be *distant* from the real concerns of selves, nonhuman nature and society and encourage "his" worshipers to be the same. The recommended solution is a panentheistic God whose being is intertwined with that of the world and selves. A theological discussion of social alienation theologically (chapter seven), however, will reveal that conflictive perspectives and an emphasis on God's transcendence carry more weight in this sphere.

Though appreciating much that current spiritual writers and ecological theologians affirm, I will find their panentheistic orientation questionable not only in light of Scripture and more traditional theology but also in response to various concrete issues raised in public discourse. Therefore part three will contain my constructive theological response. I will argue that the Christian God is transcendent but also trinitarian, and therefore *distinct* but by no means *distant* from selves and the world. My trinitarianism will be rooted not in philosophical considerations but in God's historical activity climaxing in Jesus Christ. Chapter eight will show, through dialogue with today's "Jesus Seminar," how I am approaching the history of the Christ. Then chapters nine, ten and eleven will sketch my constructive approach to the psychological, ecological and social issues raised in previous sections.

Many ecological theologians claim that traditional Christian theology is outmoded for reflecting on current issues. (Sallie McFague, for instance, exclaims that we face a "genuinely novel context" where "the 'old ways,' the old solutions, will not do" [1987:ix-x].) This work is written, in part, to introduce a more traditional and biblical perspective into the discussion.

Biblical and traditional resources will often be used differently from the way they sometimes have been (and quite differently from what current stereotypes might lead a person to expect). I will be maintaining, however, that the essential orientation points for addressing the issues (though certainly not all the details) can be found within them. Such a standpoint, I hope to demonstrate, hardly exempts theologians from critical and creative thinking.

To recapitulate: this work is primarily a theological exercise concerned to analyze the most basic assumptions, intellectual frameworks and worldviews through which people approach psychological, ecological and social phenomena. It begins by describing current *public discourse* in these three areas (part one). It then initiates a "critical conversation" with the views presented there by outlining today's most widely read *theological discourse* on these same themes (part two). Finally I develop my own constructive position on these issues (part three). Mine is a "public theology" in that it engages current issues directly, but it is also one that contributes a distinctly Christian perspective to them.

The Term *Alienation*

Readers may have noticed that a key term—*alienation*—recurs throughout this investigation. It has been used so frequently over the past few decades and with so many diverse meanings that it might seem too overworked and diffuse to guide any focused investigation. Why use it?

In contrast to more general words such as *conflict* or *division,* alienation has the advantage of showing that the kind of separation under discussion is deeply internal in a profoundly paradoxical way to the realities under discussion (see Petrovič 1967). *Alienation,* in my usage, signifies not mere discord but a pervasive condition in which elements that belong together, which should be supporting and sustaining each other and which ultimately cannot survive apart, are profoundly estranged and hostile. Alienation occurs when deeply moving experiences are repressed from consciousness, when rains pouring off eroded hillsides wash away life-sustaining crops, when ethnic groups that should enrich each other go at each other's throats.

Alienation indicates that the dividing action is somehow internal to the reality which is divided. Yet the division does not annihilate all unity in that reality, for that reality somehow participates in its own division. The whole is not simply split into parts, of which one might be more truly the whole than others (Petrovic 1967:79). Alienation, nonetheless, is a sense of rupture so irretrievable that it leads many people (particularly those whose perspective is "conflictive") to despair. Yet the conviction that the estranged elements belong together is strong enough to persuade others (especially those whose orientation is "organismic") that these will somehow be reunited.

O N E

The Roots of
Contemporary Alienation

*T*hough *alienation* is often employed to describe our current culture, this term began being used nearly two centuries ago to indicate processes which were even then leading toward the present. In fact, forces producing the situations discussed in this book have been several centuries in the making.

Many of those concerned about current alienation claim that its origins go back to the Enlightenment. Here we can find the roots of the worldview that I call "conflictive." For many organismic theorists, this paradigm lies at the heart of today's problems. Yet it is so deeply rooted in contemporary ways of thinking that many of those involved in public conversation today adhere to portions of it. Understanding of recent discussion requires a grasp of this legacy and of how twentieth-century science is questioning it.

The Scientific Success of the Newtonian Paradigm

The Enlightenment can be regarded as roughly synonymous with the eighteenth century, though it commenced several decades earlier. Its main task consisted in taking principles that had gained unprecedented success in the scientific revolution (sixteenth century) and making them the guiding principles for society as a whole. According to the Enlightenment's "meta-narrative," which has shaped Western culture, the scientific revolution consisted in the triumph of observation and reason over tradition and authority. Up till then, scientific views, much like religious and social ones, had been based on what the Bible and ancient philosophers (especially Aristotle) had said. These views were taught for centuries by the institutional church and continued to be repeated by its authoritative leaders.

Over against this reliance on tradition—the metanarrative continues—the scientific revolutionaries insisted on empirical observation. Rather than simply assuming, for instance, that heavier bodies would fall faster than lighter ones, as Aristotle had taught, they actually dropped objects of different weights and observed what happened. They found that objects of different weights fell at the same rate. (This is what Galileo allegedly proved at the leaning tower of Pisa.)

The new sciences, however, were based not only on observation but also on a new view of human reason. Scientists proceeded on the assumption that once the empirical facts had been discovered they would prove to be linked by unbreakable natural laws. The most far-reaching discoveries occurred in astronomy and physics. Here laws were expressed as precise mathematical relationships (such as those governing planets' orbits). As scientists discovered laws in other fields, they asked whether these might also be variants of the former laws. The new science pressed toward finding several basic laws that could describe mathematically all relationships among all observable phenomena, for reason was the primary capacity by which humans could understand and govern the world.

This scientific revolution also involved a new notion of scientific explanation. Aristotle had insisted that proper explanation must describe, among other things, what a thing's nature is (of what matter it is composed) and what was its final goal or purpose.[1] (For instance, he said that heavier objects would fall faster than light ones because they were composed of more earth and that they would fall downward because the goal of all things composed of earth is to reach the earth itself.) Modern science, however, began by disregarding questions as to what things' actual natures and final purposes were. For physics and astronomy it was sufficient to know an object's mass and the strength of the forces that set or kept it in motion. All these could be described mathematically.

Modern science, therefore, began by discarding the more metaphysical questions about what things really are and what their ultimate purposes were and restricted itself to mathematical descriptions of how they behave. It began, we might say, by separating questions of essence, purpose and value from questions of fact.

To describe how things behaved, it proved fruitful to divide them into minute units and to construe their behavior as interactions among these parts. Eventually Isaac Newton (1642-1727) was able to explain the motions of all heavenly and earthly bodies by assuming that they could be subdivided into tiny, inert particles which attracted or repelled each other following three basic laws.[2] In so doing, Newton set forth a paradigm, or theoretical picture of the universe, which was to govern science until the present century.

Every particle occupied a precise point on a homogeneous, undifferentiated *absolute space* stretching infinitely in all directions, and every event occurred at a precise moment on an uninterrupted, evenly-flowing continuum of *absolute time*. All interactions among particles could be described by one master formula, which determined gravitation: the *inverse square law*.[3] Though Newton believed that God had originally created this universe, God was distant and uninvolved in its daily operation, which ticked away in self-regulating, clocklike perfection.[4]

Over the next two centuries fields of study came to be accepted as "sciences" when basic units were identified that could be treated mathematically. Electricity and magnetism, for instance, had been regarded as mysterious, perhaps even occult forces. But under Newtonian influence, scientists began conceiving of them as composed of distinct charges or particles and started measuring the force with which different amounts of particles attracted and repelled each other.

By 1800 it was determined that these forces obeyed the same inverse square law as gravitation. This set the stage for incorporating electricity and magnetism into increasingly sophisticated unified theories of forces during the nineteenth century. Chemistry, moreover, attained a scientific status around 1800 when John Dalton showed that its phenomena could be reduced to basic elements that combined according to specific numerical proportions.

Biology took much longer to be incorporated into Newtonianism. The final chapters of this attempt are still being written. In the early nineteenth century many biologists believed that an energy peculiar to life, some kind of *vital spirit*, was needed to explain organic beings. In 1828, however, Friedrich Woehler synthesized urea, an organic compound (a product of the kidney), from inorganic elements and proclaimed that all biological phenomena could be reduced to chemical ones. His conclusion, however, was debated, partly because Louis Pasteur (1822-1895) succeeded in showing that microorganisms are involved in fermentation, a process some thought to be purely chemical.

Biology, however, began isolating its particular unit of study, the cell, in the 1860s and asking how it passes on its characteristics genetically. By 1900 Gregor Mendel had shown how genetics can be studied mathematically.[5] In experiments with garden peas, he treated each inheritable trait (color, skin texture and so on) as a distinct factor and noted that each was passed on independently to succeeding generations. He then provided exact mathematical formulae for combinations among many such factors through numerous generations.

By the middle of the century the main carriers of genetic transmission had been identified as two acids (DNA [desoxyribonucleic acid] and RNA [ribonucleic acid]) consisting of a small number of chemical bases. To some, this discovery fulfilled the Newtonian dream of reducing biology to basic units and of attaining "the ultimate aim of the modern movement in biology . . . , [which is] to explain *all* biology in terms of physics and chemistry" (Crick 1966:10).

These characteristics—empirical observation, analysis of phenomena into basic units, joining these units by means of mathematical laws, disregard for issues of essence, purpose and value—gave Newtonianism unprecedented scientific success until the beginning of this century. But what of the Enlightenment's larger attempt to make these principles guiding ones for all other areas of human life? And what of the claim that this process engendered alienation?

Social Implications of the Newtonian Paradigm
The Enlightenment's leaders regarded the traditional hierarchical laws and customs of European society, which deprived the masses of power and wealth, as analogous to the faulty organizing principles of medieval science. The "scientific" task was to analyze society into its most basic empirical units, to find the actual laws which should operate among them and to reconstruct society according to this pattern. As in physical science, autonomous human observation and reason, operating without reference to any tradition or authority, were to accomplish this.

According to John Locke (1632-1704), the most basic social unit was the individual. Originally individuals had not been bound by social ties or laws but had roamed freely in a "State of Nature," doing whatever they pleased.[6] But since humans were preeminently rational beings, each person's reason provided a "Law of Nature" telling one how to act toward others. Occasionally, however, some individuals would violate this and rob, beat or otherwise oppress others. Since individuals were vulnerable to such mishaps when they dwelt alone (or in small family groups), they decided to ban together and to hand over some of their freedom to rulers who would govern and thereby protect them.

This kind of analysis, Locke claimed, indicated the proper function and limits of government and its laws. Governments (and by implication all social groups) possessed no inherent authority; they existed solely to meet the specific needs of those who formed them. Consequently a government's authority was limited to carrying out what was entrusted to it by "consent of the governed." This consent was to be determined chiefly by voting. If rulers undertook to do more than was entrusted to them, they could be expelled from office—by voting or, if necessary, by force. Locke's theory provided intellectual foundations for democracy and for the many revolutions against royalty that sprang up toward the end of the Enlightenment.

Notice again that individuals, analogous to Newton's smallest particles, are the ultimate real entities that make up society. Laws or social groupings that shape their behavior are regarded as secondary and external to these final realities. Though Locke claimed that individuals are guided by reason, he also attempted to describe their behavior in a more scientific way, as determined by sensations of pain and pleasure. Seeking to define moral terms scientifically, Locke declared that whatever "is apt to cause or increase pleasure, or diminish pain" is "good," and whatever "is apt to produce or increase any pain, or to diminish any pleasure" is "evil" ([1689] 1965:143).

Later Jeremy Bentham (1748-1832) argued that the decisive characteristic which gives a being moral rights is not rationality but sentience: its capacity to experience pain and pleasure ([1789] 1948:311). This perspective constituted many animals, in addition to humans, objects of moral obligation. Consequently it has greatly impacted today's animal rights movement (see chapter three).

In any case, the main goal of Locke's society is to leave individuals as free as possible to pursue whatever brings them pleasure and mitigates pain. Government must protect each individual from serious harm from others, and all of them from foreign enemies. Otherwise, however, it has little positive function. Government would greatly exceed its limits if it sought to legislate or in some other way tried to bring some highly ideal state of piety or justice into being.

Locke realized, of course, that in voting and advocating different government actions, individuals would often disagree. Nonetheless, he believed that if conflicting viewpoints were expressed freely, they would balance each other, much as attracting and repelling forces balanced Newton's particles, so that the most congenial solution for all would be found. Although Locke realized that some persons might remain quite dissatisfied, he affirmed a major claim of the Enlightenment, or Newtonian, paradigm: that free play among conflicting elements leads not to alienation but to the best possible overall harmony.

David Hume (1711-1776) carried this kind of moral and political thinking further. He denied more clearly than Locke that reason can discern abstract ideals of how society *ought* to be. Instead, following Locke's lead of basing moral notions on sensations, he affirmed that moral and social philosophy must be based on what *is* in fact desired by our passions.[7] For Hume too the individual was society's basic unit, for "each person loves himself better than any other single person" ([1739] 1888:487), and no one really knows what another is feeling. Yet if that is so, how can social life be more than the struggle of individuals against each other to fulfill their passions?

Hume answered, first, that despite the separations among individuals we can infer from another's external behavior that that person often feels something like we do. When this occurs, we can feel a very great *sympathy,* which involves genuine concern, for that individual. *Sympathy* enables people to join together in common causes.[8]

Second, Hume affirmed, like Locke, that primitive people sometimes sought to seize each others' possessions. However, through the chaos and insecurity spawned by this behavior they eventually learned that goods would be more secure if they adopted rules of *justice* which would protect each person's property and punish any who sought to take it. This solution worked, Hume stressed, not because justice was some stronger passion or more rational principle than selfish "love of gain," for no mental principle is stronger than self-love. Instead, when people eventually realized that rules of justice opened up better opportunities to procure and keep possessions, this acquisitive self-love itself induced them to adopt these rules. Self-love, that is, curbed itself or acquired a new direction (p. 492).

Hume acknowledged a major objection against the Newtonian social paradigm: if conflicting individual passions are allowed to operate freely, society might be thrown into chaos. Hume responded that the egoistic direction of these passions can be significantly modified by sympathy and by the experience that it can often be better satisfied by adopting some rules of restraint. Notice, however, that Hume's justice is no rational, positive notion of social balance or distribution but consists mainly of sanctions against those who would take others' property.

Adam Smith (1723-1790) applied Hume's kind of thinking to the economic sphere. He insisted, even more than Hume, that sympathy is a basic human affection, enabling deep ties among people. However, sympathy also makes people so sensitive to others' opinions that it arouses strong desires to be thought well of. This, rather than physical needs, arouses the striving for wealth, the basis for economic activity ([1759, 1792] 1976:50-51). Smith also affirmed that each person "is, no doubt, by nature, first and principally recommended to his own care" (p. 82). His *Wealth of the Nations* (1776), which became capitalism's virtual manifesto, presented this kind of self-interest as the basic human motivator ([1776] 1985:16).

Smith believed in a divine purpose for humanity: the maximization of happiness throughout the race. But he believed that this would be best attained if individuals were left free to follow their economic inclinations. Then the best economic systems would emerge spontaneously and gradually—like Locke's governments and Hume's rules of justice—from interplay among short-range, self-interested passions. To understand why Smith considered this plausible, envision a situation such as Locke's State of Nature. Here everyone would be free to produce, sell or purchase whatever they wished and to employ or be employed by whomever they chose.

Assuming that everyone would follow their self-interest, no one would produce something unless others would pay enough to profit the producer. The quantity of any item produced (supply) would thus depend on how many would pay the requisite price (demand). If demand increased, a producer might raise the price, but promise of profit would soon draw other producers into the business. That would increase the supply, and the price would eventually drop. Conversely if demand decreased, the price would drop as long as supplies remained the same. But decreasing profits would move producers to reduce the supply—often forcing some out of business—after which prices would eventually rise.

Workers' wages would be similarly regulated. Though employers, following their self-interest, would want to pay workers as little as possible, demand for labor throughout the economy would mean that workers could go elsewhere, so employers would have to offer competitive wages. Conversely though workers would want wages as high as possible, they would have to accept what employers were willing to pay in light of the labor supply.

In the short run, labor shortages could raise wages and squeeze employers, whereas surpluses could lower wages and endanger workers. Yet in the long run, Smith theorized, wages, like prices, would gravitate around equilibria most beneficial to all parties. Moreover, labor supply would be regulated like any other commodity. Increased demand for laborers would produce more (prosperity would induce laborers to have more children), whereas decreasing demand would mean that fewer were produced (pp. 81-82). Since Smith believed that industry could expand almost indefinitely, he expected the number of laborers and the prosperity of all classes to increase. Yet, since natural resources were limited, he did foresee a day in the far future when growth would cease and wages decline toward subsistence levels (p. 96).

Observe that this model, consistent with the Newtonian paradigm, allows its variables (supply, demand, prices, wages, labor pool and so on) to be quantified mathematically and relations among them to be described by equations of proportional variation. It presents a vision of a massive but intricate machinery that despite short-term conflicts might operate almost as harmoniously as Newton's natural world, could its motivating forces (individual human passions) be allowed to operate freely, unhindered by idealistic ethical notions or governmental interference.

Not surprisingly, Smith granted government only a few limited functions. First came defense. Second was justice, which, much as for Hume, meant such things as protecting property and enforcing contracts. Third came tasks too large for private effort, such as building roads, controlling bank note issues and even education.

Criticisms of the Newtonian Paradigm

I have described the origins of what I will call the "conflictive" paradigm, a paradigm which many "organicists" and others blame for much contemporary alienation. To get some sense of the current conversation, it will be helpful to briefly examine several common criticisms of it. One should not assume, however, that these remarks foreshadow an entirely negative stance toward it in later chapters.

Reductionism. Many have asked whether a person can really get at the most basic nature of anything by dividing it into its smallest units. To do so assumes that tiny "things" are the most real entities and that relationships among them are secondary and external to their true nature. In physical science this tends to imply that all things are really no more than inert matter. But biologists especially would object: are not the complex structures and interrelationships which characterize living things equally real dimensions of what they are?

This paradigm also tends to imply that human activity is directed entirely by impulses and sensations. But might not human planning, hoping and creating indicate the presence of more complex personal functions? Finally, this paradigm makes individuals the ultimate shapers of the desirable society. But might not customs, laws and corporate groupings also shape individuals even in the best of worlds? Critics charge that Newtonianism's devaluation of the more complex dimensions of organisms, persons and societies may be rooted in its basic methodological decision: to eliminate issues of essence, purpose and value.

Domination. The Newtonian paradigm claims that if individuals and their passions are allowed to connect and conflict freely, reasonably harmonious balance among them will emerge. But is that really so? Or is unregulated conflict likely to lead to greater alienation and finally to domination? Critics complain that some individuals have advantages over others and that if unregulated competition reigns among them, the latter will be victimized. This will be more true the more it is the case that social structures (governments, business corporations and so on) inevitably exert power over individuals. The more they do, the greater power will those who control such structures wield.

Several economists who followed Adam Smith predicted a dire future for many workers. Thomas Malthus (1766-1834) argued that, whereas food supplies increase arithmetically, population multiplies geometrically. Thus prosperity would increase population at a rate that would outstrip food supplies. This would force increasingly marginal land, whose produce could never keep pace with the rising demand, into cultivation. Inevitably population would decrease (many of the poorest would die). In contrast to Smith, Malthus foresaw alternating cycles of relative prosperity and want, with many workers on the margins of existence. David Ricardo (1772-1823) drew similar conclusions and defined labor's "natural price"—the equilibrium toward which market forces drive it—as subsistence.

A major reason for such predictions, of course, was that natural resources are limited, as even Smith acknowledged. If humans exploit them at whatever rate their passions urge, these resources will eventually vanish, depriving first the poor and then the larger populace of the material basis on which all economic activity depends. For this reason many current environmentalists insist that exploitation of nature cannot proceed unchecked at whatever pace people may desire but must be constrained by nonhuman nature's limits and character.

Many recent philosophers have argued that the Enlightenment notion of reason led toward domination. According to Theodor Adorno and Max Horkheimer, this concept of reason had two sides. Reason was, first, a positive means for transcending prejudices and limitations to find agreement and fashion a universal, utopian society. Yet rational knowledge also functioned negatively as a means for subjugating and controlling nature and society (1972:83-84). Adorno and Horkheimer argued that reason is likely to function in the second way when it is used simply to order and control phenomena without consideration of overall goals or purposes (p. 88). But elimination of such issues characterized both the scientific and social uses of Enlightenment reason.

Rationalism. The Newtonian paradigm has been critiqued for the superior value it accorded reason. Is reason really a sufficient guide to life? Can it reach far enough, and with enough certainty, to satisfactorily cope with questions of ultimate meaning? In dealing with such issues, might there still be some place for tradition? Moreover, to become fully developed persons, is it enough to be guided by reason, or must other capacities, such as emotions, also receive attention, lest we become alienated from our very selves?

Alienation. Consideration of the Enlightenment legacy led thinkers as far back as G. W. F. Hegel (1770-1831) and Karl Marx (1818-1883) to claim that it was creating alienation. Hegel's use of the term is many sided, and consideration of it may divert us briefly from our immediate task. Nonetheless it provides a significant background for many issues raised in coming chapters.

For Hegel the heart of reality was a cosmic rational mind called the *Absolute.* This mind, however, was originally unconscious. It began coming to Self-consciousness through an evolutionary process. At the beginning the Absolute somehow unconsciously projected (or "created") physical, then chemical, and then biological realities from itself. Eventually glimmers of self-consciousness began emerging through human beings. Each human, however, normally thinks of its consciousness as separate from that of others and of itself as over against its physical environment.

For centuries human groups regarded themselves as very different from others and experienced all sorts of conflicts among themselves. Only gradually, through the insight of philosophers such as Hegel, did it become evident that there was but one consciousness, that of the Absolute, immanent in all individual awarenesses; different individuals and groups were in fact one in their deepest essence, which was the Absolute itself. Moreover, even nonhuman nature was at one with humankind, being at bottom another of the Absolute's Self-expressions. The increasing awareness of all this was the very process of the Absolute's own coming to Self-awareness. For the Absolute, though it was far greater than any human mind, existed nowhere but in the sum total of human minds.

In this process of evolving Self-awareness, Hegel called the production of nonhuman creatures and the divisions of humans into individuals and groups the Self-alienation of the Absolute from itself. For in order for the Absolute to become Self-conscious, it somehow had to produce others who were seemingly different from itself and then, through knowing them, to eventually realize that they were not really different from itself. Alienation, for Hegel, thus consisted in the paradoxical divisions of something that was originally one.

In a certain sense, these differentiations were real, for individual and group differences were not mere illusions, and tragic conflicts often erupted among those marked by them. Yet such differentiations were not ultimate ontological distinctions, for everything was, at bottom, a Self-manifestation of the Absolute. Hegel was striving to articulate a vision of oneness more profound than mere sameness: a kind of unity-in-differentiation where unity was richer and more profound precisely because of the diversities it incorporated.

Hegel provided a comprehensive theory of physical and cultural evolution. Chapters three and six will show how it has influenced some contemporary organismic views of ecological alienation. For now, observe two ways in which Hegel related alienation to the Enlightenment.

At one stage in the Absolute's coming to Self-awareness, those persons in which this is occurring have to free themselves from an impersonal, collective sense of identity (as simply members of a state) and develop a sense of individuality. One way to do this is through pursuit of wealth. Wealth can initially give them freedom to be their own persons over against society's collective demands. Eventually, however, wealth can become an

> impersonal force which rules; men have created a monster in whom all are alienated. The quest for self-identity has culminated in the complete loss of self-identity. . . . "Capital" has become the all-embracing impersonal force which controls the whole of life. . . . "Personality" has reached its nadir, alienated in a totally impersonal power. (Lauer 1987:197; see Hegel [1807] 1931:536-39)

Hegel was claiming that during the Enlightenment, in large part, pursuit of wealth unrestrained by government seemed to be an expression of freedom. But eventually this pursuit brought the whole society under the dominion of collective economic forces which alienated everyone's freedom (pp. 559-98; see Lauer 1987:201-11).

Hegel also argued that Enlightenment individualism consisted simply in critique of collective entities such as the state and religion and had no positive content of its own. But for Hegel the type of authentic reason through which the Absolute comes to Self-expression not only criticizes impersonal collective institutions but also creates dynamic new forms of social life.

Thus Enlightenment intellectuals, by simply criticizing the reigning authorities and traditions and not creating more authentic collective traditions, alienated themselves from the sort of social life through which the Absolute could come to Self-expression. For Hegel, then, Enlightenment individualism does not bring true freedom. It either alienates its proponents from authentic social life or brings them under new collective tyrannies (such as capital).

In his own critique of capitalism, Karl Marx took up Hegel's notion that a conscious being discovers its authentic self through producing something different from itself. He emphasized that this happens for humans through labor. As I create an art object, for instance, I see myself reflected in that object; I recognize and appreciate what is "in me" only through being able to embody it somewhere outside of myself and also by having others use or appreciate it.

Before capitalism, Marx claimed, when most people worked the soil or produced crafts, they could find themselves embodied in their work and experience that embodiment, or product, being used by others. But capitalism, according to Marx, alienated humans from their labor in many ways. By manufacturing things through repetitive, mechanical motions (as on an assembly line), workers were alienated from the products of their labor—lost all sense of their work as expressions of themselves. By being divorced from the sale of these products, workers were alienated from having their labor contribute to others. By creating competition among workers, capitalists alienated workers from other workers, who should have been comrades engaged in common tasks. And these actions further alienated the working class from the capitalist class as a whole. Finally in order to fill the voids created by these alienations, workers were left with only their wages and whatever manufactured products they could purchase with them. Deprived of self-realization through the laboring process, they became passive beings condemned to search for gratification through objects produced by that very manufacturing system which had alienated them.

Summary. I have briefly traced some scientific and social effects of the Newtonian paradigm over several centuries. I have noticed various ways in which it has, according to critics, produced alienation. This paradigm has been charged with several things:

☐ fragmenting the social whole into individuals who become alienated from each other

☐ allowing massive economic forces to alienate social classes from each other and the masses of people from their true potential

☐ permitting unregulated exploitation of nature and thereby alienating industrial society from its material base

☐ alienating human reason from emotion and human creativity from its material products

Coming chapters will investigate how criticisms such as these are arising in regard to current issues and some responses to them. For now, we should perhaps notice one response that advocates of the "conflictive" paradigm often make. They acknowledge that free interaction among individual desires and economic forces involves some conflict, for the Newtonian paradigm, when socially applied, never promised perfect balance. Yet the only alternative seems to lie in granting some state significant power to set social goals and regulate individual behavior. But might not such control alienate people even more deeply from actualizing their own potential and creating meaningful relationships with others and nonhuman nature?

Twentieth-Century Scientific Challenges to the Newtonian Paradigm
The Newtonian paradigm still impacts scientific research, as my remarks concerning DNA indicate. Nonetheless its overall adequacy was successfully challenged by discoveries in physics about a century ago. Some contemporary thinkers argue that these discoveries heralded a new organismic worldview that can help overcome alienation. I will outline only the chief discoveries in physics, leaving recent biological perspectives for chapter three.

The new physics. According to Newton all objects are composed of tiny particles located at exact points in an *absolute space,* and every event occurs at a precise moment in *absolute time.* All things and processes, then, including their masses and lengths, exist within an objective framework, which is the same for all observers. However, Albert Einstein's special relativity theory, which proposed that the velocity of light was constant for all observers, produced some surprising results.

Let us picture two observers: one in the middle of a moving train, and the other standing next to it on the ground. Let us then suppose that, at the exact moment when the middle of the train passes the observer on the ground, light signals are sent out in opposite directions from the middle of the train, proceeding toward its equidistant ends. For the observer on the train, the light signals will travel *equal distances* and arrive at the two ends at the *same time.* For the observer on the ground, however, the light signals will travel *different distances* (because the front end of the train will be farther away and the back end closer when the light signals arrive there). Since the velocity of the light will be constant, the second person will observe the signals arriving at the ends of the train at *different times* (at the back end of the train before the front end) (see Gamow 1961).[9]

This thought-experiment indicates that the length of objects and the duration of events will vary for different observers—at least when processes approaching the speed of light are involved. In addition, it has been found that the lifetime of some particles traveling at very high velocities will increase when measured from a stationary point *(time dilation)* and that the mass of particles can increase at greater speeds and that their length can contract in the direction of motion.

Special relativity also broke down Newton's apparently clear distinction between matter (composed ultimately of particles) and energy (the forces operating among them), for it equated energy (E) with mass speeded up to the square of light's velocity (mc^2). Moreover, Einstein's general relativity theory converted space from an undifferentiated, empty container into a *field* contoured by gravitational forces. It also transformed material objects from discrete points into regions where these forces were constellated. Such a field is hardly independent of this matter but is "bent" by it and "curved" by gravitation and is consequently finite. In the Einsteinian paradigm, then, space, time, matter and the human observer—each of which Newton regarded as distinct—all appear to be interrelated and conditioned by each other.

Similar interrelationships began emerging as physicists investigated this paradigm's smallest entities—*quanta.* Electrons exhibited the incompatible characteristics of both particles and waves.[10] Yet it proved useful to describe electrons using both models even though, according to the *complementarity principle,* neither was reducible to the other, and the more one was employed, the less could the other be.

Further, it became apparent that whatever characteristics emerged (particle or wave) depended on which experimental system the observer chose. Quanta, that is, could never be described "in themselves" apart from an observing system. Yet even when a given system was employed, a person could not predict the precise behavior of an individual quantum but only the probability of its falling within a certain range. Laws of quantum mechanics, that is, are statistical laws concerning behavior of large groups. It is no longer possible, even in theory, to describe the exact movement of the smallest particles by deterministic laws, as under the Newtonian paradigm.

Such quanta cannot be treated reductionistically—as parts whose sums straightforwardly compose wholes. For when such particles are added to or removed from a larger system, its overall behavior alters markedly. Properties appear that did not characterize the particles separately, and the behavior of the new entity cannot be reduced to that of the sum of its components (Barbour 1990:104-6).

Additional scientific findings indicate that time moves directionally, from a beginning toward an end. According to the second law of thermodynamics, the energy available for work in the universe is continually decreasing. General relativity theory predicted that the universe is continually expanding. Hubble's Law (1929) affirmed that galaxies are rushing away from each other and that space itself is expanding. In 1965 a faint background radiation, predicted from relativity theory and conceivable as the afterglow of an explosion when all matter was infinitely compressed, was detected coming from all spatial directions. Most scientists now believe that space, time and matter themselves originated from a "Big Bang" some eight to twenty billion years ago. All events, then, apparently take place in an irreversible sequence, so the universe as a whole has a history.[11]

Some possible implications. To what extent can implications for the social sciences (and for ethics, religion and worldviews in general) be inferred from scientific theories? This issue is raised by the social dimensions of the Newtonian paradigm, and it will occupy us frequently in coming chapters. However, it will be helpful to indicate briefly the kinds of broader perspectives that many claim are at least consistent with the Einsteinian paradigm. (These persons also claim, as we shall see, that these perspectives are supported by evidence from biology and other sciences which we have not yet considered.) I am not necessarily endorsing all of them.

The impossibility of reducing all phenomena to thinglike bits of matter challenges the Newtonian assumption that individuals are the most ultimate realities. Whatever the most basic entities might be, they seem to be constituted at least as much by their relations with others as by any distinct properties. (Their relations appear to be *internal*, or dimensions of what they really are, rather than *external* to them.) Interrelatedness, then, may be at least as basic a feature of reality as "thinglikeness."

Moreover, with matter/energy distinctions breaking down, these basic entities seem to be at least as much bursts of energy as bits of stuff. Perhaps, then, life is not reducible to dead matter; matter itself may be in some sense alive. This would be consistent with claiming that humans are not directed entirely by physical impulses and sensations but may possess personal functions that transcend these. Modern physics' holistic perspective at least renders questionable the assumption that societies are ultimately composed of individuals.

Modern physics also questions whether observed reality can be sharply distinguished from human observers and whether it can be described in one straightforward factual way, equivalent for everyone, apart from issues of purpose and value. Instead, it seems that human intentions and values shape the ways in which reality is perceived and that we are deeply immersed in nonhuman actuality. That would be consistent with insisting that humans are partners with natural creatures and participants in natural processes, rather than masters over them.

Finally, physics' emphasis on time's directionality, along with general acceptance of an evolutionary outlook (see chapter three), has made process intrinsic to current science. But process seems to imply the notion of universal goals and positive directions, which were banished from the Newtonian paradigm.

To be sure, not all the above affirmations can be derived directly from the Einsteinian paradigm. My purpose, however, has been to indicate only some broader assertions that might be consistent with it.

Summary

Accelerating complexity and change in life have made the task of finding one's "self" increasingly difficult near the turn of the twenty-first century. A careful look at this struggle reveals that it is not simply a matter of individual psychology but is profoundly shaped by socioeconomic features of contemporary society. Perhaps surprisingly today's sense of our being estranged from ourselves may be closely intertwined with current industrial society's estrangement from nonhuman nature. These estrangements may be called "alienations."

Contemporary alienation is at least rooted in processes stemming from the Enlightenment. This chapter has traced the development of some of those, particularly the ones that many current thinkers connect with the Newtonian paradigm. Consequently I have sketched this paradigm's scientific foundations, its social character and some twentieth-century developments in physics that have challenged it.

Alienation signifies not simply discord or distance but that a reality which should be whole, whose various dimensions should be sustaining and contributing to each other, is tragically and destructively divided within itself. The following chapters are concerned with the alienations that appear in today's psychological, ecological and social spheres and with their interconnections.

PART ONE

Contemporary
Public Discourse

T W O

Psychological Alienation

*H*ow can a person be alienated from his or her self? At first glance the very notion seems odd, for each of us has immediate access to a constellation of memories and hopes, feelings and thoughts, delights and fears that are clearly and obviously "me." How, then, could "I" be estranged from, or fundamentally mistaken about, who my "self" really is?

A little reflection should reveal that various impulses and values inconsistent with this constellation are also experienced, and sometimes acted upon, by what is evidently "me." From beneath, as it were, disjointed, unpredictable urgings, affections and dreads press for recognition. From outside, so to speak, my behavior is molded by customs and values that I partly or strongly resist. If I am sometimes at odds with my "self," it is in part because these less acknowledged elements mesh and clash with those more familiar ones within an overall composite which "I" am.

A century ago, when Freud began deciphering the intrapsychic conflicts plaguing his civilization, the main problem might have been called one of too much depth. Faced with rather severe, widely approved restraints of a traditionalist society, individuals repressed "seething caldrons" of urges from consciousness. But in our day perhaps the chief issue is one of too much surface. Many individuals are not confronted by firm, uniform famil-

ial and social systems but by a swiftly shifting kaleidoscope of heterogeneous lifestyles, values and commercial appeals.

Fewer selves are formed through internalizing or resisting one social
option. More people struggle to discern, among the fragmentary and contradictory self-images projected on our mobile social screen, any coherent
pattern for becoming a self. Whereas Freud's Victorian clients generally
possessed a sense of identity, but wondered how their deeper urges might
be reconciled with it, many modern people wrestle with finding any deep
and lasting sense of identity at all (Frosh 1991:42-45).

In the voluminous current psychological literature on what it means to
be a self, two general, contrasting perspectives are found. The first can be
called *psychoanalysis* and is traced back to Freud. For psychoanalysis, selves
are formed through a three-sided struggle. Between internal drives on one
side (the *id*) and external, social pressures on the other (the *superego*), a
fragile *ego* slowly arises in an effort to reconcile their conflicting demands.
For psychoanalysis, the self tends to be not so much initially given as
sequentially forged and reforged amid pressures which may split, distort or
fragment it.

The second perspective may be called *organismic* and derives from Kurt
Goldstein and Carl Jung. Here the struggle is more nearly two-sided. The
ego is an initially given potential which begins developing in a coherent,
self-actualizing direction in harmony with its internal drives. Conflict arises from outside, when parental and social forces repress authentic longings and encourage inauthentic ones, thereby restricting and rechannel-
ing this natural process. A person can find his or her self by reconnecting
with that inborn drive toward wholeness, which involves identifying and
resisting these external influences.

This chapter will explore how both perspectives approach personal
alienation. Whereas psychoanalysis expects that some degree of alienation
will always characterize the self-process, organismic psychologists hope
that it will be more fully overcome. From these two hypotheses, quite different approaches to personal and social healing can be derived.

The Psychoanalytic Perspective

Its origins. Before he entered medicine Sigmund Freud labored for six
years (1876-1882) as a research neurologist. By this time the Newtonian
paradigm—the effort to explain all phenomena as interactions among
minute particles operating according to forces described by the inverse
square law—had been successfully extended to electricity and magnetism.
But though most scientists conceded that Newton's laws applied to all inor-

ganic matter, many drew a sharp line at organic entities. These scientists, called *vitalists*, insisted that living processes, such as the nervous system, could not be explained by Newton's reductionistic, deterministic schema.

Freud, however, identified himself with a group of neurologists called *mechanists*. As far back as 1842 they had taken the following oath:

No other forces than the common physical chemical ones are active within the organism. In those cases which cannot at the time be explained by these forces one has either to find the specific way or form of their action by means of the physical mathematical method, or to assume new forces equal in dignity to the physical chemical forces inherent in matter, reducible to the force of attraction and repulsion. (quoted in Fancher 1973:15-16)[1]

In his research, consequently, Freud treated nervous transmission as a kind of electrical impulse and the most basic units of the nervous system (soon to be called neurons) like the particles between which it operated.

In 1895 Freud attempted to reduce all psychic functioning to such impulses. Let us consider the body of an infant, regarded as a relatively closed energy system, with electriclike energy coursing along its neural pathways.[2] Each neuron, Freud hypothesized, is capable of holding, or *cathecting*, a certain amount of this energy. When a neuron fills up with too much energy, though, it discharges it down a pathway, producing muscular activity. Freud believed that all organisms find the filling up, or excitation, of neurons uncomfortable, and that the resulting movement always aims to return the organism to quiescence, or *homeostasis*.

When neurons of human infants (say, the neurons connected with hunger) are uncomfortably excited, diffuse responses such as kicking and crying occur. Fortunately these responses are often met by external activities (feeding) that satisfy the need. Through repeated association of uncomfortable neural excitations with events that bring relief (appearance of the mother's breast) the image of that event will by itself bring satisfaction. Freud argued that the basic physiological drives, which he later called collectively the *id*, cannot distinguish organic sensations from external reality. A specific hunger pang can be equally satisfied by food or an image of food.

Ideally, recurring infantile discomforts will be followed by satisfying parental responses; neural energy will flow smoothly and habitually from need through images associated with fulfillment to actual fulfillment. Seeking to explain human behavior wholly in such terms, Freud proposed that it is determined by responses to excitations in sensitive bodily areas central to a child's development at different stages, the three "erogenous" zones: oral, anal and genital.

In this development, however, the initial neuronic current will often be blocked. Some excitations and their spontaneous expressions may elicit parental anger and become associated with painful images. Thereafter, to avoid the painful experience, energy from the same excitations may be channeled into responses less suitable for fulfilling the need or simply into dwelling on images of fulfillment. These responses will continue, however, because the original energy must be discharged, even if in these less satisfying ways. Much neurotic behavior consists in such continuing maladaptive responses or in acting out wishes or fears associated with the original blockage. Yet such wishes and fears have usually become unconscious. Psychotherapy consists in helping us recall and reexperience them, which should alleviate the blockage.

For neural circuits to operate efficiently, the developing child needs some capacity to distinguish inner excitations and images from external reality and to delay and channel its responses in some organized way in light of the latter's demands. Freud called this capacity the *ego*. It operates on the *reality principle* (rather than the *pleasure principle* of the id). But where does this capacity come from? Freud answered that it somehow emerges and derives its energy from the id's instinctual strivings. This elicits two important considerations.

First, for Freud human existence consists originally not of individual selves—not even primitive, undifferentiated ones—but of diverse instinctual drives. These are not really directed toward objects—toward things or people in the world—but toward internally experienced satisfactions. The sense of being a self, of being a person whose desires are organized within a body distinct from other entities, arises only in order that these drives may find satisfaction. In the Freudian paradigm, it is not selves involved in a world of others that come first. The instinctual drives come first, and gradually become organized as selves in order to achieve instinctual satisfactions.

Second, sharp differences exist between id and ego. The first lunges directly toward immediate satisfaction and cannot distinguish its sensations from anything else. The second repeatedly delays, shapes and modifies the former's impulses, based on its own continuous discrimination among reality's features. Could something so different from, and often opposed to, the id really emerge from it mechanistically? Or must the ego involve certain features of consciousness, choice and rationality irreducible to this Newtonian explanation?

Freud never published this 1895 reduction of psychology to physiology, acknowledging that he had not succeeded in making it convincing. Yet he continued to believe that such an explanation was possible, although he never again attempted it. Since that time psychoanalysis has often swerved between emphasizing behavior's biological roots and emphasizing an ego which seems to transcend them.

Although psychoanalysis originally sought to explain mental life within the Newtonian paradigm, the resulting portrait varied significantly from the Enlightenment's. Human behavior, to be sure, was rooted scientifically, in physical processes. Yet rather than these being directed by enlightened, conscious reason, they largely directed, deceived and subverted it. Against Western humanity's confidence in controlling itself and the cosmos, Freud raised the menacing likelihood that we often are controlled by impulses that distort our very efforts to decipher them.

In 1920 Freud reduced all such impulses to two underlying drives: the life-wish *(eros)* and the death-wish. The former strives to combine cells and then individuals into larger unities. But in the end the latter prevails. Freud believed that he had discovered "a universal attribute of instincts and perhaps of organic life in general. . . . An *instinct is an urge inherent in organic life to restore an earlier state of things* which the living entity has been obliged to abandon under the pressure of external disturbing forces" ([1920] 1955:36). To put it more crudely, *"The aim of all life is death"* (p. 38). Though many found this shocking, it was perfectly consistent with Freud's earlier views that all activity aims at homeostatic quiescence and that all life forces are variants of those ruling matter.

Behavior is not only driven by the id but also shaped, and often twisted, by other human beings who forbid its direct expression. So to the struggle between the blind, primal id and the fragile ego Freud added (in 1923) the superego. This is the internalized voice of society's moral standards. But it hardly conveys enlightened ethical principles. Instead, it seeks to block the id, prohibiting gratification of its impulses entirely.

The superego arises chiefly during the *Oedipus conflict*. Here the child of five or six, longing to possess the parent of the opposite sex, is strongly forbidden by the same-sex parent. Obeying this prohibition, the child is forced to recognize itself as a distinct individual who can no longer fuse with either parent. By internalizing this prohibition the child begins incorporating the entire, rigid social code connected with it.

Freud usually described the Oedipus conflict as it was experienced by the boy—and in genital terms. The little boy, finding that his mother lacks a penis, wants to supply her with his own, taking the place of his father's phallus. But the boy experiences the father, who is angered at the boy's wish to take his place, threatening to castrate him. This terminates the boy's wish.

Two important affirmations about women underlie this account. First, women, for Freud, were largely defined in terms of "lack" (of a penis).[3] Second, Freud believed that all infants experience an initial, gratifying sense of oneness with their mothers. This gives rise to an *ego ideal*, a sense of one's ideal self experienced mainly through fantasy and imagination. In desiring his mother, the little boy also hopes to return, in a way, to that infantile state. But that would be regressive and contrary to the mature stage of individuality that his father's prohibition forces him to occupy. Maturity for Freud therefore involved rejecting ties of closeness, as represented by the maternal or feminine, and accepting the separation imposed by the paternal or masculine.

In the end, the fragile Freudian ego struggles to attain a modicum of balance between two enormous, conflicting magnitudes shaped by unalterable physical and social forces. Consequently individuals cannot help but feel alienated from much that is within and around them, even though these also form ineradicable aspects of themselves. Still, within limits, there can be hope of forging some sort of balance and, with it, some kind of personal identity.

Not that individuals will ever discover some deeper, inner self wholly in harmony with its instincts and free to unfold joyously under present social conditions, for the Freudian self is not nearly so much discovered as it is created and recreated amid conflicting pressures. Since these pressures will not really change, there is no realistic hope of social transformation either. Freud's approach to social life was basically conservative: adapt to most social conventions, put up with some repression. Yet within his or her narrow life-space, perhaps along with a few significant others, a person might find some degree of contentment and creative expression.

Social construction of the self. Within the Freudian framework greater weight can be placed on either the ego's organizing activity or its social conditioning. Object relations theorists, as we shall see, stress the former. But some with a postmodern bent, who distrust all talk of centralizing agencies, can treat the self simply as a social construct.

Jacques Lacan follows Freud's claim that at birth no ego, but only a bundle of discordant instincts, exists. A child nonetheless will come to experience itself as a unit at two important points. The first occurs when its mother *mirrors* it: reflects back how she experiences it as a consistent presence and how she responds to its needs, affection and aggression. This mirroring offers the child an image of being a stable, identifiable self. The child, in response, will project its discordant drives upon, and narcissistically identify them with, this image, which includes the ego ideal. Yet since it exists only in the mother's eyes, such an image, even though it offers the infant experiential unity with her, will be strictly *Imaginary*.

Later, at a point corresponding to Freud's Oedipus conflict, the child will need to take a position in the social order, which Lacan calls the *Symbolic* and whose structures are enforced by "the name of the Father." This will consist in assuming a location in a system of social coordinates (for instance, in the younger generation so that the child can no longer merge erotically with its parent). Incorporation into this system, which descends upon the child from outside, as it were, will split it from the *Imaginary* (the unity with its mother).

This split will arouse fierce longing for incorporation in *the Real* (a perfect wholeness of desire and gratification). Yet desire will never find fulfillment in the Symbolic order, for selves constituted by it will be nothing but their positions within these coordinates. And so desire will be repressed, forming the unconscious. Existence will be irretrievably marked by absence and lack. Relative mental health will require some awareness that desire can never be fulfilled and acceptance of alienation from all centers of unity, including any self center.

In Lacan, as in Freud, primordial unitive experience is again symbolized by the maternal and feminine and by the unavoidable separation and aloneness necessary to adult existence enforced by the paternal and masculine. Lacan, however, postulates a social order even more rigid than Freud imagined. For on the social level nothing but pregiven systems and networks exist. Societies themselves possess no centers or norms by which they might be critiqued and reformed.

Lacan has been charged with affirming a social determinism within which self-identity can be attained only by adjusting to the dominant structures. Such a vision demands acceptance not only of continual unsubstantiality, lack and alienation on the personal level but also, paradoxically, of unalterable solidity and rigidity on the social level.

Psychoanalysis and social critique. For both Freud and Lacan the particular shape of a neurosis—the specific ways in which the id's urges are repressed and distorted—is determined largely by the social constraints with which the neurotic must cope. Accordingly if certain neuroses are common in a given culture, they might be read as mirrors of that culture's social patterns. Psychoanalytic tracing of their formation could provide detailed insight into how repressive forces in that society operate.

Those who assume, as did Freud and Lacan, that given social structures are inevitable might have little interest in this. But for those who believe that some changes are possible, psychoanalysis has become a powerful tool of social criticism. This is one of its main functions in today's general public conversation.

Before World War I, Marxists and many socialists urged workers in all countries to unite against their common enemy, the capitalist classes. But when war broke out, workers in each nation rallied to their own capitalist rulers. After the war the neo-Marxist "Frankfurt School" wondered what had gone amiss. Why had workers been so unaffected by economic and political arguments concerning their best interest?

Herbert Marcuse, along with Erich Fromm, answered that social structures are internalized through repressions and fears at deep psychic levels during a child's first years. Social change, accordingly, requires thoroughgoing transformation at this level. Marcuse eventually influenced the protest movements of the 1960s and 1970s and is still admired among radical social critics today.

Marcuse, like Freud, affirmed that large doses of repression had been necessary for building civilization and that capitalism had originally required long hours of toil for deferred rewards. Immediate expression of urges, including sexuality, had to be restrained. Due to technological advances, however, workers no longer had to repress their urges in order to meet basic needs. Still since such toil increases employers' profits, capitalism keeps encouraging the repression that undergirds it. Marcuse insists that since this repression is no longer necessary, it is a *surplus repression*. He also argues, against Freud, that restraints against libidinal impulses no longer constitute an unalterable *reality principle* but a *performance principle* demanded by capitalism (1966:35).

With increasing abundance, however, capitalism must not only control people as workers to sell its products; it must constitute them as consumers too. Through advertising it promises to fill voids left by lack of meaningful work and relationships with increasing arrays of commodities. Especially through mass media it attracts the instincts now to this, now to that superficial promise of fulfillment, which will soon prove dissatisfying, leaving consumers with intensified cravings for ever newer products and docilely submitted to the labor necessary to purchase them (pp. 100-5).

Individuals, then, are locked into capitalist socioeconomic patterns and alienated from other possibilities for living. They are locked in and alienated not by external political restraints, for in modern democratic societies they appear quite free; instead, behaviors necessary for capitalist productivity are inscribed into their very instinctual structure. But if, as a

Freudian, a person maintains that social forces shape instincts that deeply, can he or she also affirm that this can be overcome?

To do so Marcuse interpreted Freud somewhat creatively. He noted that for Freud imagination, or *phantasy*, still gave direct expression to instinctual cravings in adults. For Marcuse the persistence of this activity despite severe social restraints witnesses to a primordial protest against them by instinctual impulses which could have developed in other directions. Phantasy, he argues, retains an image or archetype of an original unity between instinct and gratification (p. 142). This arose from a libidinal, narcissistic union between infant and mother well preceding the Oedipus conflict, during which the ego ideal was apparently formed (pp. 229-30). Throughout life, despite its suppression, phantasy points toward "reconciliation of the individual with the whole, of desire with realization, of happiness with reason" (p. 143).[4]

Marcuse also stresses that the life instinct, for Freud, combines things into ever greater unities. Marcuse claims that if this instinct, guided by phantasy, can be liberated from current repressive conditions, a society of individuals freely pursuing gratification can emerge. Some struggle, to be sure, might arise as they begin living together. Yet Marcuse is confident that sexuality, when released from surplus repression, "tends to its own sublimation" (p. 202)—that instincts will then manifest a "libidinal rationality" (p. 199), a "*rationality of gratification* in which reason and happiness converge" (p. 224). All this will create "its own division of labor, its own priorities, its own hierarchy"[5]—even though this order would be simultaneously "founded on and sustained by the free gratification of individuals" (p. 191).

To paint this vision, Marcuse drew on images of primordial wholeness associated with the Greek god Narcissus. Whereas narcissism for many psychoanalysts involves regressive longing for the mother-infant relation, Marcuse protested that Narcissus imagery conveys the intuition that "'everything holds within itself, as potentiality, the intimate harmony of its being—just as every salt holds within itself the archetype of its crystal. . . . Everything strives towards its lost form'" (Marcuse 1966:163, quoting André Gide, *Le Traité de Narcisse*). For "Narcissistic Eros awakens and liberates potentialities that are real in things animate and inanimate, in organic and inorganic nature—real but in the un-erotic reality suppressed." When this eros is liberated "opposition between man and nature, subject and object, is overcome. . . . Fulfillment of man is at the same time the fulfillment, without violence, of nature" (pp. 166-67); nature will be treated "not as an object of domination and exploitation, but as a 'garden' which can grow while making human beings grow" (p. 216).

Marcuse's confidence that the instincts tend naturally in this holistic direction, and when freed can overcome personal, social and ecological alienation, sounds like organismic psychology. Nonetheless his insistence that instincts themselves are socially shaped and that the ego cannot rediscover and flow along with unobstructed libido under present social conditions is strongly Freudian.

Object relations theory. Freud, Lacan and Marcuse stressed the roles of instincts and social structuring in shaping the self. But what of that fragile mediating agency, the ego, whose function is so crucial in psychoanalysis yet whose origins and nature are so difficult to explain by biology?

Freud, remember, claimed that instincts can be as content with images associated with satisfaction as with objects providing it. In fact, he maintained, instincts are initially directed not toward interactions with external realities but toward inner tension-reduction. Only when instinctive reactions fail to attain this does a structure—the ego—arise to distinguish external objects from internal states and to direct drives toward the former.

According to W. R. D. Fairbairn, however, Freud's distinction between instinctual energy (id) and a structure that channels it (ego) resulted from his Newtonian dissolution of the person into inert components, which then had to be activated by extraneous forces (1952:127).[6] This reductionism, Fairbairn claimed, obscured the fact that the ego itself is a coherent energy system operating in certain directions.

Object relations theorists generally assume that an ego, even if only in very primitive form, is operating from life's beginning.[7] They insist, second, that the person and whatever instinctual drives it might have (many refuse to ground behavior in instincts) are inherently relational—directed from the beginning toward objects. Bodily drives and "zones," then, are not originating sources of activity but vehicles or pathways through which object-seeking tendencies operate.

By *objects* these theorists mean chiefly persons or aspects of persons— above all, the mother—for they focus on the infant's first few years with her. Their main point is that a child's self-concept is built up around images that he or she internalizes from other persons, shaped both by those individuals' actual conduct and by projections upon them of the child's needs, fears and loves. Given its emphasis on the infant-mother relationship, object relations is enormously concerned with how separation between them happens. Many regard this as the fundamental experience of alienation which will shape the way all other alienations are felt.

D. W. Winnicott (like Freud, Lacan, Marcuse and most object relations theorists) believes that infants initially experience a pleasant, undifferentiated oneness with their mothers. Winnicott endorses a *primary maternal preoccupation* during the first few months. If the mother regularly meets its needs, the infant will experience reality as a coherent whole and itself as omnipotent. This, he argues, will lay the basis for a healthy self-concept. Before long, however, the *good enough mother* will respond more slowly, allowing the infant, through painful though tolerable frustration, to begin experiencing itself as a separate being. All along, its self-concept will be formed, as Lacan stressed, by the way its mother mirrors its actions, showing it what kind of person she perceives (Greenberg and Mitchell 1983:191-94). If the mother and other early caretakers are generally attentive and supportive, the child will *introject* such objects and build its self-concept around them.

However, if the mother never establishes the primary bond, withdraws too quickly or is inconsistently absent and present, the child may become narcissistic. To survive the intolerable absence of her containing, supportive presence, the infant will begin identifying its inner self with some powerful object—perhaps its earlier image of omnipotence, or a "good" breast or "good" parents coming to the rescue. The latter two objects, however, will be merely aspects of parents that the infant *splits* from the parents' broader negative behavior, which it finds too threatening to fully retain in consciousness. It will bury its resentment and rage against these caretakers beneath the omnipotent object around which it seeks to construct its fragile sense of self.[8]

The child will cling to this object as protection against the terrifying emptiness of feeling helpless and the threatening otherness of a world it cannot control. Throughout life, narcissists will seek to overcome this painful uncertainty either grandiosely, by seeking control over other persons and events, or regressively, by searching for the kind of undifferentiated union that most theorists believe they originally experienced with their mothers (Frosh 1991:63-94; Lasch 1984:163-85).

Feminists have generally appreciated object relations' maternal orientation in contrast to psychoanalysis's usual paternal emphasis. Yet they attribute the fact that mothers perform the great bulk of early parenting to social factors, which, they argue, adversely affect both boys and girls. Early capitalism, they say, in order to build its complex factories and business networks, separated the growing productive sphere from the domestic one. Capitalism's demands for worker mobility broke down extended families, drawing fathers into the productive sphere and isolating mothers in the domestic sphere with their children. But the largely maternal parenting that resulted is experienced differently by boys and girls.

Nancy Chodorow affirms, like almost all psychoanalysts, that infants experience a union with their mothers "which all people who have been mothered want basically to recreate" (1978:201). But since the mother is of a different sex from her son, she will likely experience this for a shorter time and less intensely than with a daughter. Moreover, in order to identify with his same-sex parent, a growing boy will have to break this maternal symbiosis sharply (often with the trauma described by the Oedipus conflict).

This kind of parenting will produce men with a greater sense of separateness from others and from tasks of early child rearing; women will have a greater sense of connection with others and with early child-rearing tasks. In addition, since men will be less comfortable with closeness and often provide less than women desire, women will more often want babies to satisfy this need. Thus through psychic experiences inscribed on very young children, the social phenomenon of nearly exclusive infant mothering gets transmitted from generation to generation. Yet it alienates many men from close relationships and many women from developing firm enough self-identities to undertake many tasks in our contemporary world. The solution for feminists such as Chodorow is "that primary parenting [be] shared between men and women" (p. 215).

The fact that boys experience the early break with their mothers more sharply throws interesting light on the early unitive experience with her. Psychoanalysis, we have seen, usually describes it as "feminine" and its sense of unmediated union as something men must avoid. But since, as feminist object relations shows, boys experience its breaking more drastically, perhaps this longing for primal oneness, lauded by Marcuse, is at least as often desired by men.

A narcissistic society? If, as psychoanalysis claims, social structures significantly shape neuroses, then analysis of neuroses common in a given society can tell much about its structures. Current American society has been called a "culture of narcissism." Narcissists find early experience with caretakers unstable and threatening and cannot form stable selves around objects derived from them. They therefore attempt to build selves around objects that promise them omnipotence. But since their inner world often feels uncertain, empty and subliminally pervaded by rage and fear, and since their surroundings also seem unstable and fearful, they often cannot clearly distinguish self from not-self.

To others, however, narcissists seldom seem frightened or self-preoccupied. Since they are uneasy about events around them, narcissists become skilled at deciphering appearances and fitting in with situations and others' expectations. Their aura of omnipotence gives them a competent, confident air. They usually seem friendly and efficiently busy. Only gradually might a person suspect that, haunted by a deep emptiness, they are really manipulative, despising of others and incapable of close relationships.

Our society has been called narcissistic, first, because people who can adjust to constantly changing circumstances, operate efficiently with outward friendliness and yet move on unhindered by close personal ties are often very successful (Lasch 1979:91-103). Second, clinical cases of narcissism have increased in recent decades. Third, circumstances commonly encountered in seeking self-identity seem quite like those which produce narcissists. Christopher Lasch has argued that contemporary problems in self-formation are mirror images of societies without stable traditions or structures. They reflect families where parents are often absent, inconsistent or emotionally distant. They mirror a proliferation of moral, religious and lifestyle options.

Most of all, Lasch argues, problems in self-formation reflect a society lured by images of satisfaction obtainable through commodities. Such satisfactions, as Marcuse observed, are short-lived and often disappoint, but they are immediately replaced by more glittering images of yet more novel ones. This constant parade of surface attractions makes it difficult to discern the real from the unreal and dissolves distinctions between self and not-self:

> Commodity production and consumerism . . . create a world of mirrors, insubstantial images, illusions increasingly indistinguishable from reality. The mirror effect makes the subject an object; at the same time, it makes the world of objects an extension or projection of the self. . . . The consumer lives surrounded not so much by things as by fantasies . . . a world that has no objective or independent existence and seems to exist only to gratify or thwart his desires. (1984:30)

In such a society people's desires are freed from repressive controls. But if psychoanalysis is correct, these desires will not immediately flow in self-actualizing directions. Instead they will clash among themselves and become prey to powerful stimulations: "'Impulse is stimulated, perverted and given neither an adequate object upon which to satisfy itself nor coherent forms of control'" (Lasch 1979:90, quoting Kovel 1976:252). Phantasy, or imagination, is freed "from external constraints but . . . exposed more directly than before to the tyranny of inner compulsions and anxieties" (Lasch 1984:32-33). Individuals allured by vast ranges of commodities may feel that they are exercising real freedom. Yet they may merely be making consumer choices among products which differ little and which dissolve them into streams of short-lived longings, satisfactions and frustrations.

Lasch argues further that such consumerism undermines people's "confidence in their capacity to understand and shape the world and to provide for their own needs" (p. 33). As affairs seem managed by ever larger industries and bureaucracies, people increasingly sense that they are being watched and manipulated and become more vulnerable to images of cataclysm and fear. As traditions and values erode, people lose hope for a meaningful future and grasp oftener after those fleeting images of gratification and safety in the now. They increasingly gravitate toward one of the two narcissistic directions for alleviating external reality's inconstancy and the self's hollowness: either regressively, toward some undisturbed sense of primordial union, or grandiosely, toward Promethean control over reality or identification with some figure who promises it.

If this analysis is correct, alienation from ourselves today is not, as it was in Freud's time, chiefly a problem of too much depth, of impulses buried under fairly well-defined personas by rigid social controls. Today's socioeconomic forces influence people not by suppressing their impulses but by enticing them to pursue whatever they wish. The problem becomes not too much external structure but too little. Our deeper longing to become a self becomes fragmented among myriad alluring images competing to form its surface. That is not to say that current socioeconomic forces exert no control over us. Instead, they control precisely by encouraging a sense of freedom from all controls—and then manipulating the impulses, hopes and fears which emerge.

In describing the dissolution of structures that promote self-formation, Lasch lamented the emotional absence of today's fathers and mentioned the stabilizing social function that the Oedipus conflict can have. But because the Oedipus, since Freud, has often been regarded as affirming "progressive" masculine traits over "regressive" feminine ones, Lasch was critiqued for promoting a paternalistic social ideal. Stephanie Engel proposed that selves should be formed by both the Oedipus (which promotes individuation, differentiation and limitation) and the ego ideal (that positive sense of optimum self experienced through phantasy and desire, stemming from early union with one's mother; 1980:77-104).[9]

In general Lasch affirmed this balance. For him the ego ideal functioned wrongly only when a person sought unmediated union with it—when an individual lapsed into that regressive narcissistic effort to identify with an omnipotent object and hide psychically from his or her own limitations and disturbing differences between self and external reality. But if pursued as a goal, tempered by realistic awareness of a person's limits and of real differentiations in reality, the ego ideal could provide a guide for self-construction (1984:178-82).

Lasch also critiqued all goal-oriented activity guided by *grandiose* narcissism: that sense that one is already identical with a self exercising omnipotent control over others, society and nature. This form of narcissism also sought to deny the disturbing limitations which reality's otherness placed upon a person. It could do so by exaggerating a legitimate emphasis of the Oedipus experience (a person's distinction from others) into a sense of total, unrelational superiority over them. Lasch found this narcissistic tendency especially active in modern technological efforts (traceable to the Enlightenment) to completely remake society and nonhuman nature (pp. 244-59).

Nevertheless, Lasch criticized Engel's proposal. He read her and other feminists as advocating the ego ideal (with its features of affectivity, receptivity and union with others and nature) over against the Oedipus (with its emphasis on rationality, productive activity and distinctions from others and nature). Lasch felt, moreover, that feminists were labeling the second set of traits as "masculine" and the source of modern alienation but the first as "feminine" and the solution to alienation. Thus whereas Lasch's feminist critics regarded him as valorizing the masculine over the feminine, he saw them advocating the reverse.

It seems, however, that both sides were really affirming a similar balance between a "feminine" emphasis on the ego ideal and union and a "masculine" stress on the Oedipus and differentiation.[10] But if both are involved, the process of self-formation is highly paradoxical. Lasch describes it as involving

> the acknowledgment of our separation from the original source of life, combined with a continuing struggle to recapture a sense of primal union by means of activity that gives us a provisional understanding and mastery of the world without denying our limitations and dependency. Selfhood is the painful awareness of the tension between our unlimited aspirations and our limited understanding, between our original intimations of immortality and our fallen state, between oneness and separation. (p. 20)

Despite her criticisms of Lasch, Jessica Benjamin seems to endorse a similar vision, but she supports it by a more recent understanding of the union/differentiation dialectic. Citing recent studies on infant behavior, Benjamin claims that "the infant is never totally undifferentiated (symbiotic) from the mother, but is primed from the beginning to be interested in and to distinguish itself from the world of others" (1988:18).[11] The earliest mother-infant interchanges, Benjamin says, involve both *assertion* of each participant's individuality and each one's desire for *recognition* of him- or herself as having an identity by the other, who is recognized as having a distinct identity (1988:11-48).

This delicate interaction can degenerate into a fusion where one side is dominant and from which the other will eventually struggle for separation. Nonetheless self-formation need not be conceptualized as marked by early undifferentiation, from which a person can emerge only through sharp separation (as typical Oedipal accounts have it). Instead, the lifelong task of attaining unity with *and* differentiation from others can be regarded as the actualization of potentials operative from the beginning. However, whether Benjamin or the typical Oedipal account is more accurate, differentiation-denying tendencies such as those of regressive and grandiose narcissism are common in current society.

Summary. What basic affirmations about today's struggles with psychological alienation can be derived from the psychoanalytic perspective?

One is that alienation is partly rooted in our instincts, which strive toward short-term satisfactions that will always conflict among themselves. Their contrary pullings will never cohere perfectly with any direction the ego may set. However, not all psychoanalysts affirm, as did Freud, that the ego is ultimately derived from the id. For many, an incipient ego, which seeks personal (object) relations and not mere drive satisfaction, exists from life's beginning. Psychoanalysis, then, does not always follow the Newtonian paradigm's reductionism, though it maintains its conflictive orientation.

Second, social forces struggle against instinctual expressions and the ego's efforts to guide them, deeply shaping both activities and inducing a sense of alienation on both levels. A person can regard this shaping in a deterministic fashion (Freud, Lacan). In that case, individuals will seek not to alter social restraints but to adjust to them and be content with what little expression of desire they permit. A person can also hope that social structures might change (Marcuse). Yet so intertwined are they with individual psychic structure that both would need to be transformed together. Individuals cannot significantly change unless institutions do, but neither will institutions unless the overall impact of socioeconomic forces on personal development alters. For such transformation to occur, instincts must have some plasticity, some capacity to develop in different directions.

Third, for psychoanalysis, alienation can never be completely overcome, for we will always struggle between discordant demands from instincts and social forces. This persistent process of forging and reforging a self, never feeling centered in ourselves or at home in the world for long—this is the agony of human existence, but perhaps also an indispensable source of its creativity. Some psychoanalytic theorists, however, provide a goal toward which we can strive and through which we might occasionally experience oneness with others and the world: the ego ideal.

Today, however, objects and images for self-formation are often so inconstant and threatening that many tend to identify themselves narcissistically with the ego ideal or some other omnipotent object. This shields them from feelings of helplessness and disconcerting differences between themselves and other people, society and nature. Discussions of narcissism, however, propose that viable selves are formed neither by fusion with the ego ideal nor by sharp separation from it, as in classical Oedipal theory. Instead, the ego ideal can function as a future goal toward which we strive; on the way, we can experience both closeness to and distance from other people, society and nature. For psychoanalysis, coping with alienation will involve finding a way to work within it rather than seeking a way out.

The Organismic Perspective
For organismic psychologists, the basic conflict underlying alienation from ourselves is not three- but two-sided. On one side are what Freudians usually call drives and the self, which are in essential harmony. On the other side, and responsible for their disruption, are social standards and demands. These social influences, however, do not penetrate into the fundamental shaping of the instincts and ego, nor place them in as deep an antagonism, as Freudians believe. Greater potential unity exists between the self and its impulses.

Organismic theory and therapy. Freud formed his psychoanalytic model under Newtonian influence. He originally divided the acting subject into small, discreet units (neurons) and psychic activity into excitations transmitted among them. Larger, constant transmission patterns were gradually built up from repeated singular ones, though these latter still conflicted with each other. The psychic subject was a complex mechanism, the sum of discreet parts added together.

Organismic theorists, however (somewhat like Fairbairn), insist that such atomization artificially isolates behavior from its overall context. The effect of a specific excitation, for instance, depends on more than its strength and the immediate reaction of the organ it impinges. For example, suppose an animal is struck with a blow to the shoulder—a blow strong enough to knock it over were its body inert. The animal will not necessarily fall, however, for, upon being struck, other parts of its body (such as its feet) will likely reposition themselves to retain its balance. Quite often, in fact, similar stimuli (such as blows when the animal is and is not alert) will provoke very different responses. Contrariwise, two quite diverse stimuli (say, a blow to the right shoulder and one to the left thigh) can elicit similar responses (say, groping for balance). Behavior, in other words, is not simply the sum of discrete stimuli and responses but depends on the organism's overall interaction with its total environment.[12]

According to Kurt Goldstein (organismic theory's most influential early proponent) organisms are always seeking to maintain a balance, or an even distribution of energy, throughout their systems. This global process, called *equalization,* includes reactions to individual stimuli, but chiefly it involves establishing consistent behavioral rhythms in response to environmental pressures and internal needs. *Equalization* differs from Freud's *homeostasis.* Freud, remember, thought that organisms basically seek rest. Stimulation is therefore painful. Organisms endeavor to discharge it quickly to return to inactivity—ultimately to the inertia of dead matter. For organismic theory, however, organisms are ceaselessly active. Stimulation, which comes chiefly from without, arouses tendencies to master the environment that are intrinsically enjoyable.

Further, organismic theory claims that since organisms are units, dividing them into distinct parts is artificial. It further postulates that organisms, apart from interference by alien forces, will function harmoniously. Organisms inherently sense what they need to survive and to expand their spheres of activity. Organized functioning does not need to be built up out of conflicting processes, as psychoanalysis claims. Conflict, instead, results from the breakdown of, or unnatural interference with, spontaneous unified functioning.

Since this functioning is harmonious, organismic theory finds no need to postulate what psychoanalysis calls diverse instincts. Instead, it regards such tendencies as aspects of one master drive, usually called *self-actualization.* According to Carl Rogers this is "the urge which is evident in all organic and human life—to expand, extend, become autonomous, develop, mature—the tendency to express and activate all the capacities of the organism, to the extent that such activation enhances the organism or self" (1961:35). Humans, much as animals, know innately what they need to balance their various potentialities and needs. In other words, nothing in the basic human organism need lead to alienation—of some "drives" from others or of any of these from a person's authentic self.

Conflict arises, however, because some of what each human experiences is not admitted to the field of conscious perceptions and values, which Rogers calls the *self* (1951:498). Some experiences are fearful or unwelcome and never fully registered. Others are consciously retained but in ways dictated by the social environment rather than by a person's initial apprehension (for instance, early experiences with sex which parents find disgusting). In both cases, discrepancies arise between what is experienced on the organic level and the awareness and values that become the conscious self.

Psychological maladjustment occurs when tension arises between the two (p. 510). It can only be overcome when "all the sensory and visceral experiences . . . are . . . assimilated on a symbolic level into a consistent relationship with the concept of self" (p. 513). Overcoming of intrapsychic alienation, in other words, must be "a process whereby man becomes his organism"—in which "he fully experiences the feelings which at an organic level he *is*" (1961:103, 111).

As often practiced, organismic psychotherapy offers alternatives to some criticized features of psychoanalysis. Psychoanalysis has been charged with probing too deeply for hidden meanings and being generally suspicious of patients' self-reports. Organismic therapists insist, however, that patients have access to their important experiences. Although unconscious (or at least preconscious) experiences exist, the most significant are recoverable. Only socially acquired fears and habits prompt patients to distort or repress them. Accordingly if therapists can provide a safe, nonjudgmental, often nondirective atmosphere, patients can begin exploring disturbing experiences again.

In this process, by learning to listen to "the deepest recesses of his physiological and emotional being" (p. 176), a person moves away from façades, from "oughts," from meeting others' expectations and from pleasing others. He or she moves toward contrasting behaviors such as self-direction, experiencing self as process, openness to experience, acceptance of others and trust of self (pp. 165-75). Psychological struggle, that is, takes place not nearly so much among aspects truly inherent in the self as between the deeper self and distorting social expectations.

Whereas organismic theorists admit that such struggle involves uncertainty and pain, this emphasis diminishes when moving from Goldstein to Rogers to some current figures whom we will soon discuss. Goldstein underlined the inevitability of deep anxiety: "Shocks are essential to

human nature and . . . life must, of necessity, take its course via uncertainty" (1940:112; compare pp. 108-19). When Rogers discusses conflicts and
uncertainties, however, he tends to stress the organism's self-balancing
abilities:

> [One must] permit his total organism, his conscious thought participat-
> ing, to consider, weigh and balance each stimulus, need, and demand,
> and its relative weight and intensity. Out of this complex weighing and
> balancing he is able to discover that course of action which seems to
> come closest to satisfying his needs in the situation, long-range as well as
> immediate needs. (1961:118)

Though this process might involve mistakes, a person would still "have
access to all of the available data in the situation," and Rogers is confident
that any consequences which were "not satisfying would be quickly cor-
rected" because decisions "would continually be checked in behavior" (pp.
190-91).

Moreover, whereas such a process would have to involve thinking,
Rogers often values visceral in-touch-ness with feelings far more highly
than reason's more detached perspective. Goldstein, however, regarded
the "abstract attitude"—the ability to separate the self from the world, give
reasons for actions and formulate future plans—as a sine qua non of fully
human functioning (1940:58-68).

Organismic theory and society. Organismic theory insists that things be studied not in isolation but only within the wholes of which they are parts. It is
surprising, then, that individualism often marks its social perspective. Kurt
Goldstein claimed that the individual alone is real in nature; all species
and classes are simply thought categories (pp. 208-11). Nevertheless life in
social groupings is intrinsic to being human.[13] This involves *self-restriction,*
limiting ourselves for the sake of others, which is "inherent in human
nature."

Self-restriction is the source of ethical norms, which are essential to positive human development and not, as Freud thought, simply external
impositions on hedonistic impulses (p. 208). Self-restriction is balanced by
encroachment, the necessity of occasionally depending on and restricting
others. Goldstein believed that humankind's ethical task consisted in working toward balancing each person's "right and the inner necessity to actualize oneself" with making this possible for everyone else (p. 217). Yet he
insisted that no "pre-established harmony" exists among all self-actualizing
tendencies (pp. 203-4). This goal will be difficult to attain; social life will
probably always involve "a certain degree of restriction" (p. 214).

Carl Rogers is more individualistic:

The separateness of individuals, the right of each individual to utilize his experience in his own way and to discover his own meanings in it—this is one of the most priceless potentialities of life. Each person is an island unto himself, in a very real sense; and he can only build bridges to other islands if he is first of all willing to be himself. (1961:21)

Rogers has few worries that this freedom to explore and express self's organismic experience will lead to selfish behavior:

We do not need to ask who will socialize him, for one of his own deepest needs is for affiliation and communication with others. . . . We do not need to ask who will control his aggressive impulses; for as he becomes more open to all his impulses, his need to be liked by others and his tendency to give affection will be as strong as his impulses to strike out or to seize for himself. (p. 194)

Here Rogers includes individual and social needs among those which each organism, if properly heard, will naturally balance. Yet this claim seems to imply a much broader one: that some sort of preestablished harmony exists among the inclinations of all persons so that, if freed from undue constraints, they would all balance. The more open anyone is to his or her experience, "the more his behavior makes it evident that . . . the human species tends in the direction of constructive social living" (p. 353). Any such person will take on "balanced and realistic behavior which is appropriate to the survival and enhancement of a highly social animal" (p. 194).

Rogers maintains that application of organismic principles to nations would lead toward world peace, toward a harmony that now allegedly reigns in the animal kingdom (pp. 177-81).[14] He seems to be assuming, that is, that unfettered expression of each person's organismic tendencies would lead toward, and ultimately harmonize with, unfettered expression of everyone else's.

This kind of self-actualizing expression can be stated as an explicit ethical criterion. Abraham Maslow asks, "What is good? Anything that conduces to this desirable direction of actualization of the inner nature of man. What is bad or abnormal? Anything that frustrates or blocks or denies the essential nature of man" (1954:341). However, the fact that a person's tendencies *do* take a certain direction might not mean that this direction is good and that a person *ought* to follow it, for some such tendencies might conflict with needs of others. In such cases a good action would involve what Goldstein called *self-renunciation*.

A person's following his organism could be uniformly good only if free expression of his desires always harmonized with free expression of everyone's. Yet Maslow thinks that this ideally should happen, for he believes in the possibility of "institutional arrangements" which would guarantee that "when I pursue my selfish gratifications I automatically help others, and when I try to be altruistic I automatically reward others and gratify myself" (1965:103).

Whereas recent organismic psychology is quite critical of social restraints, it seems optimistic about human social potential. For apparently it often assumes that if such restraints vanished and individuals followed their organismic desires, harmony among everyone's desires would arise. This assumption, however, bears striking affinities with the Newtonian paradigm. It is parallel to claiming that if government ceased regulating business, leaving everyone to pursue their financial advantage, the optimum economic situation for all would emerge.

Is it possible, then, that in encouraging free expression of desire, organismic psychology promotes adjustment to capitalistic societies? Organismic therapists might reply that their clients are listening to deeper, authentic organismic drives, undistorted by social pressures. But what if social shaping of drives runs deeper than organicism suspects—or, indeed, if drives never exist apart from some social structuring? Then organismic psychology might not be so much recovering a primordial oganismic balance as helping individuals adapt to a certain kind of society. It has been argued, in fact, that Rogers's therapy best helps not those who reject their social formation but those who, after having been granted space to question it, readopt many of its values.[15]

The emergence of the inner child. If the self-actualizing drive exists from birth and if its unfolding is inhibited only by social forces, there is a sense in which the child might be called a person's natural, or spontaneous, self. And if that childlike spontaneity somehow remains alive, despite social distortion, could this inner child form a person's chief hope for self-actualization? Today such an inner child is widely emphasized in treating victims of abuse, alcoholic homes and other dysfunctional systems. This notion emerged most directly out of the movement known as transactional analysis (whose original direction was not organismic).

Eric Berne, transactional analysis's (TA's) chief founder, began as a psychoanalyst. His theory that psychic functioning involves three agencies—*Child, Adult* and *Parent*—is reminiscent of Freud's id, ego and superego. Yet whereas Freud's id and superego were impersonal instinctual and social forces, Berne's Child and Parent are actual *ego states*, virtually complete personalities, existing alongside, and sometimes in conflict with, an individual's mature personality, the Adult.

A person's Child is the youngster the individual actually was, feeling the former hopes and fears, sometimes emerging in the grown person's behavior with the very expressions, intonations and impulsive behaviors manifested years earlier. The Parent is the person's primary caretaker, or an amalgam of several, expressing the same values with the same emotional tone that the Child formerly heard. Mental illness involves severe conflict among the three ego states: for instance, when the Parent exerts too stifling a control over the Adult or Child, or when the Child's desires erupt to disturb the Adult's functioning or the Parent's standards.

In speaking of the Child, Berne usually meant that ego state which "tends to react more abruptly, on the basis of pre-logical thinking and poorly differentiated or distorted perceptions" (1961:19). He referred often to the *Adapted Child* ("the archaic ego state which is under the Parental influence") and occasionally to the *Natural Child* ("an archaic ego state which is free from or is attempting to free itself from such influence") (p. 25).[16]

The Natural Child became the forerunner of today's inner child. It includes the individual's spontaneous perceptions and inclinations. For psychological maturity to be attained, it must be freed from the Adapted Child, which has been formed in response to the Parent's demands. Yet mental health, for Berne, could hardly be acquired by simply adopting the Natural Child's attitudes and feelings. Psychological maturity, instead, consists in the Adult's recognizing, controlling and synthesizing various aspects of the Child and Parent.

Berne assumed that everyone possesses a fully functioning Adult, even when it is being overrun by the Child or Parent. Mental health therefore involves not laborious construction of an Adult self but finding ways to activate the one already present. Therapy, accordingly, need not include as much digging and dissecting as in psychoanalysis. Berne's popularity, like Rogers's, stemmed largely from developing a more easily understandable, straightforward, brief brand of psychotherapy.

TA's popularity soared with Thomas Harris's *I'm OK—You're OK*. Berne had described four positions, or attitudes, that people take toward themselves and others. His first position, the "healthy" one, consisted in accepting ourselves and others: saying, "I'm OK—you're OK."[17] Harris, however, insisted that every infant adopts another position: "I'm not OK—you're OK" during its first year. This occurs because some needs of all infants are unmet or rebuked, leading them to feel "I'm not OK." Yet they desperately need to believe in their caretakers' goodness: to feel "You're OK." Most people retain this position throughout life.[18]

Whereas the other three positions are based on the Child's feeling,

Harris insists that the first ("I'm OK—You're OK") is based on Adult *"thought, faith, and the wager of action"* (1967:50). In fact, this healthy position is not so much an organismic awareness as an ethical decision. It is rooted in a determination to treat ourselves and others as having ultimate value, as worthy of unconditional respect. Reminiscent of Goldstein, Harris discusses the challenges and difficulties of building societies based on this principle (pp. 213-23).[19]

This position can be fully attained only by getting in touch with and grieving over painful ways in which the desires of our Natural Child were blocked. This will "enable the Natural Child to emerge once more . . . free to hear and feel and see in his own way" (p. 124; compare p. 27). Yet this involves far more than a simple unfolding of the Child's organismic tendencies. It is, as Berne said, chiefly the responsibility of the volitional, rational Adult, who alone can assess the complex contemporary reality within which these desires must find expression (pp. 55-60).[20]

Harris's approach includes a religious dimension. (We will find that the more the inner child is emphasized, the more distinctions between "public" conversation and "religious" considerations will blur.) He regards religious experience as "a unique combination of Child (a feeling of intimacy) and Adult (a reflection on ultimacy) with the total exclusion of the Parent." The former may be more fundamental, for "the Adult's function in the religious experience is to block out the Parent in order that the Natural Child may reawaken to its own worth and beauty" (pp. 233, 234). Harris also proposes that the evolutionary process may be moving toward, and perhaps even be ready for, a mutational leap to an "'impossible, unprecedented' *transcendent man*" who will live according to "I'm OK—You're OK" ethics (p. 242; compare p. 224).

Whereas the Natural Child received modest attention in these pivotal works of TA, it fairly explodes onto the scene in many self-help books of the last decade or so. Charles Whitfield, for instance, equates the "Child Within—the part of us that is ultimately alive, energetic, creative and fulfilled," with our "Real Self." He also calls it the True Self, the Inner Child, the Divine Child, and the Higher Self (1987:9; compare p. 7). John Bradshaw introduces his *Homecoming: Reclaiming and Championing Your Inner Child* with verses from Christopher Morley:

The greatest poem ever known
Is one all the poets have outgrown
The poetry, innate, untold
Of being only four years old. (1990:4)

In prose, the description runs like this:

Although a child is still immature, he still has an organismic sense of wholeness, of I AMness. In other words, he feels connected and unified within himself. The feeling of unified wholeness and completeness is the true meaning of perfection, and in this sense every child is perfect. Unified wholeness is also what makes each child *special, unique,* and *wonderful. . . .* Children are also naturally spiritual. . . . Wholeness and spirituality are synonymous. . . . Spirituality involves what is deepest and most authentic in us—our true self. . . . Spirituality also involves a sense of connection and grounding in something greater than themselves. (p. 38)

For Bradshaw, this Wonder Child is the "essential self," the "soul" which will inform us of our real needs and desires if we can let it naturally emerge. For Whitfield, the inner child is an actual spiritual entity. He identifies its highest reaches with a transcendental or "observing self," which "'is not part of the object world formed by our thoughts and sensory perception because, literally, it has no limits'" (1987:137).[21]

As our inner child emerges, spontaneously tending toward self-balance, it is really this infinite awareness of cosmic harmony making itself known. In light of this eternal consciousness, each of us is not only going Home, "we *are* Home, already and always." In its perspective, "separation, suffering and evil are the absence of realizing Love, and are therefore ultimately illusions. . . . Evil or darkness is thus ultimately in the service of love" (p. 138). Realizing that some readers will find such language incredible, Whitfield insists that "spirituality is *experiential. . . .* We cannot know it ultimately through our intellect or through reason. . . . It is only be-able" (p. 127).

Bradshaw also encourages readers not to debate whether they really believe all this but to follow their inner child, who is innately religious (pp. 210, 258). The child needs to trust something beyond itself, the Great I AM. Yet each one possesses an I AMness "like God's I AMness. When I truly *am,* I am most like God."[22] When we view reality through our Wonder Child's eyes, we will see that our "whole life is perfect." Bradshaw exclaims that even his own "dysfunctional family, my alcoholic dad and co-dependent mom, my poverty—all were perfect. *They were exactly what I needed to experience in order to do the work I am now doing*" (p. 262).

To this point it may seem as if the Wonder Child does everything in these popular writings. Yet in many concrete discussions it is the Adult who recovers and releases the Natural Child from the wounded Adapted Child. Bradshaw suggests ways for the Adult to hear the Child's long-muffled voice and to help it work through suppressed grief. The Adult must then re-parent the Child by inculcating realistic structures and restraints in a caring way, which the Parent failed to do.

Though these writings stress getting in touch with feelings, and often treat thinking as a way of controlling or submerging them, they also insist that the Adult must teach the Child to distinguish thought from feeling. For instance, they critique *magical thinking*, which supposes that certain behaviors, thoughts and feelings can automatically and instantly make things better.[23]

This inner child movement has doubtless helped many make contact with and work through childhood wounds. But what, precisely, does it regard as the agency that overcomes this psychic alienation? Often it seems to be, as it was for Berne and Harris, the Adult—the mature, rational, volitional self who must rediscover, reclaim and restrain the Child. Yet when one remembers how much this movement's appeal depends on self-help books, brief intensive seminars, videos and TV images, the suspicion arises that this agency is usually the vision of a virtually omnipotent Child, effortlessly emerging to resolve the most complex modern problems in the simplest way.

Notice, for instance, how often this movement falls prey to that magical thinking which, in its Adult moments, it recognizes as inadequate. Despite reminders that genuine change takes time, more books will sell by claiming that "making contact with our inner child is a way to change our core material immediately" (Bradshaw 1990:xiv).[24] Despite repeated acknowledgment that working through such material requires help from others, such books stress the highly individualistic parenting of oneself. Despite the emphasis on grieving through what actually did happen, Bradshaw introduces a technique of reimaging the past, whereby "if you didn't get your infancy needs met . . . *you can give yourself a new infancy*" (p. 180).[25]

Perhaps magical thinking is most evident in the boundless confidence placed in the Wonder Child itself. This Child bears disturbing similarities to the omnipotent object with which narcissists seek identification.

Yet does the immensely popular notion of this self as a virtually perfected person inside one, a nearly divine preschooler (from whose perspective evil experiences appear good), provide an adequate solution to today's struggle for self-identity or an escape from it?[26] Is such a notion an inevitable outcome of the increasing simplification and optimism I have traced from Goldstein to Rogers, and from Berne and Harris to Whitfield and Bradshaw? Or can organismic psychology deal more subtly with self-formation?

C. G. Jung. Jung was one of Sigmund Freud's first disciples. Before long, however, Freud's approach seemed too simplistic. For though Freud spoke of many instincts, a single, sexually charged energy *(libido)* operating mechanistically, activated them all. For Jung, however, psychic energy, which he declined to reduce to physio-chemical forces,[27] flowed back and forth among multiple aspects and systems of the psyche, seeking equal distribution or balance. The *ego,* the *personal unconscious* and the *collective unconscious* are such contrasting systems. Jung's *ego* (much like Rogers's *self*) contains all contents of individual consciousness. People often identify it with their total personality. But beneath it lies the *personal unconscious* (corresponding to Freud's *preconscious*), where experiences that were forgotten, ignored, repressed or too weak to attract the ego are stored. These are potentially available to consciousness.

Even deeper is the *collective unconscious,* perhaps Jung's most novel and controversial concept. This consists of latent memory traces acquired during the history of the race, stretching back to its animal ancestry. Its components are *archetypes,* predispositions to experience people and events in ways which correspond to humankind's collective experience.[28] For instance, each man possesses an archetype which Jung calls the *anima,* the product of countless generations of men's experiences with women. Certain common images associated with women (such as the moon) are closely connected with this archetype, as are energies of a man's own feminine side.

When a particular male encounters specific females, these archetypal patterns shape the way he experiences them. Perhaps a particular woman arouses fear. The man usually supposes that the woman herself is threatening. But often characteristics of his own anima that he finds threatening are simply being aroused by her, and he identifies them with her (or projects them onto her). However, since the anima belongs to a transpersonal realm far greater than himself, the man experiences the threat as emanating from outside himself. Jung believes that women's experiences of men, and of their own masculine sides, similarly constellate around an animus archetype.

Every person, then, male or female, has feminine and masculine sides or characteristics between which psychic energy flows. Among other archetypes are the following: birth, rebirth, death, power, magic, unity, the hero, the child, God, the demon, the wise old man and the earth mother.

Jung's ego is not borne aloft by a smoothly flowing organismic current but assailed by subterranean energies pulling it to and fro. Moreover, society dictates which of these energies a person can and cannot express. So the individual develops a *persona:* a public personality which conforms to social expectations. Often the ego identifies itself with the persona . . . but only to be assaulted by an opposed system, the *shadow*. This is also an archetype, consisting of age-old animal instincts, together with socially disapproved urges and behaviors. Yet the shadow also contains the vitality necessary for being a complete person, which the persona only with great effort keeps in check. Jung rated the shadow's potential quite positively, estimating it as "90% gold."

Since persona and shadow pull behavior in competing directions, neither can be the individual's true center. Nor can the ego, so often opposed by the personal and collective unconscious. Instead, the true *self,* an archetype constituting the midpoint of all these systems, emerges slowly. Since the psyche's different polarities are actualized only through repeated energy interchanges among them, the self, which is their increasing balance, can emerge fully only during life's second half. It exists, as it were, midway between the conscious and the unconscious. It must be apprehended by attention to dreams and feelings as well as to projects and thoughts.

During life's first half, the ego often identifies itself with the persona. Then as the *self* begins arising from the unconscious, this persona-ego often feels threatened. It might feel vaguely restless, because established habits and relationships keep seeming less meaningful or else assaulted by and adrift among dangerous impulses and energies. The self acts as a final cause, the goal of each person's development or *individuation*. Jung also called this process the *transcendent function:* "the realization, in all its aspects, of the personality originally hidden away in the embryonic germplasm; the production and unfolding of the original, potential wholeness" (*CW* 2:110).

The self, like other archetypes, usually appears to consciousness in symbolic form. Among the most common are *mandalas*—figures in shapes such as squares, globes, lotuses and quadrated circles which represent balance and completeness. Other self-symbols are indistinguishable, psychologically, from God-symbols. The most adequate archetype is *Christ,* who represents not only complete human self-actualization but also its perfect merging with reality's infinite source. Although Jesus of Nazareth somehow elicited the self, the *Christ* symbol's continuing power, for Jung, depends on its archetypal foundation in all humans, not on any intrinsic connection with him (*CW* 11:152-57).

Yet the Christ symbol, according to Jung, lacks one thing: It is divorced from the shadow (which early Christians symbolized by Antichrist and the devil). Jung, however, insists that evil is terribly real, in both the struggles of mental patients and the horrors of the modern world. To underline this, he often insists that the devil be included in symbolization of God—as a fourth divine person, not merely as an inferior, opposing force (*CW* 11:164-92; 9:36-71; compare pp. 355-470). Yet if evil is intrinsic to psychic symbols of wholeness, would not *individuation* involve actualizing evil potentialities as well as good?

Though Jung often spoke as if radical evil were essential to both divine and human nature, he apparently intended to underline two main themes: that wholeness cannot be attained without acknowledging one's darker sides and that many tendencies which society suppresses must be incorporated into self-actualization. Neither emphasis requires that radical evil be as fundamental as good (Browning 1987:190-203).

Given this stress on struggling with our shadow and with inhibiting social forces, a person might wonder whether Jung's self might actually be constructed through conflict between social structures and impulsive forces, as in psychoanalysis, or whether it unfolds naturally along pregiven lines, as in organismic theory. An answer can be found by investigating the extent to which social realities and decisions imprint the self's actual shaping. The more they do, the more will his theory incline toward psychoanalysis.

The notion of a collective unconscious would seem to highlight the social dimensions of self-formation. Jung, especially in commenting on World War II, stressed that each person participates in collective guilt. Our shadow operates largely through *projection* of tendencies we fear in ourselves to other persons and groups. Irreconcilable hatreds for some groups (such as Jews) mirror the split between ego and shadow in individuals who hate. Even people relatively aware of their own shadows (who recognize anti-Semitism's psychological roots) still project certain hatreds and fears—by criticizing all Germans, all Europeans and so on (*CW* 10:194-226; 1957:83-125).

What, then, can free the self from this social guilt? For Jung modern society's collective tendencies—leaving decisions to bureaucratic states, "scientific" treatment of individuals as statistics and so on—discourage taking responsibility for our own individuation, including recognition of our shadow. Does this mean that, to change individuals, society should be transformed? Not really, for a political state "is nothing but a convention of independent individuals." Therefore, the only real solution, even for massive social problems, is for individuals to break from the mass and begin individuation: "The individual human being [is] that infinitesimal unit on whom a world depends" (1957:124-25, compare pp. 52, 68).

Jung finds this underscored in the *Christ* archetype: "Christianity holds at its core a symbol which has for its content the individual way of life of a man, the Son of Man, and . . . regards the individuation process as the incarnation and revelation of God himself" (p. 60).[29] A person might respond that Jesus was at least as concerned with transforming others and their relationships as with his own individuation and that personal development in a social context must involve mutual *self-renunciation* (Goldstein).

Jung, however, tends to interpret Jesus' stress on loving our neighbors, and even our enemies, as imperatives to accept the despised, shadow side of ourselves: "To accept himself in all his wretchedness is the hardest of all tasks." Accordingly, "acceptance of oneself is the essence of the moral problem and the epitome of a whole outlook on life" (1933:235). We must encourage this "sacred egoism," for it is our "strongest and healthiest power . . . a true will of God" (p. 238).

Consequently despite Jung's emphasis on humanity's collective character, he tends to regard self-actualization as a highly individual process, achieved more through a break from than a transformation of social relations. And though the complexity of this process, given the variety of Jung's contrasting systems, far surpasses that of other organismic psychologies, it still consists in the natural unfolding of a pregiven potential. Though Jung often describes the struggles of intrapersonal alienation more vividly than other organismic theorists, he assumes that the developing individual is essentially continuous with its deeper, original self and probably (as chapter five will show) with all other selves and with the heart of the cosmos.

Summary. What basic affirmations about today's struggles with psychological alienation can be derived from the organismic perspective? Unlike psychoanalysis, organicism does not regard drives or instincts in themselves as sources of alienation but as aspects of an harmonious overall self-actualization drive. Organicists tend to encourage free expression of our desires. Yet this may be congruent with a capitalist ethos, the very orientation which some psychoanalytic theorists (Marcuse, Lasch) blame for undermining self-formation.

Whereas social forces often alienate people from their deeper selves, these forces need not be altered to overcome alienation. For individuals are able, at least within an affirming relationship, to distinguish these forces' impact from their own self-actualization process and to follow the latter. This means that organismic psychology, in contrast to the general organismic orientation (which considers entities as parts of larger wholes), tends to have an individualistic focus. It also tends to suppose that unhindered expression of anyone's self-actualization process will harmonize socially with everyone else's, another assumption congruent with capitalism.

Since organismic psychologists locate alienation's main source in inappropriate social expectations, they often characterize today's society as too rigid. Many psychoanalytic commentators, however, who believe that selves must be formed around stable objects, find current society too fluid.

For organismic psychology, alienation is overcome by discovering and activating some original, naturally unfolding self-process. This may emerge almost magically (perhaps even narcissistically) as a Wonder Child or far more slowly and complexly, as in Jung's psychology. Organicism's basic message is that an authentic core self already exists and is more to be found and followed than forged. Which perspective offers the best hope for contemporary psychological alienation: *finding* a self (organicism) or *forging* one (psychoanalysis)? Is psychoanalysis more realistic about the extent of personal fragmentation, or does it overestimate the impact of instincts and social forces? Are organismic psychology's affirmations about underlying wholeness reliable or is it too idealistic and optimistic about the human situation?

Finally, how might a Christian view of self contribute to this public conversation? Might it take personal and social brokenness or sinfulness seriously, somewhat like psychoanalysis? Or might it emphasize humankind's created goodness and positive potential, somewhat like organismic psychology? Or might it combine elements of both themes? Chapters five and nine will explore these questions.

T H R E E

Ecological Alienation

lthough public discourse on psychological alienation may not often mention the environment, current conversation about the environment is often shaped by two similar overarching paradigms. The Darwinian perspective, like psychoanalysis, is a variant of the Newtonian paradigm. It divides its field of study into discrete units (individual organisms for Darwin, genes for neo-Darwinism) and emphasizes conflict among them.

Sigmund Freud believed that selves consisted of temporary harmonies among clashing instincts and social demands. In a similar fashion Charles Darwin believed that order in nature was but a tentative balance among organisms struggling for survival. Yet much as the resulting self could be relatively stable, though fragile, the emerging ecological order proved to be highly complex and balanced, though constantly threatened. Since conflict characterizes both the psyche and nonhuman nature, people need to be assertive and impose relative order on both, according to psychoanalysis and Darwinism.

Challenges to Darwinism often proceed from an organismic ecological perspective. Organismic psychology insists that a harmonious self-actualization process already exists within everyone. Authentic selves, then, need not so much to be *forged* from conflicting elements as *found* and, by learning to listen to their natural rhythms, *followed*. Similarly organismic ecology[1] argues that nonhuman nature is much more cooperative than Darwin imagined and that its order, like the psyche's, flows largely from inherent self-balancing processes. Consequently humans need not impose order on nature; they need only discover and then cooperate with those rhythms it manifests.

In today's public discourse organicism's response to Darwinism is often polemical. It blames the Newtonian paradigm in general for current environmental degradation. Newtonianism's reduction of life to dead matter, its dissection of ecosystems and organisms into externally related parts, its unconcern about goals or purposes (see chapter one)—such features are held responsible for modern humanity's tendency toward unlimited manipulation of nonhuman nature (see, for example, Merchant 1992:41-59).

Although organismic psychology tends to be individualistic (and even Newtonian in its social assumptions), organismic ecology often relates psychological and social phenomena holistically to the environmental. It portrays the contemporary socioeconomic world as driven by competition for financial gain and material possessions. Competition and struggle, which only few can win, separate not only individuals but races, cultures, genders and classes. Psychologically people are pictured as individuals isolated from and fearful of each other, emotionally undeveloped and empty, seeking to fill the voids with ever-multiplying goods and conquests. This same unlimited drive for acquisition and domination despoils the physical earth.

What kinds of positive responses do the organismic and psychoanalytic/Darwinian paradigms make to this critical portrait? In particular, how might they relate its ecological and psychological dimensions? Though this latter relationship has not often been discussed in detail, I suggest that our paradigms might conceive it as follows.

Organismic psychology stresses listening to our organism. This organism certainly involves the body, or physical nature. It would seem likely, then, that to the degree that we humans are out of touch with nonhuman nature, we might have proportional difficulty appreciating and deciphering that dimension of ourselves so closely related to it—our own physical bodies. Conversely, it would seem that the less appreciation and awareness we have of our bodies, the less we will respect and understand nonhuman nature. Accordingly, psychological alienation from our organism and ecological alienation from our surroundings would deepen and reinforce each other.

Contrariwise, drawing closer to one should greatly facilitate drawing nearer to the other. Such closeness to our organism and to other organisms would be mainly affective. Organismic theorists root alienations largely in contemporary people's lack of such affectivity. Organismic environmental advocates stress that behavior toward nonhuman creatures will not really change until we come to feel, on an affective or spiritual level, some deep affinity with them—which we cannot do unless we feel in tune with our own bodies.

The psychoanalytic and Darwinian perspectives would respond otherwise to the above portrait, based on a different understanding of the relationship of selves to their individual organisms and to the organism of nature. Affective awareness of these organisms' movements would not be enough to overcome the alienations depicted. For even when these organisms' movements are apprehended, they do not always flow in directions which best actualize selves or selves' relations with nature. Selves and societies will still be faced with conflicts among impulses, organisms and social forces that have no perfect solutions. To arbitrate these, people must make decisions that enlist volitional and rational powers—not only affectivity.

Remember Christopher Lasch's warning: desire for deep fusion with nature may stem from a regressive narcissism which cannot accept unsettling differences. Psychoanalysis and Darwinism would insist that both psychological and ecological alienation require wrestling with difference.

But how, in seeking self-fulfillment and interacting with nonhuman nature, might we employ mind and will in a way that affirms difference? One way, which might seem to flow most directly from Darwinism, would be to use them in struggling against individuals, other social groups and nature in seeking material gain. One response to the above organicist critique of this approach is arguing that competition provides the best route to everyone's socioeconomic fulfillment and that advancing technology, spurred on by industrial competition, can overcome environmental damage.

Lasch warns, however, that such an attitude may spring from a grandiose narcissism which does not really respect difference but seeks to destroy it. Might there be other self-fulfilling ways of approaching nature which use mind and will and assume some degree of basic conflict? That will be the crucial question to answer as we examine Darwinism further.

The major task of this chapter will be to examine the scientific views underlying our two ecological perspectives and to explore what is involved in developing an ethic for environmental involvement in relation to each one. For in current public discourse, different scientific orientations are commonly invoked as grounds for diverse environmental praxis. First, we will look at the Darwinian scientific perspective and show what kinds of environmental approaches it has inspired. Then we will do the same for the organismic perspective. I will keep asking how environmental issues are related to those of self-formation.

The Darwinian Perspective

Scientific foundations. Despite nineteenth- and twentieth-century efforts to reduce biology to a Newtonian science, many hold that it differs from Newtonian science in at least one respect: in explaining living creatures, it often seems necessary to speak of purpose. It seems natural to describe organs as being used "for" seeing, digesting and so on and organisms as acting "in order to" feed, rest and so on. A major feature of any biological theory, then, and especially of its impact on other fields, will be the explanation it gives of purpose or design.

When Charles Darwin (1809-1882) undertook his extensive scientific explorations (aboard the H.M.S. *Beagle* along the South American coast) between 1831 and 1836, most scientists thought that the entire world, whose intricate interrelatedness they were increasingly discovering, was supernaturally designed. Darwin, a former theology student, had been deeply impressed by the influential arguments in William Paley's *Natural Theology* to this effect.

Darwin's exposure to South America's creatures, however, began challenging certain expectations raised by this teleological orientation: first, that each species would occupy the environment most suited to it; second, that every kind of creature formed a link in a "Great Chain of Being," ordered in increasing complexity of matter through plants and animals to humanity (Bowler 1989:59-97).[2]

Darwin's observations challenged the notion that each species fits an optimal environmental niche. Some species ranged through many environments, some of which seemed unfriendly. Darwin found diverse species competing for the same niches and evidence that occupants of many niches had altered over time. Further, quite different species filled very similar niches on different continents.

Darwin also began questioning whether species were related like precisely graded chain links. In the Galapagos, Darwin found many diverse yet similar species on different islands. Would an all-wise Designer create numerous slightly different species, each to occupy just one locale? It seemed more likely that similar species had branched out by natural means from a common ancestor. Life seemed to be arranged not along one vertical stem of increasing complexity but into many radiating, horizontal branches of bewildering variety.

Darwin also began questioning the dominant geological school of the time, *catastrophism*. It held that prominent features such as mountain ranges had been suddenly formed during episodes whose violence enormously surpassed anything presently experienced. (Noah's flood was thought to be one of these.) Throughout his voyage Darwin was imbibing Charles Lyell's new theory called *uniformitarianism,* which proposed that all past geological changes were wrought through the same processes that are observable today. (Canyons, for example, were formed through millennia of erosion.)

Lyell also assumed *uniformity of rate:* that past processes had always operated at speeds like those we see today (Gould 1987:117-26).[3] This meant that change had almost always been slow, gradual and incremental. Darwin eventually accepted not only Lyell's uniformitarian methodology but also his *uniformity of rate.*

What was Darwin to make of his discoveries and this new geology? Back in England he observed how breeders, by selecting certain kinds of plants or animals for reproduction, could produce varieties with enhanced characteristics (juicier apples, woollier sheep and so on). Though breeders were not actually producing new species, it seemed to Darwin that closely related species, such as he had found in the Galapagos, could have arisen through extension of such a process. In fact, given enough time (and Lyell provided plenty) all species could have arisen from others this way. Yet species were also distributed, through space and time, in apparently random ways: some occupied favorable niches, others far less favorable ones; some species flourished while many had died out. If no Designer had selected among the variations thus produced, by what natural mechanism could this have occurred?

The answer came from economics. Adam Smith had assumed that if economic processes operated free from government interference, the wealth of all participants—workers and owners, buyers and sellers—would greatly increase (see chapter one). But Thomas Malthus argued that whereas food supplies increase arithmetically, population multiplies geometrically. Eventually, then, population will outstrip available food, and many of the poorest will die. After reading Malthus, Darwin exclaimed, "I had at last got a theory by which to work" (Barlow 1958:120).

It became obvious to Darwin that most organisms produce far more offspring than can survive, for if all those of a species did survive, "no country could support the product" (Darwin 1859:64). Accordingly population pressures set off "a struggle for existence" in which

> individuals having any advantage, however slight, over others, would
> have the best chance of surviving and of procreating their kind. On the
> other hand . . . any variation in the least degree injurious would rigidly
> be destroyed. This preservation of favourable variations and the rejec-
> tion of injurious variations, I call Natural Selection. (p. 81)[4]

Natural selection provided the cornerstone for Darwin's theory. Since
organisms that survived by means of it would be best adapted to their habitats, natural selection could explain the extraordinary, seemingly
designed, fit between creatures and environments. Yet one needed no
Designer—only a genetic process which produced occasional variations,
environmental constraints and millions of years. This approach assumes,
of course, that a creature's environment is of a given, often hostile, magnitude and that life consists in adapting to it.

This Darwinian perspective could acknowledge evolutionary "progress"
in only a very limited sense. To be sure, evolution produced increasing specialization; yet specialization limits the range of adaptability, and when
environments alter, that can lead to extinction. Darwin also believed that
populations seek to expand constantly and occupy every possible niche,
which perhaps is a kind of progress. Finally, though more complex life-
forms appeared over the very long haul, no intentional behavior, either by
organisms or by a Designer, was involved—only pure chance. Most branches on the evolutionary tree led to dead ends. The overwhelming majority
of creatures had become extinct.

Like the Newtonian and Freudian schemas, the Darwinian regards all
large-scale patterns and relationships as by-products of interactions among
much smaller units. For Darwin, these were individual organisms—though
a person could, taking his approach further, reduce them to components
such as cells, genes or Freud's neurons. Darwin avoided references to
properties, such as vital spirits, unique to life. Like Freud, Darwin eliminated all references to overarching design. Yet the clashes among his
organisms, like those among Newton's particles, Adam Smith's economic
units and Freud's instincts, produced an enormous amount of order—an
order, though, ever threatened by conflict and subject to disruption.

The reception of Darwin's theory. Generally speaking, *On the Origin of Species*
(1859) led most scientists and many educated persons to accept the general notion of biological evolution. Yet it convinced far fewer about natural selection. Most wanted to retain room for a divine design or progressive
life principle. Many found Darwin's work largely convincing, not because
it provided flawless solutions to particular problems but because it illu-

mined a large range of difficult questions.[5] Nonetheless, it involved several major weaknesses.

One was the fossil record. If Darwin's gradualistic scheme were correct, numerous transitions between species should have been preserved. Yet available fossils were of species that had endured for very long periods with little change, separated distinctly from each other. Moreover, the earliest fossils, those from the Cambrian era, were quite complex. Darwin attributed the absence of intermediate forms to the record's fragmentary character. Still, he lamented that "the absence of innumerable transitional links . . . pressed so hardly on my theory" (1859:307).

Second, Darwinism could not explain how genetic variations became dominant over generations.[6] So long as it provided no mechanism for so basic a function, many biologists favored *inheritance of acquired characteristics.* Jean Baptiste Lamarck (1744-1829) had supposed that traits acquired during an organism's life—greater strength and so on—affected its own genetic material and were passed directly to its offspring. By repetitions of this process such traits could be strengthened in succeeding generations. Perhaps most important, "Lamarckism," unlike Darwinism (which allowed this kind of inheritance only a minor role), allowed "life itself to be seen as purposeful and creative. Living things . . . *choose* their response to each environmental challenge and thus direct evolution by their own efforts" (Bowler 1989:258). In late nineteenth- and early twentieth-century society, where effort and innovation were applauded, evolution was more often understood in Lamarckian rather than in the more fatalistic Darwinian terms (Bowler 1988).

During the late nineteenth century, various optimistic interpretations of evolution appeared, all Lamarckian to some degree. Russian émigré and anarchist visionary Peter Kropotkin (a forerunner of *social ecology*) argued that animals frequently cooperate and that the success of such social instincts, not selection, was evolution's major force (Bowler 1983:55).[7] Henry Drummond similarly affirmed the survival value of altruism, a willingness to cooperate with others for the good of all, claiming that it guided evolution and is a witness to a loving God (Bowler 1989:215). For Samuel Butler, God promoted evolutionary design not as an external director but as an immanent vivifying force enabling organisms to fulfill their desires and thereby shape their futures (Bowler 1983:53, 73-74). Paleontologist Edward Cope, not unlike Hegel, identified this immanent God with consciousness, the ultimate cause of evolutionary progress (pp. 122-26).

To what extent were such theories based on scientific evidence and to what extent on efforts to soften the harsh alienations at Darwinism's core? Lamarckism's popularity illustrates the difficulties of basing a worldview and ethics directly on Darwinism.

By the early twentieth century, *inheritance of acquired characteristics* had been discredited and a fundamental "Newtonian" unit of heredity, the gene, discovered (see chapter one).[8] Gradually Darwinism was generally accepted. It became possible to conceptualize a species as a gene pool which sought to widen, filling as many environmental niches as possible. Evolutionary studies became largely statistical ones concerning populations, carried on in laboratories. Genes could even be regarded as evolution's major agents and organisms' bodies simply as "survival machines— robot vehicles blindly programmed to preserve the selfish molecules known as genes" (Dawkins 1989:195).

A mature neo-Darwinian synthesis was articulated in the late 1930s and early 1940s.[9] Neo-Darwinists, apparently recalling Darwin's severe outlook, sharply denied that any teleology had guided evolution, most of whose numerous branches had split off toward dead ends. They stressed that extinction and degeneration were common and that elimination or survival of genes occurred by pure chance. They denounced conceiving "progress" in terms of approximation to human status as anthropocentric. Moreover, they argued that human *cultural evolution,* though it emerged directly from organic evolution, was "essentially different in kind" (Simpson 1949:288). Therefore they tended to stress that ethical standards cannot be derived from the preceding naturalistic history (pp. 288-93). Only humans can formulate values and notions of progress (J. Huxley 1942:570, 575).

Nonetheless, neo-Darwinists discerned various "directions" in prehuman history to help us discern those values. According to George Gaylord Simpson (1902-1984), the fossil record witnesses chiefly to life's rapid increase and expansion—to "invasions of new realms of life and the continual creation of still more new realms, with the packing of each by organisms adapted to all its variations" (1949:115). Humanity, then, can be judged progressive for features which open up new adaptational possibilities: rapid population increase, control over its environment, ability to cope with many environments, capacity for specialization and others (pp. 244-52). Julian Huxley (1887-1975), considering animals which radiated most widely and became "dominant types" in their eras, concludes similarly that two basic criteria of progress are greater control over the environment and greater independence from it (pp. 558-66). Characteristics peculiar to *cultural evolution,* however, must be added. Huxley emphasizes the human capacity for thought, including its affective and aesthetic dimensions, which provides a third criterion of progress (pp. 572-76). Simpson stresses knowledge, which includes a responsibility to propagate and use it wisely (1949:309-24).

Though these scientists seek to base their socioethical conclusions on sober, stark Darwinian premises, have they done so? Or have they, somewhat like "Lamarckism," gone beyond what the former strictly imply? It does not seem entirely coincidental that neo-Darwinism valorized being independent from our environment yet controlling it, spreading vitality into as many new realms as possible and adapting and specializing rapidly with great skill. Is that not a mirror image of an efficient, expanding global capitalism?

Recently a neo-Marxist *dialectical biology* has proposed that many criteria by which neo-Darwinism determines advance (fitness,[10] complexity,[11] diversity and stability—along with its gradualism[12]) have little biological warrant. Yet these mirror the dynamic stability desirable in contemporary capitalistic societies, where rapid changes must be consistent with overall order. "Although individual elements in the system are changing place, the system as a whole remains in a steady state; in the same way individuals may rise and fall in the social scale, but the hierarchy of social relations is thought to be unchanging" (Levins and Lewontin 1985:22).[13]

If some of this is so, might this neo-Darwinist portrait be disconnected from organic evolution in a way its authors did not suspect: because it is less derived from natural history than read back into it? In any case, it shows how Darwinian evolution, despite the amoral arbitrariness and massive suffering it involves, can be correlated with some versions of human progress.

The challenge of punctuated equilibria. Neo-Darwinism, like Darwin, theorized that evolutionary change is very gradual. Yet today's fossil record yields the same general impression as did that of Darwin's time—of long periods of little change punctuated by rapid transitions to new forms. Few undisputed records of transitional forms have been unearthed. Accordingly a significant group of evolutionists has argued that this is exactly how life's history has run: through lengthy spans of equilibrium *(stasis)* punctuated by rapid introduction (say, five hundred years long) of new species.

Punctuated equilibria challenges the assumption, prevalent in modern society as well as in biology, that change is naturally progressive—that given enough time (and enough space through which to spread) natural processes will automatically bring improvement (Eldredge 1985:24-27). It challenges the notion that every process is dynamic, possessing inherent resources for progress. It proposes, instead, that whereas the overall life-system is dynamic, many aspects of it are static (Stanley 1981:189).

Punctuationism also questions what inferences can be made from laboratory studies, or from present processes in general, to what actually happened in the past. For history involves contingent events which were not necessitated by general laws and might have been other than they were. Like Darwin, punctuationists do assume that past events followed the general processes operative today (many include themselves in the broad Darwinian tradition). But, like catastrophists, they challenge the common uniformitarian assumption that these always occurred at the same rate.

What sorts of events, then, might have triggered rapid speciation? Most likely those that isolated small populations in rather desperate circumstances, forcing them to adapt quickly or perish.[14] Some such events were indeed "catastrophic." Earth's history has witnessed at least five major mass extinctions that exterminated at least 60 percent of extant species. Many smaller mass extinctions have also occurred. Numerous scientists believe that some were initiated by sudden extraterrestrial impacts.

In any case, in the then-current ecology survival would hardly have gone to "the fittest" (which probably perished *en masse*) but to "the luckiest" (those with some variation of no apparent value which suddenly conferred a wholly unforseen advantage).[15] Given this emphasis on widespread, unpredictable environmental disturbances, punctuated equilibria renders any notion of progressive patterns even less tenable than neo-Darwinism.

Extended to the social sphere, neo-Darwinism might lead a person to expect that progress will occur slowly but steadily and will balance opposed tendencies, as Adam Smith expected. Neo-Darwinism seems consistent with the Newtonian social paradigm. Punctuationism, however, might lead a person to expect that social institutions will tend toward long-term stasis and be altered only by revolutionary events (Stanley 1981:203-7).

Darwinism, especially in the form of punctuated equilibria, permits very little talk about evolutionary progress. Yet many who modified Darwinism's harsh implications (late nineteenth century), and even those who meant to affirm them (neo-Darwinism), could draw progressive consequences from it. Since notions of progress can have significant implications for environmental ethics, let me consider the plausibility of this endeavor before I turn to that theme.

Whereas certain directions of change can be discerned in evolution (for instance, from smaller to larger organisms), any claim that progress has occurred involves the additional value judgment that such change was for the better (Francisco Ayala in Nitecki 1988:78).[16] I agree with Ayala that such judgments cannot be derived directly from scientific study but always reflect the evaluation of an observer. Nonetheless though many scientists try to avoid making such judgments, others claim that various trends are clearly evident in the overall record and may be judged as positive.

However, some trends (for example, toward increasing complexity) seem almost intuitively obvious because evolutionary theory by its very nature tends to assume that they were occurring and reads them into time gaps where no actual evidence exists. We will find, though, that due to great diversities in organisms and time periods, significant difficulties attend the defining of comprehensive terms (for instance, *complexity*), deciding how to measure them, which units to measure (genes, species, orders and so on) and what establishes or falsifies claims (for example, that complexity has "increased").

Although humans are clearly more complex than prokaryotes, a common standard for comparing complexity among organisms is hard to find. One measure, proposed by the esteemed geneticist John Maynard Smith, is the number of cell types, or "amount of coding DNA present in the genome" (Nitecki 1988:219). Smith finds a very slight tendency for organisms that we think of as structurally more complex to have more coding DNA. Yet according to Ayala, there is presently "no way of measuring the amount of genetic information present in any one organism," for genetic information is not precisely equivalent to amount of DNA (p. 83). In cellular DNA content, moreover, humans come out well behind certain reptiles and plants (p. 98).

On the other hand, William Wimsatt and Jeffrey Schank believe that *"an increase in the possibilities for, and capability of, producing and maintaining a larger variety of more complex adaptations through evolutionary time"* can eventually be demonstrated in a very nuanced way, though they have not yet gathered enough evidence (p. 233). Yet Dan McShea, having measured vertebral columns in five species spanning more than thirty million years, found "complete absence of a trend in complexity"; George Boyajian and Tim Lutz found similar results investigating ammonoid shells from 615 genera (Oliwenstein 1993). Thus although many current creatures are more complex than Precambrian ones, difficulties in defining and measuring this term, along with dead ends and extinctions along the way, make it extremely difficult to affirm a clear general trend in this direction.

George Gaylord Simpson, as we saw, lauded life's expanding *diversity*— its invasion of new realms, leading to "creation of still more realms, with the packing of each by organisms adapted to all its variations" (1949:115).

Simpson claimed that this involved increase in the number of species, number of individuals, bulk of living matter and total rate of energy flow. Increase in species diversity (or the kinds of ways information is stored) is affirmed by Ayala and John Bonner (Barlow 1994:40-49; Wimsatt and Schank's definition also involves diversity).

Yet even today estimates as to the number of species that exist vary widely: from five to thirty million. And since about 75 percent are insect, a person might question how fully sheer numbers can be correlated with significant diversity (Nitecki 1988:86). Punctuated equilibria, moreover, maintains that species richness has never surpassed the Cambrian period. Estimates of its rise and fall vary greatly among diverse approaches, partly because they define species differently (pp. 40-43; compare pp. 222, 304). David Raup warns about the pull of the recent: since fossils of more recent organisms are more numerous and better preserved, many assume that less diversity existed earlier (Nitecki 1988:298).[17] Ayala, however, affirms that increase in number of individuals and their bulk since the Cambrian "seems certain" and that energy flow has increased faster than bulk (pp. 87-88). Yet increases in number of individuals and total bulk can be disadvantageous for species in many circumstances.

In any case, one aspect of diversification does involve a broad directional trend: spread of life to new niches. It seems that land was first inhabited by plants in the Silurian Period, by amphibians in the Mississippian, by reptiles in the Pennsylvanian and the air by birds in the Jurassic. Otherwise, whereas more diversity surely exists now than in the Precambrian seas, it seems about as difficult to speak of a clear, general evolutionary trend toward diversity as it does of one toward complexity.

Finally, Ayala suggests a line of progress along increasing "ability to perceive the environment, and to integrate, coordinate, and react flexibly to what is perceived" (p. 91). This ability, he claims, underlies Julian Huxley's two main criteria: independence from and control over the environment.[18] Ayala argues that this ability, in general, is more advanced in animals than in plants, in vertebrates than in invertebrates, in mammals than in reptiles and in reptiles than in fish (p. 92). This advance is generally correlated with increases in the nervous system and brain size. Nevertheless in humans this characteristic becomes an "incomparable advancement" which "sets apart *Homo sapiens*," for while "other organisms become genetically adapted to their environments, humans create environments to fit their genes" (p. 91).

Clearly, then, this is no general trend increasing at somewhat similar rates through many evolutionary branches but one that has taken an enormous, unparalleled leap in one species. Ayala asserts that that is "not a general characteristic of the evolution of life" (p. 92) and that by some other standards, such as synthesizing organic materials from inorganic, humans are about the least "advanced." Gould, moreover, questions how often brain size can be correlated with increases in this ability discussed by Ayala (p. 329).

In conclusion, I find the evidence for overall directional evolutionary trends ambiguous at best. Today complex creatures, highly diversified environments and one species capable of discriminating perception and flexible reaction to all this exist. As one glances back over evolutionary time, phenomena appear that might be viewed as trends toward these. Yet they are too widely scattered, too open to differing readings and too surrounded by opposing tendencies to be confidently interpreted this way. They offer evidence for progress only if the current situation and its values are read back into the past.

Environmental implications. As in psychoanalysis, conflict and struggle are inherent in the Darwinian perspective. Purposeful order arises only by chance. Always is it threatened with disruption, much as are psychoanalysis's fragile selves. Taken seriously, this perspective presents a dark, chaotic picture of the cosmos. It cannot, I have argued, instill realistic confidence that evolutionary history is progressive. It can arouse fears about finding ourselves or any consistent meaning in life. People shaken by such fears can seek security from commercial possessions or appealing images of them.

Darwinism can also arouse heroic striving for purpose. It can encourage participation in highly competitive societies and affirm such competition despite the large numbers who lose out. But in stressing conflict with the environment, and perhaps the evolutionary success of independence from and control over it, might it not increase today's ecological and social alienation? And might not such striving resemble grandiose narcissism (see chapter two)?

Still, a Darwinian environmental ethic is not likely to be read off directly from nature's rhythms but will probably involve some constructive use of mind and will. Might creative inquiry into the Darwinian schema yield some principles for resolving environmental dilemmas?

1. Social Darwinism. Since Darwin's time the ethical and social implications most often connected with Darwinism, at least in the popular mind, have been associated with this term, even though the perspectives linked with it historically have been quite diverse. Consideration must be limited to its best-known advocate, Herbert Spencer (1820-1903), even though he developed his main views before *On the Origin of Species* and preferred Lamarck's view of inheritance. Spencer greatly influenced magnates of American industry such as Andrew Carnegie and John D. Rockefeller.

Science, according to Spencer, had shown that matter is continually changing. This change, he postulated, involves progress. Though Spencer gradually came to appreciate Darwin's emphasis on evolution's branching and many dead ends, he always insisted that progress was inevitable in the long run (Greene 1977:82-86). The main force producing biological and social improvement was constant environmental pressure. Spencer concluded that governments should not shield people from such pressure by providing education, health care or aid to the poor. Though critics accused him of wanting to eliminate the unsuccessful, Spencer replied that he simply desired to remove all obstacles which prevent people from exerting their best efforts.

Because society and ethics evolve, the latter can provide no permanent values. Individuals should do whatever will most likely benefit themselves within their social framework, trusting that this will aid progress in the long run (Bowler 1984:227). Spencer did believe, however, that the sympathetic instinct, emphasized by Hume and Smith, had been expanding during social evolution. Eventually it would balance so perfectly with the other basic moral impulse, the one for personal rights, that coercive government would be unnecessary. Although these two instincts had originally conflicted, the former was being so transformed through Lamarckian inheritance that altruistic behavior would eventually become fully associated with feelings of pleasure.

In the meantime, however, individuals, groups and nations who were losing the survival struggle were simply proving their unfitness for modern life. Social Darwinism, by founding ethics as directly as possible on Darwinian evolution, could legitimate their exploitation and eventual extinction. Consistently followed, it would most likely regard human transformation of the environment, especially in competition with other peoples, as part of the same survival struggle, where the same self-interest and disregard for weaker rivals should prevail. (This is the meaning I give to social Darwinism in what follows.) One should remember, however, that Spencer viewed all this as necessary for hastening the time when sympathy should permeate human affairs and produce so much happiness that government would fade away. Still, social Darwinism does not so much interpret evolution creatively as attempt to derive ethics directly from it.

2. Extension of natural feeling. Though self-interest motivates all action in a Darwinian universe, some argue that creative appropriation of this principle, or of another foundational in this universe, can support environmental altruism through an extension of natural feeling.

In his *Descent of Man* (1871) Darwin extended Hume's and Smith's emphasis on *sympathy* somewhat as Spencer had. He argued that in evolution sympathetic instincts carry adaptive value, for creatures drawn together by them often have advantage over those who remain isolated and can successfully rear more offspring than the latter. (Kropotkin and Drummond developed this claim much further than Darwin.)

Darwin also affirmed that although individualistic and social tendencies often conflicted sharply, the latter gained ascendancy the more that humans were shaped by culture and religion and were enabled, through development of reason, to appreciate the long-range consequences of their actions. Human sympathy, in his view, could expand to ever wider circles, eventually even to animals, especially when reason showed that others' fate has a bearing on our own. Contemporary moral theorists, such as J. Baird Callicott (1991), have erected on this basis an environmental ethics extending to the ecosystem. It claims that the biological drive for survival, when shaped by interaction with others, eventually gives rise to tendencies which greatly modify its self-regarding direction. These can encourage environmental involvement by increasing sympathetic feelings toward other creatures and appreciation of the value of cooperation with them.

In "Newtonian" ethical systems, *self-interest* underlies all behavior. Yet, contrary to initial appearance, it also can become a foundation for other-regarding acts even if sympathy is lacking. For if the well-being of others is somehow connected with our own well-being, value can be extended to those others simply for that reason. When environmental issues first became major public concerns, most ethicists assumed that only humans could be direct objects of ethical consideration. If values were ascribed to other creatures, it seemed that they could be only *instrumental values*—values derived from their capacity to fulfill human interests. Wilderness and its species could be preserved, for example, because present and future generations would need these resources.[19]

The 1973 Endangered Species Act granted unprecedented protection to all species as groups and to the "critical habitats" on which they depended. However, their basis for receiving this was their "aesthetic, ecological, educational, historical, recreational, and scientific value to the Nation and its people" (Nash 1989:176). Thus it has allowed protection of some species to be compromised or overridden when these interests seemed inferior to greater—usually economic—ones. Yet, in general, most environmental legislation passes and most environmental projects succeed only when people are persuaded that human benefits, at least in the long run, will be attained from them.

Nevertheless, in any environmental issue the number of interconnected factors involved (for example, habitat size, air quality, number of species), including effects on future generations, is enormous. Can human self-interest, or sympathy, provide a vision holistic enough for deciding what values should accrue to *all* these factors? Will not certain human interests (for instance, maintaining a lumber operation which reduces habitats and pollutes air) at least seem to override some—and perhaps many? And whose human interest will be considered: local residents or those far away; prosperous groups or impoverished ones; the present generation or distant future ones? In short, can any one self-regarding perspective, rooted at least initially in struggle against others, provide a perspective holistic enough and undergird a praxis cooperative enough to adequately consider the value of all other factors involved? And will nonhuman creatures be sufficiently respected if they have only *instrumental* value?

3. Animal rights. We have seen that John Locke rooted the human individual's value, which gave it certain inalienable rights, in its possession of reason. This perspective underlies America's Declaration of Independence. But Locke also sought a scientific basis for ethics and defined good as that which leads to pleasure or diminishes pain and interpreted evil as that which produces pain or diminishes pleasure. Applying this second criterion more broadly, Jeremy Bentham argued that "the question" for deciding whether creatures have rights "is not, Can they *reason?* nor Can they *talk?*, but Can they *suffer?*" ([1789] 1948:311; see chapter one).

Over the last two centuries the "inalienable rights" principle has wielded explosive liberating force when applied consistently to blacks, women and voiceless people in many places. In the 1970s Peter Singer and Tom Regan began arguing that extending rights to animals—on the basis not of reason but of sentience—was the natural expansion of other liberation movements.[20] The consistency of this claim with Darwinism resides not in an extension of human interests to animals (granting them *instrumental value*) but in claiming that an *intrinsic value*, rooted in the organism's basic urges, should be extended to more creatures.

For Singer, capacity to feel pleasure and pain renders all creatures with this ability equal. We consider it wrong to harm noncognizant infants and mentally impaired adults, he points out. Should we not think the same about animals? This forbids killing of animals under any circumstances and mandates vegetarianism. Singer has been especially concerned to curb animal research, factory farming, zoos and hunting practices such as whaling. Out of respect for democratic procedures (a very Lockean tendency), he advocates working within political channels whenever possible. If this fails, other approaches can be considered case by case. Civil disobedience can occasionally be justified; violence seldom can be, though violence against property in freeing laboratory animals might be (Nash 1989:169-70).

Animal rights ascribes value to individuals, though Singer can allot some secondary value to habitats as the indispensable contexts for animal well-being (p. 141). But many argue that among animals, species are more important; thus one member of an endangered species may be more valuable than many members of a nonendangered one. And why refrain, for instance, from culling a deer herd if continuance of all its members will bring some to starvation, and thus greater suffering? Moreover, is not the value that humans are asked to grant individual animals quite inconsistent with the value they have had in evolution?

Animal rights is also critiqued for limiting value to sentience (to "somewhere between a shrimp and an oyster" [Singer 1975:188]). Are not plants, and perhaps rocks and rivers, just as essential to the existence of habitats? And do not habitats, which support many creatures, possess more broadly encompassing and sustaining value? This movement has also been criticized for simply extending, but not essentially challenging, the atomistic concept of society which has helped produce much environmental damage (Rodman 1977).

One might ask, in sum, whether this attempt to base rights and value on an aspect of self-interest, even though its range has been greatly extended, is not still too narrow. Given the interconnectedness of all creatures which modern environmentalism—especially its organismic forms—so strongly impresses upon us, can value be limited to any portion of them and can the self-interests of these be the basis for assigning values to all others (ecosystems, for instance)?

4. Evolution versus ethics. If the Darwinian perspective is commonly thought to sanction actions such as those recommended by social Darwinism, it is not surprising that some might draw an opposite conclusion: Ethics can never be based on evolution. Such a thesis was promoted not only by Darwin's critics but also by Thomas Huxley (1825-1895), one of his staunchest defenders, especially against religious objections. (We have seen how his grandson, Julian, sought to separate ethics from a neo-Darwinian basis, even though he carried some evolutionary values across the gap.)

Since Huxley was not about to ground ethics in reason or revelation, he, like Hume, Smith, Darwin and Spencer, had to derive it ultimately from the sympathetic or social instincts (1989:84-88). Yet he was convinced that "the ethical process is in opposition to the principle of the cosmic process" (p. 89). Consequently he had to face the issue confronting all Darwinian ethics in its sharpest form: If ethics originated in evolutionary struggle, how could ethics come to oppose it?

Huxley's answer was that, although one energy permeates the cosmos, it produces incessant conflict. Accordingly this energy, which works in "nature" through survival of the fittest, can work through humankind to oppose this principle (pp. 70-71). Huxley repeatedly affirmed that evolution can give no reason "why what we call good is preferable to what we call evil" (p. 138) and that "social progress means a checking of the cosmic process at every step and the substitution for it of . . . the ethical process" (p. 139).

Unlike Spencer, who believed that Lamarckian inheritance was increasing the strength of altruistic sentiments and their harmony with egoistic ones, Huxley felt that conflict between these would always remain intense, in both individuals and society.[21] In this and in denying inevitability to progress, Huxley was more Darwinian than Spencer. And precisely because natural processes could not be trusted to improve social conditions, Huxley rejected Spencer's laissez faire, insisting that social institutions must do much of the work. Yet Huxley also opposed liberal and radical movements, finding that they too overestimated humanity's potential goodness and progress.[22] His insistence that ethical life would always involve tension is reminiscent of Freud.

Huxley offers little specific input for environmental involvement.[23] Yet he raises questions crucial for all the approaches we are considering: To what extent can environmental ethics be derived from evolutionary science? Or, to put it in general ethical terms, to what extent can ethical *oughts* be derived from scientific descriptions of what *is*? And, to the extent that they cannot, from what other sources might they come?

Summary. Darwinism, when taken seriously, depicts a stark universe where conflict is inevitable. It contributes to that contemporary sense of reality as constantly shifting, without stable reference points around which to constellate some sense of self. Individuals lacking these often thirst after ever-multiplying possessions, or images of them, to fill the void. According to psychoanalysis, such conflicts cannot be resolved simply by listening to our organism, for that organism itself is in conflict.

Similarly, Darwinism affirms that human conflicts with nonhuman nature cannot be resolved merely by listening to its organisms or ours, for conflict exists among them all. To overcome psychological alienation, one must also employ reason and will in developing a sense of self. To overcome ecological alienation, in a Darwinian perspective, we must employ reason to develop criteria for environmental involvement. This chapter has explored four kinds of criteria so far.

First, we have seen how biological evolution is often incorporated into some view of progress and then used to sanction the latter. I have argued that neither Darwinism nor the best available evidence offers firm support for any theory of progress.

Second, social Darwinism legitimates using reason and will in self-interested struggle against nature by the strongest human groups. I must concur with organismic ecology's criticism of this attitude: it is too much a cause of environmental problems to be their solution.

Third, some principle operative within Darwinian evolution can be creatively appropriated and considered capable of redirecting it. I have discussed three: sympathy, self-interest and sentience. I have wondered whether the first two can provide a vision holistic enough or a praxis cooperative enough to overcome the self-concern at their basis and whether nonhuman creatures should be granted only *instrumental value,* as in the self-interest perspective. Yet whereas the sentience principle grants some of these creatures *intrinsic value,* I have wondered whether it extends value widely enough, particularly in relation to species and ecosystems.

Fourth, evolution can be regarded as too contrary to ethics to provide any basis for it. In this case a person's approach to environmental issues must be rooted in some other source.

The Organismic Perspective

I have asked whether the ethical principles often derived from a Darwinian perspective can extend far enough to provide adequate responses to today's environmental problems. Can a holistic perspective be extrapolated from individualism, cooperation from self-interest, regard for nonhumans from instrumental value, concern for species and ecosystems from sentience—or can ethics even be derived from evolution at all?

The organismic perspective, while answering yes to the last question, critiques the Darwinian for faulty assumptions. The insights crucial for environmental action, it claims, will be missed if we treat organisms or genes as externally related individuals on the model of Newtonian physics. For then we notice conflicts among them but fail to realize that they are already elements of functioning organic wholes. We do not perceive that underlying harmony among nonhuman and human creatures already exists and needs not so much to be forged, by reason and will, or extended from specific evolutionary principles as to be *found* within the whole and then *followed*. Purposiveness can be attributed to organic wholes themselves and need not be regarded as the paradoxical outcome of clashing impulses or individuals.

Scientific considerations of this sort have most vividly entered public discourse with the *Gaia hypothesis*. In brief, it affirms that the various life forms on our planet so interact with, balance and modify each other that "the entire range of living matter on earth . . . could be regarded as constituting a single living entity . . . endowed with faculties and powers far beyond those of its constituent parts" (Lovelock 1987:9).[24] In other words, the earth itself, or at least its living systems, throughout its history, constitute a single self-regulating organism.

Though few scientists have endorsed this hypothesis in so strong a form, and whereas some dismiss it as overly metaphysical, its claims have brought many compartmentalized disciplines into dialogue—a necessary step in directing scientific resources toward environmental issues. Yet Gaia is more than a scientific principle. Gaia was the ancient Greeks' earth goddess. Perhaps, then, it functions as a primordial unconscious symbol *(archetype)*. For many today Gaia evokes a profound sense of interconnectedness among all earthly beings. And although this affective or religious dimension frightens away some scientists, it raises many people's consciousness and energy for environmental involvement, while enhancing appreciation of their own organic selves.

James Lovelock and the atmosphere. In the 1960s NASA asked this versatile British scientist to find some way of detecting whether life existed on Mars. Finding no generally accepted scientific definition of *life*, Lovelock devised his own approach.

According to the second law of thermodynamics, the energy available for work in the universe as a whole is constantly running down, or tending toward equilibrium (the tendency called *entropy*). Living systems, however, counter this trend, for they move toward greater complexity. They decrease their internal *entropy* by taking in free energy from their environment. Now entropy can be conceptualized in terms of mathematical probability. Molecules in a closed system tending toward equilibrium move toward their most probable distribution—complete disorder. Life, then, which moves in the opposite direction, involves a highly improbable distribution of molecules.

Consequently, if life existed on Mars, its atmosphere would contain gases associated with life and be characterized by disequilibrium. Mars's atmosphere, however, proved to be in virtual equilibrium, so Lovelock concluded that the planet was lifeless. (Thereupon NASA, which was looking for arguments supporting the possibility of Martian life to boost its funding, dismissed him.)

Lovelock next turned to earth's atmosphere. He found it, in stark contrast to Mars's, in high disequilibrium, representing "a violation of the rules of chemistry to be measured in tens of orders of magnitude" (1987:10).[25] This presented a new problem, for Lovelock, like most scientists, had been taught that all this "could adequately be described by the laws of physics and chemistry" (Thompson 1987:83). But something else was apparently contributing to the atmosphere. Since improbable chemical combinations and high disequilibrium point to life's presence, Lovelock concluded that this was the missing factor.

Eventually Lovelock offered evidence like the following to support this hypothesis. Nearly all the oxygen produced by photosynthesis in plants is used up through human and animal respiration. Yet despite this, the amount of oxygen in the atmosphere has increased over life's history, enabling more life to flourish. Moreover, during the same time temperatures reaching earth from the sun have risen about 30 percent—enough to kill most life-forms—yet earth's temperature has remained relatively stable. How have these two results been attained?

Lovelock notes that temperatures rise as certain gases, such as carbon dioxide, increase in the atmosphere and correspondingly fall as these gases decrease. Now when plants die, some carbon is buried with them; eventually it is washed down rivers and deposited on the ocean floor. This process reduces slowly the carbon dioxide in the atmosphere, gradually lowering temperatures in a way which would balance increasing warmth from the sun. At the same time as the carbon molecule from the CO_2 is removed from the atmosphere, however, an oxygen molecule is added, slowly increasing the overall amount of oxygen (Lovelock 1987:69-72; Joseph 1990:126-27).[26]

Thus through a process regulated by living creatures (plants), oxygen has gradually increased and carbon dioxide gradually decreased in a manner favorable for spreading life. Atmospheric concentrations of methane, nitrous oxide, nitrogen and ammonia have been governed by the same and interrelated processes (1987:72-83).

Along these lines Lovelock eventually developed an argument for Gaia's existence: "Wherever we find a highly improbable molecular assembly it is probably life or one of its products" (1988:34). Further, "where these profound disequilibria are global in extent, like the presence of oxygen and methane in the air . . . we have caught a glimpse of something global in size which is able to sustain and keep constant a highly improbable distribution of molecules" (p. 38).

Lovelock often claims that talk about Gaia as "living" or as an "organism" is not meant to attribute conscious or purposeful behavior to some entity. It is intended to point out ways in which earth's processes interact with and balance each other. It aims at countering tendencies to study phenomena as isolable entities, ignoring their interrelations with everything else. Most important, it is a *hypothesis*. The main issue is not "whether the Gaia Hypothesis is right or wrong, so much as whether it causes one to ask valuable questions" (Joseph 1990:79).

Yet for Lovelock, Gaia really seems to be more. Psychologically Gaia also symbolizes or evokes a sense of life's unity, which "makes it seem, on happy days, in the right places, as if the whole planet were celebrating a sacred ceremony" (1988:65). Lovelock, however, is not a formally religious man. To him, a transcendent Father seems remote and belief in him confining. Questions about the cosmos's ultimate origins seem too abstract. But Gaia, a

living organism a quarter as old as the Universe itself and still full of vigor is as near immortal as we ever need to know. She is of this Universe and, conceivably, part of God. On Earth she is the source of life everlasting and is alive now; she gave birth to humankind and we are part of her. (p. 206)[27]

Lovelock draws further implications from this general religious awareness. A person can likely infer "that the universe has properties that make the emergence of life and Gaia inevitable" (p. 205). This counters gloomy evolutionary portraits of a wholly purposeless cosmos (1987:12). Nonetheless Gaia, as known through natural processes, is not only nurturing and comforting, she is also "stern and tough . . . ruthless in her destruction of those who transgress" nature's rules (1988:212; compare p. 208). Gaia teaches, however, that death is an inevitable part of life and not evil in itself.

Finally, Lovelock believes that evolutionary history indicates that the human race is becoming something like Gaia's brain or nervous system: "She is now through us awake and aware of herself. She has seen the reflection of her fair face through the eyes of the astronauts. . . . Our sensations of wonder and pleasure, our capacity for conscious thought . . . are hers to share." Perhaps humanity's growing awareness of this will lead us to renounce all greed, nationalism and tribalism and join "the commonwealth of all creatures which constitutes Gaia" (1987:148).[28]

Lynn Margulis and the microsphere. While James Lovelock has been occupied with the large atmospheric layers surrounding earth, Lynn Margulis has focused on earth's tiniest organisms. Out of admiration for these minute creatures, she often criticizes the assumption that humankind plays creation's foremost role. Her most widely-read volume— *Microcosm* (coauthored with her son, Dorion Sagan)—seeks to "deconstruct" this traditional perspective by rewriting evolutionary history from the bottom up—"from the vantage point of microbes" (1986:33).[29]

Margulis and Sagan argue that evolution's most important steps were taken, or "invented," by microbes. As the first bacteria began swimming in ancient seas, early earth's highly volatile climate annihilated many. Yet these crises forced bacteria to diversify. Fortunate mutations and genetic recombinations survived by "inventing" processes such as fermentation, nitrogen fixation and then photosynthesis, "the most important single metabolic innovation in the history of life" (p. 78; compare pp. 17, 95-96).[30]

Margulis and Sagan affirm that bacteria, and hence early life, took over the globe "not . . . by combat, but by networking" (p. 17). Since bacteria are not surrounded by membranes as are cells, genetic material can pass quickly among them, producing new forms constantly. Interrelated in this way, "all bacteria" form "one organism" (p. 89).[31] Each bacterium is a "team player" which "never functions as a single individual"; together bacteria form, as it were, "a worldwide decentralized democracy" (pp. 91, 96). Spreading over the planet, this "bacterial superorganism" transformed its environment, cycling and recycling its elements through various metabolic processes. As Lovelock stresses, these processes helped produce and regulate atmospheric gases. The environment became so interwoven with bacteria that, from then until now, we can hardly determine where life ends and the inorganic begins (p. 93).

Combining and recombining at rapid rates, these bacteria were "functionally immortal" (p. 93). And since our own DNA derives in unbroken sequence from them, "the microcosm lives on in us and we in it" (p. 22). Today bacteria still "support the entire biota"; each creature, in fact, should be regarded as "a microcosm—a little universe, formed of a host of self-propagating cells, inconceivably minute" (pp. 18, 20).[32]

For full-blown nucleated *eukaryotic cells*[33] to emerge, however, early life had to endure a severe crisis. Bacteria needed hydrogen, a gas which was originally abundant, whereas oxygen, which was scarcely present, was lethal for them. Gradually, however, the available hydrogen began decreasing. Although the omnipresent waters contained much hydrogen, no early bacterium could sever hydrogen's bonds with oxygen. Eventually in some ancestors of today's cyanobacteria, which were already using sunlight for photosynthesis, mutant DNA produced a second photosynthetic reaction center. With the sunlight transmitted through this center, these bacteria began splitting water molecules into hydrogen and oxygen. Gobbling up the freed hydrogen, these microbes multiplied quickly.

Yet the rapidly increasing waste product of their labors, oxygen, began annihilating other bacteria in "a holocaust that rivals the nuclear one we fear today." More than half of all species were extinguished. Yet out of it "came one of the most spectacular and important revolutions in the history of life" (p. 109). Without this aerobic respiration and the far greater energy it released, eukaryotic cellular life would have been impossible.

Oxygen, which had once composed .0001 percent of the atmosphere millions of years ago advanced to today's level of 21 percent, as Lovelock stresses. The "microcosm did more than adapt: it . . . changed life and its terrestrial dwelling place forever" (p. 109). If this oxygen level were slightly higher, most things would be incinerated; if slightly lower, most organisms would asphyxiate. Margulis and Sagan, like Lovelock, believe that this consistency results from cooperative "cybernetic control of the Earth's surface by unintelligent organisms." For Margulis, this "calls into question the supposed uniqueness of human consciousness" (p. 111).

The difference between prokaryotic and eukaryotic cells, however, is still so great that Margulis and Sagan believe that it could not have been bridged gradually. Instead, a new process called *endosymbiosis* must have leaped the gap. For example, mitochondria, membrane-bounded, oxygen processing components within nearly every eukaryotic cell, may have originated from fierce, oxygen-breathing bacteria which burst their prey asunder, devouring them slowly from inside out. But when the host cells died, so did the invaders. Eventually, the invaders learned to keep the hosts alive, and to benefit from some of their host's functions, while providing them oxygen-processing and other services. Gradually each microbe surrendered some individual functions, and the two lived on as one in symbiotic fashion.

Despite the ferocity of the original relationships, Margulis and Sagan extract some general lessons from the process. "In the long run the most vicious predators bring about their own ruin by killing their victims. Restrained predation—the attack that doesn't quite kill or does kill only slowly—is a recurring theme in evolution" (p. 130). More broadly, microbial activity throughout history has shown that "symbiotic cooperation is at least as important as 'survival of the fittest' competition; in order to compete—in order to get into the game in the first place—you have to cooperate" (Margulis, quoted in Joseph 1990:36-37; see pp. 34-51).[34]

Though Margulis and Sagan trace life's history to the present, their interpretive principles are largely formulated by the time they pass that "fundamental division in life forms," between prokaryotes and eukaryotes (p. 17). Let us, then, consider those trends that they predict, far more confidently than does Lovelock, will continue.

"Life"—despite the difficulty of defining it and distinguishing it from nonlife—is often the subject of their sentences. "Life" creates "its own problems and solutions;" it "so far has proved to be immortal" (pp. 243, 263). Life's history, of course, has passed through terrible sufferings, such as the "oxygen holocaust" and mass extinctions (stressed by punctuated equilibria). Yet out of such disasters, "like the phoenix rising from its own ashes, DNA regenerated into new long-lasting forms."

Indeed, like an artist whose misery catalyzes beautiful works of art, extensive catastrophe seems to have immediately preceded major evolutionary innovations. Life on Earth answers threats, injuries and losses with innovation, growth and reproduction (p. 197).

Among the catastrophes, Margulis and Sagan include Hiroshima and Nagasaki, which cleared the way for the rise of modern Japanese industry (p. 237).[35] Lovelock counts at least ten catastrophic collisions with planetesimals and marvels at Gaia's quick recovery (1988:86; compare Joseph 1990:103-11; Lovelock and Allaby 1983). Despite all this, life's evolution keeps accelerating; cooperation increases, for "symbiosis is the rule in evolution" (Margulis and Sagan 1986:229; compare pp. 246, 248, 250).

Margulis and Sagan keep trying to "deconstruct" humanity's traditional self-estimate by insisting that humans must learn to cooperate with other species and that life will achieve its aims even if *we* self-destruct. At the same time, they stress that the microcosm is now "evolving *as us*," for we are "a permutation of the wisdom of the biosphere" (pp. 67, 195). At present, in fact, life "may be nearing 'the greatest turning point in four billion years'"—something that "relative to former evolutionary advances . . . may occur nearly instantaneously," something which will make the future "as different from our world as we are from bacteria" (pp. 230, 261, 235). Gaia is "struggling . . . to give birth. . . . Across the black rivers of space, we are the biosphere's bridge to the stars" (Sagan 1990:18).

Life will expand into this *supercosm*, of course, only through advanced technology. We should not regard technology as alien to nature, for just as "no clear line can be drawn between organisms and their environment" so can none be drawn "between what is 'natural' and what is not" (Margulis and Sagan 1986:260).[36] In the future, new species will arise from humans.

Perhaps remnants of what we are now will become parts of machinelike creatures, just as microorganisms have become parts of us. Yet even if we disqualify ourselves by blowing up the present biosphere, life will inevitably take this step.

Responses to Gaia. Though other expressions of today's organismic ecological perspective exist, Lovelock's and Margulis's well illustrate its general features. Lovelock points to one self-balancing macrosystem; Margulis eulogizes countless microentities which operate as one interlocking organism. In both cases, biota function not as competitive individuals but as interactive, creative, purposive unities. Contrary to Darwinism, where life must adapt to a hostile environment, life transforms its surroundings. Life evolves in a progressive, even inevitable, direction. Extinctions and massive sufferings are appraised as making novel development possible. We can become attuned to this process by apprehending it as the expression of a nurturing goddess who interconnects all things—yet sometimes destroys many, giving expression to terror like that aroused in a Darwinian cosmos. (Jung described the Earth Mother *archetype* as both nurturing and devouring.)

Humans are alternately described as irrelevant to the life process and as the agencies through which it becomes conscious and advances further. The overall portrait yields glimpses of Hegel. Organismic psychology's main message is that a self-balancing *self* process already exists and that we need to *find* and *follow* it more than we need to *forge* it. Organismic ecology claims that a creative, self-balancing world process exists and that we must find and follow it or ignore it at our peril.

Some of Lovelock's, Margulis's and Sagan's wilder speculations show why the Gaia hypothesis makes some scientists nervous. Yet in the late 1980s several high-level Gaia conferences were held. Almost all scientists would endorse this hypothesis in a weak form: *The biota influence the global environment.* Many are considering a moderate version: *The biota modify the overall system in some significant ways.* Few, however, accept the strong form: *Life controls the environment* (Joseph 1990:89-93). In any event, the hypothesis is probably too comprehensive to ever be decisively affirmed—or rejected. Its value will lie in bringing many compartmentalized biological and geochemical fields into invigorating dialogue.

Some scientists, however, charge that Gaian claims are inaccurate, or at least confused. Paul Ehrlich, a neo-Darwinian and outspoken environmentalist, cautions that coevolution strictly speaking, carries no overtones about cooperation: "Coevolutionary interactions in which each player gains a net benefit are much less likely to occur than coevolutionary interactions based on attack and defence or simply competition. . . . Most coevolutionary relationships undoubtedly end with a loser." Further, "one cannot say that coevolution is itself stabilizing or destabilizing, because it may be either, and changes in other factors may alter the balance" (1991:19-22). Meanwhile, among ecologists

> the idea of the balance of nature and the fragile interdependence of all the elements of an ecosystem are regarded in many quarters as being more fiction than fact. Natural systems seldom display the long-term tendencies toward stasis that would justify such notions of balance, nor are they so fragile that any change will throw the whole system into convulsions. (Visvader 1991:36)

The chief environmental implications drawn from Gaian theory do concern cooperation and ecological balance. Yet even here confusion arises. For Gaia is credited with guiding systems toward regularizing homeostasis (Lovelock's main emphasis) *and* propelling them toward unprecedented innovation (as Margulis often stresses). During the oxygen holocaust, the biota formed "one of the most destabilizing forces ever." But if "Gaia stabilizes, and Gaia destabilizes . . . then is there any possible behavior that is not Gaian?" (Kirchner 1991:41).[37] What, then, is the value of postulating any such all-encompassing agency or of turning to it for practical guidance?

Others attribute much of Gaia's popularity to its apparently more benign portrait of evolution. Richard Dawkins complains that "the Gaia theory thrives on an innate desire, mostly among laypeople, to believe that evolution works for the good of all" (Joseph 1990:56). This complaint recalls earlier efforts to interpret evolution progressively and touches the theory's inner consistency. For despite its emphasis on cooperation, it presupposes much of the traditional evolutionary view. It takes for granted several evolutionary beliefs:

□ that more than 99 percent of all species which existed have perished

□ that an overwhelming percentage of mutations are deleterious

□ that nature, even when preserving species through balancing processes, seems entirely indifferent to individuals

□ that countless highly developed animals become prey for each other, or otherwise perish, in ways which surely include suffering

But to what extent can an emphasis on cooperation, purpose and progress be integrated with what still is such a painful struggle for survival? Which aspects of Gaian behavior should humans follow in relating to their environment? Might the organismic emphasis on cooperation suggest some possibilities that the Darwinian paradigm cannot?

Environmental implications. Since Darwinism pictures humanity and non-humans in conflict, some find that it legitimates continuing struggle against the latter (social Darwinism). Yet others, we have seen, claim that principles operating within Darwinism's conflictive cosmos (sympathy, self-interest, sentience) can, if extended through human thought and effort, ground a different environmental ethic. I have wondered whether these principles can be extended far enough. (Can individualism give rise to a holistic perspective, self-interest to cooperation, instrumental value to true regard for nonhumans, sentience to species and ecosystem concern?) Organismic ecology, however, affirms that reciprocal, self-balancing rhythms between humans and nonhumans already exist. What contributions to environmental ethics might be derived from this different scientific perspective?

1. *"Let Gaia do it."* If Gaia is the self-regulating rhythm balancing all biotic (and perhaps abiotic) systems and if humanity is one of these, whatever environmental damage we cause, other natural processes will eventually counteract it. Dorion Sagan points out that landscapes fouled by today's technology were once polluted burial grounds for the oxygen holocaust's countless bacterial victims. Perhaps since technology has arisen from evolution, today's environmental blights are an unavoidable phase in life's journey to the stars (Sagan 1990:17-18; compare pp. 27-28, 175, 182).[38]

In the 1970s, James Lovelock was first to demonstrate that chlorofluorocarbons (CFCs) were accumulating in the atmosphere, threatening the ozone layer. Not until 1988, however, did he urge banning their emission. Why? Lovelock was so impressed by Gaia's self-regulating capacities that he kept waiting for some counteracting natural process to begin.

If all human activity is a direct expression of Gaia, this organismic perspective could legitimate vast environmental devastation. Organismic ecologies, however, do not go this far. They generally affirm that humans, having developed self-consciousness, are able to diverge from, or intentionally cooperate with, nature's activities. We must model our behavior not on every tendency evidenced in evolution but on the cooperative ones.

2. *Deep ecology.* One of today's most activist and most publicized environmental approaches calls itself "deep"—first in the sense of "ever-deepening questioning of ourselves, the assumptions of the dominant world-view in our culture, and the meaning and truth of our reality" (Devall and Sessions 1985:8). This process leads to basic intuitions about nature and ourselves—intuitions shared by most primitive peoples—which are deep ecology's norms (pp. 65-66).[39]

The first norm is *Self-realization.* We recognize it as a basic principle of organismic psychology. For Carl Rogers, self-realization was attained by allowing our organic processes to flow naturally, unhindered by inhibiting social expectations.[40] Deep ecology's Self, however, includes the cosmos. We realize our small selves only as we participate in the actualization of the Cosmic Self, which includes all creatures (Devall and Sessions 1985:67). This awareness implants the kind of profound, affective communion with every being emphasized in organismic ecology; ethically it shows us that "if we harm the rest of Nature then we are harming ourselves" (p. 68).

Moreover, "alienation subsides. The human is no longer an outsider, apart," for our roots are in other creatures, back through evolutionary time. We are "only recently emerged from the rainforest," so the saying "'I am protecting the rainforest' develops to 'I am part of the rain forest protecting myself. I am that part of the rain forest recently emerged into thinking'" (p. 243).

The second norm is *biocentric equality*. It articulates Warwick Fox's intuition that "we can make no firm ontological divide in the field of existence. . . . To the extent that we perceive boundaries, we fall short of deep ecological consciousness" (quoted in Devall and Sessions 1985:66 from Fox 1984:5-6).[41] It means that all creatures have an equal right to live and attain their own forms of self-realization within the larger Self-realization (p. 67). It also entails that all things—including plants, rivers, rocks, species and ecosystems—have *intrinsic value* derived neither from human self-interest nor from a capacity for pleasure and pain (p. 70). This base-line equality is thought not to blur over but to emphasize and promote great diversity. Evolution, through increasing symbiosis and complexity, has been producing this over time. The greater the diversity among organisms, then, the richer and fuller the universe and "the greater the self-realization" (p. 76).

The fact that most organisms, including humans, must prey on others for survival presents problems for such thoroughgoing equality. Though deep ecology forbids humans to reduce diversity, it must add "except to satisfy *vital* needs" (p. 70). But "vital needs" is deliberately left vague, for it can be variously understood in different geographical and social settings (p. 71). Vegetarianism, for instance, is not always mandated.

Deep ecology also seeks to reduce humanity's negative environmental impact by favoring a decrease in human population (p. 70). Some deep ecologists have carelessly suggested that AIDS and African famine may be performing such a task.[42] Moreover, with the self-regulating Whole at its center, deep ecology, like other organismic approaches and in contrast to animal rights, values wholes over parts. Since ecosystems make possible the existence of individual members, deep ecologists often accord the former the greatest value.[43] Herds can be culled to further their overall well-being, and a single member of an endangered species might carry greater worth than many humans.[44]

On a practical level most deep ecologists stress preservation of full ecosystems—of wilderness—as arenas where natural evolution can keep occurring (Foreman in Bookchin and Foreman 1991:72).[45] Yet they seldom invest great effort in national or global *reform environmentalism* (through standard political and social channels). They are usually skeptical about society's ability to reverse its destructive ways and feel that moderate political approaches tend to get coopted (pp. 71, 75, 113).

Instead, they often promote *bioregionalism*—efforts of small, committed groups to live in local areas in life-enhancing ways. Such groups seek to be models, to incarnate visions, of how humans might live in harmony with Earth (Devall and Sessions 1985:18-29, 162-77). They claim not to reject all authority but only centralized, hierarchical, enforced authority. They seek to be self-regulating communities, like those found in nature. Such an approach could be called "deeply conservative" (p. 21).

In social and political matters, deep ecologists follow a minority tradition of direct, often dramatic, action. They share some similarities with the Peace Movement. Some organizations, such as Greenpeace, stress that means must be consistent with ends; although they harass seal-pup slaughters or whaling expeditions, they avoid all violence. Others, such as the radical Earth First!, may "monkey wrench" bulldozers intended for logging operations, but usually they limit violence to property.

Theoretically, however, can an ethic which rejects any clear distinction between humans and other creatures denounce all violence against other life? Most other creatures are ready to defend their vital interests this way. Dave Foreman, founder of Earth First!, regards himself "as part of the wilderness defending myself" and considers "one hundred percent nonviolence as life-denying" (Nash 1989:196). This issue again raises Huxley's question about how directly ethics can be derived from evolution, or even from ecology.

3. *Ecofeminism.* Like deep ecology, ecofeminism affirms for all entities *"the freedom to unfold in their own way unhindered by the various forms of human domination"* (Fox 1989:6). Both are "deep" philosophies calling for inward transformation and self-realization. But whereas deep ecology regards *anthropocentrism* as the main problem, ecofeminists single out *androcentrism*.

Feminism is commonly subdivided into three orientations, which each approach the environment somewhat differently. *Liberal feminism* affirms that women have the same basic abilities and should be accorded the same rights and privileges as men. It generally supports *reform environmentalism*. Both *socialist feminism* and *cultural* (sometimes called *radical*) *feminism* note that women have been largely identified with nature in the West and that both have been subjugated in similar ways. *Socialist feminism*, however, regards "nature" and "women" as we know them as social constructions of capitalist patriarchy and believes that both will be freed only when it is altered. *Cultural feminism* asserts that many female-male differences are biologically based and that women are more in tune with, and will better promote liberating attitudes toward, nature.

Many cultural feminists believe that patriarchy arose several millennia ago as hunter-gatherer societies who worshiped an earth Mother succumbed to agricultural and urban civilizations (including the Hebrews) that worshiped a male sky-god (Diamond and Orenstein 1990:23-34). Many of these feminists worship the goddess, "the Divine as immanent in and around us" whose "'good book' [is] nature itself." They stress "the experience of *knowing* Gaia, her voluptuous contours and fertile plains, her flowing waters that give life, her animal teachers." In such experiences "the distinction between inner and outer mind dissolves, and we meet our larger self, the One Mind, the cosmic unfolding" (pp. 5, 8; compare pp. 112, 153).

Though this kind of ecofeminism has probably received most publicity, many feminists do not embrace its spiritual sensitivities and caution that identifying the feminine with nature reinforces, rather than challenges, the patriarchal mentality.[46] In any case, these holistic intuitions sound much like deep ecology's.

Other ecofeminists, however, suspect that deep ecology's Self may be the product of male psychological processes, as described by the feminist appropriation of *object relations* (see chapter two). According to this approach, remember, boys split from their primary, maternal care-giver much more sharply than girls and experience a sense of lonely particularity. This can give rise to longing for reunion with the mother, which can be projected on to other things that promise to provide a safe, containing wholeness—including nature. Deep ecology's Self may be a product of this longing for fusion, which Christopher Lasch would associate with regressive narcissism.

Yet this notion of Self-realization, by promoting indiscriminate union with the Whole, overlooks commitment to specific relationships (p. 136). It implies that a person becomes a full Self without concrete interactions with others. On the ethical level, simply insisting that *all* creatures have *intrinsic value* either fails to give guidance for specific decisions (which involve choices among competing values) or produces "a kind of ecological totalitarianism in which the good of individuals is subservient to the good of the whole" (p. 147). Women's experiences of embodiment, however, involve "a *lived* awareness that we experience in relation to *particular* beings *as well as* the larger whole" (p. 137). They imply that genuine relationships with nonhumans will be possible only if these creatures are somehow truly *different* (p. 151). In general, ecofeminists seek to avoid "isolated egos on the one hand and unconscious blending on the other" (p. 147).

Yet although deep ecology's norms of Self-realization and biocentric equality may clash conceptually with appreciation of particularity and diversity, its practical emphasis on bioregionalism affirms them and shares with ecofeminism values such as the following. Bioregionalism involves becoming native to a particular place and learning to live on its terms, rather than transforming it to fit our predetermined tastes (p. 158). Bioregionalism counters centralization of power and encourages self-government in which all participate. Moreover, bioregional living gives importance to physical tasks and to interpersonal conciliation, activities in which women have gained much skill (p. 160).

In broader political matters, ecofeminists can stress concrete dimensions which can escape deep ecologists. For example, whereas deep ecology promotes general population decrease, ecofeminism warns that population control often involves patriarchal domination of women and that for Third World women, especially, living standards must rise—and thus economic transformations occur—before limiting families becomes realistic (p. 12).

4. *Social ecology.* Like many ecofeminists, social ecologists fear that movements such as deep ecology, which blame humanity in general for environmental problems, fail to realize that particular groups and structures carry the major responsibility and that oppressed humans also need liberation from them. Social ecologists also worry that the mysticisms of both deep ecology and cultural feminism encourage blind submission to what may seem to be nature's demands (for instance, a decrease in human population), which rather than liberating humans will simply reverse the domination humankind now exerts over the rest of nature (Bookchin 1990:8-9; Bookchin and Foreman 1991:30-32).[47]

Actually social and deep ecology have quite different foci and sensitivities. The former emphasizes grassroots urban organizing, supports workers and minorities, and does little with wilderness. The latter finds some minorities and many workers blatantly antienvironmental, can regard

commitment to wilderness as a litmus test and fears that any group stressing social dynamics will assume that once these are resolved environmental problems will solve themselves. Tensions between the two movements
escalated in the late 1980s, but serious reconciliatory efforts were made to
avoid splintering the environmental movement.[48]

Murray Bookchin, the best-known social ecologist, argues that human
domination of nature is rooted in human domination over other humans.
Much like cultural ecofeminists, Bookchin paints a rather romantic picture of early hunter-gatherer societies. They did not struggle for survival
against nature, for nature was nurturing (1990:32-33). Society's main problem, as feminists affirm, is hierarchy; but Bookchin insists that it was initially political, neither gender related nor economic. (I will explore this
further in chapter four.) Hierarchy's growth climaxed in the state, "a pro-
fessional system of social coercion" (p. 66). The nation-state is allied with
capitalism, a wholly evil force (p. 94) which "must *continually* expand until
it explodes all the bonds that tie society to nature" (p. 128).

Bookchin critiques deep ecology's tendencies to treat humans in biological, rather than social, categories. Of course, humans, according to our
"first nature," are entirely the product of a natural, "*cumulative* evolution
towards ever more varied, differentiated, and complex forms and relationships" (p. 36). Yet this process is "of a nature rendered more and more
aware of itself" that eventually produces our social, or "second nature."
This enables us "to choose, alter, and reconstruct [our] environment—
and raise the moral issue of what *ought* to be, not merely live unquestion-
ingly with what *is*" (p. 41).[49] Consequently humans are, or at least can be,
"the voice, indeed the expression, of a natural evolution rendered self-conscious" (p. 203). Yet if we continue down the capitalist path, we can destroy
the biosphere. How can we avoid this?

We must recover possibilities for sounder social and ecological living
that were by-passed in history. Bookchin deplores environmental romanti-
cisms which elevate affective and aesthetic experience and swamp rational
capacities for remembering and reconstructing history (pp. 21, 73, 108,
110, 116, 118 and so on).[50] With hints from such sources, social ecologists
seek—like deep ecologists—to construct and live out contemporary visions
of egalitarian, ecologically sound community life. Yet, though they begin
with local groups, social ecologists envision eventually decentralizing great
cities and intermixing agriculture, soft technology, small urban centers
and wilderness throughout large areas (we will see how in chapter four).

Though Bookchin stresses that the environmental crisis forces people to
begin thinking about options like this, he clearly regards social recon-

struction as the key to it. Nonhuman nature remains in the background. And though Bookchin agrees with ecofeminism that hierarchy is the major problem, his program will work only if people, despite diversities, unite around universal human values. Movements putting gender, race or bioregional concerns above these will make poor allies.

Summary. Organismic ecology's most basic emphasis is that since harmony and cooperation appear often in evolution (more often than Darwinism supposes), environmental involvement should build directly on these tendencies. Even more directly than Darwinism, organicism draws the ethical *ought* from its reading of the scientific *is*.[51] Much as organismic psychology bases self-formation on listening to our individual organism, organismic ecology bases environmental action on discerning nature's harmonious organic patterns.

Yet this procedure involves a fundamental flaw, for organicism regards evolution as inherently progressive. And it credits nature or life or Gaia with spearheading this process through destructive calamities as well as with promoting harmony and cooperation. But if ethics are derived strictly from evolution, no reason can be given for preferring the latter tendency. A person could equally infer, as do social Darwinists, that humans are to promote evolutionary advance by emulating Gaia's disruptions. Indeed, glimpses of this inference appear when Earth First! considers violence or Dorion Sagan ponders whether technological devastation heralds Gaia's birth pangs or when tragedies such as Hiroshima and Nagasaki are valorized for allegedly positive consequences. Yet organismic ecologists clearly intend to derive ethics from Gaia's harmonizing, stabilizing activities.

I must conclude, then, that the evolutionary portrait, even on an organismic reading, contains strongly conflicting tendencies. It is highly ambiguous, and cooperative implications can be derived unilaterally from it no more than theories of progress can.

How does organicism respond to the specific environmental attitudes that Darwinist ethics seeks to establish? Darwinism, first, derives cooperation from sympathy and self-interest. Can organicism ground cooperation more convincingly?

Aside from the general tendency to base cooperation on evolution, the most common approach, stressed in deep ecology and often found in cultural feminism, points to experiences of oneness with an all-encompassing Cosmic Self. Psychologically this is one form of that affective communion with nature which organicism encourages. Ethically, it is claimed, cooperative conclusions emerge from such experiences, for they entail that "if we harm the rest of Nature then we are harming ourselves" (Devall and Sessions 1985:68).

Yet this approach, like Darwinism, derives other creatures' value from self-interest. Further, as other feminists insist, it avoids recognizing that differences are essential for genuine cooperative relationships. Psychologically this kind of Self-realization resembles the regressive narcissism that cannot cope with real difference.

Second, some forms of Darwinism grant nonhumans *instrumental value,* whereas others extend *intrinsic value* to all sentient creatures. Can these kinds of value induce humans to regard others seriously enough?

Deep ecology responds by broadening intrinsic value to all beings— including inanimate ones, species and ecosystems. This would likely deepen respect for every creature, yet intrinsic value hardly seems derivable from evolution, which is often ruthlessly indifferent not only to countless individuals but to species and even ecosystems.

Further, deep ecology bases intrinsic value on *biocentric equality.* Yet deep ecology itself realizes that humans (not to mention all other animals) must use other creatures to satisfy "vital needs." Otherwise said, many creatures have instrumental as well as intrinsic value. But simple affirmations of equality (such as the theme of Self-realization) do not adequately recognize difference. Though they claim to appreciate diversity, they fail to acknowledge that creatures' diverse functions give rise to different values which must be recognized in making ethical decisions. Though every entity may have some intrinsic value, ascribing equality to them all helps little when choices involve competing values.

Third, I have asked whether an adequately holistic perspective can arise, as Darwinians claim, from individualism.

Organicists answer with a fundamental vision of all things being interconnected. If interconnectedness is clearly distinguished from identity and involves creatures that are truly different, this awareness seems more intrinsically comprehensive and compelling than any that Darwinians can attain by extending some evolutionary principle (sympathy, for example) indefinitely. Such a vision, functioning psychologically or spiritually, can energize that affective sense of communion crucial for authentic environmental involvement. I agree with organismic ecology that awareness of interrelatedness with all creatures should humble human arrogance. Yet I find this arrogance reaffirmed in its frequent assertion that humans now guide the entire evolutionary process, for we are (progressive) evolution become conscious.

Holistic awareness, then, does seem to be better established on an organismic than on a Darwinian foundation. However, neither cooperation nor intrinsic value seems to be convincingly derivable from organicism or Darwinism. Both cooperation and intrinsic value, I will maintain, are basic Christian values. But if they cannot be grounded in either scientific perspective, we must ask the question Thomas Huxley raised: Whence do they come?

Finally, I note that organismic environmental ethics, unlike the Darwinian, usually recommends significant social change. This flows from the organismic perspective itself, which regards all things as so intrinsically interrelated that changes in any one realm involve changes in others (even though organismic psychology does not apply this logic to society). Darwinian ethics, however, which starts by valuing individuals, cannot deeply challenge societies rooted in this same axiology. Interestingly, however, the organismic environmentalisms I have discussed do not stress overall structural social change so much as establishing particular communities which challenge the status quo by living out different values. I will consider this kind of social strategy further in chapters four, seven and eleven.

How might a Christian view of nature contribute to this public conversation? Would it tend to see nonhuman and human nature as permeated by hostility and sin, analogously with Darwinism? Or would it stress all nature's potential goodness and harmony, much as does organicism? Or would it be compatible with various insights from both perspectives? Chapters six and ten will consider these questions.

FOUR

Social Alienation

Much public discourse on contemporary psychological and ecological alienation occurs between proponents of two major paradigms. One, the Newtonian (which includes the psychoanalytic and Darwinian perspectives), divides reality into individual units. It proposes that any harmony among them arises, paradoxically, out of underlying conflict. It assumes that such harmony will always be imperfect and that humans must work creatively to enhance it. The psychological task involves using reason and will to help construct a self—a continuous ongoing challenge—out of conflicting impulses and social demands. The environmental task involves either discovering ethical norms within the evolutionary struggle (sympathy, self-interest and sentience have been proposed) or deriving them from some other source.

The second, the organismic paradigm, proposes that the ultimate realities are not individuals but organic wholes, of which particular entities are internally related components. Conflict is a more "surface" phenomenon, for harmony, except where humans have disturbed it, already exists in self-balancing rhythms among these components. We need not *forge* harmony out of conflict so much as *find* these underlying rhythms and then *follow* them. The psychological task involves learning to hear our unified organic rhythms and to be drawn into their self-actualizing process. The environmental task involves learning nature's rhythms and experiencing affective unity with the dynamism of Gaia, Life or a cosmic Self-actualization.

It has become clear by now that psychological and ecological alienation and their overcoming are shaped by social forces. According to many psychoanalysts, our society's fluidity increases the difficulty of forging selves out of conflicting elements. According to some psychoanalytic social critics, capitalism's dissolution of traditional customs and structures and its intensifying of human appetites accelerate this fluidity. Organismic psychologists claim that social restraints and expectations cripple our organismic selves, and organismic ecologists blame environmental problems on socioeconomic forces which seek to reshape nature and society without limit.

It is now time to consider directly those current perspectives which shape social awareness and action. The Newtonian paradigm is perhaps most clearly expressed today through the libertarian perspective. Previous chapters have mentioned organismic criticisms of Newtonianism, but we now need to hear it on its own terms.

Libertarianism treats individuals as the basic social realities. Though it acknowledges that their economic and social desires do not perfectly harmonize, it argues that the best balance among them can be attained by allowing them free interplay, which requires sharply reducing government. Quite unlike psychoanalysis, however, which regards significant social shaping of selves as inevitable, libertarianism strives for maximum emancipation from all social restriction, for it regards the state in particular as the chief force which alienates people from their individual and social potential. Libertarianism's major goal is more to weaken than to reform the state, and it rejects restructuring society in line with social visions and values.

In public discourse of social alienation we find what I shall call a *holistic perspective* similar to the organismic psychological and ecological perspectives (though organismic psychology's social orientation, in practice, has been more individualistic than holistic). I do not call it organismic, however, because this term implies that underlying unifying rhythms already exist, even if disturbed by humans. But holistic social theories include an element that has so far appeared only in Newtonian ones: the depth and pervasiveness of conflict. It seems that few thinkers, surveying social situations in which people actually live, can regard conflict as more or less surface, capable of rather rapid resolution if the right underlying rhythms are discerned and followed.[1]

In fact, holistic theories (especially socialist ones) usually view today's social alienation as more serious than do individualist-capitalist ones. They regard cataclysmic conflicts, perhaps revolutions, as necessary for its overcoming. Nonetheless these theories, quite unlike libertarianism, articulate visions of better societies as integrated wholes, involving balance among interrelated elements. For this reason they are holistic, even if they are not, precisely speaking, organismic. The holistic perspective assumes that individuals are and always will be shaped by some social structures. Consequently reformation of these structures, rather than emancipation from them, is its goal.

This chapter will explore the libertarian perspective first, then the holistic perspective. A final section will summarize similarities and differences between them. As I proceed, I will ask what implications they carry for psychological and ecological alienation.

The Libertarian Perspective
Enlightenment foundations. Although current libertarian social philosophy may not have gathered an overwhelming, explicit public following, many of its arguments provide sophisticated expressions of the "conservative" mood sweeping many Western countries since the 1970s. Libertarianism is actually an effort to recover much of what the Enlightenment called "liberal" social theory.

According to John Locke's social outlook, human individuals take the place of Newtonian physics' distinct particles (see chapter one). Each is ultimately moved by sensations of pleasure and pain, but each is also governed by reason and possesses intrinsic rights to life, liberty and property. All social and political arrangements can be viewed as features of a "social contract" to which each one has voluntarily agreed and whose specific provisions can be altered if, and only if, a majority concurs. Government has no business restraining anyone more than necessary for mutual protection and should allow individuals maximum liberty in ordering their possessions and lives.

David Hume, we also recall, was more skeptical than Locke about what reason could grasp (see chapter one). It could not know, and therefore could not direct action toward, what society *ought* to be. Instead, reason can only guide us toward attaining what *is* in fact desired by our passions, or feelings. Now, "each person loves himself better than any other single person" (1888:487), and this self-love expresses itself especially in desire for possessions. But if each person wants as many possessions as possible, how have humans learned to live peaceably in society? Would not this passion lead rather to continual warfare?

Hume argued that through trial and error people gradually learned that each person has a better chance of acquiring and keeping possessions if they agree on rules of *justice* which punish any who seek to take another's property. Such justice does not consist in positive personal or social qualities but chiefly in restraints against interfering with others. The social virtue of justice, that is, is not some ideal known chiefly through reason, and to which all social practices should conform. Instead, it consists of practical rules which people slowly developed as their self-love curbed itself or acquired a new direction (p. 492). Rules of justice worked out in diverse sociohistorical circumstances are therefore somewhat different.

This notion that practical social wisdom emerges gradually through ordinary interaction, producing better results than rational utopian idealism or long-term centralized planning, is central to the libertarian perspective (Barry 1986:19-43). It parallels Adam Smith's claim that the best economic arrangements emerge spontaneously and slowly from interplay among short-range, self-interested passions. To keep government from interfering with these activities, Smith limited its functions to (1) defense, (2) administering justice (protecting property, enforcing contracts and so on), and (3) projects too great for private effort, such as road-building, issuing bank notes and education (see chapter one).

Smith also asked what moral virtues were necessary for society to function. The first he named was *prudence*—looking after yourself and bettering your situation. Prudence, however, had to be pursued within the framework of (second) *justice.* The third virtue, *benevolence,* was positive activity for the benefit of others. However, although benevolence would greatly enhance society, Smith claimed that only prudence and justice were strictly necessary for it to function. Smith and Hume also stressed that relationships among their separate individuals could be strengthened by *sympathy,* the virtue that Darwinian ethicists extend to other creatures and sometimes even ecosystems.

Later economists such as Thomas Malthus and David Ricardo predicted that Smith's capitalistic system would not increase everyone's wealth but would, on the contrary, drive many workers toward subsistence and even starvation. Nevertheless capitalism seemed so successful in creating wealth that it was not widely challenged in the United States (very broadly speaking) until the Great Depression. This catastrophe sharply challenged faith in the economy's ability to regulate itself, and a "social democratic" consensus arose. It granted the government significant authority to set and revise overall social goals and to stimulate the economy by financial measures (largely following the economic theories of John Maynard Keynes [1883-1946]). It assumed the benevolent, or at least the objectively neutral, character of the state. Faith in mechanistic, self-regulating economic and political processes sharply declined.

Recent libertarianism. By the mid-1970s, however, dissatisfaction with the social democratic consensus was becoming vocal in many countries. In the United States increase in real income, which had been almost uninterrupted throughout the sixties, had slowed to a crawl. Heavy government welfare expenditures seemed to have produced little fruit. Some libertarians pointed to statistics suggesting that poverty, illiteracy and racial and class tensions had grown considerably worse (Murray 1984; Gilder 1981). Government expansion into many spheres had increased that uneasy sense of being controlled by faceless, unresponsive forces—of the average individual's alienation in mass society. At the same time, despite the benevolent intentions of government social programs, alienation among classes and races seemed to have increased. I will sketch some main features of the libertarian response by looking briefly at three chief spokespersons[2] and then discussing some ecological and psychological implications of their views.

1. *F. A. Hayek* critiqued government planning by challenging the human capacity to know enough about the market and society. Reminiscent of David Hume, Hayek insisted that "the concrete knowledge which guides the action of any group of people never exists as a consistent and coherent body. It only exists in the dispersed, incomplete and inconsistent form in which it appears in many individual minds" (1953:29-30).[3] How, then, can these fragments of knowledge, which no person or group can coordinate rationally, be brought together to guide social and economic action (1949:54)? Hayek answered, much as Hume and Smith had, only when these fragments are allowed to interact spontaneously through market mechanisms developed gradually and unreflectively through the centuries.

Hayek added, however, that this lengthy process was continuous with biological evolution. Thus its social phases, like its prehuman ones, had passed through disruptive changes, such as the advent of machinery, "the severity of which is proportional to the speed of advance" (Schumpeter 1979:83). Yet precisely because certain customs, institutions and practices had survived this lengthy competitive process, they should be greatly honored (as "the fittest").

The duration of this process, furthermore, indicates that its tendency toward economic betterment is discernible only over the long haul. Even were the market to be freed from government intervention tomorrow, its processes would hardly be perfect. (Libertarians emphasize this by speaking of such things as a "natural rate of unemployment," which no current measures can alleviate [Friedman 1975]). The libertarian conviction is simply that over time the market's unhindered operation, while occasioning short-term disruption and suffering, will eventually check and correct itself, yielding the greatest possible economic improvements.

Hayek, like Hume and Smith, defines justice largely as noninterference with others. It includes such things as freedom of contract, inviolability of property and duty to compensate those we damage (Bosanquet 1983:38). (He also believes that government should assure "minimum sustenance for all" [Hayek 1960:259].[4]) Yet Hayek complains that governments are enticed beyond these limits by modern democracy, for democracy appears to have increased everyone's appetite for larger portions of the public good. To obtain these, people form competing special interest groups, which heightens social alienation. Then politicians, in order to be elected, promise such groups ever greater slices of the pie. Yet the cost of meeting such demands is self-perpetuating inflation, which hinders the economic growth that alone can meet them.

Consequently politicians disappoint everyone by delivering less than they promised and increase the competition for public favors. Hayek complains that "the real exploiters in our present society are not egoistic capitalists or entrepreneurs, but organizations which derive their power from the moral support of collective action and the feeling of group loyalty" (1979:96).

2. *Milton Friedman,* somewhat like Hayek, grounds libertarianism in a restricted view of the scope of knowledge. Friedman accepts the general tenets of logical positivism: that true knowledge can be had only of logical definitions (which are merely decisions about how terms are used and say nothing about existing things) and empirically grounded relations among facts (1953:7-9). All assertions not subject to strict empirical verification are regarded as literal "nonsense."

Thus "positive economics [is] . . . in principle independent of any particular ethical position or normative judgments" (p. 4). By this means, all rational definitions of the good person and the good society are excluded from economics' scope. So is all argument about values. Friedman simply assumes that Western industrialized persons value freedom and prosperity (Barry 1986:48). Economics can then consist in showing what empirical courses of action lead to, or defeat, these goals. Economics, in other words, can focus simply on what is the case and cease worrying about what things ought ideally to be.

Following this approach libertarian economists seek to demonstrate the shortcomings of major social democratic policies. They contend, for instance, that minimum wage laws, by fixing labor prices above market rates, always increase unemployment (Stigler 1975:chaps. 5-6). Other studies seek to show that neither the increasing number of public officials (Buchanan and Tullock 1962), nor the rising power of special interest groups (Olson 1965, 1982), affect the public interest benignly. Yet however much such correlations may have held in the recent past, they cannot demonstrate that these must always obtain in the future. Neither can they show that libertarian alternatives would produce markedly better results.

Friedman, however, seeks to correlate capitalism and important social values in an additional empirical way. He claims that throughout history greatest progress has never been achieved by governments but solely by individuals who took risks—in business, the great entrepreneurs—possible only in societies permitting much diversity (1962:3-4). Moreover, there has never been a society "marked by a large measure of political freedom" that has not organized most of its economic activity by "something comparable to a free market" (p. 9).

Friedman and his wife, Rose, stress that such a "combination of economic and political *freedom* produced a golden age in both Great Britain and the United States in the nineteenth century" (1980:3). That was true especially because the greatest threat to freedom (as history confirms) is concentration of power; and capitalism, by removing the market from government control, greatly reduced the government's power (1962:15).

3. *Robert Nozick,* in contrast to Hume, Smith, Hayek and Friedman, seeks to establish the libertarian concepts of these themes on firm philosophical foundations. Hume, Smith, Hayek and Friedman all argue in practical ways. They seek to show that, as a matter of fact, when government is restricted and individuals are allowed maximum freedom, the economy functions best. But all four refrain from enquiring deeply into the nature of the individual, of government and of the rights of each.

One of Nozick's chief theses is the separateness of individuals and the inviolability of each one's rights. Many people suppose that society can require some individuals to bear greater costs than others (say, in welfare payments) "for the sake of the overall social good." For Nozick such talk about some collective entity is unwarranted: "There is no *social entity* with a good that undergoes some sacrifice for its own good. There are only individual people, different individual people, with their own individual lives" (1974:32-33).[5]

What makes an individual so inviolable? It is neither rationality nor free will nor moral agency by themselves. Deeper than these is the individual's "ability to regulate and guide its life in accordance with some overall conception it chooses to accept" (p. 49). No one else can dictate what this conception might be or how a person might strive to actualize it. Basically for this reason, individuals must be allowed to pursue their goals by any means they choose—including ownership of whatever property they can acquire, so long as they don't violate anyone else's equally valid right to the same pursuits.

Nozick claims to be following Immanuel Kant's principle that persons should always be treated as ends and never as means. (Interestingly Nozick seems to argue that animals, or at least "higher" ones, also have inviolable rights. The apparent criterion for this is Jeremy Bentham's: that animals can suffer [1974:35-42].)

Pronounced as this individualism is, Nozick believes that it is compatible with the existence of a minimal state. To establish this he contends against a position to the "right" even of libertarianism—anarchism. Whereas anarchists agree that humans must live by laws and are entitled to protection from those who violate others' rights, they hold (as Nozick does) that each individual has the right of self-protection; they conclude that mandatory surrender of it to a state violates personal freedom. Most anarchists argue that those who want greater protection can purchase it, as they do other services, from various providers on the open market. Nozick, however, beginning from a State of Nature like Locke's (where each person has the right of self-protection) argues that a plurality of protection services cannot coexist in the long run. Instead, through gradual processes which no one really plans (just as no one deliberately devises principles of justice or procedures of market exchange), a single state can eventually emerge without violating anyone's free consent (pp. 10-146).[6]

Against anarchism, then, Nozick concludes that a state can exist which protects people's rights but does not usurp freedom. Such a state would have geographical integrity, a system for making public law, centralized institutions and would prohibit private enforcement of justice (Barry 1986:140). Yet its functions would be strictly limited to protecting individuals' rights. No limits could be placed on acquisition of property unless it were acquired by force or fraud. The Nozickean state would have no welfare, redistribution of wealth, taxation or limits on drugs and voluntary sexual activity (p. 159). Nozick does insist, however, that any wealth gained unjustly, even if this originated several generations back, be returned to its original owners if possible.

Libertarian environmental perspectives. If more than minimal government involvement harms the economy and if individuals should be free to acquire as much property as they can, two imperatives would seem to follow regarding the environment: greatly reduce government's environmental regulations, and let more natural resources be privatized.

According to Hayek the chief arguments for government controlling natural resources are that it (1) knows and (2) cares more about preserving them than do individual entrepreneurs (1960:370). But whereas Hayek concedes that government may know more about general future developments, he does not agree that it understands as much as local businesses about particulars of managing a mine, a forest and so on. Overall, local knowledge provides better guidance about the future than general government mandates (pp. 371-72).

Hayek and others also insist that entrepreneurs care about future availability of resources.[7] If resources begin running out, entrepreneurs will produce lesser quantities or raise prices (Rothbard 1973:259-61). In a free market this will stimulate technology to develop alternatives. Libertarians repeatedly critique environmentalists for supposing that if a natural resource becomes exhausted, nothing can take its place, so government must regulate its use. Yet technology has been producing new fibers, new energy sources and so on for generations. In fact, few things can be called resources until technology creates means for making them available and distributing them (p. 262).

Hayek affirms that "most consumption of irreplaceable resources rests on an act of faith" that they or alternatives will increase (p. 369). Libertarians often complain that predictions of resource scarcity and irreparable environmental damage are exaggerated and believe that free enterprise technology can rectify these. Libertarians also argue that many of the worst environmental problems occur when things are owned by government (water, air, forest, grassland and so on) and that privatization would solve most problems. If most rivers and lakes were private property, anyone polluting them could be quickly stopped. If air on a person's property were considered his or her own, individual and class actions suits would bring air polluters to court (pp. 269-78). Moreover, many grasslands and forests, particularly in the west, are government owned and leased to ranchers, lumber companies and others. It is because these users have no continuing responsibility for the land itself that they exploit it as quickly as possible for as much profit as they can (Hayek 1960:368; Rothbard 1973:263-65).

Karl Hess complains that American government has enforced inappropriate single-minded management visions on its western lands for more than two centuries. The latest is much influenced by deep ecology and seeks to reduce human "intrusion" and commercial ventures greatly. Hess finds this approach supported by the early ecological theories of Frederic Clements.

Clements proposed that the various plants in a region all develop toward a particular configuration, a *climax community*, which is the inevitable product of their collective evolution. (Tallgrass prairie before white settlement was one such configuration.) As in organismic ecology, this nicely balanced climax community provides an ethical criterion for environmental action: whatever hastens or preserves it is right; whatever retards or alters it is wrong. Humans are regarded as intrusive on this natural order (pp. 183-84). Hess finds this current insistence on one appropriate environment consistent with the monovisions that government has consistently imposed on the west.

Hess, in contrast, finds nonhuman nature more indeterminate and liable to disturbance. Balance and equilibrium are not the rule. Claims about how *climax communities* should look involve conjecture. Hess regards plant groups as different species which happen to be evolving together and not so much as ecosystems. Above all, significant diversity seems to be most characteristic of and important for healthy ecosystems (pp. 218-19). This overall view is much more Darwinian than organismic.

Moreover, Hess believes that human involvement should be considered in any ecological assessment. Humans have shaped landscapes for millennia and have enhanced the survivability of domesticated plants and animals. Furthermore,

> despite the accelerating rate of species extinction and the accompanying simplification of the global environment, humans have the potential to enhance diversity. . . . Through such diversity, it is even conceivable that species extinction may be slowed or reversed. As long as humans are able to exercise their special informational skills and respond to their environments creatively and with dispatch, flourishing and viable landscapes are possible and probable. (p. 222)

Nonhuman life best flourishes when it can develop diversely, unregulated by single-minded management systems. Human life also flourishes when people are free to initiate diverse economic ventures and follow varying lifestyles, unhampered by government regulations.[8] Is there some way of allowing both to occur on America's western lands?

Hess makes a proposal which, whether practical or not, well articulates a libertarian vision (pp. 223-41). All lands now controlled by the National

Forest Service and Bureau of Land Management would be surrendered in a twenty-year process. (Hess [p. 233], like Hayek [1960:275], exempts national parks; apparently they are unique and meaningful enough to enough people to be exempted from privatization.) Every American will be credited with one hundred "shares" of this land, which they can either "purchase" or sell to others. Thus all such lands will come under private control and be developed in myriad ways.

No one's project will be backed by government, so its success or failure will depend on whether it fits the market and is appropriate to its environment. In this way both human and natural diversity will flourish, and human communities and landscapes will constantly change. There will be no final criterion of what is environmentally sound (no one rhythm such as movement toward climax communities which simply needs to be followed). Instead, people will need to make creative rational and volitional choices. Risk will be involved—but it always is where there is freedom (p. 246).

Hess's vision, surprisingly, seems to stress something like deep ecology's and ecofeminism's bioregions. Like Bookchin, Hess envisions decision-making operating as it did in early New England town meetings (p. 247; see below). He calls his final chapter "The Ecology of Freedom," the title of Bookchin's 1982 work.[9] Deep ecology, social ecology and this libertarian view, despite their differences, stress local decision-making and reject governmental macromanagement. Yet the latter, unlike the first and somewhat like the second, rejects any single vision of future society—though it strongly encourages multiple visions. Again unlike deep ecology and somewhat like social ecology, libertarianism promotes continuing human transformation of the earth.

Libertarianism and psychology. Though it is difficult to find explicit libertarian discussion of self-formation, some general remarks may be advanced from what has been studied so far.[10] It might seem that libertarians, with their individualistic and conflictual emphases, would be inclined toward psychoanalysis. Yet their stress on everyone following their conscious wants fits uneasily with an emphasis on the unconscious, which implies that our real motivations are often hidden to us. Psychoanalytic explanations, which are often authoritative interpretations of what a person really wants and does, tend to be unwelcome. Libertarians are also uncomfortable with the notion that social forces shape our very instincts and thus all our wants.

Libertarian psychiatrist Thomas Szasz sharply critiques psychoanalytic notions of mental illness and psychotherapy, as indicated in the titles of two major works: *The Myth of Mental Illness* (1974) and *The Myth of Psychotherapy* (1978). Psychiatry does not really deal with anything that can be called illness; rather it deals with moral and political issues involved in finding ourselves (1974:xii).

A major feature of mental-moral soundness is taking responsibility for ourselves, neither placing blame on others nor expecting them to solve our problems. Though the impulses that move us should be heeded, reason and will must be employed in attaining their satisfaction. "The crucial moral characteristic of the human condition is the dual experience of freedom of the will and personal responsibility" (1977:xiii). But exercise of freedom will arouse conflict, and that means that life will be "unimaginable without suffering" (p. xv). Yet one should never succumb to efforts of government or other institutions to abolish suffering and take away risks. Even drugs should be legalized—we have a right to them as property and government should not protect us from their dangers (Szasz 1992).

In some respects, the libertarian orientation is reminiscent of Carl Rogers (see chapter two). Like libertarians, Rogers stresses the damaging force of social expectations and restraints and the importance of being in touch with who we really are and what we really want. Rogers plays down the role of the unconscious and emphasizes letting our felt desires flow. Rogers, like libertarians, seems to assume that if each of us follows these desires to our own self-realization, the best possible social harmony will emerge at the same time. Once again it appears that an organismic psychology can well suit an individualistic, capitalist society.

Summary. Libertarianism affirms, as do psychoanalysis and Darwinism, that conflict between individuals is inevitable. Still, it maintains, the unregulated natural flow of events and relationships, though sometimes rough and oppressive, produces surprisingly well-ordered societies and economies. It also alienates people less from their individual and social potential than does state control, the chief source of social alienation. Psychologically, big government alienates people from the necessity of taking responsibility and therefore from fully experiencing freedom. Ecologically, the placing of property in governmental rather than private hands increases environmental devastation. And government forces single-minded schemas on development, denying both nature and humanity full development of their diverse potentialities.

Moral bonds voluntarily formed through *sympathy* and *benevolence* may be imperfect, but they are better than legislated social ideals, for authentic morality cannot be legislated. Government has no right to infringe on anyone's basic decisions about guiding his or her life. Societies and economies should be based on what *is* actually desired by people, not on someone's notion of what they *ought* to want. To claims that society should be directed by lofty values, libertarians respond, Whose values will be chosen, by what criteria will they be selected and why assume that any government installed to realize these values will not act instead in its own selfish, shortsighted interest?

The Holistic Perspective

Do limited government and a "free market" really lead to the greatest freedom for most people and avoid the alienation produced by dominating social structures? Will they enable nonhuman nature to best actualize its diverse potentialities? Will freedom from social restraints and institutional programs designed to avoid suffering release people to develop true freedom and responsibility? Or does the free market impose its own kind of restraints and alienations on social processes? Does it alienate technological society from its natural foundations? And does it make its own, perhaps subtle, contributions to psychological alienation?

Holistic thinkers answer these last three questions in the affirmative. They do not regard limited government and the free market as socially, ecologically or psychologically neutral. They generally assert that alternative, more ideal, social systems must be envisioned and brought into existence.

Some contradictions of capitalism. Not all of capitalism's critics are strongly socialist. Daniel Bell is usually labeled a "neoconservative." Bell distinguishes three main realms in modern society: economy, polity and culture. Each has its own *axial principle:* efficiency, equality and self-realization, respectively. Bell claims that in current society these realms are becoming increasingly independent and contradictory (1976:10-16).

Capitalism's axial principle of efficiency produces corporate structures which are hierarchical, bureaucratic and impersonal. Individuals fill roles where a "person becomes an object or a 'thing,'" (p. 11)—roles which can be altered or deleted as efficiency demands. These clash with democracy's axial principle of equality. Although capitalism and democracy arose together historically, Bell discerns no intrinsic connection between them (p. 14), in opposition to libertarianism's usual claim (especially the Friedmans') that one is necessary for the other.

Further, Bell senses a contradiction between the disciplines which capitalism requires to produce goods (thrift, delayed gratification, hard work) and the attitudes it must encourage to sell them (heavy spending, immediate satisfaction, enjoyment). He argues that capitalism worked well in nineteenth-century America because religion (mainly its Puritan emphases) provided a value framework which encouraged the productive attitudes but restrained the consumptive ones. But with religion's decline, a search for self-realization—the desire to explore our nature and expand its desires and experiences without limit—broke loose to become the axial principle of current culture.

Unchecked by any moral framework, capitalism now spawns, chiefly through its advertising and marketing, an individualistic hedonism that contradicts the very attitudes it needs for production. Bell also roots that interest-group clamoring for greater public benefits which libertarians abhor in desires that capitalism arouses for having more and more (p. 23).

Bell does not celebrate today's society, insofar as it has been shaped by capitalism, as truly free. For him people are free only when they have some framework for coping with larger questions of purpose, interpersonal relationships and death. He finds modern people fearful of the nothingness that arises when they have no answers to these. Yet refusing to recognize their finitude, they hurl themselves into "the megalomania of self-infinitization," the never-ending search for deeper experiences of the self (p. 49).

Capitalism, however, has been largely responsible for the disruption of older social structures and beliefs and for releasing this ever-intensifying thirst for self-gratification (pp. 16-17). Bell believes that without some general sense of goal and purpose in life and society, people will be unable to make the sacrifices necessary for public well-being and to decide among competing social values. The "ultimate sources" for this are "religious conceptions" (p. 83).

Herbert Marcuse's critical theory. Although I placed Marcuse on the Newtonian (psychoanalytic) side of public discourse in chapter two, I noted that his view of a liberated society was quite organismic. This, with his strong views on how social forces shape persons, place him on the holistic side in this chapter.

Like Marx and Freud, Marcuse believed that early humans had to struggle against nature. He agreed with Freud that civilization was constructed, and modern individuals are constituted, only through painful repression of many primordial urges. Society was built through increasing domination by oppressive elites and enforced by internal guilt and the decreasing influence of the life-instinct, which strives to bring people together. Yet though Freud believed that societies and persons must always be constructed through repression, Marcuse, like Marx, felt that this is unnecessary now that technology has overcome nature's scarcity.

Marcuse's hope for a nonrepressive society is based largely on *phantasy*, which points towards a future "reconciliation of the individual with the whole, of desire with realization, of happiness with reason" (1966:143). Phantasy's images recall the infant's primordial oneness with its mother and witness to those earlier, maternal phases of society emphasized by feminists.[11] These images point toward a *primary narcissism* where the ego felt connected with the entire universe (1964:168), and they seek to reactivate a narcissistic Eros through which the "opposition between man and nature, subject and object, is overcome" (p. 166).

This emphasis on phantasy's creative power sets Marcuse against positivism, as employed by Friedman, which he finds to be the dominant outlook in capitalistic society.[12] Positivism, Marcuse feels—along with all outlooks focusing on what *is* and ignoring what *ought* to be—accepts current reality as given and unalterable. By branding all nonempirical ideals of humanity or society as "nonsense," it induces people to put up with today's repressive reality. By denying that imagination and rational ideals have more than subjective meaning, positivism rejects the full potential of what humans can become and their creative visions of liberation.

But if current social reality is alienated from its future potential, how is this manifest? Marcuse associates much of today's alienation with the welfare state, which libertarians also deplore. As more sectors of society clamor for government funds, the state, by channeling benefits through its expanding bureaucracy, administers increasing dimensions of their lives (1964:48-50). Yet even as they fall further under government control, the burgeoning groups of beneficiaries are unlikely to challenge the source that is improving their lot.

For Marcuse, however, capitalism does not challenge a growing state, as libertarians claim, but capitalism's hierarchical structure (which Bell emphasizes) colludes with and furthers the latter. Governmental administration is paralleled by businesses' increasingly sophisticated administration of their workers. Today almost everyone is a proletarian in the sense of having no say over means of production and in that "decisions over life and death, over personal and national security, are made at places over which individuals have no control" (p. 32). As governments engage more in economic planning, their interests and those of business converge, and the interests of both are increasingly intertwined with the military's.

In general, capitalist social repression exists where producers (whether business, government or military) rather than choices of consumers or citizens determine what will be produced and how, and where they control the marketing and servicing of products (p. xv). This happens not only through administration but also through advertising (see chapter two). To keep increasing production, modern capitalism needs to expand its markets. To this end, rather than impoverishing its workers (its domestic ones, at any rate), it seeks to constitute them as consumers. That is largely accomplished, Marcuse says, by advertising, which intensifies human needs and keeps creating new ones. Myriad new products promise sensations and comforts greater or other than people had ever thought of.

Marcuse's main point is that when people so influenced make market choices, they are not free, independent individuals choosing what they really want or need, as libertarians suppose. Instead, the very character of most "needs" is shaped by social forces, is "superimposed upon the individual by particular social interests in his repression" (p. 5).

Consumers, their appetites continually intensified and expanded, keep chasing after images of happiness whose respective products satisfy partially at best—yet which incessantly give way to more images making more elusive promises. Though they experience their market choices as decisions for self-fulfillment, they increasingly lose any capacity to act as creative, self-determining agents, envisioning and actualizing possibilities of enjoyment and freedom which transcend the present order (what *is* the case). Even political information is so shaped into commercialized images which invite immediate, stereotyped, positive or negative response that little room exists for authentic choices.

In such a society, Marcuse complains, reality's complexity—its variety, its oppositions, its transcendent possibilities—is flattened into "one dimension." For instance, opposition between labor and management is largely overcome by allowing the former to pursue the system's products, giving them a stake in its continuance and absorbing them into it.

Another flattening out is the absorption of "high" culture into "mass" culture (pp. 56-74). Great art of the past—with its heroes, villains, daring feats, romantic quests—conveyed intimations of a world higher and deeper than the present. Though this art was undesirably limited to a particular class, its breadth of vision contrasted with, and thereby protested, the current reality's meanness, limitations and misery. (Since it is phantasy that projects a better future, art, for Marcuse, is a major medium through which this is expressed.)

Today, however, high culture (for example, themes of great symphonies, quotations from great literature) has been absorbed into commercialism. Fictional characters such as the "vamp, the national hero, the beatnik, the neurotic housewife, the gangster, the star . . . are no longer images of another way of life, but rather freaks or types of the same life, serving as an affirmation rather than negation of the established order" (p. 59).

This absorption of high culture by mass culture is paralleled by loss of depth in the contemporary self. With their inner psychic functions increasingly shaped by commercialism, whose images reach into unconscious depths, individuals lose any deeper dimension from which to challenge and transcend the present. Marcuse regards this as an advanced stage of psychological alienation in which the subject "has become entirely objective, . . . is swallowed up by its alienated existence" and is also reduced to one dimension (p. 11).

Marcuse finds capitalism so adept at incorporating opposition that he often exudes pessimism about the concrete historical future. Still he insists that another kind of world is feasible—though we cannot be certain that it will ever come (pp. x-xii, 220). This world would be chiefly concerned with the *pacification of existence* in which not only humanity but nature also would fulfill its ultimate potentialities (pp. 236-37). Working would continue but would coincide with gratification and be assimilated with play (p. 214). Reason, now also aiming toward gratification, would create a new social hierarchy and division of labor (1966:224), whereas libido would unfold its own kind of sociality and regulation (p. 213). The instincts would generate a new *reality principle*, characterized not by impulsive striving but largely by their conservative character (pp. 197, 223). The superego, in fact, would often ally with the id (p. 228). Earlier libidinal stages, repressed today, would be reactivated (p. 198), and libidinal cathexis of a person's own body would provide the path to enjoyment of the world (p. 169).

Marcuse is envisioning a world where individuals would still remain different, and decisions about organizing their work and social interrelationships would need to be made. Yet he is confident that the rationality of such decisions would be easily understood and approved by all (p. 225). In envisioning this world as springing forth rather spontaneously, despite lack of connection with the present, Marcuse shows his organismic side. Despite the terrible alienation which always has and still does dominate our world, he is confident that underlying individual and social potentialities exist which, if given their chance to flower, would spontaneously eliminate all of this.

Fredric Jameson's neo-Marxism. This literary critic has been much involved in discussions about postmodernism. Many proponents of postmodernism, such as Jean-Francois Lyotard, regard rejection of *metanarratives* as one of its main features (Lyotard 1984). Metanarratives are interpretations of history that explain and justify the rise and success of given cultures. The story of the "modern" world's Enlightenment origins and its subsequent scientific and social progress is the one that postmodernists most vehemently abjure. They proclaim that that "modern" world is past and that we are now in the postmodern era. We must no longer view the world as dominated by one monoculture; rather we must recognize the myriad cultural forms that exist.

Jameson disagrees with this perspective for two main reasons. First, the claim that modernism has ended and postmodernism has begun is inconsistent, for it is itself an overarching historical interpretation—a metanarrative (1991:xi-xiii). Second, Jameson believes that all societies are being increasingly controlled by totalizing power and that neglect of this simply subjects all groups to deeper social alienation. Jameson thus rejects any sharp break between modernism and postmodernism. For him, postmodernism is the cultural expression, or "logic," accompanying a global stage of capitalism (pp. 35-36; Mandel 1975).

In the West, capitalism has been characterized by the decline of industrial production in favor of service economies and of explicit class struggle. This has given rise to claims that Marxist historical analysis, which emphasizes industry and class conflict, is no longer valid (Bell 1973). Globally, however, this stage has been marked by the expansion of American economic and military power. Jameson regards it as "the purest form of capital yet to have emerged, a prodigious expansion of capital into hitherto uncommodified areas" (1991:36). Jameson approaches postmodernism as a cultural critic. In many realms, he finds culture characterized by at least the four following symptoms, which alienate people from their individual and social potential.

The first symptom is the commodification of almost everything. During the modernist period, the economy could be distinguished from the culture. But much of today's most innovative artistic work is done in advertising, which constantly engenders aesthetic innovation and experimentation. Almost all commodities are repeatedly presented in highly artistic ways, and it seems that almost everything is being marketed. In the typical advertisement we are not only being motivated to buy the product itself but are being induced to believe that we can purchase the pleasurable sensations imaginatively connected with it, as well as the benefits (happiness, health, popularity and so on). The lines seem increasingly blurred.[14]

Nature too is being commodified—developed and polluted. We seldom experience it directly; we are exposed only to sentimentalized simulacra of it. The unconscious also is penetrated by the media's images to arouse new cravings, as Marcuse affirms, leaving no realm free of commodification (pp. 34-36; 1971:36).

Second, the distinction between the economy and culture is further blurred, as Marcuse also noticed, by the breakdown of the difference between high and low culture. Classical music and modernist architecture, for instance, were produced according to specific structural principles, and they conveyed a sense of reality and value distinct from commercial culture. Today symphonic themes mix with current jingles, and postmodern buildings mingle motifs from popular sources. "Lowbrow" people may welcome the "superior" culture's demise, feeling that their tastes are now receiving recognition. Yet this breakdown could mean that no realm is exempt from capitalist penetration.

Jameson finds, third, a new depthlessness, which includes the loss and dispersal of the subject. Andy Warhol's repeating Campbell's Soup cans or Marilyn Monroe photos perhaps best exemplify art that is pure surface, without subtlety or tension. Much modern art suggests that the distinct though perhaps anxious subject formed by the classical family has been dissolved by the world of organizational bureaucracy. As Lasch noticed, the older problem of alienation from a deeper self is being replaced by the self's fragmentation (see chapter two). Postmodern people may be liberated from "the older *anomie*," but they are also freed "from every other kind of feeling as well, since there is no longer a self present to do the feeling" (1991:15; compare 1981:124-25, 260).

Connected with this depthlessness, fourth, is the loss of a sense of history. Through examples from literature and film, Jameson shows how snatches of older works are incorporated into recent ones in ways that take them out of context and create or reinforce stereotypes. This deprives the former works of their critical capacity. It means that "we are condemned to seek History by way of our own pop images and simulacra of that history, which itself remains forever out of reach" (1991:25). Deprived of a coherent flow of events with which to connect, private temporality becomes schizophrenic.[15] The future either stretches out as a meaningless blank or becomes filled with images of apocalyptic catastrophe (p. 46).

Jameson claims that space has taken priority over time. He examines postmodern architectural works (especially Los Angeles's Bonaventure Hotel) in which it seems impossible to orient oneself spatially. He finds such presentations of overwhelming, unmanageable space symbolic of "a network of power and control even more difficult for our minds and imaginations to grasp: the whole new decentered global network of third stage capital itself" (p. 38). This loss of historical and spatial coordinates in culture symbolizes a loss of critical distance for challenging the present.

Jameson believes that we cannot evaluate the present without a sense of history, including a vision of future potentialities. He affirms Marcuse's notion that phantasy reminds people of a primordial plenitude of psychic gratification and points, especially through art, toward the possibility that work can become as play and that subject and object, inner and outer, humanity and nature can be as one (1971:112-15, 86-90). He criticizes the positivism of Friedman and others for reducing reality to what can be immediately and unambiguously perceived (1971:367-74; 1991:266-73). He believes that hope for a liberating future is largely repressed—by oppressed groups so they can endure the present, by dominant groups because its realization would dismantle their power (Dowling 1984:117).

What kind of practical approach to social alienation does Jameson propose? Against the fragmenting character of much postmodern analysis he advocates "mapping" international capital's overall workings and uniting those who oppose it. Whereas postmodernism's focus on particular oppressions can aid specific groups' struggles, blindness to the global forces affecting every group can only harm them all in the long run. Jameson finds the inability to locate ourselves in contemporary social space—to discern how we are impacted by the bewildering intersectings of local, regional and international forces—a major cause of victimization (1991:399-418).

Jameson retains some commitment to traditional working-class politics, while recognizing that its significance is declining as Western blue- and white-collar workers become increasingly similar. Chiefly he calls for alliances among various oppressed and marginalized groups, hoping that they can collectively provide an inventory of kinds of contemporary domination and a common front against them (Best and Kellner 1991:190-91).

Murray Bookchin's social ecology. Bookchin (who was introduced in chapter three) calls his outlook "organic"; among the perspectives discussed here it is the most "organismic." For him nature is benign toward humans. He endorses the Gaia hypothesis (1982:359-60) and, quite unlike Marx, Freud and Marcuse, finds that early human "labor" in the natural world was pleasurable and nonexploitative and usually produced surpluses. Early hunter-gatherer societies regarded differentiation among their members as complementary, affirmed their substantive equality, used persuasion to decide issues, provided each member an "irreducible minimum" of goods and treated all resources as sharable (1990:46-53). Women had great prestige, and many communities worshiped mother-goddesses (1982:52-63). The original situation was anarchy, which meant not that no rules were followed but that no one surrendered their freedom to coercive authorities.

Gradually, however, the authority of elders in primitive groups increased, eventually giving way to that of "big men" who, in agricultural and then in urban contexts, became warriors (pp. 81-88; 1990:54-66).[16] Hierarchical domination subordinates whole groups to others and is the principle underlying all particular social alienations. It did not originate in a human struggle with nature but is the root of human exploitation of nature. It did not consist, contrary to feminism, in subordination of women by men, which is but one form of it. Yet hierarchy is not simply a social category. It denotes systems of command and obedience, of superiority and inferiority, which are internalized and control the ways persons regard themselves and respond to the world. Hierarchical relationships can exist even where there is no economic or social subordination. Consequently, Bookchin warns, if they are not uprooted from consciousness, they can structure and cripple even organizations dedicated to freeing humanity from them (p. 4).

Although hierarchy has dominated human life for millennia, Bookchin finds some alternatives in Western history upon which social ecologists can draw. He claims that urban centers such as early Athens (1990:176-79) and free European cities before the industrial revolution (pp. 87-89) displayed great potential for local self-government and for uniting diverse peoples. The anarchist tradition (Robert Owen, Charles Fourier, Peter Kropotkin and so on) preserves visions of societies combining work and play, reason and sensuousness and persons of all types and ages (pp. 119-26). Early New England town meetings, as Karl Hess stresses, were an ideal kind of participatory government.

How can change occur? It will begin with small groups committed to egalitarian ways of living. These will engage in grassroots organizing characterized by "an almost cellular form of growth, a process that involves organic proliferation and differentiation" (Bookchin and Foreman 1991:83). Gradually people in various urban districts will take affairs into their own hands until an entire metropolis is governed by alternative, face-to-face assemblies. During this time the economy will be municipalized and reforms will spread to the country. Hopefully such changes will then spread from community to community, with affairs in each being managed in ways that suit local desires and conditions.

Productive and domestic spheres, separated by capitalism (compare Chodorow in chapter two), will be integrated; urban and agricultural life will mingle, and wilderness will be honored. Small-scale, environment-friendly technology will be utilized. The most comprehensive political form will be a confederation of municipal structures. Affairs as a whole will approximate a healthy ecological system: diversified, balanced and harmonious (Bookchin 1971:80). Bookchin regards this process as at least worth beginning because it would, apparently, follow the dynamic he finds in evolution. Yet it also allows for the unexpected and for spontaneity, which also occur there.

Bookchin's scenario is like Karl Hess's libertarian scenario in that minority groups with unique visions take the lead, the evolutionary tendency toward diversity flowers and humans creatively "choose, alter, and reconstruct the environment" (Bookchin 1990:41). Bookchin's minorities, however, are guided by social visions, whereas many of Hess's are motivated by economic goals to be realized in a capitalist way. The various visions of Bookchin's groups, despite their variations, seem ultimately harmonizable, whereas those of some of Hess's groups may clash. Most important, for Hess capitalism is a loose framework which allows numerous diverse ventures to flourish. For Bookchin, in contrast, capitalism is a rigid system based on inflexible principles such as maximization of profit, which inexorably allies itself with the nation-state's oppressive domination and the destruction of its own natural base.

Despite hierarchy's pervasive shaping of consciousness and society, Bookchin finds "every reason to hope for a degree of personal and social enlightenment for which there are no historical precedents." That is partly because the mother-infant relationship regularly plants "seeds of a human nature that can be oriented toward selfless endearment, interdependence, and care" (1982:340). It is also because every person, even if only in daydreams, experiences and longs for pleasure, the satisfaction of their desires. This experience or anticipation of pleasure, as Marcuse says, arouses everyone to long for a society and world free from domination and alienation. "Precisely in this utopistic quest for pleasure," Bookchin declares, "humanity begins to gain its most sparkling glimpse of emancipation" (p. 9).

Finally Bookchin hopes for a greatly transformed world because of his faith that "all mature individuals can be expected to manage their social affairs directly" (p. 336). He therefore has confidence that social affairs can be managed in face-to-face gatherings where everyone has opportunity to speak. Here all individuals, of whatever race, class or gender, will be regarded as equals. All social alienation based on such characteristics will cease. Bookchin calls such structures *libertarian*.

However, given his rejection of even a minimal state such as Nozick's and of capitalism, his social theory is better called *anarchism*. Bookchin's strong affirmation of primordial social and social-natural harmony and his confidence that unprecedented social alterations could arise rather spontaneously if natural human affections, abilities and pleasures were allowed to flower, probably classify his views as "organismic" in the usual sense.[17]

Summary

In opposing social alienation, both libertarian and holistic theorists value personal freedom. All of them regard expanded governmental power as a major source of alienation. None proposes an ideal superstate as a solution. Both perspectives also find diversity among social groups as essential to society's health. Yet their evaluations of capitalism differ enormously.

For libertarians, capitalism provides a loose framework within which a multitude of economic and social ventures may be pursued. It does not restrict freedom but makes maximum freedom possible. For holists, capitalism is a hierarchical system whose inexorable principles—efficiency, profit maximization and so on—deeply shape individual lives and social structures. For libertarians, capitalistic economic forces, which maximize freedom, are antithetical to expanding governmental control. For holists, capitalism, which is based on enormous concentrations of wealth and power, allies naturally with other forces—government, media, the military—seeking expanded social control. Yet capitalism usually controls people not so much through legal strictures as through its pervasive imprint on social and psychological structures.

Underlying these disagreements are different psychological understandings. For libertarians, our impulses operate in fulfilling directions and our will is basically free apart from formation by social traditions and forces. We should follow these impulses and seek to satisfy them by use of will and reason, resisting all social restraints. Social freedom consists in rules safeguarding pursuit of individual goals and absence of limitations on this. For holists, however, individuals are shaped far more by social forces, and significant individual change is possible only within altered social contexts. Freedom therefore intrinsically involves not merely pursuing our own goals but forming meaningful relationships with others and grappling with issues of ultimate meaning (Bell 1973). Social freedom includes positive ways of relating to others and is not merely absence of restraints.

Since libertarians view individual impulses and desires as expressions of freedom, they regard capitalist structures, which are designed to fulfill them, as responses to human choices. But holists, who believe that capitalism shapes desires, see capitalism not responding to genuine needs and desires but creating them. Capitalism, they believe, accomplishes this largely by dissolving structures and traditions which provide frameworks for forming stable selves and by stimulating appetite and imagination to pursue elusive pleasures which promise to fill the resulting inner voids but seldom do.

Whereas libertarians emphasize both desires and the will, holists reviewed in this chapter place special emphasis on phantasy, which envisions fulfillment of the desires. Phantasy, operating through art and in other ways, arouses vivid hope for a better future society. Marcuse and Bookchin link phantasy especially with early experiences of union with our mothers. Does phantasy, then, express a particularly masculine longing (Chodorow, ecofeminism)? Does it promote a regressive narcissism, where desire for union hinders our ability to cope with difference (Lasch, compare ecofeminism)?

It is possible, however, since such "recollections" of union help people construct a new society through rational and volitional powers as well as affective ones, that they function in the positive way that the ego ideal can in psychoanalytic theory (see chapter two). In any case I note that despite libertarianism's strong emphasis on will and the acknowledged roles of both will and reason in holistic theory, both perspectives stress the psychological importance of desires for pleasure and efforts to fulfill them.

Our two perspectives differ, however, over the function of visions of a better social future. Libertarianism can affirm the flourishing of *diverse* visions (especially Hess). But to stress *one* vision for civilization is to gear society toward an ideal which only coercive government can implement— to base society on what *ought* to be rather than on what it *is* that people desire. For holistic philosophies, however, visions of a unified human future which transcend present reality are essential for overcoming social alienation. For if we believe that a single, integrated force (global capitalism) underlies social alienation, we will need a unified, global vision of an alternative future to effectively combat it.

Since such a vision is somewhat discontinuous with present reality, holistic theories usually affirm that sweeping changes will need to herald its actualization. (Whereas organismic psychology and ecology tend to suppose that such a potentiality underlies, as it were, the *present* situation, holistic social theorists, directly pondering the magnitude of current social alienation, refocus it toward the *future*.)

For holists, gradual increases of *sympathy* or *benevolence*, which are possible sources of social amelioration for libertarianism, will produce neither vision broad enough nor action radical enough to introduce the changes necessary. This conviction parallels organismic ecology's claim that self-interest cannot produce action sufficiently cooperative, nor individualism a perspective sufficiently holistic, for needed environmental change (see chapter three). It also parallels the claim of organismic psychology and some object relations theorists that the id's self-regarding impulses cannot produce an other-regarding ego (see chapter two).

For libertarianism, the social diversity that unrestricted capitalism can produce can also enhance an ecological diversity appropriate to nonhuman nature. For nature is more open to indeterminacy and disturbance and less characterized by balance than organismic ecologies suppose. Holism's ecological vision is reminiscent of that harmonious unfolding of natural and human rhythms found in organicism. Yet Bookchin affirms that the differentiation and surprise found in evolution will mark the future of ecological societies.

Libertarians acknowledge that "free market" societies cannot be perfect and that some persons in them will suffer. But to protests that society ought to be guided by higher standards, they repeatedly respond by asking, Who will decide on such social values, and how can a more "ideal" society come into being except by granting extraordinary power to a government that is almost certain to abuse it?

Finally, what might a Christian view of society contribute to this public conversation? Would it see social relationships permeated by selfishness and conflict? If so, would it recommend a strong government or a weak one, as do libertarians, as the best way to cope with social sin? Or would a Christian view encourage striving toward higher social ideals and greater social harmony? Or might it include emphases from all these perspectives? Chapters seven and twelve will show us.

PART TWO

Contemporary Theological Discourse

*T*his book is a work in Christian theology. It is asking a crucial question: What contribution can a Christian perspective make to understanding and grappling with the sense of alienation prevalent in today's world? My basic task is to develop my own theological contribution to current conversation on this issue.

Part one considered the broad arena of public conversation. The kind of discussion most often heard within this arena is what I have called *public discourse:* general kinds of argumentation designed to appeal to broad spectra of persons. I distinguished this from *religious discourse,* which is argumentation clearly grounded in premises of specific religions (see introduction). Even within public discourse, however, general religious themes occasionally emerge, especially when organismic psychology and ecology are considered. This strengthens my assertion that actual public conversation on these issues cannot be confined, as some theologians claim, to people who affirm a fairly definite body of assumptions, beliefs and kinds of evidence considered "rational." The Enlightenment ideal of a "secular sphere" distinct from religious influence does not correspond to today's public reality.

Because I sought to hear this public discourse on its own terms, however, I refrained from raising theological considerations in part one. I want my constructive theology to deal not only with issues that Christians find important but to engage in critical conversation with what is actually being said in our culture.

In part two I begin building my response by investigating today's *theological discourse* on alienation themes,[1] especially in light of what issues are being raised and how they are being treated from Christian perspectives. I will interact with various theologians and begin developing my own perspective on some issues raised by them and in part one. In the process I will listen carefully to their conversation and seek to describe it as accurately and as fairly as possible.

Alienation means not simply conflict or discord but a deeper, paradoxical rupture among elements that belong together, which should be nourishing and supporting each other and which ultimately are part of the same whole. In psychological alienation, we find ourselves in conflict with or unable to connect with or incapable of shaping or forming our own self. This estrangement separates aspects of the very same self. In ecological alienation, technological society is distant from, and destroying, the natural basis on which it depends and with which it is inextricably interconnected, since humans are also natural creatures. In social alienation, political and economic forces in which people participate willingly or unwillingly are the same forces that estrange them from their individual and corporate potential.

Part one showed that much public discourse about these three kinds of alienation is conducted by adherents of two overarching paradigms: the Newtonian and the organismic (which is similar to the holistic social perspective). Of course, it can be debated whether some thinkers belong under one heading or the other, and any such schematization can marginalize or omit some important individuals. Nonetheless the particular features of different viewpoints, and specific disagreements among them, are so often connected to and explicable in light of the basic frameworks overarching them that this categorization has had value. It yields two main theories as to how different dimensions of alienation are related and how alienation can be overcome.

According to the Newtonian, or conflictive, paradigm, alienation is rooted in the very nature of things, for all things are composed of conflicting basic elements. Even though some incipient self may exist at life's beginning, selves must be constructed in a never-ending process out of clashing impulses and social expectations. The natural world, which includes humans, consists of organisms competing for life's necessities, and humans must devise tolerable ways of adjudicating the needs of diverse individuals, species and ecosystems. The socioeconomic realm is constituted out of conflicting wants and efforts to satisfy them; different people must fashion their own ways of satisfying wants in particular settings but refrain from organizing overall systems in so doing. In all three realms, according to the conflictive paradigm, basic alienation among components exists, and it is up to humans to *forge* the best harmony they can among them, though it will never be perfect.

According to the organismic paradigm (and the holistic social perspective), alienation is not inherent in the basic nature of things, for all things are, or at least can become, self-balancing wholes. Alienation arises from human imposition of false structures upon them. To become ourselves, we should disregard inauthentic social expectations and restraints, then *find* and *follow* our organismic self-actualization process. To attain ecological health, humans should look beneath the ways that society has shaped nature and find and follow those natural rhythms that guided evolution and now balance ecosystems. To enjoy social wholeness, humans should look beyond today's unhealthy socioeconomic systems to future possibilities of integrated, balanced ones visualized through creative imagination and attainable through revolutionary action. In all three realms, according to this outlook, self-balancing harmony among components already exists or can naturally emerge, so humans should find and follow its direction (though social holism puts greater emphasis on *forging* harmony).

As we explore today's theological discourse, we will find that some issues that appear in public discourse will reappear in it, while others will not. I will not deal much with some of the latter until part three. We will find that theologians also address some matters not raised in part one. We will also observe that many theologians prefer, and some simply assume, the validity of organismic or holistic perspectives. I will ask why that is so.

Chapter five will show how psychological alienation is being handled in the upsurge of interest in spirituality that is currently sweeping Christian churches. Chapter six will explore the emerging field of ecological theology and also consider creation-centered spirituality. Chapter seven will explore how socioeconomic issues are handled in "realistic" and liberation-oriented theologies.

FIVE

Spirituality & Psychological Alienation

Many have characterized our current situation as one in which the struggle to become a self is extremely difficult. Chapter two surveyed several current perspectives on the nature of this struggle. Is it, as psychoanalysis maintains, an ongoing process of forging and reforging a tenuous sense of self-identity? Will some irreducible tension between the self and its biological drives always persist? Will both wrestle against, and yet be deeply imprinted by, their social context? Or, as organismic psychology proposes, does greater potential harmony exist between ourselves and our drives, and can a good measure of it be actualized despite social constraints?

Throughout this chapter I will ask whether today's theological discourse helps answer some of the major issues raised in chapter two.[1] Will we, for instance, find religious writers complaining that current society is too rigid (as organicism often does) or too fluid (as some psychoanalysts do)? Or will much attention at all be given to the social shaping of selves? Will we find further indications that organismic psychology fits, or does not fit, a capitalistic ethos? Will we find tendencies similar to those of regressive or grandiose narcissism, or structures similar to psychoanalysis's ego ideal?

This chapter will first explore four current approaches to spirituality—

two generally organismic ones and two more conflictive efforts. Then, to examine the interrelation of spirituality and psychology in depth, I will consider a Jungian interpretation of Teresa of Ávila and John of the Cross. After this I will summarize my findings.

Trends in Recent Christian Spirituality

Within Christian circles the discipline of pastoral psychology has been developing over the last century to address many of the above issues. Much that is relevant to our questions could be gleaned from it. However, for several reasons I will be concerned chiefly with the rapidly expanding interest in Christian spirituality.

First, pastoral psychology has developed somewhat outside of, and often in some tension with, Christian churches and theology as a whole. Its procedures and perspective, in some cases, have tended to parallel secular ones.[2] Interest in spirituality, however, has often arisen from dissatisfaction with psychology by itself and a desire to recover truly religious resources rooted in Christian tradition. Second, a significant amount of current spirituality, unlike most pastoral psychology, addresses ecological and social issues. And third, many current spiritualities do make use of psychology, enabling us to consider the potentialities and problems involved in its direct encounter with Christian tradition.

Most recent spirituality is Roman Catholic. Historically Protestants have been suspicious of specific methods for enhancing the inner life. Such procedures, they have feared, can obscure the priority of simple, direct faith and become schemes of "works righteousness." To be sure, many groups emerging throughout Protestant history have placed emphasis on spiritual and ethical formation: Anabaptists, Baptists, Quakers, Pietists, Methodists . . . all the way up to recent charismatics. But even these have produced relatively few detailed writings or programs for bringing about spiritual and ethical formation.

In fact, Catholic spirituality itself became somewhat truncated after the sixteenth century. At that time Ignatius Loyola (1491-1556) developed a method of imaginative contemplation: of visualizing, say, a Gospel scene, placing oneself within it and then "applying" our five senses by asking questions. (What did the place look like? What did I hear the characters saying? How did they or the place feel to my touch? What spiritual fragrance and savor did I experience?) Ignatius's *Spiritual Exercises* also involved more *discursive* applications of the memory, intellect and will: of remembering a point, drawing lessons from it and resolving to put it into practice. Ignatuis's overall aim was practical—to lead people to decisions regarding personal reformation and vocation, especially vocations devoted to bringing the Christian message to the world.

Two other great Spanish spiritual writers, however, taught a quite different approach. Teresa of Ávila (1515-1582) and John of the Cross (1542-1591) stressed experiences with God that go beyond anything expressible through the senses, imagination or intellect. John especially warned that exercises using these faculties could impede such experiences. In loftier moments God's presence would be *infused* directly, by-passing all ordinary human processes, bringing the soul into an inexpressible, ineffable union with the divine. In seeking to articulate these experiences, Teresa and John employed images which frequently appear in depth psychology.

Over the next few centuries, however, as Catholicism frequently took a defensive stance against Protestantism and the emerging modern world, intense, individual experiences such as Teresa's and John's were often regarded with suspicion or considered as reserved for the exceptional few. Practices such as the discursive portions of Ignatius's *Spiritual Exercises* became standard fare in Catholic spirituality even up to the Second Vatican Council (Keating 1986:19-32). Since then, interest in rediscovering classical spiritual authors has exploded among Catholics and has spread swiftly into Protestant and even non-Christian circles.

In a society which has been intrigued ever since Freud by the psyche's mysterious depths—yet one where shifting surface images of pleasure, power and multiple lifestyles seem to splinter efforts at forming coherent selves—it is no wonder that Christians have ransacked their traditions for resources to help them attain authentic personal depth. This search, of course, has been stimulated by the rising appeal of other religions (especially Hinduism, Buddhism, Native American religions and various "shamanistic" approaches). To many seeking expanded consciousness, and often more ecological and socially egalitarian lifestyles, these seemed to offer what Christianity lacked (Egan 1982:40-76). Though the Christian response has been far too variegated to be covered in a brief discussion, I will outline several approaches representing some of its main features.

The emphasis on depth. The techniques of *centering prayer* have been developed from the ancient Benedictine practice of "sacred reading" *(lectio divina)*. This involved four stages, often interwoven: first came careful "reading" *(lectio)* of a biblical passage, then discursive "reflection" *(meditatio)* on its meaning, followed by "prayer" *(oratio)*, or affective response to this meaning, and finally "contemplation" *(contemplatio)*, a simple resting in God's presence where *infused* prayer might be experienced.

Centering prayer attempts to overcome current obstacles to contemplation by moving directly to the fourth stage. "Its modest packaging appeals to the contemporary attraction for how-to methods" (Keating 1986:34). But can the first three steps be safely omitted? Thomas Keating claims that they can today because people have been taught "to analyze things beyond all measure" and need to recover those intuitive faculties repressed by "the Cartesian-Newtonian world view" (p. 30). Nonetheless, centering prayer should be practiced within the framework of Christian faith-commitments and church participation.

Centering prayer's basic aim is direct union with God, much as Teresa of Ávila and John of the Cross experienced it, beyond all images, thoughts and even awareness in the usual sense. This is possible because everything actively participates in God and shares God's being (Pennington 1977:44). "The chief thing that separates us from God is the thought that we are separated" (Keating 1986:44). Moreover, because Christians have been baptized into Christ, they "are in some very real, though mysterious way, Christ . . . the Second Person of the Blessed Trinity." So when we pray, we come forth from the Father in Christ and "return to the Father in that perfect love which is the Holy Spirit" (Pennington 1977:47).

Centering prayer seeks to focus on this inner unity with God by gently suspending the attention of our faculties—by ceasing to focus on particular sensations, images or thoughts. To attain this concentration it is helpful to slowly repeat a single significant word ("love" or "God," for instance). It is often said that the problem lies not in our faculties themselves but in their "habitual functioning," which attaches us to particular lusts, fears or other distractions. However, centering prayer proponents sometimes speak as if sense and reason themselves were barriers to God (Keating 1986:85; Pennington 1977:63). Emptying of ourselves to receive God is often identified with an emptying, or *kenosis,* of the contents of these faculties (Merton 1968:75).

The main road to God is said to be faith, which is opposed to any kind of sight. For sight is not needed, since God is already within us (Keating 1986:35). Nonetheless the aim is not to contemplate ourselves but to pass beyond ourselves and find God (Merton 1978:32). Thomas Merton affirms that efforts to merely darken our senses and remain alone with ourselves could lead to "inert, primitive and infantile narcissism" (1969:90).

The experience at which centering prayer aims is

immediate experience of Being. . . . It is completely non-objective. It has in it none of the split and alienation that occurs when the subject becomes aware of itself as a quasi-object. . . . It is not "consciousness of" but *pure consciousness,* in which the subject as such "disappears." (Merton 1968:23-24)

Such an experience is also "instantaneous . . . an act without time" (Pennington 1977:53). It divinizes us: we become by participation and by gift what God is by nature. Yet its authenticity will be confirmed by the life of service that flows from it, which will provide a channel for the energies it releases.

The life process which leads to such union unfolds in organismic fashion. Our "true self" consists in a "basic core of goodness" which is "capable of unlimited development" (Keating 1986:127). It is "dynamic and tends to grow of itself" (p. 129). Acceptance of our basic goodness "is a quantum leap in the spiritual journey" (p. 127), for we "were made for boundless happiness and peace," and "there is nothing wrong in reaching out for it" (pp. 43, 88). The ultimate goal of this process is "to integrate our whole being with its active and passive, masculine and feminine, expressing and receptive aspects" (p. 91). Whereas this journey will involve many mistakes, and sometimes sins, these will be "insignificant compared to the inviolable goodness of our true Self" (p. 129).

This journey will also involve confrontation with and rooting out the false self. A "structural change of consciousness" will occur (p. 95). Experiences of darkness and emptiness will take place. Yet we can only prepare ourselves to let this happen; God alone can put an end to the false self. As we let go of thoughts and images connected with the false self, the centering process will loosen them up and begin sweeping them away. This dynamism will be "a kind of divine psychotherapy, organically designed for each of us, to empty out our unconscious and free us from the obstacles to the free flow of grace in our minds, emotions, and bodies" (p. 93). However, no process for getting at these obstacles or being freed from them is mentioned besides letting them go and letting God wash them away.

In summary, centering prayer recognizes certain features of contemporary psychological alienation. It emphasizes a false self whose habits, including its roots in the unconscious, must be loosened so that the "true self" can be re-formed. All our senses, drives and faculties participate in a self-splintering, accentuated by the analytical bent of the Newtonian worldview. We will pass through darkness and emptiness in becoming detached from them. Yet the true self is not something to be constructed; it is an existing, organismically unfolding "basic core of goodness," far outweighing any sinful tendencies, with which we must experientially assimilate. We need to be absorbed in a reality which is always truly present, for "God and our true Self are the same thing."[3]

Yet given centering prayer's adaptation to the popular "how-to" market (which separates it from its historic biblical framework), one wonders how thorough its encounter with darkness, sinfulness and the unconscious will be. Can all the self-deceptive distortions of the unconscious simply be swept away? And how often should our desire for "boundless happiness and peace" be encouraged—or might this simply appeal to desires for undiluted pleasure intensified by today's commercial ethos?

Moreover, could not some apparent experiences of merging with God resemble, as Merton acknowledges, a "primitive and infantile narcissism"? Here the caution that an energetic life of service flows from authentic divine encounters seems warranted. However, if centering prayer seems a bit shallow, a more profound version of this approach will be shortly explored in Teresa and John.

The emphasis on the body and feelings. Whereas some current spiritual writers advocate suspending the operations of our faculties, others question this approach. We do not reach God, William McNamara protests, by "sinking down into a subrational condition." Instead,

> the truly prayerful person activates his senses to the highest possible degree until they become so saturated, so filled, so highly developed, that there is nothing more they can do. . . . We do not reach the source of being . . . by recession, regression, withdrawal, or a diminution of human powers, but by the fulfillment of our human powers . . . sensing as much as we can sense, feeling as much as we can feel, knowing as much as we can know. (1983:12-13)

For McNamara, passion and desire, sometimes even anger, are at the heart of spirituality. True mysticism must be "earthy"—engaging all our bodily energy and involved in this world's realities. I will return to McNamara (who does have a place for emptying our faculties) later. First, I will consider a focused attempt to put into practice a pervasive theme in most recent spirituality: the importance of our body. Current spiritual writers, even as they seek to recover much traditional wisdom, often criticize the Christian past for underplaying the body and overemphasizing the soul (see, for example, Miles 1990).

Bio-spirituality adapts the techniques of *focusing* developed by psychologist Eugene Gendlin into several sensible steps for getting in touch with the *felt meaning* of events and situations carried in our bodies. However, bio-spirituality claims that this meaning is almost always different from rational awareness or explanation. The mind's "instinctive tendency to control everything" is the greatest barrier to true spirituality (Campbell and McMahon 1985:52). Bio-spirituality, in contrast, helps us work toward "allowing *anything* that happens to have a kind of here-and-now organismic energy to come forward and be recognized" (p. 32). Its authors, citing Carl Rogers, affirm "that the most accurate scientific instrument available on this planet is the human organism functioning non-defensively in the presence of a problem" (p. 45). The focusing process proceeds as follows.

□ First, take inventory of the feelings going on at your bodily level and simply experience their organismic energy.

□ Second, identify which feeling is "no. 1" for you right now.

□ Third, ask yourself if it is OK just to be with that feeling now. (If it is not, go back to the original inventory and find another.)

□ Fourth, let yourself go into that feeling, sensing the whole of it. If the feeling is painful, that may be a frightening, wilderness experience (p. 74). Maybe you will have to just put your arms around it, as you would hold a hurt child (p. 18).

□ Fifth, allow this feeling to express itself by means of an image. The right image will bring *resolution,* a "distinct sense of inner release you feel in your body . . . which *always* feels good" (p. 44). This release, moreover, will be the beginning of a movement, something *"meant to unfold!"* (p. 80). Thus the right image, or a combination of several, will lead us toward appropriate action.

□ Sixth, the process and its results should be shared with another person.

As we move into these steps, we will begin entering "a realm where *we are carried* more than we carry" (p. 43). Experiences of our authentic feelings will come to us as gifts. A "True Self" will begin emerging, deeper than our "ego-perception" (pp. 43, 71). For this to occur, we must believe—believe with and in our body (p. 55). We will learn to balance striving with letting go of the reins (p. 48).

Although *focusing* is one specific technique, it concretely illustrates the kind of attention to the body and feelings advocated in most current spiritualities. I can hardly dispute that getting in touch bodily with *felt meanings* of experiences is indispensable for psychological and spiritual growth. But can we be sure, as Carl Rogers apparently was, that intouchness with our organism will direct us to the right ethical actions in a world where many needs and claims must be considered? What is bio-spirituality's approach to larger issues?

Considered more broadly, *resolution,* that inner release which initiates a movement *"meant to unfold!"* (p. 80), is really "an open-ended invitation drawing each person along a path of further unfolding" (p. 81). The sense of being carried means that we are caught up in a process with "destinations beyond human comprehension" (p. 78). The sense of being an organism means that we are also intertwined with the organism of the universe (p. 89). By getting in touch, through feeling, with our organism, we can sense that we are part of a vast cosmic adventure—the evolution of, and a "new Copernican revolution" in, consciousness (p. 97).

The authors claim that certain biblical terms express this mystery, though they mention no texts and offer no exegesis. For instance, the New Testament word for "body," *(sōma)* indicates "some primordial organicity or *bodily felt tied-togetherness*," (p. 90), which constitutes "an incredible bond *in our very openness to evolution!*" (p. 95). "Sin," they claim, is "slipping away from the mainstream of advancing consciousness and deserting the bio-spiritual quest" (p. 93). *Metanoia,* or conversion, means "A return to the way . . . coming home once again in openness to the unfolding inner destiny which calls us ahead" (pp. 93-94).

Further, "within the heart of this movement lies a Greater Word waiting to become Flesh and to dwell among us" (p. 88). In fact, all Christian doctrines can be expressed to indicate this process, so long as we realize that Christian revelation "from the vantage point of human development . . . *is not first about God—but about ourselves!*" and that it highlights "aspects of *human self-awareness and human self-process*" (p. 97).

Despite its great differences from centering prayer, bio-spirituality is also an organismic approach. It too is a centering technique—though it focuses on bodily experiences rather than trying to get beyond them. In the process, uncomfortable negative feelings must be embraced and the false ego faced. Yet none of these tensions really involves the unconscious, for our conflicts can be directly interpreted by ourselves. The overall direction sounds highly positive, pleasurable and progressive—qualities much valued in a capitalistic society.

Whereas sensations, images and thoughts are equally distrusted in centering prayer, the first two are valorized but the third strongly critiqued in bio-spirituality. Yet after repeated warnings that intellect can never get at spiritual truth, readers are asked to accept an extraordinarily wide-ranging theory of cosmic history and a radical recasting of biblical terms. By means of this leap, we are assured that whatever feels natural for each of us will correspond with what is "right" and makes for progress in society and non-human nature.[4] We will see that organismic personal spiritualities are often linked with progressive socioecological evolutionary theories.

An emphasis on struggle. Centering prayer and bio-spirituality, which provide representative glances at widespread emphases in current Christian spirituality, are clearly organismic. So is most recent spirituality. In a way, this should not surprise us. In chapter two I noted that organismic psychology, with its overarching emphasis on wholeness, often took religious concerns seriously. But psychoanalysis, largely due to its Freudian origins, has often been regarded as hostile to religion. Moreover, organismic theory produces many optimistic, short-term, comprehensible and therefore popular approaches to healing, whereas psychoanalysis is more convoluted and less "client-friendly."

Both centering prayer and bio-spirituality direct persons experiencing internal alienation to a realm where that does not really exist. They seek to focus an all-encompassing sort of attention on a realm where things are already whole, or at least inherently tending that way. Though they acknowledge that we must pass through conflict, pain and darkness, these phenomena seem to reflect not the way reality is but simply the way that humans in their incompleteness and imperfection experience it. In the current revival of spirituality, are there others who, somewhat analogous to psychoanalysis, regard brokenness and struggle as more characteristic of the way things are? Two writers—William McNamara and Alan Jones— do.

1. *Passionate mysticism.* William McNamara, we have already seen, regards spirituality as an expression and outworking of passion. Prayer, our most basic communion with God, is for him "a cry of the heart." But we do not simply utter our own cry. "Strictly speaking," McNamara continues, "there is only one prayer in the whole world": the prayer of "the Spirit in the heart of the historical, mystical, and cosmic Christ, calling, '*Abba,*' 'Father'" (1983:18). This cry was uttered on the cross by Jesus, who was "wholly human, wholly free, wholly loving, and *therefore* helpless to achieve what he sought." He was answered only when he was resurrected.

McNamara calls "crucifixion and resurrection, the prayer of Christ and the response of the Father," the "archetype and source" of prayer. Apparently he is referring not simply to a universal symbol, with which the Jesus-events happen to correspond, but to originating historical occurrences.[5] Though he can speak, somewhat like bio-spirituality, of the Word becoming flesh from the beginning, he stresses "the supreme initiative of the One who acts" (1983:2).

Humankind became alienated from God, but Christ entered the gap and took on "the cosmic conflict, the whole conflict of the universe, the conflict of disordered, chaotic man" (p. 34). This intercession on our behalf was the root of his death cry, where "Christ suffered the loss of God more radically than any other man in the history of the world. Any other form of atheism is a drop in the . . . ocean compared to the loss of God"

(p. 37). In our prayer, we enter into this conflict and death cry.

Yet on the cross Jesus was also abandoned by humankind, especially because he collided "with the 'empire' of human egotism" (p. 19) and its world systems. Jesus identified with the oppressed of his day, and identification with him in our day calls us into conflict with "the way things are, with the brokenness of our world and our lives, with the rape of the earth . . . [with] a demonic empire that thrives on our immediate gratification and our ultimate degradation" (p. 27). It is this kind of commitment, and not simply inner struggle, that calls us away from comfortable lives into a desert experience ([1977] 1991:84-102). It is identification with Jesus that calls one to combat "the body of used flesh marketed by the empire for the maintenance of a safe and soft civilization" and for this reason to deny "the false self, the skin-encapsulated ego, separate, alienated, loveless" (1983:84).

This kind of spirituality contradicts our longing for "boundless bliss, cosmic consciousness, an oceanic feeling," for "God is not a life-force" but deeply personal (pp. 49, 56). Although McNamara can say that God "is my inmost self," God is also "an Otherness that transcends my own subjectivity even when I respond to it from the subjective ground of my being and know it only in my contact with it" (pp. 21, 95). McNamara can affirm that "there is no separation between the transcendent God and the material world," but the two seem to exist in dynamic, tense interaction (p. 5). In reality God is not our Self, for our "existence is fragile and contingent; we are next to nothing" (p. 98); "we need a savior, because we cannot sanctify ourselves" (p. 63). As we are sanctified and unite with God and others, we retain our identities: "We do not merge" (p. 88).

2. *The mystical journey.* For Alan Jones, spiritual life can be expressed in the form of a journey, an archetypal motif appearing in many religions and cultures. Jones's *Journey into Christ* commences not with heroic enthusiasm but with foreboding: "Storm and flood begin our journey. There are no promises, no guarantees, not even an itinerary. We travel lightly, just as we are. The sky is overcast. There is a heavy promise of tempest, fire, and flood" (1992:18).

The voyage will involve much unlearning; we must admit that we are lost (p. 40). Of course, "we are forever seeking to attain a secure if cheap equilibrium" (p. 27). But true prayer is disquieting: "There are enormous dangers to be found in the deeper recesses of the soul" (p. 22). We will encounter "formlessness, the emptiness, the void . . . that which lies at the heart of human consciousness" (p. 30). Though the journey will indeed have its lighter moments, we will sometimes need to wait in darkness for a

God who is hidden—yet whose hiddenness safeguards our freedom and the character of divine love as free gift (pp. 22, 31, 55).

Jones correlates many journey themes with those of psychoanalysis. (He especially likes Jung but resists the common "temptation to interpret the whole of reality in Jungian terms" [p. 68].) Spiritual birth, like physical birth, is often closely related to death. In both we struggle to be born and against being born (p. 60). Our mother is both a source of bliss and, because of her possible absence, a potential source deprivation and destruction. "This sense of terror and wonder continues to operate in that vast treasury of our subconscious" (p. 64). We must resist succumbing to the devouring Mother. We must differentiate from her and be stricken by the wound of transcendence, which both arouses hope and drives us mad (pp. 67, 72). The only real route will be through cross and resurrection (p. 66).

Our journey will also acquaint us with defilement, with the feeling that there is something horrible and unmentionable about us, much as a child experiences in the anal stage (p. 68). We may try to escape this by regarding ourselves as nothing—yet this too will be an act of pride (p. 72). The only way out will be to acknowledge that, despite being prey to emptiness, we are freely and undeservedly loved (p. 93). Then, much as a child enters the genital stage, we will need to get in touch with our sexuality and unite our feminine and masculine dimensions (pp. 76-86). Finally we will need to reckon seriously with the way socialization, through our original families and the Oedipus conflict, has shaped us, even though we are not totally determined by these.

Although Alan Jones gleans rich insights from many myths, he warns that some can be dangerous (p. 38); therefore the Jesus-story is the criterion of them all. Classical Christology is, for him, the one dogma which releases us from all other dogma (p. 53). It is crucial because it is in Jesus that human faith and divine faithfulness—those obscure movements that mysteriously stretch out toward each other through the dark journey—come together (p. 23). Jones stresses the real, if limited, values of reason (p. 56) and Christian tradition (p. 34). He warns against relying solely on experience, which can become a drug, requiring ever greater doses (p. 66). Revelation, Jones insists, is essential for sorting out truth in a venture so profound and obscure as the journey.

Jones stresses that God is not nature but nature's creator (p. 46) and that creatures are truly distinct from each other. Like McNamara, he regards the cross as the supreme symbol of human lostness and divine love:

It stands in direct contradiction to the success-promising symbols . . . the house, the car, the robust sexual life, the persistent cheating of the final enemy—death. The cross is a shocking and blasphemous symbol in a success-oriented world. It is a sign of the brokenness and vulnerability of God . . . of his hiddenness and his love. (p. 48)

A realistic appraisal of modern reality shows it to be cruciform—that we really are bound together in tragedy and evil.

3. *Summary.* For William McNamara and Alan Jones, reality itself and not just our experience of it is scarred with genuine conflicts, uncertainties and gaps. Emptiness and hiddenness mark our inner selves, outer reality, perhaps even God. The wrenching away from the false self, the journey through the wilderness, hardly seem smooth or predictable. Some experiences of ourselves and God can even be deceptive. Creation, which is distinct from God, is still riven with a cry of alienation and pain, and the unknown toward which we journey may not yet fully exist. Our journey is initiated by our sense of lostness and the wound of transcendence—not by desire for an oceanic feeling or primordial reunion. Though we can hope to be filled with God, we must often search, and sometimes simply wait, as did Jesus for resurrection. We journey toward differentiation from, as well as union with, God.

This differentiation goes along with other distinctions. Though we can be "in Christ," we are also different from him—the pioneer, divine as well as human—who broke the path for us and still intercedes for us. Basic affirmations about him are chiefly about the divine Other, not, as bio-spirituality has it, about human consciousness. Reason, which makes distinctions, has genuine, if limited, value. Experience, which by itself can blur all distinctions, can delude us about reality. For in this kind of spirituality, reality itself is marked by actual differences. Alienation, though it may one day cease, cannot be overcome through straightforward immersion in a reality where things are already whole. Alienation can be confronted only by accepting its tragic reality, even as did Jesus on the cross.

Finally psychological and spiritual maturity requires sharp differentiation from a society driven by desire for ever greater pleasures, possessions and success, and which in consequence forgets and victimizes the weak. Yet even in so doing we are following and participating in Christ.

A Closer Look: Jung, Teresa of Ávila and John of the Cross

In an era when many feel alienated from any satisfying sense of self, can the Christian faith offer insight as to how self-identity is formed? Can it give counsel as to whether some continuing struggle with our drives and social context is to be expected, as psychoanalysis predicts? If so, can it offer help for enduring this? Or can Christian faith enable persons to find more immediate harmony among their impulses and self-longings, as organismic psychology envisions?

We have just seen that contemporary spiritual writers propose diverse answers. My comprehensive response must await chapter nine. But the complexity of the issues just considered indicates a need to examine them in greater depth in this chapter. Fortunately a creative, detailed effort has been made to integrate the teachings of two of the mystics most often mentioned today—Teresa of Ávila and John of the Cross—with the psychologist most frequently incorporated into current spirituality, C. G. Jung. Examination of John Welch's attempted synthesis will help us pinpoint the issues at the intersection of these two fields most crucial for the problem of alienation.

Teresa of Ávila's Interior Castle. Teresa imagines the individual soul, or self, to be like a large, circular castle. This castle has six levels of rooms, each running all the way around it, so that each encircles those within it. The outer wall of the castle is the body; it connects the self to the world. At the center, in the seventh chamber, is God. Teresa portrays the spiritual life as a journey toward this center. The mystical journey toward God, then, is at the same time a journey into the depths of ourselves, which must involve increasing self-awareness.

Teresa images God's presence in the seventh chamber as that of a light, or sun, which illumines all the rooms, as a brazier exuding aromatic scents and often as a fountain watering the soul, for this castle is also like a garden. Sin, she says, darkens this sun, as when a black cloth covers a crystal. Alternatively she speaks of us uprooting our souls and planting them in other, foul-smelling waters (Teresa of Ávila [1577] 1980:1.2.2-3).

Persons in the outer level of rooms, says Teresa, are preoccupied with their bodily appetites and with daily concerns and distractions. Little light from the center reaches them, yet not because of flaws in the rooms. Instead, because such people are preoccupied with daily affairs and demonic "things like snakes and vipers and poisonous creatures," they are not aware of the light (1.2.14). The journey inward must begin with humility, with awareness of our lowliness in contrast to God—this is what Teresa means by *self-knowledge* (1.2.8-9).

We enter the second level through prayer and reflection. Here, however, demonic forces increase their attacks. They make those preoccupations which we are now attempting to take less seriously seem of eternal importance ([1577] 1980:2.1.3). To keep on, it is essential to "embrace the cross your spouse has carried" (2.1.7): to focus on Jesus and his sufferings for us and to follow his difficult way. Teresa stresses that the aim of this journey is not sublime experiences but increasing conformity with God's will (2.1.8). Discursive meditations on Jesus' life and death—on his path of obedience—are important here (2.1.11; [1562-1565] 1960:129, 135, 144).

Those who occupy the third rooms maintain a consistent prayer life and regular church involvement and perform charitable works. Many admirable Christians (especially laypeople) are of this sort. Yet they can still become attached to ingrained sins they refuse to correct. Such persons experience dryness in prayer and may never move beyond this stage.

Describing the fourth dwellings, Teresa distinguishes *consolations* from *spiritual delights*. The former are exercises, such as discursive meditations, where we make the initial efforts through our faculties (imagination, reason and so on) and eventually experience something of God. The latter are initiated and infused directly by God without our specific preparations—they transcend the range of our faculties. Teresa compares the former to our filling a trough with water, the latter to the trough being filled, without our effort, by an aqueduct so that "this water overflows through all the dwelling places and faculties until reaching the body" ([1577] 1980:4.2.4).[6] Teresa says that demonic forces seldom enter the fourth rooms but that when they do they are usually defeated, bringing the soul great gain (4.2.3).[7]

Experiences of union with God which go beyond the faculties begin in earnest in the fifth dwellings. Teresa repeatedly cautions that the faculties cannot be forced to shut down; we can only detach ourselves from their operations gradually, in response to God's gentle inward drawing. She compares what we contribute to a moth building a cocoon: suddenly "to the little we can do, which is nothing, God will unite Himself, with His greatness," making the soul like a butterfly ([1577] 1980:5.2.5). But now distress begins. The little butterfly flutters above earth, where no creature satisfies it (5.2.8), yet often it feels far distant from God. It is anguished that most people dishonor God (5.2.10). But Teresa reminds us that however we feel, the only important thing is to continue loving God and neighbor (5.3.7-8).

In the sixth rooms the soul is betrothed to God. Here God may visit the soul in ways intense enough to be frightening, yet alternating with even more anguished experiences of absence. Through these absences the soul "knows clearly its wretchedness and the very little we of ourselves can do if the Lord abandons us" ([1577] 1980:6.1.10). Teresa discusses the many communications that may come from God. Very few, she says, come through the imagination. She calls most of them "intellectual," by which she means truths immediately impressed on the soul, not ones reached through reasoning.

Finally in the seventh and central chamber, the soul and God are wed. The ups and downs of the sixth dwellings subside, and life becomes more integrated. We might suppose that the human Jesus, so important at the journey's beginning, would have long ago been left behind. Many mystics in Teresa's time claimed that this was so. But Teresa insisted that we never transcend our need for Jesus. He enters the sixth and seventh rooms as a constant companion, and visions of his "sacred humanity" (which leave some impression on the imagination) can be frequent (esp. 6.7.5—9.5; 7.2; [1562-1565] 1960:209-19). In the seventh room, Teresa also sees how the three trinitarian persons "are one substance and one power and one knowledge and one God" through an "intellectual vision" in which "all three Persons communicate themselves" ([1577] 1980:7.1.6).

In this spiritual marriage God and the soul become one, as "when rain falls from the sky into a river or fount; all is water," or "like bright light entering a room through two different windows; although . . . separate when entering the room, they become one" (7.2.4). She also depicts the soul as a "tiny fount" swallowed up in a "full-flowing river" (7.2.6). We might suppose that a soul so immersed would abandon the world. But Teresa insists that this interior calm enables it to be more involved in serving and to cope with far greater exterior disturbance: "The faculties, the senses, and all the corporeal will not be idle [for] the soul wages more war from the center than it did when it was outside suffering with them" (7.4.10).

John of the Cross's dark nights. John's *Ascent of Mt. Carmel* begins by considering recent entrants into monastic life. Full of enthusiasm, they gain much delight from discursive meditations (using their imagination and reason) and church ceremonies. Yet, John observes, such persons are frequently hooked into subtle, religious forms of sin such as pride (over their many hours in prayer), avarice (for spiritual experiences) and so on. Then without warning, many such persons find these exercises becoming stale. Inwardly they feel empty. They fear that they somehow may have sinned, for God seems to have disappeared. Yet, John says, they are really being drawn into a deeper, direct, experience of God. They will pass through one, perhaps two, "dark nights."

The first, the *dark night of the senses,* will purge their five external senses and their internal, image-forming functions of dependence on sensations and images. It will unite the lower, sensory part of their soul, to its higher, spiritual part. Then after many years, some will go through the *dark night of the spirit,* which will purge the powers of the spiritual part—intellect, memory and will—in order to unite it (and the sensory part) to God. Each night will have an active dimension (where we can do something) and a passive one (where we must simply let God work). The second night will be more painful because alienation from God is rooted in the spirit.

In describing these journeys John often portrays God as distant from the soul through images of vast height. Only in works which depict journey's end does imagery of God at the soul's center frequently appear. Since John's major works are commentaries on his poems, it is important to first be moved by his poetry. Let us begin with "The Dark Night," even though John's detailed explanations cover only the first two stanzas. (The first stanza, he says, chiefly describes the *dark night of the senses,* whereas the second depicts the *dark night of the spirit* and the last six express some beneficial results of these.)

The Dark Night

One dark night,
fired with love's urgent longings
—ah, the sheer grace!—
I went out unseen
my house being now all stilled.

In darkness, and secure,
by the secret ladder disguised,
—ah, the sheer grace!—
in darkness and concealment,
my house being now all stilled.

On that glad night
in secret, for no one saw me,
nor did I look at anything
with no other light or guide
than the one that burned in my heart.

This guided me
more surely than the light of noon
to where he was awaiting me
—him I knew so well—
there in a place where no one else appeared.

O guiding night!
O night more lovely than the dawn!
O night that has united
the Lover with his beloved
transforming the beloved in her Lover.

Upon my flowering breast,
which I kept wholly for him alone,
there he lay sleeping,
and I caressing him
there in a breeze from the fanning cedars.

When the breeze blew from the turret,
as I parted his hair,
it wounded my neck
with its gentle hand,
suspending all my senses.

I abandoned and forgot myself,
laying my face on my Beloved;
all things ceased; I went out of myself,
leaving my cares
forgotten among the lilies.

The dark night of the senses involves the purging of our appetites. By *appetites* John does not simply mean physical impulses but inordinate cravings that conflict with our adherence to a moral or spiritual good. Nevertheless his language could often suggest that he regards our bodily nature, and the whole physical world, as evil. He insists, for instance, that "all creatures of heaven and earth are nothing when compared to God." One can only come to God, then, by turning from creatures, for "there is no likeness between what is not and what is." John continues: "All the beauty of creatures compared to the infinite beauty of God is the height of ugliness." "Compared to the infinite goodness of God, all the goodness of the creatures of the world can be called wickedness" (*Ascent* 1991:1.4.3-4).

In describing the appetites John reminds one of Freud. An appetite, he says, "as such is blind . . . because, of itself, it has no intellect" (1.8.3). Appetites, then, spring forth in different directions toward diverse gratifications and in so doing weary, torment and weaken the soul. "They resemble little children, restless and hard to please, always whining to their mother for this thing or that, and never satisfied" (1.6.6). The more satisfactions they crave, the more do they disperse and weaken our basic "force of desire" (1.10.1). The appetites, as it were, place enticing images before our eyes, blocking us from seeing farther ahead (1.8.3).

The "active" role we can take in the dark night of the senses is to "imitate Christ in all [our] deeds by bringing [our lives] in conformity with his." For John, this involves remaining empty "of any sensory satisfaction that is not purely for the honor and glory of God" (1.13.3-4). He advises us to be always inclined "not to the easiest, but to the most difficult; not to the most delightful, but to the most distasteful. . . . For Christ, desire to enter into complete nakedness, emptiness, and poverty in everything in the world" (1.13.6).

Yet our response to this night must be mostly "passive." When discursive meditations no longer bring joy, when we feel empty, listless and distant from God, we can do little but wait. John advises that such persons no longer attempt to meditate but "be content simply with a loving and peaceful attentiveness to God, and live without the concern, without the effort, and without the desire to taste or feel him" (*Night* 1991:1.10.4). For although God is beginning to infuse a burning fire of love, it is so delicate and unlike what sense or imagination can grasp that we seldom feel it (1.11.1).

This Night's "chief benefit," meanwhile, will be an increasing *self-knowledge* by which John, like Teresa, means awareness of our lowliness and misery. The soul "considers itself to be nothing and finds no satisfaction in self because it is aware that of itself it neither does nor can do anything" (*Night* 1.12.2; compare 1.3.3).

Although many dedicated to the religious life will pass through this night of the senses, very few will enter the dark night of the spirit—and even then much later (*Night* 1.8.1; *Ascent* 1991:2.7.3). The only path through this Night is faith, which John defines as the opposite of sight—and therefore also of the intellect, which ultimately depends on the senses.[8] Again Jesus is the model, for "during his life he certainly died spiritually to the sensitive part," and at his death "he was certainly annihilated in his soul, without any consolation or relief" (2.7.10-11).

Although John acknowledges that God normally draws people beginning with the senses (2.17), in this Night the intellect must be emptied and blinded. None of its concepts can lead it to God. In general, "a soul must strip itself of everything pertaining to creatures . . . (of its understanding, satisfaction, and feeling), so that when everything unlike and unconformed to God is cast out, it may receive the likeness of God" (2.5.4).

Since imagination and memory also rely on sensory images, God will not be reaching persons in this Night through images or recollections (2.12, 16;

3.2).[9] John advises them to disregard all visions, even if they might be from God. (He does, however, approve veneration of images proposed by the church, so long as they remain means to, and not objects of, faith [3.15.2].) Much as imagination and memory must be purged of reliance on images, so the will must be purged and reformed through charity so that it will no longer be ruled by the appetites. Then its energy and passions (joy, hope, sorrow and fear) will be directed only toward what is for God's honor (3.17.2).

With the normal operations of intellect, imagination, memory and will darkened, the "passive" suffering of this Night is intense. By stripping us "of the habitual affections and properties of the old self to which the soul is strongly united, attached, and conformed," God "so disentangles and dissolves the spiritual substance . . . that the soul at the sight of its miseries feels that it is melting away and being undone in a cruel spiritual death. It feels as if it were swallowed by a beast and being digested in the dark belly" (*Night* 2.6.1). Moreover,

> persons feel so unclean and wretched that it seems God is against them and they are against God. . . . The soul understands distinctly that it is worthy neither of God nor of any creature. And what most grieves it is that it thinks it will never be worthy. . . . This divine and dark light causes deep immersion of the mind in the knowledge and feeling of one's own miseries and evils; it brings all these miseries into relief so the soul sees clearly that of itself it will never possess anything else. (2.5.5)

While one is in this weakened, despairing state, the devil does all he can to inflict additional horror and dread (2.23).[10]

Yet all this is necessary because "the divine experience . . . is foreign to every human way." The soul, accordingly, must be made "a stranger to its usual knowledge and experience of things so that, annihilated in this respect, it may be informed with the divine, which belongs more to the next life than to this" (2.9.5). Nevertheless the divine light which causes this pain is itself warm and gentle. Gradually the soul becomes capable of sensing and absorbing its goodness (2.13). John depicts the climax of this ascent, so far as it can be attained in this life, in almost opposite imagery.

The Living Flame of Love

O living flame of love,
that tenderly wounds my soul
in its deepest center! Since
now you are not oppressive,

now consummate! if it be your will:
tear through the veil of this sweet encounter!

O sweet cautery,
O delightful wound!
O gentle hand! O delicate touch
that tastes of eternal life
and pays every debt!
In killing you changed death to life.

O lamps of fire!
in whose splendors
the deep caverns of feeling,
once obscure and blind,
now give forth, so rarely, so exquisitely,
both warmth and light to their Beloved.

How gently and lovingly
you wake in my heart
where in secret you dwell alone;
and in your sweet breathing,
filled with good and glory,
how tenderly you swell my heart with love.

Explaining the first stanza, John exclaims:

> The soul now feels that it is all inflamed in the divine union, its palate is
> all bathed in glory and love, that in the intimate part of its substance it
> is flooded with no less than rivers of glory, abounding in delights, and
> from its depths flow rivers of living water (John 7:38). (*Flame* 1.1)

Switching from water to fire imagery, John calls the flame "the Spirit of its
Bridegroom, who is the Holy Spirit."

> The soul feels Him within itself not only as a fire that has consumed and
> transformed it but as a fire that burns and flares within it. . . . every time
> it flares up, [it] bathes the soul in glory and refreshes it with the quality
> of divine life. . . . The interior acts He produces shoot up flames . . . in
> which the will of the soul united with that flame, made one with it, loves
> most sublimely. . . . Thus in this state the soul cannot make acts because
> the Holy Spirit makes them all. . . . All the acts of the soul are divine,
> since both the movement to these acts and their execution stem from
> God. (1.3-4)

John can also call this state, as Teresa did her seventh chamber, spiritual marriage (1.27). Indeed, "the Blessed Trinity inhabits the soul by divinely illumining its intellect with the wisdom of the Son, delighting its will in the Holy Spirit, and absorbing it powerfully and mightily in the unfathomed embrace of the Father's sweetness" (1.15). John now speaks, as Teresa often did, of God as the soul's deepest center. The soul is like a crystal which absorbs so much light that finally "the crystal is indistinguishable from the light, since it is illumined according to its full capacity, which is to appear to be light" (1.14).

A Jungian interpretation. What kind of relationship might exist between the spiritual journey as reported by a saint and the developmental journey as described by modern psychology? Christians would affirm that the saint indeed has moved toward and attained, albeit in an unusual way, the ultimate goal of human existence. One manner of relating a given mystical and a given psychological account, then, would be to regard them as parallel versions of the same process. This assumption undergirds John Welch's creative and stimulating effort to interpret Teresa of Ávila and John of the Cross in Jungian categories. Both of their journeys, he proposes, exemplify Jungian *individuation.*

Welch claims that the foremost language for both saints is imagistic. Teresa's main images (castle, water, cocoon-butterfly, marriage) and John's poetry are the "primary" and "first" expressions of their God-experiences (1982:3; 1990:1). They are necessary, indispensable means of communicating realities too subtle for concepts (1982:20). Even more, their key symbols are archetypal, indicating that a more universal human story is unfolding through their journeys. Welch does acknowledge, with Paul Riceour, that "the symbol gives rise to thought" (p. 25) and that the saints' voluminous pages of didactic writing have some valid function (thought and imagination are not as polarized as in bio-spirituality). Yet he insists that Teresa's and John's basic language is the one Jung found fundamental for the psyche.

Jung's *individuation,* remember, is the process through which the *self,* our authentic center, emerges chiefly during life's second half (see chapter two). Until that point the ego has needed to develop a persona—a public personality conformed to the demands of our society. The ego will more or less identify itself with the persona. But then energies from the unconscious begin pressing for recognition; familiar routines and relationships start feeling stale; we begin feeling restless and inexplicably afraid.

According to Welch, Teresa's first three rooms cover the beginnings of this process. The main barrier to spiritual growth in the first two is preoccupation with daily, public life. By the third, a stable, admirable persona has been established; yet the individual clings to it, along with its flaws, and experiences growing spiritual dryness. Welch also proposes that John's newer monks who are enthusiastically practicing religious exercises are in fact developing religious personas which hide more subtle defects. The religious and imaginative objects among which they move are in fact ego projections which cannot fully represent themselves and God. When these exercises go dry in the first dark night, as does the religiosity of Teresa's third-level occupants, what is happening?

Welch emphasizes that, for Jung, self-images are indistinguishable from God-images (pp. 104-5). He also finds a close correlation between God and the self in Teresa, for she places God as fountain or Sun in her castle's center. Welch also often refers to John's affirmation, "The soul's center is God" (1990:47; though without John's qualification: "through grace and his self-communication to it" [*Flame* 1.12]).

Accordingly, Welch proposes, the dryness and restlessness just mentioned correspond psychologically to the beginnings of the self's breakthrough. The saints' dramatic experiences (Teresa's anguish at feeling torn away from creatures, yet suspended in emptiness even farther in her smallness and sinfulness from an infinite and holy God; John's terrible struggles with a darkness assaulting and undoing his very being from its roots) express the ego's experiences in surrendering its persona-shaped self-understanding and allowing unconscious energies to emerge. Later on, Teresa's ineffable ecstasy in spiritual marriage and John's immersion in the streams and fires of love express the ego's integration into the deeper self.

According to John Welch, then, God's action in these two Carmelites' experience can be correlated with the emergence of Jung's self. Interestingly, a similar attempt to compare John of the Cross with Carl Rogers correlates the same process with the latter's organismic self-actualizing tendencies. According to Kevin Culligan, "God's interior guidance of the person to divine union is experienced psychologically in the human organism's natural tendency to develop all its capacities" (1982:117). What mystics call centering one's life in God can be explained psychologically as increasing congruence between a person's *self* (Rogers's definition) and his or her experiencing organism (pp. 120-21).

Returning to Teresa and John, what can psychology make of the encounters with demonic forces (Teresa's snakes and vipers) that they describe? Welch notes that both writers speak of the soul being strengthened through such meetings. He recalls Jung's emphasis that each person's *shadow* is "90% gold." Welch concludes that these mystics are speaking symbolically of encounters with and appropriation of their lesser known and socially unapproved, though potentially positive, sides.

But how should the centrality that both mystics ascribe to Jesus be understood? Welch answers that the Jesus story—which he understands as the ego's path to and through crucifixion and into resurrected union with the self—is the most basic human story (p. 29). Jung saw in "the image of the Savior crucified between two thieves . . . a crucifixion of the ego, its agonizing suspension between irreconcilable opposites." In this image the "human psyche can fully recognize itself" (p. 199 [quoting *CW* 9:79]. Alternatively, a person might regard Jesus' crucifixion as the ego's effort to resist, or crucify, the self (p. 200). In any case, Welch approves Jung's affirmation "that the journey of the psyche through the individuation process is almost perfectly expressed in the dogmatic truths of the Christian Church" (p. 104).

Welch also emphasizes that, for Jung, Christ is a chief symbol for the self. Thus when Jesus reappears in Teresa's sixth and seventh rooms, she is meeting her true self. Marriage, for Jung, was an archetypal expression of the union of the feminine and masculine—of a man with his *anima* or a woman with her *animus*—inside the self. Accordingly, Teresa's language of betrothal and marriage and John's erotic imagery refer to such a reconciliation within themselves.

In his book on Teresa, Welch differentiates very little between the religious and psychological journeys. He can call the relation "between the human and the divine . . . the large context within which the psyche's healing takes place" (p. 160), but it is not clear how the former is any different from the latter. Welch's later book acknowledges, however, that for John the crucifixion symbolizes not simply the ego's "agonizing suspension between irreconcilable opposites" but that of the entire self, "which has passed over to the realm of the holy in surrender to the Mystery in its deepest center" (1990:84; compare pp. 160-61).

This volume also suggests "that we never find a final place of complete meaning and heart's fulfillment." In the face of John's awful Nights the main issue is no longer "lack of consciousness, or more appropriate images and understandings, but the very limitations of life itself are faced . . . the impossibility of life, no matter what the human development, to finally and fully satisfy life's promise" (pp. 166-67). Sounding somewhat like McNamara and Jones, Welch affirms that in the struggle with psychological alienation a person should, at the end of the day, not count on "ultimate reconciliation of opposites in a heightened consciousness" but, as Jesus did, "bear the suffering trusting in the dark, incomprehensible love of God" (p. 164).

Yet despite this, he places Jesus', Teresa's and John's journeys in an upward movement of consciousness, such as bio-spirituality and some ecological movements laud. Through human consciousness, which Welch traces back to African primates, the evolutionary journey first becomes aware of itself (p. 43)—or, as Jung said, "Human consciousness created objective existence and meaning" (p. 34).

Welch celebrates the *axial age* (about 500 B.C. to A.D. 500) when humans first became aware of their "core of autonomy and freedom" (1982:205). Jesus intensified this, speaking of "a transcendent core in the human personality, the Kingdom which is within." His life, death and resurrection "confirmed a divine presence in the depths of the human co-constituting the self. The long history of the development of consciousness is revealed as the tracing of God's intimate presence within the human" (1990:64). Teresa and John further explored the depths of this presence. Then the Enlightenment discovered "the role humans play as creators of their own history," for "each individual is a free and active cause, a self-creating subject" (1982:206). Nonetheless, as Hegel observed, this emphasis on the individual brought about psychic and social alienation. Teresa and John, however, while affirming human autonomy, can show the way back to our psychic depths.

Limitations of a Jungian interpretation. Those interested in the relationship of psychology to current spirituality can be grateful for John Welch's careful, creative work. He has discovered many intriguing connecting points among his authors. Still, his attempt to treat the two sixteenth-century mystics and a twentieth-century psychologist as giving parallel accounts of nearly the same path leads me to ask, To what extent can what these saints intended to say be translated into Jungian concepts, and to what extent did it transcend or differ from them?

The two Carmelites' profound images express certain dimensions of their themes better than could concepts. They are primary in the sense of giving immediate, vivid expression to many of these. But does *primary* in this sense always mean most accurate, valid and helpful? They repeatedly emphasize that images must be transcended to attain deeper communion with God. Moreover, their prose discussions differentiate at length among alleged God-experiences and are designed to discern their *truth*. They rank imaginative visions fairly low, saying that they are often likely to be deceptive.

Their overall approach might be better expressed by saying that neither images nor concepts can grasp mystical truth but that both are necessary and therefore constitute *alternative* languages, each of which does some things the other cannot. The symbol does indeed give rise to thought; but the two are on more equal footing in Teresa and John than Welch claims. The epistemological priority of images reflects an organismic preference for the affective realm.

Teresa's and John's encounters with demonic forces ultimately yield positive results. According to Welch, then, these two are really talking about their *shadows*, which are "90% gold." Yet I find no passage where they attribute any positive quality to these forces; they appear entirely as hostile enemies. Good results only when God uses such encounters to strengthen the pilgrim. Whatever we may think about demonic powers today, John and Teresa believed that alienation was intensified by uncanny forces which existed beyond themselves, yet which could subtly penetrate their intrapsychic conflicts.[11]

Though Jung sought to underline modern evil's massive scope, his organicism, where everything must function as an element in positive self-balancing wholes, ultimately amalgamated most evil into good. But the two Carmelites' world is less monistic, and evil is much more thoroughly opposed to good and God.

Welch, following Jung, treats Jesus as an archetype of the self, and his crucifixion and resurrection as a pattern fundamental for all individuation. For Teresa and John, Jesus' suffering and raising clearly provided the model to which they sought to conform and, beyond that, a continuing reality in which they participated. Yet can the significance of Jesus for them be reduced to an archetypal pattern? Teresa especially expresses a continuing gratitude for all she owes Jesus. Her spiritual life began in earnest when a picture of his suffering aroused "distress when I thought how ill I had repaid Him. . . . I felt as if my heart were breaking, shedding floods of tears" and "quite lost trust in myself" ([1562-1565] 1960:115; see [1577] 1980:6.11.7).

Jesus' coming was God's "pledge of the love which He bears us," and Christ was always the source of all her good ([1562-1565] 1960:217, 211). Teresa regards him as her constant, indispensable friend and companion, although his "presence bears such extraordinary majesty that it causes the soul extreme fright" ([1577] 1980:6.9.5). Can one for whom she expressed such gratitude, dependence and love really be (unknown to her) her deeper self? Can such a relationship be reduced to a self-relation?

Similar considerations are relevant to the question of how far Teresa's and John's experiences of God can be equated with those of the self. Both, to be sure, affirm some substantial union between themselves and God in their souls' "centers." In imagery such as that of light merging with another light beam or a crystal the two may seem to merge completely. But other powerful imagery must be balanced with this.

John often speaks of the soul as bearing no likeness to God, probably overstating the usual Christian emphasis on divine transcendence. The anguished struggle of the Nights is presented as the clash of two utter contraries (*Night* 2.5.4). And though John encourages individuals to make what "active" preparation for the Nights they can, the divine activity is so foreign that "they cannot actively purify themselves enough to be disposed in the least degree for the divine union" (*Night* 1.3.3).

Similarly, Teresa stresses that even though "we can do much by disposing ourselves" (like the moth building a cocoon), in God's deeper works "we can do nothing" ([1577] 1980:5.2.1) We should "reflect again and again on our poverty and misery and on how we possess nothing that we have not received" (6.5.6). As Teresa comes closer to her center in the fifth and sixth rooms, God paradoxically often appears as greater and more distant. The farther off God is, the more often she is wounded with love and desires God more vehemently. The soul, in "getting to know ever more the grandeurs of its God and [seeing] itself so distant and far from enjoying Him, the desire for the Lord increases much more" (6.11.1).

If this love and awe were simply for the greater self, it would be terribly narcissistic. And if some reality which Teresa and John regarded as so utterly different from them were simply this deeper self, they would be victims of projection, not guides to overcoming it. However closely God may be connected with their selves, especially through grace, Teresa and John also experience Someone terrifyingly and wondrously Other, calling and commanding, wooing and hiding, slaying and resurrecting them.

The extent of alienation from God these saints feel is probably greater than Jungian conceptuality can describe. Welch interprets Teresa's stress on humility as simply "another way of saying that we must be anchored in reality" (1982:76). Yet Teresa's repeated references to this theme reflect, for better or worse, far greater self-abasement. In waiting for God to move, we must "beg like the needy poor before a rich and great emperor, and then lower our eyes and wait in humility" ([1577] 1980:4.3.4). "Almost everything lies in finding oneself unworthy of so great a good and in being occupied with giving thanks" (4.3.8).

John, on the other hand, experiences such fierce fragmentation among his "appetites" that they hardly tend toward any organismic balance or deeper, quasi-divine Self. Indeed, such distorted patterns are so deep that only a disentangling and dissolving of a person's substance that feels like dying can cure them (*Night* 2.6.1).

Finally, to what extent can Teresa and John be designated pioneers in consciousness's cosmic journey, announcing itself through human freedom and autonomy? Though they certainly experienced and expressed a freedom and initiative unusual for—and threatening to—their era, it has little to do with the kind celebrated by the Enlightenment and its modern heirs. Their freedom is actualized through strict mortification and thorough conformity to Another's will. Their persons attain wholeness through complete surrender to this Other, whose very acts become their own. The gaps, darkness, suffering and breathtakingly tender affection in this relationship forbid the conclusion that they are simply actualizing their deeper selves. The chief resource they offer for overcoming alienation is not simply reconnection to our depths but the paradox of liberating submission to Another.

Summary

I have traced a careful effort to interpret two classical mystics who have received much attention in current spirituality in terms of Jung's organismic psychology. Much of value has emerged. It may well be, for instance, that painful experiences of distance from God occur when deeper levels, or potentialities, of our self are emerging. I also find the complexity of Jung's approach—his appreciation of the unconscious, of lengthy struggle with our *shadow* and *persona* and so on—more realistic than implications that such issues can be quickly dealt with in centering prayer and bio-spirituality.

In one way, organismic explanations in general are open to religion. Since they regard all things as interconnected, they can incorporate spiritual dimensions into their basic descriptions of, say, the earth's biota or the self's emergence, more easily than can Newtonian accounts. In another way, though, these explanations tend to be reductive. Since they conceive the divine as so closely integrated with the self, for instance, the divine can be regarded as little more, or perhaps as nothing more, than that self. Divine agencies (such as Christ) can be reduced to symbols or archetypes for immanent processes. Specific religious events (such as Jesus' cross) can become illustrations of general (archetypal) patterns, not actual sources of historical and personal change.

I have argued that the reductions made by John Welch do not really do justice to Teresa of Ávila and John of the Cross. God and Christ, as they experienced them, cannot be reduced to (be interpreted as archetypes of) the Jungian self. Their demons cannot be reduced to Jung's shadow. The freedom they experienced cannot be interpreted as no more than awareness of "a divine presence in the depths of the human co-constituting the self" (1990:64). Yet Teresa and John emphasized the immanence of God and religious realities more than most of Christian tradition. If even their religious notions cannot be reduced entirely to this level, it is unlikely that those of most Christian theologies can.

Conflictual spiritualities also resist such reductionism. Jesus' cross and resurrection, his death-cry and the Father's answer—these are historical and vital sources, not simply symbolic illustrations, of authentic prayer (McNamara 1983). Jesus is the incarnation of the divine Other, of divine faithfulness reaching out to us in our darkness, not simply an archetype of the human journey (Jones 1992). The basic element which resists reductionism in these and the two Carmelites' spiritualities is the conviction that God is transcendent: not only greater than but also distinct and different from the cosmos.

It is because God is truly different that the spiritual journey involves divine hiddenness, unpredictable occurrences, deep convictions of our littleness and sinfulness and growing differentiation from as well as union with God. And because God is really different from humans, other creatures that God has made (including those that are now demonic) are more diverse from us than organicism, with its monistic outlook, usually implies.

Moreover, God as transcendent, or distinct from the world, is certainly not distant from it, as organismic ecological theologians often claim (see chapter six). It is that very transcendence, with the difference it involves, that makes divine involvement in the spiritual journey so personal and often conflictual. Because it renders this dimension of spirituality more realistically, I welcome many emphases in the conflictive perspective. Yet I also appreciate various themes in the organismic perspective, as I will show in chapter nine, where my positive understanding of psychology and spirituality can be developed more directly and fully than here.

Further, my appreciation for some conflictive emphases hardly means that I wholly endorse psychoanalysis, especially in its Freudian form. I can affirm neither that human behavior is best understood by analyzing it into physiological impulses, nor that selves are nothing but products of clashing instincts and social constraints, nor that all motivation is ultimately libidinal.

Still several emphases found often in organismic spiritualities give me pause. Affirmation of the near-identity of God with our true self and apparent assurances that experience of this can be realized rather swiftly can appeal to narcissistic inclinations. They can help us escape, rather than confront, the issues of psychological alienation. I do not doubt that experiences of intense union with God, as reported by Teresa and John, can be authentic. Yet these saints reached these through a process involving deep experiences of enormous differentiation. If desires for and experiences of union lead us along a path of differentiation, especially one that motivates loving and serving others, those desires and experiences may function somewhat as does the ego ideal when pursued as a goal in psychoanalytic theory (see chapter two).

Second, I can as yet find no reason for preferring feeling and imagination over reason. The former capacities unite us with our organisms and others, whereas reason makes distinctions and differentiations. Both seem equally essential to healthy self-formation.

Third, neither the organismic nor the conflictive spiritualities we have discussed pay great attention to the social dimension. They do not answer some questions from chapter two, such as whether society is too rigid or too fluid. Organismic spiritualities apparently assume that major personal change can occur while social contexts remain the same.

Further, centering prayer encourages desires for "boundless happiness and peace," while bio-spirituality affirms that inner resolution "*always* feels good." Moreover, by uniting expanding awareness with evolutionary advance, as Welch also does, bio-spirituality assures individuals that what feels natural for them corresponds with social progress. Such emphases, like those of much organismic psychology, might promote adjustment to capitalistic society. Conflictual spiritualities, however, do mention that spiritual transformation involves opposition to societies based on progress and pleasure. Chapter six will indicate what social attitudes organismic spirituality adopts when it incorporates ecology.

SIX

Theology, Spirituality
& Ecological Alienation

*C*hapter three showed how much current discussion of our
nonhuman environment, like discussion of our personal
selves, is shaped by two contending perspectives. The
Darwinian perspective, much like the psychoanalytic, presents conflict as intrinsic to reality. Nature is marked by
struggle, where only "the fittest" survive. Insofar as it has presented our
environment as simply something to be conquered to promote human survival, this paradigm has helped cause ecological alienation. Yet some who
embrace it propose that the self-concerned impulses undergirding all
struggle (chiefly sympathy, self-interest and sentience) can expand into
positive environmental attitudes toward all creatures.

I wondered, however, how thoroughly such self-regarding impulses
could be transformed into genuinely cooperative activities. I questioned
too whether such individualistic, narrowly focused, short-range concerns
could give rise to the holistic, long-range perspective which modern ecological awareness demands. I also asked whether the instrumental value
which such theories ascribe to nonhumans (and even the degree of intrinsic value extended through sentience) would move humans to regard
them seriously enough.

Chapter three also showed how environmental discussions are shaped by a second, organismic perspective. Much like organismic psychology and spirituality, it affirms that alienation can be overcome by identifying and incorporating ourselves into larger cooperative trends already tending toward wholeness. Some such approaches, especially deep ecology and some ecofeminism, seek to overcome our self-concern by cultivating an affective sense of communion with all other creatures. Like bio-spirituality and John Welch, they find an all-embracing cosmic consciousness arising from, and now spearheading, an evolutionary process.

Yet I pointed out that the cooperation derived from such experiences was still rooted in self-interest and did not adequately recognize differentiation. Deep ecology in particular sought to overcome instrumental value's limitations by extending intrinsic value to all creatures. Yet I maintained that its biocentric equality, once again, did not fully appreciate differentiation. However, I did find value in organismic ecology's effort to overcome individualism and stress holistic perspective through emphasizing interrelatedness.

Nonetheless I noted that organicism, though finding more cooperation in nature than Darwinism, still presupposes much of the Darwinism's struggle and suffering. So I questioned how consistent organicism is in deriving its ethics from cooperation alone. I also challenged the general organismic assumption that evolution is progressive. Consequently I concluded that both ecological perspectives raise questions about the extent to which an adequate environmental ethic (affirming what we *ought* to do) can be derived from consideration of evolution (what *is* the case, scientifically).

Chapter five showed that most current Christian spiritual writers assume an organismic, rather than a conflictive, orientation. Among Christian ecological theologians, however, all seem to adopt organicism, leaving no clear Darwinian-conflictive alternative to sketch.

This chapter will outline two popularized approaches which have impacted theological discourse, mainly by expressing a new ecological sensibility. These are the "Common Creation Story" developed by Brain Swimme and Thomas Berry and the "creation-centered" spirituality of Matthew Fox. Then I will examine some major ecological theologies: process theology (Charles Birch, John Cobb, Jay McDaniel), Rosemary Ruether's ecofeminism and Sallie McFague's proposals. Finally, I will undertake extensive interactions with all these writings.

Ecological Sensibility
Organicism stresses that today's environmental situation will not really

change unless humans develop a new sensibility toward nonhuman nature. Accordingly, works that express this sensibility have made important contributions to theological discourse on the environment.

The first dimension of such a sensibility is a new vision of cosmic evolution—one allegedly integral to, and buttressed by, the scientific perspective which has emerged during the twentieth century. (Physics' contributions to this perspective were sketched in chapter one.) The most widely read version of this vision, well known to and often acclaimed by environmental theologians, is Brian Swimme and Thomas Berry's "Common Creation Story."

The second dimension of this sensibility is an affective spirituality congruent with this story. The most popular version, which frequently cites Swimme and Berry, is Matthew Fox's "creation-centered" spirituality. It is well known to environmental theologians, but they acclaim it in a more qualified manner than they do Swimme and Berry.

"The common creation story." To instill a sensibility which counters ecological alienation, Rosemary Radford Ruether calls for "scientist-poets who can retell . . . the story of the cosmos and earth's history, in a way that can call us to wonder, to reverence for life, and to the vision of humanity living in community with all its sister and brother beings" (1992:58). For Sallie McFague, "the common creation story" is the "heart" of the current scientific view of reality (1993:104). Process theologian Jay McDaniel recounts a "new myth concerning the origins of the cosmos" (1990:109-11), which is most fully expressed in Swimme and Berry's work.[1] Although Swimme and Berry apparently intend their volume to be a "public" presentation based on scientific findings available to everyone, it is religiously flavored enough to function like a natural theology.

Swimme and Berry repeatedly stress this story's novelty: it "was never known before in the course of human affairs. It compares only with those revelatory narratives" that founded great ancient cultures (1992:238). Though these authors frequently critique Newtonianism, they trace the "momentous change in human consciousness" which gave rise to this story to the scientific revolution and Enlightenment. This process crystallized when evidence for an expanding cosmos was discovered (p. 235), revealing "that the universe has emerged into being through an irreversible sequence of transformations" which they call *cosmogenesis,* leading to greater structural complexity and greater variety and intensity of conscious experience (p. 223). The newness of this story mirrors the universe itself, which "at each instant has re-created itself new." Here "to be is to be different . . . to be a unique manifestation of existence" (p. 74).

The universe began with a big bang, a "primordial flaring forth," a "primeval fireball which quickly billowed in every direction" and which can now serve as "a metaphor for the infinite striving of the sentient being" (p. 55). This flaring forth released the elements which have recombined in all existing things, along with untold latent potentialities, so that all things are "kin." These potentialities emerge in sequential order when energy sufficient to release them has organized itself; each level (particle, atom, cell and so on) comprises a qualitatively "distinct 'world'" (p. 73).

Great novelty often arises from episodes of cataclysmic destruction and from circumstances involving mind-numbing waste. "The cosmological power of differentiation explodes with a trillion new pathways. Let them all enter existence. Perhaps one will result in a thrilling new complex community" (p. 90). Swimme and Berry, like Margulis and Sagan, acknowledge the severity of the oxygen holocaust, yet stress that "this very obstacle" made possible "a creative advance," a cell which "invented respiration . . . and magically transformed a curse into a blessing" (p. 58). They admit that "mass extinctions rip apart the accomplished interrelatedness of Earth's community." Yet these open up "a plethora of new ways of life to explore" (pp. 119-20).

Despite this frequent disruption and constant novelty, "the universe is a coherent whole, a seamless multileveled creative event" (p. 18). Despite massive destruction and waste, each being is unique and ineffable, and the universe somehow "works to assure" each particle of its special role (p. 52). At the same time, all these distinct beings are interrelated. Each particle is instantaneously and "intimately present to every other particle" (p. 29). "At the heart of the individual is everyone else" (p. 134). If one word could express the universe, it would be "celebration" (p. 263), and earth seems to be "developing with the simple aim of celebrating the joy of existence" (p. 3).

For some readers, Swimme and Berry's effusive language may not quite ring true. Though violence, destruction and death are often mentioned, are their sharp edges really felt? They are nearly always justified as necessary for creativity, in which "stupendous variety displays its beauty" (p. 51) or as "conditions for adventure" without which "existence might tend towards the trivial" (p. 248).

But how authentically is the vastness of cosmic space, time and energy represented by fast-paced images of billions of galaxies "suddenly" exploding and trillions of creatures "suddenly" perishing? Might these rather insulate the reader, like a spectator at a Hollywood multimedia spectacular, from plausible anxieties about human insignificance and purposelessness which such vastness might arouse? And how consistent is this overall portrait? Is destruction of innumerable creatures really consistent with the special value of each—and joyful celebration by the whole? Do the novelty and diversity of each creature fit with its being conditioned by all others?

Swimme and Berry speak of most phenomena as self-creative. Like Margulis and Sagan, they credit microorganisms with initiating and inventing. They regard the earth (often called *Gaia*) and the universe as self-regulating.[2] How does this work? Well, billions of years ago, for example, "suddenly the universe constellated into a trillion separate clouds of hydrogen and helium. . . . Powers of self-determination erupted within each of these clouds. The galaxies were born." Yet our authors also say that these galaxies were evoked by "the power that evoked the universe" (p. 34). Was something like a god the ultimate origin?

Swimme and Berry often mention that had conditions at the Big Bang been slightly different, nothing like life could have arisen: "In some sense the structures of the universe were 'aimed at'" (p. 69).[3] Yet no personal or rational agent is credited with this aiming. The "power that brings forth the universe" is variously styled by names such as "the matrix out of which the conditions arise" for spatio-temporal existence (p. 17), the "depth communication of primordial existence" (p. 41), "emptiness . . . the latent hidden nothingness of being" (p. 76; compare p. 20) and "pure potentiality" (p. 110). To determine what connections this power might have with the Christian God, one will have to go beyond this sort of natural theology.

Like the organismic ecologies discussed in chapter three, Swimme and Berry's *The Universe Story* regards humankind as the point where evolution becomes self-conscious. Our role is to enable "the Earth and the universe entire to reflect on and to celebrate themselves, and the deep mysteries they bear within them, in a special mode of conscious self-awareness" (p. 1). In fact, "the cosmological enterprise is at a pitch of intense creativity in our time precisely because the role of the human in the web of relationships"—especially our capacity for ecological devastation or transformation—"is changing so radically" (p. 24). As in other organismic ecologies, however, previous Western history is critiqued for granting humans too exalted a role (p. 254).

What guidelines might we follow in environmental action? For Swimme and Berry, like nearly all the authors examined in chapter three, ethics is to be derived from "that creative process whence the universe derives, sustains itself, and continues its sequence of transformations" (p. 251). And what are the chief characteristics of that process, which, they say, moves toward greater complexity, variety and intensity?

The first is *differentiation,* the production of diversity, which arises from the surprise, spontaneity and wildness—and also the chance and error—at reality's roots. Biologically differentiation arises through *mutation* (p. 126).

Second comes *communion.* Since "relationship is the essence of existence," real alienation seems to be impossible (p. 77), or perhaps the supreme evil (p. 78). Biologically communion has arisen through natural selection. Predator-prey relationships have coevolved into stable ecosystems (p. 105). For Swimme and Berry, natural selection fosters not a struggle for survival but "a deep intimacy of togetherness" (p. 134). It demands that members of an ecological community adapt to each other and work harmoniously (p. 133).

Third, the evolutionary process is characterized, as Margulis and Sagan say, by *autopoeisis,* or the self-organizing dynamics exhibited especially by biological creatures. Though Swimme and Berry claim that this emphasis does not clash with neo-Darwinism (p. 129), their repeated emphasis on purposeful development is far more Lamarckian.[4]

If we humans can learn to follow this three-fold pattern, following the great geological eras of the Paleozoic, Mesozoic and Cenozoic, we will enter the *Ecozoic,* a period of harmony among humans and all other creatures—or perhaps more precisely into a conflict between the *Ecozoic* and the *Technozoic,* a possible period of increasing human control and destruction. The Ecozoic's foremost goal is the alteration of consciousness, the fostering of a sensitivity or an *entrancement,* which enables humans to "appreciate the ultimate subjectivity and spontaneities within every form of natural being" (p. 268). We must learn to listen to nature's deep, self-regulating rhythms, as primitive peoples did, and to celebrate these through art, poetry and ritual.

Religion will play an important role, above all in preserving "the natural world as the primary revelation of the divine" (p. 243). Religion originally conveyed a sense of embeddedness in the cosmos's deep rhythms. Throughout the Paleolithic and Neolithic periods (120,000 to 5,000 years ago) humans worshiped a Great Mother who symbolized the seasons' rhythms and nature's fertility and destruction. Like cultural ecofeminism and Murray Bookchin's social ecology, *The Universe Story* portrays the hunter-gatherer societies of this era as largely peaceful, with women playing important roles. Yet many such societies were subjugated, starting about 3000 B.C., by urban, male-dominated, warrior civilizations worshiping sky-gods. (The biblical religions, however, are credited with perceiving the divine in historical events.)

Later military ventures, such as the Crusades (p. 194), Columbus (p. 208) and the rise of nationalism (p. 212) performed important tasks in bringing different peoples together. Nonetheless neolithic villages continue to exist among rural peasants and may provide models for future eco-villages (p. 179). As humankind enters the Ecozoic era, we can identify the Great Mother with "the grand curvature of the universe . . . the creative and nurturing context of all that exists" (p. 220).

Swimme and Berry sometimes acknowledge that life even in the Ecozoic will involve some hardship. To live in communion with other creatures, we must restrain frenetic efforts to intensify and satisfy all our desires (p. 57). They critique the "Wonderland vision" of ever-increasing consumption, embodied "in the Disney world ideal of the human in a nonthreatening world of fabricated imitations, or caricatures, of the universe and all its living manifestations" (p. 219). But although their criticism of myths of ever-escalating production and consumption is warranted, I wonder whether *The Universe Story* itself, at least in its rhetoric, might not tend to construct an alternative Wonderland vision.

When events of unimaginable destruction and suffering are repeatedly portrayed as grand spectacles and glorified as initiators of yet greater novelty and aesthetic harmony, when each particle is portrayed as unique and valuable despite these cataclysms, when natural selection is idealized as communion and when nature's complex, mysterious rhythms are presented as simple spontaneities, easily penetrable through entrancement—is not a nonthreatening world being fabricated by creating caricatures of the real universe? In an age whose external "reality" is increasingly constructed from enticing yet fleeting images, which ever promise fulfillment through yet more pleasurable images but ever increase our inward emptiness because they have no depth (see chapter two)—might this story function, at least in part, as a grandly attractive commercial product, displaying the greatest variety of intensities and contrasts, designed to disguise the ambiguity and anxiety that a more realistic account of evolution suggests and to place the spectator at the center of everything? Yet if the natural world and our environmental problems involve harsher aspects, will not the sensibility and enthusiasm aroused by such a story be likely to fade?

An ecological spirituality. Whereas ecological spiritualities have emerged in various forms,[5] their overall thrust is probably best represented by Matthew Fox. Though Fox, who frequently cites Swimme and Berry, has been critiqued as they have for being somewhat effusive and shallow, his work covers more themes than other environmental spiritualities and is qualifiedly affirmed by the ecological theologians we will interact with later in this chapter.[6]

Fox's spirituality, which he calls *creation centered,* affirms that the created world is a blessing. It should arouse joy and delight, giving rise to trust in reality (1983:46). That means, as Carl Rogers and bio-spirituality affirm, that we should trust our body with its organismic rhythms. This will lead us to trust ourselves, then others and then the organismic rhythms of non-human reality. *Faith,* for Fox, is this kind of trust, not trust in unseen realities (pp. 83, 120).

Fox affirms, however, that a contrasting *fall-redemption* approach has characterized most Christian spirituality. This tradition considers all nature "fallen" (p. 11). By stressing original sin, it affirms that individuals enter the world "despised, unwanted, ugly, and powerless" (p. 29). *Fall-redemption spirituality,* Fox claims, teaches people to mistrust their organisms and to project the loathing and fear they feel for themselves upon other creatures. This leads to the real original sin, *dualism,* which treats another human or nonhuman "as an object outside oneself" (p. 49) and seeks to subdue it.

For Fox the notion "that God is 'out there' is probably the ultimate dualism" (p. 89). This attitude will best be overcome by a *panentheistic* awareness, "a transparent and diaphanous consciousness wherein we can see all events and beings as divine" (p. 90).[7] Again reminding one of bio-spirituality, Fox affirms that "there is one flow, one divine energy . . . flowing through all things, all time, all space. We are part of that flow" (p. 38). Fox calls the cosmos a maternal womb; he celebrates the Great Mother (1988:29) and Gaia (pp. 235-36) as givers and takers of all life. People can discern God's purposes by listening to this cosmic flow, for "Nature itself is 'the primary Scripture'" (1983:38). Like Swimme and Berry, Fox means that evolutionary science provides an essential means for deciphering nature's voice.

Unlike Swimme and Berry, however, whose presentation is more "public," Fox often mentions Jesus. Jesus, he says, "was in love with the birds of the air, the lilies of the field" and other creatures "enough to pray to them, which means to enter into them, to be transformed by them" (p. 63). Jesus came not to be King but to redefine kingship as a dignity, or *royal personhood,* belonging to all people (p. 122). The summit of his teaching, apparently derived from his love of nature, was "Be compassionate as your creator in heaven is compassionate" (Fox's rendition of Luke 6:36 [p. 225]).

Jesus was also the *Cosmic Christ,* the pattern connecting all phenomena in the cosmos, which only modern science with its emphasis on interconnectedness has fully appreciated (1988:79). His body is the universe, and he suffers in every creature (p. 153). However, since all humans are *microcosms* of the cosmic *macrocosm*, the true self in each of us is also the Cosmic Christ (p. 65). Sounding like John Bradshaw (see chapter two), Fox affirms that "the Cosmic Christ is the 'I am' in every creature" (p. 134). Given Fox's confidence in God's presence in everyone, "Jesus" and "Christ" appear to be largely exemplars, or archetypes, of humanity in general, which do not qualify or counter what nature otherwise teaches.

Reality's basic movement, as Swimme and Berry affirm, is *cosmogenesis,* the cosmos birthing itself. Humans, as the ones through whom the cosmos becomes self-conscious (1983:180-81), participate in this through creative activity. By this Fox frequently means art. Often, like Rogers, bio-spirituality and John Welch, he privileges images over words, the right brain over the left (though he sometimes affirms their integration).

Fox's foremost spiritual technique is *art as meditation,* unfettered expression of inner or outer perceptions. Creativity involves play, the release of infantile energies, the actualization of the Child within us. Fox often makes romanticist connections among the child, the feminine, native religions, mysticism and creativity (for example, 1988:11-34). He can also call lovemaking "art as meditation par excellence" (p. 179) and sex, following C. G. Jung, a return to unconscious oneness, childhood and the divine (p. 171).[8] Out of such experiences creativity arises, and by being creative we birth "God's Son" (1983:176).

Despite this sensuous emphasis, Fox, who defines *faith* as organismic trust, has room for a *Via Negativa* (negative way) like John of the Cross, who defined faith as the opposite of touch and sight (see chapter five). The *Via Negativa* is a process of letting go of all thoughts and images and all clinging to our ego. The cross is its ultimate symbol. This process cleanses, or deautomatizes, the senses from overloads from our consumer society (1988:39). We get in touch with our pain and befriend it. (Fox, like Jung, compares this with Jesus loving his enemies.) We face fears which we project dualistically on others and learn that salvation is through pain, not from it (1983:162). We learn to trust the darkness, and even death, and as we sink deeper we experience "the unity of all things" (p. 161).

Fox affirms that a dialectic of "light *and* darkness, fullness *and* emptiness" exists in both God and us (p. 130). He even claims that "a light-oriented spirituality is superficial, surface-like, lacking as it does the deep, dark roots that nourish and surprise and ground the large tree" (p. 135). Nonetheless the *Via Negativa* is the shortest of Fox's four spiritual paths,[9] and he paints the others in exceedingly "light-oriented" tones.

Unlike the organismic spiritualities in chapter five and truer to the general organismic outlook, Fox is much concerned with social issues. He finds that the humanity-nature dualism underlies all others (p. 210; compare p. 119). This agrees with deep ecology but not with ecofeminism (for which male-female dualism is basic and then projected upon humanity-nature), nor with Bookchin (for whom general domination of humans over humans precedes that of men over women and humans over nature). Fox therefore believes that as different peoples and religions learn to revere the earth, their mutual hostilities will cease (pp. 15-16). "Approaching the cosmos with reverence and eagerness assures the approaching of others—especially those different from ourselves—with equal reverence" (p. 78).

The key to loving nature and others is compassion, which is derived from cosmic interrelatedness in a way similar to deep ecology's: "The entire insight upon which compassion is based is that the other is *not* other; and that I am *not* I. . . . In loving others I am loving myself and indeed involved in my own best and biggest and fullest self-interest" (1990:33; compare McDaniel 1990:29).

Fox's ethic also stresses justice, which he conceives in aesthetic terms, as balance in the cosmic order. Injustice, then, is a rupture in this order, which the cosmos's self-balancing rhythms—not God (1988:71)—will eventually redress. Fox insists that creation-centered spirituality is liberation spirituality, deeply concerned for the *anawim* (Hebrew for "the poor"). For they have experienced the darkness of the *Via Negativa* (p. 207) but have retained their imagination and a humility that make them "an authentic source of revelation . . . our primary spiritual directors" (p. 270). They are oppressed because of their diversity—something the dualistic mentality fears but which Fox and our other organismic authors celebrate. Fox regards the earth as "the ultimate *anawim*" today (p. 17).

At bottom, however, Fox affirms that our organisms, and thus our actions, are motivated "by preference," or pleasure (1983:55). Justice-making, then, can be thought of as "sharing the pleasure" (p. 54). But though Fox sometimes distinguishes true pleasure, or "savoring," from the sensory overloads continually emanating from our commercialized society, he is writing for people strongly conditioned by that society. As Herbert Marcuse argued, our most fundamental awareness and understanding of pleasure are deeply shaped by such processes (see chapters two, four). Thus when Fox identifies repression of organismic feelings as our chief enemy and enthusiastically champions sensory, organismic expressiveness as the liberative key, I fear that many of the energies unleashed will simply rush into preprogrammed channels. When he claims that we can harness unleashed passions and lusts by simply donning "a bridle of love" (1983:60; 1988:178), I fear that Fox seriously underestimates the kind of crucifixion-resurrection process involved.[10]

Summary. Berry, Swimme and Fox seek to arouse a sensibility which will motivate environmental involvement. They portray nature as inherently creative, brimming over with exciting possibilities and as the foremost revelation of the divine. Here all things are kin—intertwined within the panentheistic God (Fox). Each thing is both highly individual and inextricably interrelated with everything else. Nature is inherently celebrative, guided by self-forming powers and on the brink of unparalleled positive *(Ecozoic)* or destructive *(Technozoic)* breakthroughs. Humans can direct these potentialities, for we are evolution become conscious (and also Cosmic Christs [Fox]). This evolutionary movement corresponds with our own organismic rhythms, as bio-spirituality affirms, and our deepening consciousness *(entrancement)*. Attunement with it will awaken our artistic creativity, a childlike playfulness and the best possibilities for social harmony.

To be sure, the natural world displays many beautiful creative rhythms. They often resonate with our bodily rhythms and enhance our conscious creativity and delight. Any viable environmental activity will follow these patterns closely. But are these rhythms, or patterns facilitating artistic creativity or social justice, as readily discernible, as easy to follow or as revelatory of God as these authors often imply? Or does discerning them often require lengthy labor, which is liable to error, and is the best way of following them often open to debate? If we do find and follow some such natural patterns, will we quickly enter a whole new (Ecozoic) era—or simply improve life in modest ways?

I wonder whether these authors' efforts to valorize novelty, creativity and diversity and paint them in such sparkling colors might not mask some of the complexity and struggle which mark nature and human life's real challenges. Does today's commercial ethos perhaps prompt them to "sell" environmental involvement by promising ever newer, better and brighter rewards for those who buy in? If so, might not their "light-oriented" portrayals turn out to be somewhat "superficial" and "surface-like," and eventually disappointing?

Ecological Theologies
Because they advocate a new sensibility toward the cosmos, the above approaches have impacted the emergence of theological discourse on the

environment, which began appearing in print in about 1985. We should not assume, however, that any shortcomings found in these more popular presentations characterize the scholarly works as well. We must evaluate each on their own merits. Like the thinkers engaged in public discourse (see chapter three), those involved in theological discourse seek to derive their environmental perspectives and ethics largely from modern science. For clarity of presentation, then, I will distinguish their general views from what they say specifically about Jesus Christ. But first I must consider an issue that shapes the entire discussion.

Panentheism. Many current spiritualities seek to overcome psychological alienation by merging our small selves with a Divine Self (see chapter five). Similarly most environmental theologies seek to overcome ecological alienation, as Matthew Fox does, by incorporating the being of the physical cosmos into God's. They trace much of today's environmental malaise to a God-world paradigm which allegedly dominated most traditional Christian theology and which was accentuated by the Newtonian worldview. That paradigm conceives of God as transcendent in the sense that God's being is distinct from and independent of that of the cosmos—not necessarily interdependent or intertwined with it.

This God-world paradigm is criticized, first, for making God *distant.* According to McFague it portrays the world "empty of God's presence, for it is too lowly to be the royal abode. . . . Whatever one does for the world is not finally important . . . for its ruler does not inhabit it as his primary residence" (1987:65).

This paradigm is faulted, second, for depicting God as *wholly spiritual,* with the result that, in Ruether's words, "everything that changes, decays, falls into decline and death expresses this negative drag of material mutability. The dissolution side of the life cycle [is] . . . the manifestation of evil. . . . Ultimate good is escape from the life cycle"—that very cycle whose rhythms and intricacies ecology emphasizes (1992:123-24).

Other characteristics of such a distant, vastly different deity spawn social and economic problems. According to process theologians, this God is, third, an isolated *individual,* "totally independent, with no real relationships to any other actualities." Not surprisingly, recent Western culture "has been characterized by an increase in atomic individualism and isolation" (Cobb and Griffin 1976:21).

Fourth, being independent and sovereign, this God is also *absolute.* He sanctions ideologies and prejudices which, in McDaniel's words, "are usually justified by appeals to . . . conceptual absolutes" (1990:36) and often divide creatures into "'Them' against 'Us'" (pp. 26-29).

Fifth, this treating of good and evil as "opposite substances, ultimately embodied in opposite cosmic principles" is said to encourage people to align absolutely with one side, legitimating sociopolitical *domination* (Ruether 1992:86).

Finally this God-model reportedly assures people that "the world will be cared for with no help from us," fostering *passivity* and escape from responsibility (McFague 1987:69).

To counter the alleged flaws of this transcendent paradigm, which stresses God's distinctness from the world, ecological theologians probably stress no theme more than the "fact" of "universal interconnectedness." This entails for most of them that "the universal web of interconnections . . . is itself holy or sacred, being the source of all value and power" (Griffin 1990:3, 2). The God-world paradigm consistent with this emphasis is *panentheism*. It means, literally, that God *(theos)* is in *(en)* everything *(pan)*.

As I shall use the term, panentheism claims, in contrast to transcendence, that God's being is necessarily interdependent and intertwined with that of the cosmos—or at least some cosmos.[11] Panentheism must be distinguished from *pantheism,* which claims that God is, or is wholly identified with, everything, for panentheists also affirm that God "transcends" the cosmos in the sense of being more than, and not being entirely reducible to, the cosmos. God's relation to the cosmos is often likened to how our total human selves relate to our bodies: though we are more than our bodies, we are not independent from them (McDaniel 1990:102-5).[12]

Clearly ecological panentheists fault the transcendent paradigm not merely for inaccuracy but also for inculcating a sensibility hostile to environmental concerns. They believe that their paradigm can nurture a different sensibility.

This paradigm portrays, first, a God who is not distant from but *deeply involved* with all creatures. If creatures form parts of God's being or "body," God can hardly be unconcerned about their welfare—and neither can we once we realize that by helping or harming them, we help or harm God.

Second, since this God is *embodied,* people can celebrate their bodies and those of other creatures. People can expect to find God by looking within rather than by fleeing or by birth, change and death.

Third, since interconnections "are internal to the very essence of things themselves" (Griffin 1990:1), this paradigm can encourage us to find ourselves and God, and to help heal nature and society, through *cooperation* with others.

Fourth, since all creatures contribute to each other and even to God, this paradigm should foster a praxis and spirituality "open to, celebrative of, and transformed by, plurality—the sheer diversity of different forms of life" (McDaniel 1990:31; compare Ruether 1992:53, 102; McFague 1993:29, 49-51). *Pluralism* will be celebrated, even among religions, for panentheistic ecologies seek to overcome dualisms based on a fear of Otherness which they believe absolutes support.

This attitude, fifth, should free individuals and societies from desires to dominate others and inculcate *compassion.* Love of neighbor will flow from the insight that others are not separate from but are "part of ourselves" (McDaniel 1990:29).

Finally realizing that we are God's hands and feet, we should become *active* and responsible, renouncing passive dependence on an omnipotent God.

Most environmentally concerned people would affirm most or all the outworkings attributed to the panentheistic paradigm. Why, then, do proponents take pains to contrast it with a wholly negative, highly caricatured one (see especially Cobb and Griffin 1976:8-10; McDaniel 1990:24-26; McFague 1987:63-65)?[13] Is the choice really so simple and clear-cut? Or might another option exist?

I will raise these questions again later in this chapter. I will examine them in depth at the end of chapter ten, where I will consider another version of the transcendent paradigm and ask how well it meets the six criteria just mentioned. At present, we need to consider our ecological theologians' work in detail.

Process theologies: General features. Most ecological theologians, like current organicism in general, trace the bulk of contemporary problems to the "modern" mindset which crystallized at the Enlightenment. The Enlightenment, we have seen, exalted reason over humanity's affective and aesthetic capacities and detached matter from all mental and spiritual forces, including God (see chapter one). Human reason became fully capable of understanding the cosmos, discerning moral values and restructuring nature and society. Enlightenment *philosophes* exuded confidence that since the key to all physical and social knowledge had been discovered, unending technological and social progress were inevitable. God, who was no longer needed to explain this process and could not act within it, was reduced to initiating it and supporting its values.

Especially during the nineteenth century, many Protestant theologians (preeminently Albrecht Ritschl [1822-1889]) interpreted this scientific and social "progress" as the advance of God's kingdom, which Jesus had proclaimed.[14] But when this culture self-destructed in World War I, most Protestant theologians, rather than seriously questioning Newtonian assumptions, simply ceased dialoguing with science. Process theologies reopened this conversation and began challenging Newtonianism in the 1960s. Yet they were often relegated to theology's margins—until environmental concerns mushroomed. Today many ecological theologians either espouse process theology or are much indebted to it.

Process theology draws heavily on certain philosophers, most notably Alfred North Whitehead (1861-1947). Reflecting the change from Newtonianism to quantum mechanics, Whitehead conceives the universe's ultimate components not as indivisible particles but as *actual occasions,* as vibratory particles of streaming energy existing for fractions of seconds. All occasions, even those composing rocks, enjoy some kind of "experience" and, through a *subjective pole,* make some kind of self-determining response to the world they encounter. No other basic kind of entity exists, for all things are composed of actual occasions. They do not owe their being to any cause, for they have always existed. Yet their form and relationships are shaped largely by other things.

Whitehead's ultimate principle is *creativity,* that characteristic of the evolutionary process through which the cosmos moves toward increasing complexity, harmony and intensity of experience. Creativity also has no cause. It is the ultimate feature, or explanation, of everything else. Yet for Whitehead form and organization do not just emerge spontaneously, as they seem to in some organismic worldviews (Margulis and Sagan, for example). For actual occasions to be incorporated into creativity's flow, it is necessary to postulate an agency—*God.* "God," however, is not the creator of anything but another actual occasion—even though God's existence, unlike any other's, is *everlasting.* God also—again unlike the rest—has a *primordial pole* which envisions all the potential patterns (or *eternal ideas*) by which occasions might organize themselves.

The universe acquires shape and occasions form relationships as the latter spurt into existence, and God, from among the possibilities envisioned in the *primordial pole,* proposes to each the pattern which will best actualize its potentials and contribute to the cosmos. All such patterns involve the occasion's relationships to all other occasions, so by choosing any pattern those entities and their structures enter into the constitution of the developing occasion. In other words, all occasions (including God) are *internally related,* not merely *externally related* through force and impact, as were Newton's particles. These choices and the patterns God offers involve some degree of novelty, so the universe is somewhat indeterminate, though not enough to contravene scientific laws.

Occasions, however, may reject God's pattern, for God operates only through persuasion—only as a *lure,* or *final cause,* presenting a vision of the best goal. Further, God's *consequent pole,* which is God as actually existing, evolves and "shares with every occasion its actual world." Thus this panentheistic God is also "the great companion—the fellow-sufferer who understands" (Whitehead 1929:406, 413). God, as Whitehead puts it, "does not create the world, he saves it; or, more accurately, he is the poet of the world, with tender patience leading it by his vision of truth, beauty, and goodness" (p. 408).

Yet process theology, like all evolutionary worldviews, must make some sense of the suffering and evil choices that occur along the way. Process theologians respond with three answers: first, such things are often necessary to produce higher and better life forms; second, God, who does not create things but simply proposes patterns to them, is finite and limited in power and is not responsible for all that goes amiss; third, in the *consequent pole* God accompanies entities in their suffering.

Process theologians, along with Swimme and Berry, believe that although the contemporary situation has spawned unprecedented threats, these can best be met by taking advantage of the latest scientific discoveries and conceptualities. Whereas the Enlightenment promoted the Newtonian paradigm, it also marked an advance in human self-consciousness (as John Welch says) and unleashed the potentialities of science. David Griffin insists that "the modern world has produced unparalleled advances that must not be lost in a general revulsion against its negative features" (1988:xii). Accordingly the modernity stemming from the Enlightenment "can successfully be overcome only by going beyond it, not by attempting to return to a premodern form of existence" (p. xii).[15]

Process theologies: Ecological theology. Charles Birch and John Cobb promote social and economic liberation. Yet they want these to be guided not simply by negative reactions to oppression but also by positive visions of life's potentialities. To this end, they argue that the concept of life itself needs liberation from mechanistic, reductionist thought-forms. Beginning with the cell and basing their arguments on science, Birch and Cobb carefully develop an "ecological" concept of life they finally root in a divine Life. Though they acknowledge that this last step involves some speculation, they connect life only loosely with the Christian God. Their approach, though more explicitly Christian than Swimme and Berry's, still approximates a *natural theology.*

Birch and Cobb accept some less optimistic features of Darwinism. They critique notions of evolution as "movement forward to new heights" (1981:65) and as having a single goal (p. 4). They affirm neo-Darwinism's stress on slow, gradual change and its statistical methods. They accept random mutation despite its usually deleterious consequences as the foundation of all variety and endorse the "inexorable necessity" of natural selection (p. 64). Yet to these two evolutionary mechanisms they add purpose—in the sense that organisms who pioneer better survival behaviors often leave more offspring. This is not Lamarckian, for behaviors themselves are not genetically transmitted. Yet it grants a special role to "'the restless, exploring and perceiving animal that discovers the new ways of living, new sources of food'" (quote from Hardy 1975:172).

Based on sciences such as quantum mechanics, Birch and Cobb argue that events are best conceived as primary and objects simply as "enduring patterns among changing events" (1981:95). Events, however, are not distinct but are constituted by relationships with other events—by *internal relations*, which ultimately include "spatio-temporal relations to all other events" (p. 88). But if something is constituted internally by events entering into its very being, how can we conceive this sort of influence, or causation? Birch and Cobb propose that "human experience"—the impacts, joys, pains, hopes, fears and so on that are felt when other things affect us—"is the ideal exemplification of internal relations" (p. 105).

This model provides a bridge to ethics. For all living organisms, experience is bound up with the urge to live. Being alive, or life, is "not a mere fact; it is a value" (p. 106). Further, all organisms desire fuller and richer living. Experience is fuller when our world is more complex and when our response to it is fresher. Both are matters of novelty: life requires new stimuli and responses and is richest when we strive for new meaning (p. 107). Life resists decay and repetition and aims for the highest perfection allowed by given conditions.

This notion carries implications for environmental ethics. The *intrinsic value* of something equals the richness of its experience (or of the experiences of its constituent parts or of their potential for rich experience). Consequently, since all experience is valuable, everything has some intrinsic value, but since nothing has infinite experience, nothing has infinite value (p. 141). Yet everything also has *instrumental value*—it can be a means to some other end.

Birch and Cobb agree that assigning limitless intrinsic value to every creature, as deep ecology does, provides no help in specific ethical decisions. Their notion of grades of value, whatever its problems, deals more concretely with diversities among creatures. (Nevertheless they regard them all as different organizational points on a monistic continuum [of nothing but Whiteheadian *actual occasions*]). Moreover, their emphasis on life's continual novelty leads them to deny any "stable, harmonious nature to whose wisdom humanity should simply submit" (p. 65). They base ethics far less on ecological balance (or on "stabilizing Gaia") than do many organismic ecologies.

Birch and Cobb generally oppose animal rights' individualism, for animal experience is far less complex than human. Animals, therefore, have more instrumental than intrinsic value. They promote preservation of animal species, however, for these contribute to the complexity, and hence richness, of overall experience (pp. 153-62).[16] The criterion for biospheric ethics is maximization of total richness of experience. Here both quantity and variety are involved. Severe reduction of human population, as recommended by some deep ecologists, is rejected, for human experience is richest (pp. 168-74). However, since ethics is rooted in how things are experienced, our actual environmental values will alter as nonhumans are experienced, and hence valued, differently (p. 144). Despite Birch and Cobb's differences with deep ecology, their insistence that all creatures share some kind of experience supports a sense of affective communion with the Whole.

Birch and Cobb's value-laden life concept, though they seek to ground it scientifically, also carries progressive implications. Though they reject a goal for evolution and resist calling it a "movement forward to new heights," they clearly attribute to it a positive directionality, or "'anagenesis . . . towards . . . richness of experience.'"[17] Moreover, they claim that this anagenesis occurs because "emergent possibilities for creative transformation" arise every moment (p. 188). Like Margulis and Sagan, they name the power of these possibilities "Life," which "actualizes creative novelty wherever it can" (p. 189).[18]

By offering new possibilities each moment, Life calls each person to decisions. If we disregard these possibilities so that our present remains "simply the product of the past and does not create something new, there entropy reigns undisturbed." But if we take the risk of actualizing these possibilities so that "the past is turned into the ingredients of a new order, there Life is present" (p. 189; compare pp. 183-84). This identification of Life with the novel and of the continuation of past or present conditions with resistance to Life underlies process theologians' insistence that an undesirable situation today "can successfully be overcome only by going beyond it, not by attempting to return to a premodern form of existence" (Griffin 1990).[19]

Though Birch and Cobb insist that Life has no overall teleology—it did not, for instance, intend to create humans but simply aims at "creation of values moment by moment" (p. 189)—they allow that it is "purposeful" in its general "cosmic aim for value" (p. 197). This permits them to affirm that, so far as we know, "human society is the utmost cosmic venture toward creation of richer integrations. Here the existing universe is groping out into that vast realm of possibility of as yet unrealized value." Consequently humans are, or can be, "the shock troops of the integrating process of the universe" (p. 192).[20] Thus even if Birch and Cobb deny any overall goal to evolution as such, they are surely, like Lovelock, Fox, Margulis, Sagan, Swimme and Berry, identifying a purpose being worked out through it.

Birch and Cobb acknowledge, however—more clearly than the authors just mentioned—that such adulation of Life raises distressing questions. Why does evolution involve so much suffering? Why the apparently pointless waste of countless creatures and their potentialities? In regard to humans, Birch and Cobb argue that we could not have developed our higher potentials without mistakes and injustices. Like Swimme and Berry, they justify some past oppressions, such as the industrial revolution, as necessary components of a "fall upward."[21]

Yet what about "natural" evil? Birch and Cobb reply that the possibility of suffering is a condition of richer experience. Therefore Life, which promotes richer experience, is actually "the reason for most of what we call evil."[22] Nevertheless, Life is greatly limited by circumstances. It is certainly not omnipotent. Life can only produce "creatures in profligate abundance so that through the process of selection some will emerge with greater intelligence and capacity for feeling" (p. 197).

Still Birch and Cobb argue that Life can be trusted and worshiped—as God. But to affirm this they need to go beyond what evolution can confirm, for much in evolution suggests that in the end death "will have the last word both for us and for all things" (p. 201). However, no force can be unreservedly worshiped unless it will ultimately win out over death.[23] To trust Life, then, requires a religious decision in regard to which "our scientific knowledge helps us but little" (p. 201). Birch and Cobb acknowledge that affirmation of Life's final victory is speculative, "the consummate speculation of . . . this book" (p. 201).[24]

Though Birch and Cobb seem more realistic than Berry, Swimme and Fox about evolution's suffering and apparent lack of direction, they have certainly identified a dominant trend working through evolution—one constantly seeking to transcend past achievements, to produce things more varied and complex and to yield experiences ever more intense. These characteristics seem to match those of our insatiably progressive, pleasure-hungry technological society, however much our authors critique various aspects of it.

This raises the question of whether rationalism, reductionism and mechanism, which they ably critique, are the only Enlightenment tendencies spawning environmental malaise, or whether valorization of ever-escalating variety and constant global transformation, with humankind providing "the shock troops . . . of the universe," are not also wreaking environmental havoc. Birch and Cobb, despite their intentions, could encourage this trend by insisting that pursuit of maximum richness of experience brings people into harmony with other creatures' experiences and an immanent divine life.

Ruether's ecofeminism. The subtitle of Ruether's *Gaia and God* is *An Ecofeminist Theology of Earth Healing.* From an ecofeminist standpoint, it critiques Judeo-Christian themes that have shaped Western environmental attitudes, yet ultimately seeks to retrieve their best elements. Like socialist feminism, Ruether analyzes these themes' social dimensions and calls for sweeping reconstruction (see chapter seven). Like cultural feminism, she probes their deeper psychodynamisms. (She rejects, however, romantic interpretations of a preurban matriarchal era.)

For Ruether, "the ecological crisis is new to human experience," and "all past human traditions are inadequate in the face of it" (1992:206). To establish a satisfactory current perspective, she employs science "as normative or as ethically prescriptive" (p. 47).[25] Science since the Enlightenment has destroyed traditional theology's cosmic framework, including any God independent of nature (pp. 32-35, 86). How, then, shall science establish an environmental ethics?

Ruether acknowledges that human self-consciousness and altruistic inclinations give us a sense of standing out from our environment, calling us to act kindly and shape the future differently from animals (pp. 31, 115). Yet this sense of human ethical distinctness can be explained as an evolutionary product. Following Pierre Teilhard de Chardin (Thomas Berry's mentor), Ruether conceives of evolution as a process in which an increasing organizational complexity of matter produces an increasing intensity of inward unity. Matter's internal "radial energy" reaches "boiling points" which produce "qualitative leaps to new levels of existence" (p. 243).

Eventually mind emerges as the interiority of matter; consciousness is the way that the "dance of energy organizes itself in increasingly unified ways, until it reflects back on itself in self-awareness" (p. 250). This means that our consciousness and ethical conscience have arisen directly from evolution, and that humans are now "the 'mind' of the universe, the place where the universe becomes conscious of itself" (p. 249; compare p. 43).

Ruether finds Chardin's twofold emphasis on mind as matter's interiority and on continuity "from the simplest molecule to the most complex organism" his most compelling thought (p. 245). Ruether makes little mention of divergent directions, dead ends, mass extinctions and discontinuity in her accounts of evolution.

Since ethical awareness has arisen from evolution and since science can describe this process, ethics "should be a more refined and conscious version" of the current situation which science describes (p. 57). Ecology teaches that the well-being of biotic creatures depends on continued balance among species and that systems are more sustainable the more diversified they are (pp. 48-54).

From these premises we can derive specific principles, such as that excessive meat-eating will disrupt our food chain (p. 52). We can also draw more general conclusions, such as that death, which keeps an ecosystem's members balanced and recycles its elements, is the "friend," not the enemy, of life-processes (p. 53). Further, the fact that each species is a distinct evolutionary form shows that it has intrinsic value. However, Ruether's ecosystemic emphasis, in contrast to animal rights, values species more highly than individuals (pp. 218-21, 227).

Ruether criticizes Darwinism as "a vastly distorted picture of nature" (p. 55). Citing Margulis and Lovelock, she names cooperation and interdependence as evolution's primary principles and grants competition a mere subsidiary role in keeping populations balanced. Ruether, understandably, is concerned that competition not be ethically justified by evolution, for among humans competition is "mutually exclusive" and "imagines the other side as an 'enemy' to be 'annihilated'" (p. 56). Nevertheless all evolutionary theory teaches that significant change occurs only when some species are annihilated. Ruether seems to have based her ethics only on what chapter three called "stabilizing Gaia" and to have largely neglected "disruptive Gaia." Yet disruptive Gaia contributed greatly to that increase of complexity and consciousness Ruether celebrates.

Ruether acknowledges that the evolutionary life force itself conflicts with her ethics, for each species and individual seeks to maximize its own existence without regard for others. She insists, however, that ethical "good" must consist in "limits, a balancing of our own drive for life with the life drives of all the others . . . so that the whole remains in life-sustaining harmony" (p. 256). Yet her preferences for the balance of the whole over the diverse drives of the parts and for cooperation over competition, cannot have been derived directly from evolution, with its conflicting tendencies.

In any case, this definition of good allows Ruether to describe the chief social value as equity—between women and men, among various human groups and between humans and all other species (p. 258). Evil can then be defined as a wrong relationship (p. 256) and human social evil as unequal distribution of power (p. 142). Humans, then, should not strive to attain dominating power but to accept their limitations, vulnerability and interdependence with all creatures (p. 268). Ruether also claims that nature teaches us how to *be*, rather than to *strive*, and to cultivate deep joy in life's goodness (p. 269). Yet evolution, I note, does not teach these values unilaterally either.

Finally Ruether's ecofeminist theology affirms something about the panentheistic reality underlying all this.[26] Beneath "the 'appearance' of nuclear, atomic, and molecular structures," she claims, modern physics has discovered a "voidlike web of relationships," a " 'dance' of movement itself, a dance without dancers, engaged in restless, continual motion" (p. 38)— something like process theology's events without objects. This web, which appears below "the 'absolute minimum' of the tiniest particles" (p. 248), includes all observers of it, for in modern physics' measurements of quantum behavior "consciousness and object . . . flow together, as two aspects of one reality" (p. 38). This web, however, is also "the 'absolute maximum,' the matrix of all interconnections of the whole universe" from which all things evolve and into which they disintegrate and return (p. 248).

Ruether asks whether, confronted with this ultimate paradox of the unimaginably large and infinitely small, humans can feel only terrified and lost. She replies that humans are really the mean, or *microcosm*, between these extremes: first, because "what we perceive can only be known and evaluated from . . . our own standpoints," and, second, because we are "the 'mind' of the universe" (p. 249). Since consciousness has flowered in us, we can be assured that it is also reflected "in the ongoing creative Matrix of the whole" and that this Matrix which "sustains the dissolution and recomposition of matter" is "also a heart that knows us even as we are known."

We can encounter this Matrix when "the illusion of otherness" breaks down, when, paradoxically, gazing "into the void of our future extinguished self . . . we encounter the wellspring of life and creativity from which all things have sprung and into which they return, only to well up again into new forms." We can surrender ourselves into this Matrix with "a prayer of ultimate trust: 'Mother, into your hands I commend my spirit. Use me as you will in your infinite creativity'" (pp. 252, 253).

This Matrix seems to be both identified with and differentiated from individuals in ways that remind us of organismic spiritualities. On one hand, "small centers of personal being dialogue" with this "great Thou" in "the conversation that continually creates and recreates the world." On the other hand, our "small selves and the Great Self are finally one" (p. 253). Similarly, whereas reflective consciousness differentiates humans from other creatures, "it does so only relatively, not absolutely," for all are "kin along a continuum of organized life-energy" (p. 250). Ruether, like most organismic ecologists, wants to emphasize and celebrate diversity. Yet, like process theology, she conceptualizes it *monistically*—as different organizations of some energy underlying all things, including whatever is divine.

Ruether grounds this monism, in large part, epistemologically with the claim, which she finds warranted by quantum physics, that no "object" can be known or described apart from, or even clearly differentiated from, a knowing "subject."[27] This monism, whose energy/matter in some way includes consciousness and personal being, apparently underlies Ruether's confidence that we all have some direct connection to the Source of consciousness and personality. Ruether evidently counters the possibility that evolution might involve irreversible ruptures and breaks and that divine being might really be distinct from the world's[28] with the claim that all things always have been, are and will be diverse forms of one underlying reality.

McFague and God's body. McFague, like Ruether and other process theologians, claims that current theologizing must be done in a "genuinely novel context" where "the 'old ways,' the old solutions, will not do" (1987:ix-x).[29] Her first ecological book, *Models of God* (1987), often italicized the importance of articulating theological convictions *"for our time."* It insisted that God's activity be understood in a way "not just commensurate with an ecological, evolutionary sensibility but intrinsic to it" (p. 80).

McFague's main goal is for readers *"to think and act as if bodies mattered"* (1993:xii). To this end, she makes the metaphor "the world as God's body" her major theme. Science shows that all things are points on a matter-energy continuum; this, she claims, "overturns traditional hierarchical dualisms" such as flesh and spirit (p. 16). McFague repeatedly styles matter the "base," "bedrock" and "source" of all things and proposes applying it to God. But the terms *physical* for God and *God's body* for the cosmos, she stresses, are not direct descriptions. If they were, they would constitute a "metaphysics of presence"—an attempt, which McFague rejects, "to cover up the absence, emptiness, and uncertainty we sense (and fear) may be at the heart of things" (1987:24). Instead, *body* as applied to God is a metaphor, a wager, an experiment to help people envision and love each creature as an expression of God's being.

McFague's second ecological book, *The Body of God* (1993), seeks to balance the body model with a more "agential" one. The best combination of models, she says, will portray both God's immanence and transcendence as radically as possible (p. 137). McFague adds that immanence is not merely God's presence in the world but also "radicality of love for the vulnerable and the oppressed" (p. 162). For an agential model, she favors "spirit." Spirit, however, does not indicate some nonphysical, qualitatively distinct level of being but is modeled on the vitality conveyed through creaturely "breath" (pp. 143-44). McFague's universe, though expressed through metaphors, is still monistic.

McFague believes that the "Common Creation Story" enables our generation to envision divine reality in unprecedented ways. This story, on one hand, portrays a radical unity, a seamless network, among all things. Yet McFague stresses even more its depiction of overwhelming diversity. For by the time she wrote *The Body of God* she was well aware that organic metaphors, historically, have usually been hierarchical, with the result that differences among members have involved subordination of some to others (pp. 36- 37). She believes that this kind of oneness can suppress real differences. For much the same reason she criticizes efforts—in Swimme, Berry and Teilhard de Chardin—to identify a single overarching evolutionary direction.

McFague endorses the punctuated equilibria emphasis that "evolution displays no . . . overriding push or pull towards some goal. It is not the 'conventional tale of steadily increasing excellence, complexity, and diversity'" and is best pictured not as a ladder but as a bush branching in many directions (pp. 78-79).[30] Nonetheless, she does affirm that evolution moves irreversibly from simplicity to complexity and diversity (pp. 42, 45), accompanied by increasing subjectivity (p. 106), and that natural evolution produces cultural evolution (p. 172). Overall, however, McFague's version of the story valorizes the "wild, strange, and unconventional" diversities among evolved bodies (p. 47). This means that God's body "is not *a* body, but all the different, peculiar, particular bodies about us" (p. 211).

How does this emphasis on interconnected diversity inform environmental ethics? It critiques deep ecology's emphasis on "an oceanic fusion of feeling" with a cosmic organic Self and affirms some ecofeminisms' emphasis on "the independence and difference of the other" (p. 127).[31] Whereas a sense of union with, say, the land, is a necessary environmental sensibility, ethics is rooted not in these feelings but in the land's intrinsic value and implemented through detailed knowledge about it (p. 128). Yet while McFague affirms everything's intrinsic value, she acknowledges, like Birch and Cobb, that they all have instrumental value too and that both must be considered (pp. 165-66).

Finally, McFague affirms, like all our organismic authors, in both public and theological discourse, that humankind is "responsible for taking evolution to the next step." She acknowledges that this is "a far higher status than being a little lower than the angels, subjects of a divine king, or even the goal of evolutionary history." She qualifies this a bit by allowing that humans are not nature's creators or saviors but only God's partners (p. 201). Still, we are necessary to the process, for "God needs us to help save the world!" (1987:135).

To this point it may seem as if McFague, like our other authors, is developing a natural theology of creation. She affirms, however, that Christian theology begins with experiences of redemption and considers creation in light of them (1993:65, 76, 181).[32] This leads to quite a different perspective on evolution, for the *material norm* of McFague's theology is the "destabilizing, inclusive, nonhierarchical vision of fulfillment for all of creation . . . illuminated by the paradigmatic story of Jesus"—especially in his parables, healings and table fellowship with outcasts (1987:49).

However, McFague insists, Jesus "in his identification with the oppressed . . . certainly cannot be read off or even imagined from the story of evolution or even from . . . the world as God's body" (1993:157). For "what consonance can there possibly be between Christianity's inclusion of the outcasts of society . . . and biological evolution, in which millions are wasted, individuals are sacrificed for the species, and even whole species are wiped out in the blinking of an eye?" (p. 171; compare pp. 161, 173, 174, 189, 198).

Interpreting the Creation Story in light of the Jesus Story, McFague proposes that once evolution reaches the human, cultural stage, the principle of solidarity actually counters natural selection (pp. 171-72).[33] Yet she acknowledges that even concern for the weak, when derived from the social instinct of solidarity, is a utilitarian extension of self-interest, as many Darwinian ethicists say. The "scandal of Christianity," however, "goes further; it insists on solidarity with the outsider, the outcast, the vulnerable. Does not this make Christian faith a surd, if not absurd, in view of postmodern science . . . ?"

McFague concludes that "the radical inclusiveness that is at the heart of Christian faith . . . is not compatible with evolution, even cultural evolution" (p. 173; compare p. 174).[34] Jesus' solidarity with the outcast, then, can be seen as combatting natural selection and extending solidarity to its farthest extreme. This includes not only outcast humans but, as Fox also proposes, nature—which we can now see as "the new poor" of Jesus' parables, healings and table fellowship (p. 169).

Still, even if Jesus opposed evolutionary selection and suffering, McFague's panentheism, which includes this whole process in God's body, leaves her with a problem. McFague forthrightly acknowledges that in any monist system "evil is not a power over against God; in a sense, it is God's 'responsibility,' part of God's being, if you will" (1987:75).[35] How can she reconcile this with divine love?

One response is, like process theology, to emphasize that God suffers along with creatures in the world. McFague can call this being "forever nailed to the cross," though she contrasts this with the few hours that traditional theology allegedly allotted to God on the cross.

Another move is to separate some aspect of God from direct involvement in evil. McFague proposes imaging God as Mother, Lover and Friend. She then insists that God as Lover "suffers with those who suffer . . . participates in the pain of the beloved as only a lover can . . . totally, passionately involved in the agony." Consequently, God as Lover "is totally opposed" to natural and human horrors "and has no part" in them. Finally, McFague invokes the Christian hope of the final resurrection and includes all creatures within it. Though the precise form of this transformation is unclear, we may hope that "all suffering bodies, will live again to see a new day" (1993:174; compare p. 202).

The role(s) of Jesus. The theologies we have surveyed seek either to forge their basic conceptualities by means of science or to rearticulate belief through scientific concepts (McFague). But when McFague comes to Jesus, he significantly affects her evaluation of scientific findings. What impact might Jesus have on our other ecological theologians? Let us consider their views and McFague's view more closely.

Process theology identifies a movement of *creative transformation* working toward greater complexity, harmony and intensity of experience throughout the cosmos. Such advances emerge when creatures respond positively to the optimum patterns proposed by God's primordial pole. In this function, God can be called the *Logos* and is that power aiming at fullness of life, which Birch and Cobb describe. Like "Life," the *Logos* always aims at novelty and affirms the past only as it is transformed by the new; it "makes us restless and condemns our desire for stability" (Cobb 1975:85). Cobb believes that the energy of creative transformation can also be called "Christ" and that it can be connected with Jesus through scientific study of his life.

Cobb accepts some skeptical results of historical Jesus study, such as that Jesus occasionally yielded to temptation (p. 130) and that stories of his wilderness temptation, struggle in Gethsemane and forsakenness on the cross are unreliable (p. 142). Still, using four quite different studies,[36] Cobb identifies several reliable features of Jesus' historical activity—most notably his call to the kingdom of God's inbreaking and to radical decision in every moment (pp. 103-5). Through Jesus' word "a permanent principle of restlessness is introduced into history" by which individuals are "uprooted from complacency" and must search for ways to actualize "the new reality proclaimed in that word" (p. 109). Cobb also argues that Jesus experienced no discrepancy between that Word, which was the Logos, and his own person. Thus Jesus' words may be regarded authoritatively as the Logos's own expression (pp. 107-10, 137-39).

Jay McDaniel applies these themes more directly to problems raised by evolution. Why do process theologians, despite the evolutionary struggle, regard the consciousness which is "the very essence of reality" as loving? The chief clue is Jesus. For he "was, or strove to be, fully loving, and . . . to the extent he realized this ideal, he revealed God's nature" (p. 43). Jesus also hoped to embody *shalom*, though he may not always have done so, and thus "at times" his will and God's will, his lure and God's lure, became one (pp. 54, 159-60). God's nature was especially "revealed in Jesus' death on the cross, [as] the one whose power includes vulnerability and unlimited love" (p. 100).

By maintaining that Jesus' revelation was likely imperfect, McDaniel indicates agreement with historical-critical skepticism and implies that his norm of infinitely tender, inclusive love can be derived, at least in part, from elsewhere. Yet it is difficult to overestimate the role that this kind of God plays for process theology in a universe whose evil and suffering no force can control and the extent to which this infinite tenderness seems to be drawn from Jesus. Whereas Cobb conceives of Jesus as filling a role which study of evolution can establish, McDaniel sees Jesus affirming something which evolution otherwise largely counters.

Ruether seldom mentions Jesus in connection with ecology. Yet he plays an important social role for her. Jesus embodied the *prophetic principle*—the critical criterion by which authentic divine revelation can be discerned in Scripture (1983a:22-23, 135-36). More specifically, his chief significance lay in the kind of lifestyle that critiqued the roots of the desire for domination. In so doing he was aiming at a kind of society where all hierarchy was overcome (pp. 119-22). However, "Christ" for Ruether indicates a fullness of humanity which cannot be wholly incarnated in one person. Jesus, then, could provide only one exemplification of this ideal, for which we need other models and whose fullness is still future (pp. 114, 138).

Jesus seems to function for Ruether chiefly as a symbol, or archetype, of a human possibility (as he does for John Welch), albeit a radical, counter-cultural one. Jesus' exemplification of this archetype was imperfect, as McDaniel affirms (though for a different reason). Ruether's view of Jesus appears not to affect her scientific findings. Yet her ethical critique of dominating power—which, I argued, cannot be strictly derived from evolution—does seem consistent with him. I will examine Ruether's Christology more fully in chapter seven.

Although McFague draws her vision of the inclusive, nonhierarchical relationships from Jesus, she, like McDaniel and Ruether, refuses to absolutize him. She insists that "Jesus is not ontologically different from other paradigmatic figures" in other religions and that for Christians he is only "our historical choice" (1987:136; compare 1993:163). She declines to investigate Jesus' history, affirming that her vision is generated as much by today's social, economic, political and ecological realities as by any portrait of Jesus (1987:49).

McFague does agree with Ruether that Jesus affirms and extends a critical prophetic principle found in Hebrew Scripture. Yet she finds the New Testament so "distorted by ideologies of power" that "no hermeneutics of retrieval would be possible" (pp. 197-98). In any case, what matters "is not primarily validation of" the paradigmatic Jesus story "but illumination of our situation" by it (pp. 49-50).

Like McDaniel, McFague emphasizes Jesus' cross. She recognizes that Christianity's theme of "the king who became a servant, one who suffers for and alongside the oppressed" was "antihierarchical and antitriumphalist," countering tendencies to regard its distinct God as distant and dominating. Yet the traditional understanding of incarnation, she claims, restricts God's intertwining with creation to one person's brief life in a distant past (1987:54-56). In contrast, McFague wants to envision the cosmos as *the* incarnation of God (p. 62). Yet Jesus' cross clearly influences her insistence that this embodied God, much like the process God, suffers evils which creatures experience. She can even affirm—in phrases such as "God becomes dependent" or "at risk" through embodiment (p. 72)[37]—that God chooses to suffer in a way difficult to ascribe to any deity whose being is intertwined with the cosmos's.

Although these authors express much skepticism about our actual knowledge of Jesus, which would seem to undermine his suitability for providing a theological norm, he often seems to function in precisely this way, especially in the crucial role of countering evolutionary science's harsh implications.

Summary and Appraisal: Darwinism, Organicism and Ethics

Progress. None of our writers advocate Darwinism. Birch, Cobb and McFague, however, in contrast to Berry, Swimme, Ruether and Fox, seek to emphasize evolution's lack of unilinearity and the enormity of its suffering much as Darwinism does. Nevertheless, all our authors emphasize evolutionary progress in some form, as do the organismic ecologies covered in chapter three.

Berry, Swimme and Fox not only valorize an advancing cosmogenesis but hope for rather immediate, wide-ranging environmental transformation is central to the sensibility they foster. Ruether makes mind's emergence from matter's interiority the primary evolutionary trend. Life's surge toward novelty allows Birch and Cobb to measure and praise its advance, even if they deny evolution as a whole a single direction. McFague, who appreciates punctuated equilibria, is most skeptical about progress, yet even she regards tendencies toward complexity, subjectivity and cultural evolution as general evolutionary trends.[38]

Our authors' progressive interpretations are most notable in their common affirmation, shared with chapter three's organicisms, that humans are evolution become conscious and are responsible for taking it further. I generally find that our authors, like the Lamarckians of a century and more ago, interpret evolution more optimistically and progressively than scientific evidence really warrants.

Diversity. In chapter three I found that organicism, particularly in the form of deep ecology, could have difficulty articulating differentiation. Deep ecology unites all creatures into a cosmic Self and claims that they all share a biocentric equality in intrinsic value. But attributing equal value to everything gives little help in ethical decisions, where choices among values must be made.

I find more helpful Birch, Cobb and McFague's claim that all things have both intrinsic *and* instrumental value and that choices revolve largely around the latter. Process theology also emphasizes degrees of intrinsic value according to capacities for experience. This acknowledges animal rights' criterion of sentience but allows for differentiations among various intensities (between, say, in a chimpanzee and in an oyster) and correctly grants nonsentient creatures some value. Process theology's and Ruether's emphasis on species and ecosystems over individuals also rightly promotes preservation of greater diversity.

I wonder, however, about the emphasis, especially prominent in Berry, Swimme and McFague, to picture nature celebrating both maximum diversity and maximum unity. It seems to imply that in environmental decisions, if we decide to maximize one, the other will automatically be maximized also. But do not choices to increase diversity (for example, by reintroducing wolves near ranches) often at least threaten to disrupt an area's unity, and vice versa? (I will take up this issue more fully in chapter ten. I will also ask how well a panentheistic monism can conceptualize diversity.)

The basis for environmental ethics. Swimme and Berry seem to agree with Darwinism that cooperation can be derived from self-interest. They affirm that natural selection yields communion, or "a deep intimacy of togetherness" (1992:134), and that humans ought to follow this pattern. This way of interpreting natural selection, however, is too problematic to yield helpful guidance. Deep ecology derives cooperation from mystical participation in the cosmic Self, which brings us to realize that "if we harm the rest of nature we are harming ourselves" (Devall and Sessions 1985:68). Yet this approach not only underplays differentiation but, like Darwinism, bases cooperation on self-interest.

Fox roots compassion in the same sense of oneness and self-interest,[39] whereas McDaniel grounds love on the same foundation.[40] With McFague I acknowledge that a certain degree of social solidarity can arise from self-interest. However, concern for creatures which seem quite other than us and of marginal importance arises from a stronger valuation of otherness and a more radical self-giving, such as Jesus exercised. (I will state my complete argument in chapter ten.)

Darwinism also claims that the holistic perspective necessary for appropriate environmental involvement can arise from individualism. I affirm, however, as I did in chapter three, that organicism's vision of interrelatedness provides a more adequate basis for this.

Chapter three also maintained that organismic evolutionists valorize both progress—which involves conflict, disruption and extinction—and ecosystemic preservation and balance. Yet they base ethics on the second kind of activity alone, though no scientific reason can be given for this preference. This discrepancy was detected in Fox who, though he lauds cosmogenesis, assumes that justice always consists in processes of cosmic balance. I also found that Ruether, who derives ethical consciousness from cosmic advance, based ethics on ecological balance. I argued that her ethical notions of good, equity, vulnerability and being (rather than doing) and her critiques of power imbalance and social domination could not be strictly derived from evolution.

None of the values I have discussed *(oughts)* seem derivable from scientific study of evolution (what *is*, except for the holistic perspective, which is not really a value). I have to agree with Thomas Huxley that environmental values must come from somewhere else. But from where? I will answer in chapter ten.

Summary and Appraisal

Panentheism. This model is compatible with the six environmental values listed in the discussion of panentheism above. But is it the most plausible God-world paradigm? To answer, we must learn whether an alternative is available (which I will treat in chapter ten). We also need to ask whether panentheism itself involves significant flaws, particularly regarding the existence of evil and human freedom.

1. *Evil.* If the cosmos is an aspect of God's being and if evil exists in the cosmos, then—simple logic seems to mandate—evil exists in God's very being. But given the scope of environmental and social evil today, panentheism would seem to undercut its aim of arousing humans to combat these things by including all things in God. How do our writers respond?

Fox, though he decries many social evils, seems to mostly ignore the issue. Swimme and Berry paint massive catastrophes and extinctions in spectacular colors and package them as necessary preludes for even more stupendous advances. Neither, in my view, deals realistically with natural or social evil.

Birch and Cobb more soberly regard the possibility of suffering as a condition of richer experience and many human evils as "falls upward" necessary for social progress. Process theology also speaks of God, who is finite and unable to prevent much evil, as patiently suffering under it along with creatures. To be an adequate object of worship, God need not be omnipotent but only omnibenevolent (McDaniel 1990:50).

But is that really enough? What of people who find evil's scope so great that it paralyzes all positive action? Will belief that God suffers with them be enough to elicit significant response against evil if they still suppose that much of it is ineradicable? Or might belief in a God who can and eventually will overcome all evil be necessary to spur action? Birch and Cobb apparently affirm a God who is more than omnibenevolent when they stress that to trust "Life" unreservedly we must believe that it will finally overcome evil and death.

Ruether seems to minimize evil by downplaying evolutionary competition and by scientifically regarding death as a necessary part—even a "friend"—of the life-cycle. But does this do justice to the deep sense of irredeemable tragedy that many people experience in suffering and death? Ruether wants to avoid abstracting good and evil from natural processes, for in this way they can become absolutized and play destructive, socially dualistic roles. Yet we have seen Ruether herself develop notions of good and other values that go beyond what natural rhythms can teach.

McFague responds to evil by affirming a God who not only suffers with creatures, like the process God, but who "becomes dependent" or "at risk" through embodiment. Yet this kind of suffering love is possible only for a God who can choose embodiment because, like the traditional transcendent God, this one was originally distinct from it. McFague's effort to separate one aspect of God—"as Lover"—from evil is arbitrary and simply inconsistent with panentheism's implications. Finally, her hope for a final resurrection of all bodies goes well beyond what any panentheism, by itself, can affirm.

It is significant that precisely when considering evil our theologians indicate a need for some power or principle that transcends their panentheistic frameworks. Birch and Cobb require a power that can finally overcome evil and death. Ruether needs a Good transcending what natural processes display. McFague requires a God who can choose embodiment and resurrect the whole creation. Panentheism, at least as represented by our authors, runs up against crucial limits when it confronts evil.

2. *Human freedom.* A transcendent, omnipotent God apparently possesses all power, while we have none, and can solve all problems so that we need face none. Therefore panentheism, where creatures share in divine activity, is recommended to help humans take responsibility and to win freedom from a dominating God. Nevertheless, McFague recognizes that if people are in some sense organic parts of God, their distinctness, and hence their freedom, may actually be compromised.[41] If we are aspects of God, can we really choose authentically whether or not to align ourselves with God?

Panentheists raise the freedom issue a second way. Since a transcendent God does not need the cosmos to exist, this God's love is often equated with entirely self-giving love, or *agapē*. But according to Cobb and Griffin, *agapē* involves "no element of responsiveness to the qualities of the loved one" (1976:46) and presents God aloof from and uninvolved with the world. Yet if God's love is portrayed through the body model, where humans are the organs God loves, "it underscores the need that God has of us." God needs us not only for God's own satisfaction but "to help save the world!" (McFague 1987:134, 135).

Theologians often call this second kind of love *eros*. It involves desire, for it arises from a need or lack that a person's beloved can fulfill. On one hand, *eros* seems to better represent the mutual caring and delight involved in Christian God-creature relations. But on the other hand, if God needs me to fulfill God's own need or lack, am I as truly free to choose or reject God as I would be if God were transcendent—distinct from me—and did not absolutely need me? Panentheism, in other words, seems to undercut true freedom of choice. (I will return to this issue in chapter ten.)

Breaking with the Enlightenment? Our authors claim that today's environmental problems are unprecedented and that attitudes stemming from the Enlightenment are much to blame. These theologians are indeed providing preferable organismic alternatives to Newtonian mechanism, atomism and individualism. They are indeed bridging gulfs between reason and affectivity, humanity and nature, and a deistic God and the cosmos. Yet their overall approaches retain many features consistent with the Enlightenment.

First, though not all Enlightenment thinkers sought to explain every dimension of reality by natural science (some, for instance, allowed for a rationalist ethics), natural science provided standards with which every kind of explanation had to cohere. It possessed an autonomy which other kinds of knowledge-claims—such as revelation—could not fundamentally challenge. Similarly whereas our authors deal with areas of experience which deepen what science can strictly establish, they seek to derive much of their content from science and to integrate it all with what science can know in a way entirely consistent with its principles. Only McFague claims that a significant discrepancy exists between the Jesus story and what evolution apparently teaches.

Second, Enlightenment savants regarded their ways of knowing as far superior to almost anything from the past. Now, whereas our authors admit that present knowledge may not avert humanity's dire end, their claims that "all past human traditions are inadequate" (Ruether) and that "the old solutions, will not do" (McFague) manifest a confidence that up-to-date methods provide far better keys to knowledge than do former ones. To be sure, all retrieve elements of Christian tradition. Some, such as Jesus' servantlike way of love, may actually function normatively. But even then, knowledge of such elements is strained through contemporary epistemological qualifiers which seem to deprive them of that role. Past elements are highly reinterpreted by modern criteria and seem to retain little capacity to challenge them.

Third, the Enlightenment effectively removed God from the natural and social worlds so that humankind could control them. God was first dismissed deistically so that humans could take full responsibility for history. Yet it was entirely consistent with Enlightenment principles to reintroduce God as an immanent force, impelling history forward, so long as God never modified processes that an autonomous science could trace or an autonomous ethics approve.

Our authors often stress that ecological science, by demonstrating humanity's interdependence with countless creatures, removes us from center stage and that this should humble us and reprove efforts to control the world. Yet all our authors affirm that humankind is where several billion years of evolution become self-conscious and that the survival or annihilation of most creatures is in our hands. Is this not an anthropocentrism far greater than traditional Christianity's, where such prerogatives were reserved for God? Is it not an intensification of the Enlightenment principle that God works nowhere but through material forces and human hands?

Finally, the Enlightenment championed ever-accelerating human progress, fueled by anticipation of continually increasing pleasurable experience and expansion of the mind. All our authors affirm a progressive direction in evolution, which it is the task of humans to extend, and resist any return to the past. Berry, Swimme and Fox paint this progressive sweep in enjoyable colors, and Fox especially promises that following it correlates with heightened organismic pleasure. For process theology, progress is marked by increasingly intense and rich experience and, for Ruether, by expanding conscious awareness. Accordingly although all our authors critique some ways of commonly measuring progress (for example, expanding GNP), they (except perhaps McFague) appeal to those desires for the ever more novel, complex and intensely experienced that launched capitalism in the first place, and they connect them with the cosmos's progressive direction.

To be sure, careful examination of our authors would show that some understand certain notions (pleasure, for example) in ways which also critique the Enlightenment. But they are writing for audiences highly shaped by this legacy. Might they not, then, often be understood as appealing to, and therefore strengthening, many of those very Enlightenment attitudes at the root of environmental problems today?

An adequate spirituality? To become meaningfully involved in environmental issues and to adopt a lifestyle compatible with the planet's carrying capacity, we need some affective sense of commonality with nonhuman creatures and of harmony with their overall rhythms. Like the organismic spiritualities of chapter five, however, the ecological spirituality examined here seeks to attain this by directing us to a realm where serious conflict is minimized (sometimes because it is glorified or justified as necessary for progress). Harmony reigns especially because in this realm not only the self (as in chapter five) but now all things are one with God.

But if real conflicts exist in nonhuman nature and will likely emerge in efforts to address environmental problems, are we best helped by encouragement to assimilate with some underlying harmonious rhythm which should heal all these rifts? Or might we better be helped by a God who is distinct from these rhythms and the conflicts we experience and who can step in to help us through them—not a God who removes us to a realm where struggle is unreal but one who companions us through, and shares in the pain of, the struggle? But is belief in such a God compatible with a plausible God-world paradigm? So far the only paradigm presented of a God distinct from nature is the transcendent one highly caricatured by panentheists. Chapter ten will articulate a third alternative.

SEVEN

Theology &
Social Alienation

*T*he previous chapters have shown that psychological and ecological alienation are both shaped by social factors. When we turned to public discourse concerning society itself, we found two opposing views as to what causes these alienations and the alienation of people from their own social potential (see chapter four).

For libertarianism the main alienating force is an inordinately powerful state. Alienation can be overcome by greatly reducing state power so that individuals can pursue their own destinies and form their own social and economic alliances. Governments and political activists should refrain from imposing their ideals (of what *ought* to be) on society and let social forms spring up from interactions among what people actually desire and do (what *is* the case).

For holists, however, capitalism, which libertarians regard as arising from free interactions, has its own dominating structures and is social alienation's chief source. Alienation can be overcome only through transforming the entire socioeconomic capitalist ethos, which has deep psychological roots. Visions of a different future society are essential to this process. If such a society comes at all, it will likely be preceded by conflict.

Ecologically libertarians expect private owners to treat land better than governments and favor diversified development over centralized planning. Holists expect more cooperative relations with nature, sometimes romantically envisioned, to accompany the widespread future social cooperation. Psychologically libertarians encourage individual exercise of free will and expression of the drives, but they discourage speculation about the unconscious. Holists believe that individuals are not so free as they think but are socially shaped by forces which penetrate the unconscious. (In this they are closer to psychoanalysis than to organismic psychology or spirituality.)

We have seen that psychoanalysis wields little influence on current spirituality (see chapter five) and that Darwinism makes almost no impact on recent ecological theology (see chapter six). Many Christians today, however, hold, if not libertarian, at least right-leaning political and economic views. Accordingly even though such persons may not often be heard in circles where spirituality and ecological theology are read, we can identify scholarly theological spokespersons for a generally conflictive social outlook.

This chapter can therefore be divided, as were chapters two, three and four, into two contrasting perspectives. First, I will consider Michael Novak, a contemporary social conservative, and Reinhold Niebuhr (1892-1971), the respected architect of a "realistic" social theology.[1] Both thinkers began as "liberal" theologians with strong socialist leanings. In what ways, I will ask, might they affirm limited government? Next, I will cover holistic social theologies and will consider Rosemary Ruether again, as well as the Latin Americans Paulo Freire and Juan Segundo. What kinds of social ideals might they propose? Finally I will summarize and raise questions about these views.

Conflictive Social Theologies

Almost all social theologies stress that current social conditions are highly conflictive. However, I apply "conflictive" to the positions in this section because they affirm that significant conflict will continue under any social system that humans adopt. By contrast, theologies discussed later in this chapter maintain that if current oppressive structures are abolished, conflict will diminish qualitatively.

Michael Novak's democratic capitalism. Novak's mature perspective on social alienation can be approached through his notion of original sin. Original sin, for him, is not a force with significant corporate characteristics. Instead, it chiefly means that evil's roots do "not lie in our systems but in ourselves" (1982:350). By contrast, Novak claims, utopian social theorists believe that sin and morality flow from social structures. They therefore think that they can eradicate alienation and sin by altering such structures. Yet the most serious social alienation arises when utopians, by legislating moral and social goals, deprive individuals of freedom to choose. Since original sin also means that humans can use power selfishly (1986:39), concentrating it in any government's hands will likely lead to domination—the greatest threat, according to all theorists in chapter four (libertarian and holistic), to any social system.

Legislation of social goals, according to Novak, will sharply curtail individual creative spontaneity, a prime source of social richness, and undermine individual responsibility for moral character. All persons, except perhaps those who orchestrate the whole, will feel alienated from their true potential, from others and from society's most creative possibilities. Thus Novak is convinced that individual freedom, even if it is often badly used, must be limited as little as possible. Social theory must begin with humans as they *are*, not as they *ought* to be.

1. *Balance among powers*. How can this kind of alienation be avoided? When society is composed of different systems whose tensions check each other. Novak is not thinking simply of the three governmental branches— legislative, executive and judicial—though he affirms this division for the political system. Instead, he practically defines his ideal society, *democratic capitalism*, as an interplay among the three realms identified by Daniel Bell: economy, polity and culture (or the "moral-cultural"). Bell, of course, identified clashes among these as the source of capitalism's contradictions.[2] Scarcely mentioning this, Novak insists that they can supplement and moderate each other.

Novak is not defending as pronounced a laissez-faire or as minimal a state as are libertarians. When complaints about capitalism are raised (it allows the unemployed to starve, for example), Novak usually replies that the political or moral-cultural system can alleviate such problems. He holds, for instance, unlike Nozick, that social welfare, some graduated tax scale and universal education are consistent with democratic capitalism (1982:217-18; 1986:38).[3] He insists that the moral-cultural system should teach not only "self-restraint, hard work, discipline, and sacrifice for the future" but also "generosity, compassion, integrity, and concern for the common good" (1982:57-58).[4]

In fact, Novak allows the economic system to be so modified by the political and moral-cultural that one wonders whether what he calls *democratic capitalism* might include what many call *democratic socialism*. Apparently it can.[5] When Novak rejects "socialism" as antithetical to *democratic capitalism*, he evidently means an alienating "unitary system, dominated in all its parts by a state apparatus," (p. 334) including ownership of absolutely all property.

2. *Strengths of capitalism.* Novak is aware that free markets and democratic processes are imperfect and that they create some social alienation. Still he praises capitalism's strengths. He claims that private property is necessary for curbing state power. He argues, unlike Bell, that capitalism is requisite for any sustained working of democracy (pp. 14-15). Novak finds that capitalism encourages many virtues, such as adventurousness and trust, for we must work with others. He regards financial investments as acts of faith, trust and fraternity (p. 100). The market system obliges people to be other-regarding (1986:42). It promotes careful long-range planning, not short-term greed, for those operating by greed will quickly come to ruin (1982:92-93; according to Bell, planning is essential for entrepreneurs, but it is discouraged—whereas greed is encouraged—in consumers).

Capitalism's ultimate goal is to place "a sound material base . . . under every single person on this planet" (1986:42). "Growth," moreover, "is not an end in itself. It is a means toward liberation from poverty" (p. 51), whereas "wealth is only a means to spiritual purposes" (p. 52).

Though original sin means, for Novak, that everyone sometimes sins, it does not mean that most are seriously depraved. He is quite convinced of people's basic decency. Like Hume and Smith, he thinks that much informal wisdom has accumulated through social and economic traditions. Unlike Bell, he believes that "the so-called Puritan ethic in the United States is alive and well" (1986:63). Novak affirms that *self-interest* understood "broadly enough . . . is a key to all the virtues" (1982:93). Following Hume and Smith, he stresses that it must be balanced by sympathy and keeping rules of justice. Self-interest must also be extended to the welfare of a person's family (p. 93).

Although capitalism has been blamed for destroying traditions and eroding families, Novak emphasizes the bourgeois family. For him, it shows that our roots are communal and, contrary to libertarianism, that the individual cannot be "the sufficient unit of economic analysis" (1982:161). Moreover, the independent family with private property opposes collectivist forces. Novak charges that every utopian movement begins by undermining the family (p. 165). Within the family we encounter the limits of gender, role, generation and society's moral code. Lasch and Marcuse might partially approve (see chapter two). Novak blames lack of restraint in families, rather than any hedonistic capitalistic ethos (Bell), for that governmental tendency, critiqued by Hayek, to bestow benefits on everyone (chapter four).

Having praised families, what does Novak say about the widespread lone-liness and sense of alienation in American society? He responds, first, by saying that this is true freedom's reverse side (pp. 52-55), for the "drive to ask questions is the most persistent and basic drive of human conscious-ness" (1970:14). Once freed from traditional authoritative beliefs, human consciousness can challenge every certainty and bring profound encoun-ters with nothingness. Novak parallels this experience with John of the Cross's dark nights;[6] it indicates that individuals have an irreducible soli-tary dimension. Socially this capacity to question everything and transcend all given answers means that the individual's ultimate freedom must be respected and that a person can never be coerced into accepting any belief.

> In a genuinely pluralistic society, there is no one sacred canopy. At its spiritual core, there is an empty shrine . . . left empty in the knowledge that no one word, image, or symbol is worthy of what all seek here. Its emptiness, therefore, represents the transcendence which is approached by free consciences from a virtually infinite number of directions. (1982:55)

Novak has a second response concerning loneliness: Americans are extra-ordinarily gregarious and form countless social organizations. He valorizes a kind of "community" uniquely appropriate to capitalist society: a "band of brothers" that forms "a community of colleagueship, task-oriented, goal-directed, freely entered into and freely left." Though Novak admits that its members "may not have much emotional attachment to each other," he finds it a very satisfying togetherness (pp. 137-38). Novak repeatedly argues that capitalism, rather than being individualistic and immoral, is communal and ethical. Able CEOs, he claims, must facilitate team deci-sions and work by moral principles. (Yet the average tenure of these com-munal persons is only six years [pp. 131-32].)

3. *Theological affirmations.* Despite his emphasis that society and econom-ics should be structured on what *is* rather than on what *ought* to be, coupled with his insistence on "an empty shrine" at society's center, Novak acknowl-edges that "without certain moral and cultural presuppositions . . . neither democracy nor capitalism can be made to work" (p. 16). Accordingly Novak sketches his own theology of democratic capitalism, touching on several doctrines which, he believes, helped lay the groundwork for democratic capitalism's emergence in history (pp. 337-58).[7]

Novak emphasizes the Judeo-Christian notion of *historic vocation*—that the world, as created, is incomplete and that humans, as co-Creators with

God, are called to unlock the secrets God has hidden within it (1986:40-42, 95; 1982:71-80). This call explains why democratic capitalism's "two favorite words are 'new' and 'improved'" (p. 72). In chapter six I found that organismic ecological theologians affirmed something like this, and I asked whether it might support a capitalist orientation. For Novak, however, this process involves intense struggle against nature (pp. 269, 356). Still, he claims that a natural evolution toward justice operates in history.[8]

For Novak *the Trinity* carries significant social meaning. It points to individuality-in-community as the highest social value. It refutes the notion that the noblest human is the conquering but solitary loner (pp. 337-38). Critics might respond that Novak values community so long as it is familial or strictly voluntary ("freely entered into and freely left") but that his great distaste for any degree of collectivity suggests that he values individuality more.

Novak also mentions the *incarnation* of Christ. It means that God has accepted history's limits, including exposure to its worst sins. But it also apparently means that God continues to accept evil. Novak does not present Jesus' life, death and resurrection as a great struggle with and decisive judgment on sin. This notion that God will continue to accept evil thus critiques all utopian visions—though Novak still sees the incarnation as supporting some hope for social improvement.

Novak finds that Christian teaching also sanctions *competition*. That is because it regards life as a challenge in which the outcome depends on our decisions.[9]

Finally there is *separation of realms.* Jesus' saying "Give to the emperor the things that are the emperor's, and to God the things that are God's" (Mark 12:17) shows that neither politics nor the economy can be run by Christian standards. Novak argues that exhortations to self-giving behavior—such as loving enemies or freely lending to all—cannot concern political or economic practices; rather they serve as ideals to critique even our best behavior (1982:352).

4. *Responses to criticisms of capitalism.* How might Novak respond to some of the more common criticisms of capitalism raised in chapter four? Most critics, we saw, treat capitalism as a self-enclosed system of economic principles pushing inexorably toward certain results. They find labor, for instance, increasingly becoming a matter of working for wages, usually in impersonal systems which alienate workers from meaningful participation in production. Novak, however, finds a positive side to this: as wage labor becomes more impersonal, occupations are freed from ties to social station and opened to people of all races and cultures (p. 44). And whereas

capitalism's critics see certain rational laws, such as those of profit, determining all economic activity, Novak responds that inventive, unpredictable, practical reason is also very much involved (pp. 46-47). But most often Novak parries criticisms by responding that he is espousing *democratic* capitalism, where economic tendencies are modified by the political or moral-cultural systems.

What of the criticism that capitalism, to sell more and different goods, devises a pseudoworld of tantalizing images that seep into subconscious processes, prompting consumers to crave one ephemeral promise of fulfillment after another? What about the reproach that most political input is packaged to arouse this restless dissatisfaction with the present and everheightened craving for the new?

John K. Galbraith and others have argued that advance stimulation of consumer desire becomes more necessary as modern industries must invest increasing amounts of capital simply to begin production. The more they invest, the less they can wait for consumer response to know if they have produced something desirable. On the contrary, they must stimulate demand for particular products well before they appear (pp. 108-9).[10]

Novak acknowledges that mass communications have created "almost as it were a new collective brain, for the instantaneous transmission of ways of looking at the world. In a sense, ideas and symbols have become more powerful than reality," and these media "are, from one perspective, institutions of the economic system" (p. 183). Yet he feels that journalists are governed more by the "domain of the word" and the moral-cultural system than the imagic commercial world. Moreover, Novak finds media and journalism controlled largely by artistic, socially left types quite hostile to capitalism (p. 184).

Although he acknowledges that Galbraith may be partly correct, Novak emphasizes the risks involved in production and that many preadvertised products fall flat. Above all, he finds people generally capable of resisting advertising's allurements and of deciding freely what they really want (pp. 107-8). Though Novak believes that external forces can greatly limit peoples' outward freedom, he apparently believes, like libertarians and unlike Marcuse and Jameson, that they are genuinely free on inward, psychic levels. Finally Novak argues that no matter how poorly people might choose, leaving economic choices up to them is preferable to the only other option—entrusting them to some government.

5. *Latin American issues.* But even if capitalism has improved in the West, many argue that its dark side appears overseas, where numerous countries serve as cheap sources of raw materials and labor. This criticism

has been raised by Latin American liberation theology, a holistic social movement to be covered under holistic social theologies. Novak has undertaken serious debate with this approach.

Most Latin American theologians affirm the theory of *dependency*—that their nations' economies are structured to provide not for their own needs but for those of more developed countries. During the 1960s, in contrast, many Latin Americans affirmed *development*—that if they simply followed the capitalistic route that had enriched the West, they would eventually experience similar prosperity. They hoped that this would strengthen the middle class and bring greater democracy. Yet despite growing GNPs, benefits seemed to accrue chiefly to a small group of elites. Most things worsened for the populations' lower halves, and hopes for greater democracy languished. These prospering elites controlled the political scene and most connections with more developed economies.

Gradually many Latin Americans concluded that these wealthier nations, in collusion with such leaders, whom they bolstered with economic and military aid, were largely determining Latin America's economic course and reaping many of the benefits. Yet this had resulted not merely from happenstance or deliberate greed but from capitalism's basic structure. For to continue making profits, it was argued, capitalism must exploit a large class of workers and basic raw materials. If the exploited proletariat had shrunk in the West, this was merely because it had now shifted overseas, to whole nations which would remain subordinate to wealthier ones by virtue of capitalism's structure (Gutiérrez [1973] 1988:81-88). Such a worldview, which roots our major cultural and social problems in the global spread of capitalism and its supportive military apparatus, generally corresponds with Jameson's (see chapter four).

Yet Novak, as we saw, believes that capitalism's goal is to place "a sound material base . . . under every single person on this planet" (1986:42). Accordingly he must deny that dependency is endemic to global capitalism and basically affirm *development*. Let us see how he regards Latin America in particular.

Novak argues that the roots of Latin America's problems arise not from current capitalist imperialism but from the continent's history. For centuries it has been ruled by a small group who reserved privileges for themselves and disdained economic development. Novak claims that Latin America today is more a feudal than a capitalist continent. He deplores situations which make it nearly impossible to start small businesses, obtain credit or invest money safely in home industries. Novak believes that government should encourage such things.

Novak concedes that the contrast between very rich and very poor is at least analogous to class struggle (p. 21). Yet in response to criticisms that U.S. imperialism lies behind this, he insists that only 16 percent of U.S. foreign investment is in Latin America (p. 131). When it is claimed that foreigners control Latin America's resources, he argues, like libertarians, that resources would not be resources if advanced technology did not discover and process them.

Novak affirms that transnational investments and corporations are usually desired by underdeveloped nations and bring many improvements—though such companies can create cultural conflicts and act high-handedly. He argues that their profits need not benefit host countries but should reward original investors (1982:228). To complaints that host governments cannot regulate transnationals, Novak affirms usual arguments against government controls. To complaints that local governments collude with transnationals to victimize their people, he blames indigenous sociopolitical structures. He does, however, recommend that living standards of the very poorest in underdeveloped lands be raised by other than market methods (p. 109).

Novak says nearly nothing about ecological consequences. Yet he challenges environmental talk about limits to growth, since he believes, with libertarians, that new inventions can transcend problems (pp. 71-72).

Novak also complains that capitalism's Latin American critics usually define it in the most stereotyped and worst possible ways. They generally describe it as a monolithic system operating inevitably by inherent principles (such as profit motive), unmodified by the cultural and political systems essential to Novak's democratic capitalism. Latin Americans often do so, he argues, because they have no real experience of a free market's benefits.

Novak also finds liberation theologians naive in their praise of "socialism." He critiques Juan Segundo's definition of it as a "regime in which the ownership of the means of production is removed from individuals and handed over to higher institutions whose concern is the common good" (Novak 1981:15). Novak finds here a naive confidence, typical of the historic Latin American tendency to entrust many things to government, that any such institution will actually act for general good (1986:28). Novak also claims that "the people," when they have their say, usually want private property (p. 169). But above all, he finds liberation theologians extremely vague as to what they mean by "socialism." Some, he suggests, might be content with a system permitting limited private ownership, occupying the left margins of his democratic capitalism (pp. 170-71).[11]

Reinhold Niebuhr's social realism. Niebuhr's thought combines paradoxical elements at its heart. Initially a leftist like Novak, he first sought to synthesize radical Marxism with a religious orientation. Deeply disturbed by the Great Depression, Niebuhr felt that only Marxist analysis could explain capitalism's dehumanizing aspects. Like Jameson and Marcuse, he was deeply impressed by Marxism's vision of a future society (McCann 1981:28-31).

By the mid-1930s, however, Niebuhr became convinced that Marxism falsely absolutized certain merely human values, which led to intolerant tyranny in practice. He began to believe that only a religion "which worships a holy God before whom all men feel themselves sinners" can maintain "decency, pity, and forgiveness in human life and can resist the cruelty and inhumanity which flow" from absolutizing some values and identifying others with evil (1934:379). From then on Niebuhr emphasized the contrast between a transcendent religious realm, which inspires high social ideals and critiques social practice, and the historical realm, in which these ideals can only be approximated.

1. *Transcendence, the self and worldviews.* Despite his strong social interests, Niebuhr's discussions of transcendence often focus on the self. The main paradox of selves, he says, is that they are fully involved in nature yet transcend it as spirit. Moreover, the self's capacity to question whether it is merely a part of nature and what the limits of reason are show that it transcends both of these. The self, further, can survey not only the world but also itself from a higher vantage point. This shows that

> it stands outside both itself and the world, which means that it cannot understand itself except as it is understood from beyond itself and the world. This essential homelessness of the human spirit is the ground of religion; for the self . . . cannot find the meaning of life in itself or the world. (1941:14)[12]

In emphasizing the self's transcendence over any finite reality, Niebuhr grounds its importance somewhat as Novak does when he claims that individuals can question everything and transcend all given answers, so that their ultimate freedom must be respected. Both thinkers, to protect individuals from absolutist claims of social forces, insist that counterbalancing tensions must exist among all such entities. Yet, whereas Novak chiefly discusses the "horizontal" tensions among systems (economic, political and moral-cultural), Niebuhr continually roots these in a finite-infinite, temporal-eternal dialectic. Humankind's paradox is that we are oriented toward both the infinite *and* the finite, with the result that all our activities are affected by each.

With this in mind, Niebuhr analyzes strengths and weaknesses of some important worldviews.[13] Unlike Novak, he finds in capitalism an inexorable, self-enclosed logic which increasingly turns people and relationships into units governed by economic calculations (pp. 66-67). Capitalism irreverently exploits nature (p. 20), and the apparently free individuality which initiated it finally becomes submerged in "more mechanical interdependencies and collectivities than anything known in an agrarian world" (p. 22).

Niebuhr believes that Marxism rightly deciphers capitalism's weaknesses at points. Yet, like Marcuse, he finds Marxism's traditional economic analysis too shallow, for it supposes that all problems can be solved by proper economic structures. Marxism does not grasp "the depth of spirit in . . . the human personality" which will undermine even the best economies by selfish striving (p. 47).

Niebuhr also critiques romanticism—which would include some organicists we have studied—in which he finds too optimistic a hope that society can be reformed by simply following nature's impulses and patterns. (He critiques Friedrich Schiller, whose emphasis on phantasy and play both Marcuse and Jameson affirm [pp. 27, 33].[14]) Romanticism, he objects, does not recognize the extent to which any apparently "natural" social form is, or will be, shaped by human spirit, including its lust for power. When romantics exalt intuition and impulse above reason, they open the way for uncontrolled expression of destructive irrational forces.

Niebuhr also criticizes biologism, with which he identifies Freud, for reducing human behavior to instincts which operate as do animals'. Niebuhr protests, as Marcuse does, that human instincts are quite malleable. They can be shaped in many ways (pp. 42-43).

2. Theological affirmations. Niebuhr provides greater in-depth analysis of sin than Novak. He adapts Karen Horney's psychoanalytic theory that both Freud's libido and Alfred Adler's "will to power" are derived from a more basic anxiety (p. 192).

Anxiety, according to Niebuhr, arises from the self's particular structure of being both finite and able to transcend finitude toward infinity. This means that in making a decision the self will need to settle on a particular option, yet will have an indefinite range to choose from. Faced with this range, and with uncertainties about the results of selecting or rejecting any option, the self will experience deep anxiety. We will be tempted to choose something which will offer security but will transgress the creaturely limits set by God (for example, in setting public policy politicians will choose what gives them greatest control over citizens). Sin involves unwillingness to put up with ambiguity.

Nonetheless anxiety, in itself, is not sin but sin's "internal precondition" (p. 182). If we could embark on self-transcendence secure in God's love, we might not sin. Accordingly Niebuhr defines sin, precisely speaking, as *unbelief,* or lack of trust in God (pp. 183, 251-52). It takes two major forms. The most common, he claims, is *pride:* exalting ourselves against God and seeking inordinate power over others. The less common, contrasting form he calls *sensuality:* regarding ourselves as less than responsible, self-transcending people and seeking security by "turning inordinately to mutable good" (p. 185).

Niebuhr insists that people sin freely and responsibly—yet that sin is also "inevitable." This unfathomable paradox lies at the heart of original sin (p. 241).[15] Socially this is visible in the fact that, since the Enlightenment, the apparently free human spirit has created a civilization of increasingly "enslaving mechanical interdependencies and collectivities" (p. 22). Nevertheless through pride the economic, political and social institutions which rise to dominance in this process will proclaim themselves as far more benign than they are. Such absolutist pretenses of self-righteousness, which institutions and movements opposing them will also adopt, are a chief source of social alienation.

Niebuhr believes that general awareness of the phenomena I have described is available to humans apart from Christian revelation. Continuous transcendence beyond ourselves can lead any of us, first, to a "sense of reverence for a majesty and a sense of dependence upon an ultimate source of being." Awareness of ethical striving and sin can lead, second, to a sense of moral obligation and unworthiness and, third, to "longing for forgiveness" (p. 131). Jesus Christ, however, especially in his atoning death, provides the ultimate resolution of these longings. For on the cross, God, our ultimate moral Source, judged sin uncompromisingly—yet also absorbed its penalty and now offers humans free mercy (pp. 142-49).

Especially through the cross Jesus is "the perfect norm of human nature," for "the final perfection of man in history" is "the perfection of sacrificial love" (1943:68). Niebuhr can even call this suffering love "the very law of history" (p. 49). Nevertheless he also insists that another form of behavior, "mutual love" (often called *eros*), which aims at receiving reciprocal benefits from others, is the "highest good" attainable in actual history (p. 69). He believes that sacrificial love (often called *agapē*) must always give freely without thought of benefit and thus cannot become a widely practiced behavior in our power-dominated history.

Paradoxically, however, sacrificial love does wield an indirect impact on history, for some of the best social practices (such as many social services) are initiated by people who actually do act for the benefit of others without thought of rewards. Then too, as Novak mentioned, Jesus' self-giving activity and commands can critique and refine our best behavior, even if we seldom put them literally into practice.[16]

If sacrificial love, history's "very law," cannot be widely actualized in history, Christianity's eschatological realities (for instance, last judgment, the perfected kingdom) will not be realities in space and time either. Whereas Niebuhr, like Novak, believes that improvements in history are possible, both deny that history tends toward a climactic spatio-temporal state. For Niebuhr, history's consummation cannot be an actual social reality but only "a divine mercy which makes something more of history than recurring judgment" (1943:29). This mercy triumphs in Jesus' cross, making it, in effect, history's fulfillment. Biblical symbols of Jesus' return and perfected kingdom, then, simply express faith in the final supremacy of God's sovereignty, love and mercy over all history, despite forces which oppose it (p. 290). History's fulfillment seems to be experienced only in the eternal realm, where individuals encounter God's judgment and love in a way that history as a whole never can (Vaughan 1983:23, 120-21).[17]

Conflict for Niebuhr, then (unlike for Hume, Smith, Darwin or Freud), is ultimately rooted in something deeper than nature or history. For these realms conflict with the eternal, divine realm, and this conflict is experienced within individuals, who participate in both. As I continue with Niebuhr (here and in chapters nine and eleven), I will ask whether he separates the spiritual realm too far from the material, the individual (who alone can transcend toward the eternal) from society and historical reality from the social visions connected with the *eschaton*.

3. *Balance among powers*. Niebuhr agrees with Novak and libertarians that inordinate concentration of power presents the greatest social threat. The optimum social situation will balance these powers against each other as symmetrically as possible. But since these power blocs will remain intact, some hostility and alienation among them will be inevitable, and some people will suffer injustice. Such balancing, however, should ensure that the absolutist pretensions of any social force will be checked by the others.

Nonetheless Niebuhr does not believe that balancing among powers will occur automatically. Each social field, especially international relations, must have some central organizing power which manages these tensions and is able to control some others, coercively when necessary (1943:266). Novak interprets Niebuhr's lifelong direction away from socialism and toward balance of powers as a move toward democratic capitalism (pp.

321-24). Nevertheless Niebuhr understands justice more positively than traditional capitalism: it means not simply refraining from infringement on others, as it does for libertarians, but includes positive "brotherhood" and caring.[18]

4. *International applications.* In politics Niebuhr wielded far greater impact than most theologians. In 1947 he joined the State Department Planning Policy Staff. During the Cold War, his belief in the necessity of a strong supervising power led him to stress American hegemony. He regarded this role for the United States as morally necessary, though one which should be accepted humbly (McCann 1981:112). For Niebuhr, British colonialism provided a good model of hegemonic responsibility, though he acknowledged its economic exploitation and racism. He strongly rejected the thesis of people such as Jameson that imperialism is a necessary consequence of capitalism (pp. 110-11).

Like many Cold War theorists, Niebuhr found U.S.A.-U.S.S.R. conflict so pervasive that he doubted whether other nations could have truly independent perspectives. Foreign intellectuals critical of the United States he regarded as Marxist dupes—though he acknowledged some degree of capitalist exploitation. Like Novak, he blamed despotic governments, along with attitudes which opposed productivity, for problems in non-Western countries (pp. 112-14). Niebuhr regarded democracy as essential for economic and social well-being and named three necessary prerequisites for it: (1) unity of community which can allow free play of competitive interests, (2) belief in the freedom and worth of the individual and (3) enough balance among social, political and economic forces to establish approximate social justice (p. 117).

Turning specifically to Latin America, the Niebuhrian approach found three problems: (1) despite common language and culture, massive illiteracy blocks many potential social contributions; (2) Catholicism has historically underplayed individual worth; and (3) society and economy have long been controlled by a feudal hierarchy (p. 119).[19] Nevertheless, a modernized middle class was gaining economic and political power. If it can "bring the semifeudal and depressed areas into the national community through education, welfare, and reform," an impending crisis fueled by Marxism may be averted. But if it cannot, "the rural areas and the downtrodden urban masses will rise up to destroy those who refuse them their economic rights" (Niebuhr and Sigmund 1969:152).

This approach regrets that American military and economic power has often sided with "feudal" elements most needing reform. However, its emphasis on strengthening the middle class, along with the "democratic-left" parties such as the Christian Democrats, cohered with the reformist thinking behind the Alliance for Progress (McCann 1981:119-21). It envisioned bringing Latin America on to the path of development.

Viewed in hindsight, Reinhold Niebuhr's international views exhibit a questionable confidence in American ways, particularly in America's ability to guide other nations. The sincerity and efficacy of America's social and ethical values are assumed, while negative effects of American military and economic power, though not entirely ignored, may well be underestimated. Other nations seem incapable of formulating truly significant, indigenous perspectives. Has Niebuhr's emphasis on paradox and balance really led toward the best international equilibrium and eliminated as much social alienation as possible? Or has it skewed things in favor of the dominant nations and capitalism? Has it allowed novel social solutions and values to emerge, perhaps even some motivated by sacrificial love, or has it tilted toward preserving the status quo?

Niebuhr's views and the status quo established by capitalism coincide on another important social issue. Capitalism, we have seen, divided American society into a productive realm and a domestic one (Chodorow [see chapter 2]). Niebuhr found sacrificial love inapplicable to the first, with its power relations, but quite relevant to the second, and especially to mothers (Vaughan 1983:117). Compatibly with this, Niebuhr regarded motherhood as woman's "primary function," which will limit her freedom in "development of various potentialities of character not related to" it (1941:282). Niebuhr, that is, limited woman's productive role and enhanced her domestic role (Vaughan 1983:189). Is the symmetry with capitalist social structure entirely coincidental?

Summary. For conflictual social theologians, government must be limited not only to preserve individual freedom, as libertarians affirm, but also to mitigate sin's consequences. Individual sin, for Niebuhr, has some of the subtle, self-deceptive features stressed by psychoanalysis. But sin also corrupts governments, especially through their pretensions of righteousness—a theological reason to avoid granting them great power. Yet theology also affirms the individual's transcendence toward the eternal and not merely his or her right to pursue a freely chosen life pattern (Nozick 1974) as an argument against state control.

The state, however, must not simply be limited, nor the economy left unrestricted, as in libertarianism. Instead, these should balance each other, and both should be balanced by morality and culture. The moral values mentioned apparently cannot all be derived from sympathy or self-interest (though Novak claims that they can). It cannot be assumed that balance will emerge automatically if government is restricted; balance must be worked at more deliberately. Yet while moral forces should restrain some capitalist tendencies, idealistic ones (such as *agapē*) and utopian social visions should have little practical import.

Novak praises capitalism provided that it is balanced by the other forces. He does not find it conditioning deep psychic levels but, like libertarians, believes that people recognize and freely pursue their true desires. Niebuhr, however, regards capitalism as a self-enclosed system of forces which increasingly deprives most people of freedom. Yet both theologians strongly oppose Marxism, and on the international scene they champion the forces of capitalism and Western democracy. Latin America's problems, they argue, arise from being behind in the process of development due to historically feudal socioeconomic structures.

In their concern to protect individual transcendence toward God from control of corrupt governments, our conflictual theologians conceive of religious fulfillment mainly as spiritual communion with the eternal realm and interpret eschatological hopes as symbols of this communion. But in their concern to guard religion from the flaws of matter, society and history, do they remove it too far from these realities?

Furthermore, Novak and Niebuhr represent privileged classes. Does this enable them to put up with the injustice which they find inevitable more easily than they would if they represented oppressed groups? In this way, do they support social alienations embedded in the staus quo? However, in response to more utopian visions of the future, they ask, as do libertarians, Who would enforce these?

Holistic Social Theologies

Rosemary Ruether's feminist liberation theology. Ruether makes no major distinction between spirit and matter (chapter six). Mind is matter's evolving interiority. For her, God is the Matrix of all things and includes both matter and mind.

1. *Dualism and alienation.* Ruether, accordingly, treats notions of a distinct, transcendent God as psychological projections. These arise when males, fearing the natural processes of birth, change and death, imagine a purely spiritual reality with which their "higher" selves can assimilate so that they might permanently escape these things. Through this same process males project things they fear—natural bodiliness, spontaneity, corruptibility and so on—onto "others" whom they seek to control or conquer. All forms of alienation spring from this dualism. The most fundamental, however, is between males and females. Yet because women are

associated with birth and natural rhythms, male-dominated societies control and exploit women and nature in parallel ways. Capitalism reduces both to manipulable things. The logical outcome of belief in a transcendent deity is nature's eventual destruction.[20]

Alienation is spread and solidified largely through social shaping of self-consciousness. Men, Ruether claims, tend to regard themselves as rational, strong and purposeful—qualities required to subdue the earth and other people—and project irrationality, weakness and fickleness upon women. Women tend to accept and internalize this projection, or at least find that they must struggle against it. Further, men (and some women) in dominant cultures apply the former sort of qualities supremely to themselves and attribute their negative counterparts to dominated races and social groups—projections which these groups, at least in part, often accept.[21]

Alienation, however, is rooted in social structures as well. The "economic structure of industrial capitalism," splits the productive sphere from the domestic one, creating "pervasive, structural discrimination against women" (1983a:219; compare 1972:116). In productive districts men lead impersonal, competitive lives (not as "bands of brothers," as Novak claims); in domestic districts women provide rest, recreation and household services to free men for that life. Women in the first districts usually fill secondary positions, and most find it impossible to function equally with men, for they are socially expected to carry the domestic burdens as well. Yet on the domestic front, as advertising arouses false needs, women are expected to be both "the chief buyer and the sexual image through which the appetites of consumption are stimulated. Woman becomes a self-alienated 'beautiful object' who sells her own quickly decaying façade to herself" (1975:198-99).

2. *Reconciliation among powers.* If society is split into alienated groups, each actualizing only a portion of full human potential, how are such dualisms overcome? Unlike Novak and Niebuhr, Ruether does not emphasize limiting by negatively balancing the powers of dominant groups against each other. She wants dominating powers overthrown and the strengths of all groups brought into liberated, positive balance. Feeling that religion's transcendent language about a better world usually diverts energies toward an unreal "spiritual" sphere, she argues that it should be interpreted horizontally as conveying an *ought* impelling people to seek a better historical world (1972:166).

This ought is often expressed through utopian visions (1975:182), not unlike those of Marcuse, Jameson and especially Bookchin. It arises when a better reality is glimpsed, even if dimly, beyond our alienated social- and self-consciousness. Ruether regards this "as an incursion of power and grace beyond the capacities of the present roles" (1983a:186). Yet this grace is not "supernatural" in the traditional sense, since it restores us to our true selves (1972:9). The vision we glimpse is not simply of our potential self but involves a renewed community including all creatures (1983a:212; 1992:258). It involves qualitative change, not merely "one-dimensional alterations" (1972:167).

Ruether apparently understands this alternative reality to also underlie the present in a way I have called organismic. For example, she argues that social and ecological solidarity are "eminently practical" because they point to "our *actual* solidarity with all others and with our mother, the earth, which is the actual ground of our being" (1975:211, italics added). Moreover, the new possibilities to which God/ess leads us "are, at the same time, the regrounding of ourselves in the primordial matrix, the original harmony. The liberating encounter with God/ess is always an encounter with our authentic selves resurrected from underneath the alienated self" (1983a:71).[22] This authentic self, moreover, we in some sense bear within us, for we always recognize it whenever we catch a glimpse of redeemed universal humanity, and it is "the foundation and ground of our being" (p. 114).

The initial turn from dominated toward liberated reality must apparently be taken by the oppressed.[23] But since this vision involves liberation of all, we must also work ultimately to liberate the oppressor. To set dominated groups as wholly good over against dominating ones as wholly evil is to repeat the dualism grounding all alienation. But the dialectic between good and evil runs through all groups and ultimately through each heart (1972:136).

Though liberation will normally begin with a few in an oppressed group and then spread through it, Ruether also hopes for "gradual conversion of large groups who are relatively established, but who come to see their deepest interests lying on the side of change" (p. 169). Ideally change will be spearheaded by coalitions of radicals, who keep stressing the transcendent vision, and liberals, who can influence actual structures (p. 172). Because male-female dualism is the most basic alienation, "the women's movement, properly understood, encompasses all other liberation movements" (1975:xi).

What kinds of specific transformations does Ruether recommend? Overall, human societies should move toward an ecological model, an interdependent organicism where "no part is intrinsically 'higher' or 'lower'" (1983b:67). Here farm and town, home and work will be closely interrelated (1975:183). Whereas capitalism has made the domestic sphere, where women create and sustain life, subordinate to the production sphere, the domestic should become the center and work be integrated into it (1983a:228). Men and women should share parenting and household tasks equally, freeing women from unfair extra burdens. Ruether recommends communal units of about fifty adults and twenty to twenty-five children within which domestic tasks would be apportioned. Kitchens, tools, vehicles and other such things would be communally owned (1975:208-9). Though private property must be challenged (1983a:85), she envisions each family having some private space—for "abolition of the home would be the total alienation of one's life to institutions" (p. 226). It would also be essential for women to have full control, reproductive and otherwise, over their bodies.

In such communities, private autos would be banned, more food would be produced seasonally in bioregions and trends toward urbanization would gradually reverse (1992:261-62). Much like Bookchin, Ruether sees industries being locally managed and owned. She suggests that communal affairs be handled by short-term committees with rotating membership, which would occasionally bring proposals before direct primary assemblies (1975:208).[24]

Yet despite this grassroots management and decision-making, Ruether acknowledges that economic planning, distribution and enforcement of standards would need control by regional, national and international bodies—though these would include representatives from local communities. Global interrelatedness would also necessitate unified management of the world's resources. She envisions subsidies undergirding development of sound technologies—such as wind and solar power—and withdrawn from less sound ones (1992:260). Even the all-important transformation of home/work relations would have to be "socially institutionalized" (1975:181). Novak and libertarians would ask how all this could happen without greatly restricting her ideal of local control.

Movement toward such structures might begin by building "base communities" ("face-to-face groups with which one lives, works, and prays") which involve themselves in local affairs, where significant changes can often be made (1992:269). Yet because all social life is interconnected, people need to think and act globally as well as locally (pp. 272-74). Ruether occasionally speaks of the church as the avant-garde of a liberated humanity. However, since she finds the church highly influenced by patriarchy and its related alienations, she often stresses that base communities within it need to create "liberated zones" and regard the larger church as one of their mission fields (1983a:205-6).

3. *Theological affirmations.* Though I have found organismic emphases in Ruether's thought, she rejects a romanticist return to primitive interactions with nature. For her, "technological rationality is itself the highest gift of nature" (1975:205). Romanticism—whether it idealizes the psyche's "feminine" depths (Jung), domestic women[25] or return to preindustrial economy—expresses the longing of alienated white male consciousness for lost ties. It leads white males to idealize not only women but also peasants, Native Americans and others who represent "the primitive"—and keep them in their place (1983a:85).

Yet despite Ruether's belief in some historical progress and the centrality of universal community in her visions of liberation, she believes that actual history has no single goal. For her, belief in an eschatological consummation, where all suffering ceases, springs from the isolated male ego's desire to escape finitude and death (pp. 245-56).[26] But in reality, since consciousness is matter's interiority, physical death must involve loss of consciousness and return to the Matrix.[27]

But even if we cannot anticipate an ideal climactic society, we can make things significantly better now. Ruether recommends that we think of "social change as conversion back to the centre, rather than to a beginning or end-point in history" (p. 69). This would accord with nature's activity, which seeks to restore balance. And balance, remember, provides Ruether's criterion for what is "good" (see chapter six). Ruether proposes the redistributive pattern of the Jubilee (Lev 25)—when debts were remitted, slaves freed, and land restored to original users—as a model for social change. She sees proclamation of a Jubilee Year as central in Jesus' ministry (1983b:68-70).[28] Another favorite organismic term for this better future, when labor will no longer be alienated, is reminiscent of Marcuse: "cultivation of the garden" (Ruether 1972:125).[29]

I have already noted several main features of Ruether's Christology (chapter six). Basically, Jesus modeled a servantlike lifestyle which critiqued the roots of the desire for domination and so sparked hope for a society free from hierarchy. Further, Jesus saw God's coming reign as a vindication of the poor and oppressed. He recognized that among oppressed groups, women were the most oppressed of all. Because he recognized this, his maleness need form no barrier to women in accepting him as a profound manifestation of "Christ" (1983a:135-38). However, Ruether finds that this emphasis clashes with classical confessions of Jesus' deity. For they ascribed the abstract, male-oriented Greek concept *logos* to him. This made him an imperial Christ, who sanctioned Rome's oppression

(1983b:48-49). For Ruether, however, Jesus functions mainly as a symbol, or archetype, of fulfilled humanity.

Remember, however, that for Ruether the human fullness indicated by "Christ" cannot be wholly incarnated in one person. Neither should we suppose that "Christ" will appear completely at some eschatological point. Ruether opposes all "once-for-all" events, whether in past or future (1983a:255). Jesus, she claims, did not refer to himself as the eschatological "Son of Man." Rather, in passages referring to this Son (for example, Mk 8:38) he was indicating One who would come later (1983a:121-22). Jesus neither overcame all evil, nor did he bring the finality of God's reign or deliverance from all sin. Through Jesus the crucified prophet we simply reaffirm his own faith that the kingdom is at hand. Faith in his resurrection simply indicates our refusal to take the victory of evil as the last word (1983b:23).[30]

Jesus' servanthood also precludes his being a king.[31] Jesus, she says, "does not evoke the hope for the Davidic Messiah"; yet if he does so, he "speaks of the Messiah as servant rather than king" (1983a:119, 136). On the cross Jesus, and through Jesus God, identified profoundly with the oppressed. Yet Ruether suggests that God completely gives up kingship here. For God as "omnipotent sovereign" is "modelled after the powers of domination," whereas on the cross God "abandons God's power into the human condition utterly and completely" (1983b:29). Still Ruether recognizes that in Scripture, calling God king and Father can have an altogether different intention. It can proclaim that since God alone has these titles, people "owe no allegiance to human fathers and kings" (p. 28). Ruether intimates that Jesus, who referred to God as father through the more personal name "Abba," had such a liberating conception of God's kingship (1983a:64; compare 1975:65).[32]

Although servanthood through Jesus becomes a norm for human behavior, Ruether stresses that "it is possible only for liberated persons, not people in servitude" (1983b:54). Preached to oppressed people, servanthood can squelch their desire for liberation and harden their bondage. Ruether also argues that since Jesus successfully resisted the temptation of being a warrior Messiah, Christians too should be forgiving and nonviolent whenever possible. However, in some situations, like those that frequently prevail in Latin America, almost any liberative action will provoke a violent response, and Christians cannot always avoid violence (pp. 29-30; see Vaughan 1983:164-70). Yet even though she concedes this, Ruether regards militarism as today's "largest system of dominating power" (1992:266).

Some Latin American liberation theologies. Since many Latin American theologians regard dependency on global capitalism as their continent's major problem, what a person decides about this issue will affect how he or she evaluates many of their claims. Is Latin America, to a significant extent, a victim of outside forces or, as Novak claims (and to a lesser extent Niebuhr), of its own history?

1. *Development or dependency?* When Novak points to and blames the continent's historic feudal structures governed by oppressive elites, he seems to overlook a fundamental point: Latin America, ever since the Spanish invasions, has always been dominated and exploited by some outside force, and its criticized elites have usually been the link that made this possible. Now that global capitalism has taken over these historic structures, this system has become the basic source of Latin America's dependence on more advanced economies—even if only 16 percent of U.S. foreign investment is there and even though local elites continue to enforce it.

In support of the dependency perspective, I affirm that intervention in Latin America's economic affairs (through austerity controls, conditions for foreign aid, support of particular governments and so on) has increased greatly in recent decades. Latin America's wealth continues to be distributed quite unevenly. Very little trickles down to the masses, and few signs exist that much more will do so in the near future. Further, this dependency seems clearly correlated with lack of democracy.[33] Consequently, however much the governing elites may have been and now are responsible for the continent's misery and however much they have profited from it, the fact remains that the overwhelming masses have almost always been exploited by someone tightly connected to foreign powers.

I find the masses' situation today much as liberation theologians describe it, and global capitalism is the main structure within which this now occurs. But must one then agree with Latin American theology in every respect?

2. *Internalized alienation.* Latin American social alienation has not only external causes but also profound internalized ones. As Ruether says, dominating structures become deeply ingrained on the psyches of the oppressed. This process has been described in Paulo Freire's *Pedagogy of the Oppressed,* a work which has greatly impacted all Latin American liberation movements.[34] Freire claims that oppressed people are deeply divided within. They long for freedom, yet they fear it. They are themselves yet also the oppressor, whose perspective has been etched into their consciousness (1972:32). On one hand, they believe themselves to be worthless and inca-

pable of creative action, as their oppressors tell them. On the other, they can visualize liberation only as becoming like the oppressor: taking over the oppressor's position and oppressing others.

Oppressed peoples are usually aware only of their concrete misery and not of overall situations in which they are caught. That is why Freire stresses "pedagogy," which involves something like Jameson's *cognitive mapping*—discerning one's location amid a world of bewildering, ensnaring relationships. In this pedagogy, instructors work alongside students, developing their ability to decipher their social positions and change them creatively. Freire contrasts pedagogy with *banking education,* where teachers deposit discrete quantities of information in passive student minds. Banking education, which he finds modeled on capitalism's quantifying tendencies, makes an organic process mechanical (p. 64).[35]

For Freire human consciousness is no passive container. It is an intentional activity, continually transcending its current awareness of its situation and even of ourselves, constantly remaking its world and ourselves (pp. 66-67). All people participate in the great "ontological and historical vocation to be more fully human" (pp. 40-41). Niebuhr would agree about this continual transcendence. However, he would stress that transcending selves eventually encounter limits: their finitude, God and awareness of their own sin. Before these limits they must bow, acknowledge sin and seek forgiveness. Freire, however, speaks of limits in a quite different sense.

For Freire each social setting involves many *limit-situations.* These block tendencies toward fuller humanization and often obscure people's very awareness of these tendencies and of the obstacles opposing them. (For example, lack of education in an area, based on an accepted definition of its inhabitants as permanent "peasants," would be a limit-situation.) Pedagogy works toward increasing the awareness of these situations and of people's capacities to transcend them. Limit-situations are overcome by *limit-acts,* which identify and strive to surpass the former (pp. 92-93). Awareness of these situations, and especially of people's capacity to transcend them, is called *conscientization.*

Liberation theologies, following Freire, emphasize the hope-arousing role played by visions of a liberated society (even though, as Novak complains, these seldom contain concrete detail). They view history as the story of humanity's growing freedom, as "the dialectical process" through which "humankind constructs itself and attains a real awareness of its own being; it liberates itself in the acquisition of genuine freedom which through work transforms the world and educates the human species" (Gutiérrez [1973] 1988:29). Though "revolution" of some kind may be required to overcome the alienation now sundering society (liberation theologians are vague about its character also), they look forward to the creation of a "new man" in whom conflict between oppressed and oppressor will be overcome (Freire 1972:42).

Freire stresses that revolution must free everyone to pursue true humanization. If the masses are simply manipulated by leaders and do not undergo conscientization, they will institute another form of oppression. Oppressors, also, must be freed from needs to dominate others. Love for others must pervade the new society and movements that usher it in (pp. 77-78). Freire acknowledges that the new society must have leadership and authority structures. Yet he is confident that because true humanization will have occurred, these will function without oppressive features (pp. 176-81). He recognizes that former masters will have to be restrained but insists that this will not be oppressive (pp. 42-43).

Although social oppression deeply impacts the psyche, one senses that the self is not structured—either for Freire or for Ruether—quite as Niebuhr or psychoanalysis would say. For the forces that warp the self's awareness seem to come solely from outside, from oppressive social structures, and participation in this warping seems to consist entirely in buying into the self-definitions they proffer. There is no mention, as in psychoanalysis, of tension among a person's inner drives also contributing to alienation, nor of a person's inner anxiety, pride or sensuality, which Niebuhr emphasizes, playing this role. Instead, despite the depth at which social forces impact self-consciousness, it seems that even underneath this people have an accurate awareness of who they really are and of what they must do to humanize themselves and society.

Niebuhr, however, understands psychological alienation in what I have called a "three-sided" sense (see chapter two). The self must struggle not only with social pressures from outside but also with internal forces. For Ruether and Freire, though, alienation seems "two-sided": imposed upon a harmonious self-process only (though very deeply) from outside. To actualize this process, people need some help to see themselves and their situation as they actually are. "Evangelization," accordingly, can be understood not so much as proclamation concerning God's acts or nature as a conscientizing function which communicates "awareness of being oppressed but nevertheless of being masters of their own destiny" (Gutiérrez [1973] 1988:116; compare McCann 1981:166-67).

Freire mentions no ultimate framework or limits (such as recognition of God or sin) that might guide or modify the socially transforming limit-acts. Is it perhaps the case that all parameters for self-discovery and social transcendence—such as religious doctrines or behavioral standards, both of which could be regarded as formulas masking social oppression—are considered negative barriers to humanization (McCann 1981:168-70)? At any rate, Freire seems quite confident that, once freed from oppressive dependency structures, people will clearly know how to construct the right kind of society—including the difficult tasks of developing new authority structures and humanely treating former oppressors. We hear no warnings, as in Novak and Niebuhr, that any social structure will yield to corruptions of power and needs to be checked by moral-cultural or theological "limits."

To be sure, pedagogy of people who have always been told what to do and what reality is like and who have been discouraged from thinking for themselves, should hardly begin by stressing behavioral or doctrinal norms. Limit-situations should indeed be challenged and limit-acts encouraged. But should Christian teaching imply, or even affirm, that no limits, such as God's reality or acknowledgement of our sin, ultimately shape Christian liberation endeavors?

To be sure, we should challenge some definitions of sin—such as Niebuhr's affirmation that its main form is pride—in dealing with people whose self-image has always been degraded. Here more emphasis on sin as considering oneself as less than a responsible, self-transcending person (infelicitously called *sensuality* by Niebuhr) is appropriate. Yet does this imply that no subtle anxieties and contradictions, apart from those imposed by oppressive structures, subvert our willing and acting? Or that no parameters carry normative force in constructing a new society? To consider this issue more carefully, let us examine a theology that may eliminate normative affirmations.

3. *Theology without normative content?* Latin American liberation theologies are diverse. Many clearly contain normative content. Some, for instance, affirm a traditional Chalcedonian Christology (Gutiérrez [1973] 1988:151-52, 175-78; Sobrino 1978). By discussing an approach which seems to challenge the notion of such content, I do not mean to imply that all such theologies head in this direction. But I wish to explore what happens when *humanization,* understood as involving freedom from limits, becomes the major theological theme.

Juan Segundo is suspicious of all political efforts grounded in a specifically Christian kind of vision. He examines the Christian Democratic Party of Chile, which advocated such a vision in the 1960s and 1970s. It was the kind of party favored by Niebuhrians, one which initially took a developmental approach to Latin America's problems. Yet after tracing this party's history, Segundo claims that such movements "turn into counterrevolutionary forces when and if revolution becomes feasible" (1976:94). Unlike Ruether, who places Jesus directly in the prophetic tradition, Segundo finds that he emphasized "interpersonal relationships" rather than "political oppression" (p. 111). Therefore unless Jesus can be disengaged from his original historical context, he will be understood in a conservative, counterrevolutionary way (p. 106).

Segundo begins by distinguishing *faith* from *ideologies*. Faith is commitment to an absolute value (for instance, Jesus Christ or love) which guides our life. However, it is impossible to define or describe what that value is (1982:17). If we ask, "What is [faith's] truth *content?"* the answer must be *"nothing"* (1976:108). Our basic faith in Jesus, for example, must be independent of, and remain unaffected by, specific content derived from historical investigation into his words or character (1982:14). However, to put our faith into action, we need specific principles by which to live. Segundo calls such principles, which span the gap between faith and the concrete world, *ideologies* (1976:116).[36] For instance, he regards both violence as found in the occupation of Canaan, and nonviolence as taught by Jesus, simply as different ideologies for applying faith to diverse situations. Segundo rejects any hermeneutic that would designate Jesus' teaching, or any other ideology, as the central biblical norm (pp. 116-17).

Segundo distinguishes *proto learning,* which consists in absorbing content, from a *deutero-learning* process, which consists in learning how to learn. The true purpose of Scripture and tradition is to lead people into this second activity—which sounds a great deal like Freire's pedagogy. *Faith* is another name for this deutero-learning through which, by wrestling with Scripture's ideologies (say, violence and nonviolence), we learn "how to create the ideologies needed to handle new and unforseen situations in history" (p. 120). Eventually even the external teacher, Jesus, will disappear from the scene. He will be replaced by the Spirit's internal work, which means that "after Christ history itself will be entrusted with the task of carrying on the process" (p. 121). In this way, the significance of Jesus can be detached from his (allegedly conservative) historical ministry.

If any "absolute" remains, it is found in the fact that Christians "absolutize one concrete pedagogical process in history," that of Scripture and church tradition, "placing it above and before any other such process" (p. 179). Yet even though this process is in some sense prior to individuals who become involved in it, they cannot do so without first being "engaged in a common quest of human liberation." In this way, such a faith "makes revelation possible" as its "necessary precondition" (1992:241-42). Moreover, the sign that God's revelation is occurring is "the liberation of the person"

(p. 249). In all these ways, then, it seems that Segundo has made faith into a liberating pedagogical process much like Freire's, without objective limits or normative content, and placed it prior to anything that could be called revelation.

Still, since Christians must create ideologies to handle current historical situations, Segundo seeks to elaborate how Jesus can be best understood today. Like ecological theologians, he takes evolution as the overall horizon for this task, emphasizing that humanity must now assume evolution's guidance (1988:21-22; 1992:236-37). Segundo identifies two major evolutionary processes: *entropy,* the tendency of energy available for work to decline, and *negentropy,* movement toward more highly organized forms exerting greater influence upon their environment. Segundo rejects the Darwinian vision of species competing against each other and a hostile environment. Organisms which survive, he argues (echoing Margulis, Sagan and Ruether), are not those who best compete against each other but those who best integrate with others—who fit into what he calls evolutionary *circuits* (1988:55-60). They are more likely to fit the more they possess the chief evolutionary value—*flexibility* (p. 99).

Segundo correlates the negentropy, which integrates organisms into circuits, with what Freud called eros, the life-force that brings things together into greater unities. Yet Freud also claimed that eros's strength was limited and that all things tend entropically toward death (see chapter two). This meant that everyone's energy for loving relationships was restricted. For this reason, Freud complained that Jesus' Sermon on the Mount, which apparently commanded love for everyone, was misguided. Everyone's limited love is very valuable to their family and friends, so if we try to expend it on strangers or enemies, we will deprive those close to us of what they need (pp. 75-76).

In light of these current evolutionary and psychological beliefs, what might Christians affirm about Jesus' relevance today? Segundo first interprets Jesus' critique of his own Israelite society as a way of saying that the oppressed were poorly integrated into its circuits, which deprived the whole of their unique gifts and energy. Jesus recommended giving up defense mechanisms which separate us from others, surrendering "our own center so that the other person's center may come out and be integrated as such by us" (p. 63). Jesus' Sermon on the Mount, despite Freud's pessimism, pointed to the possibility of injecting the highest negentropy into relationships with the greatest entropy (p. 64).

Nonetheless, Segundo insists that Jesus, like every human being, operated with limited eros. It was therefore impossible for him, as Freud noted, to express love to everyone he met. Even more, Jesus, like the rest of us, could love some people only by keeping others at arm's length—which, Segundo declares, involves doing them violence (1976:159-60). This meant, for instance, that Jesus accepted "the common prejudices against aliens" (p. 164), such as when he told the Syrophoenician woman that heeding her request was like throwing food to the dogs (Mk 7:27). Jesus, according to Segundo, also refused, unfairly, to consider the perspectives of his enemies, the scribes and Pharisees (1988:89-90).

But how could Jesus proclaim an ideal of love which even he did not fully practice? Segundo answers that the ideal envisioned what negentropy might eventually accomplish, yet it did not take time and its entropic limitations into account. Jesus' practice, however, was affected by what he could accomplish given entropy and limited time (pp. 90-91). This, however, rather than lessening his impact, made him a privileged moment when "evolution bends back on itself to become conscious." Even more, it makes Jesus "the central point of meaning for the universal process." Why? Because by combining negentropy and entropy in his vision and practice, Jesus' "life and message preserved the supreme evolutionary quality: flexibility" (p. 93).

What shall we make of Segundo's overall approach? It shows that when humanizing pedagogy becomes theology's main theme, it can (though, I would add, it need not) eliminate all biblical and other norms which might shape and limit theological construction. Teaching of truth is handed over to a historical process tending toward human liberation. Much as those experiencing conscientization will apparently know, from the nature of that process, how to construct just societies, those engaged in deutero-learning will discern how to select among biblical themes to construct appropriate ideologies. God is found within, and apparently closely identified with, this immanent process. Ideologies can be taken from many sources. Evolution's becoming-conscious-of-itself can become the backdrop for historical liberation. Yet combined with a Freudian motif, which finds conflict inevitable, human imperfection and violence can be attributed even to Jesus and legitimated in contemporary struggles.

Summary

In theological discourse about social alienation, not quite as much debate is directly focused on capitalism as in public discourse. Of course, Novak strenuously defends capitalism, whereas Latin American theologians decry dependency. Yet theologians are concerned not so much with economic questions as with the spiritual and psychological ways in which social structures affect people (and are thereby perpetuated) and with religious alternatives to their alienating effects.

For conflictive social theologies, social alienation results chiefly from the drive for inordinate power endemic to all political organizations and rooted in individuals too. Niebuhr claims that at deep psychological levels individuals fool themselves about the purity of their motives, and all states pretend to be more righteous than they are. The more a political organization glorifies itself and the more utopian the ideals it seeks to enforce, the more despotic might it become. Therefore conflictive social theologians tend to suspect lofty social visions. Yet these theologians also seek to safeguard something positive about human individuals: their capacity for relationship with an eternal God.

The main means for denying inordinate power to social institutions is not laissez-faire (as it is for libertarians) but limiting their power drives by balancing them against each other. The religious relationship also involves accepting limits—for instance, acknowledging our sin and accepting Christ's atoning work. Conflictive social theologians stress the importance of religion and the individual by ascribing greater value to the spiritual, eternal and individual realms than to the material, historical and social spheres. Yet in seeking to safeguard individuals and be realistic about social imperfection, do conflictive theologians remove the religious realm too far from history and society? Further, are they able to accept the injustices of a society where power-blocs clash because they represent the privileged classes, which are shielded from many of their negative effects?

For holistic social theologians, social alienation is perpetuated when dualisms based on male-female polarity (Ruether) or capitalistic economic oppression (liberation theologies) are deeply internalized. Yet I find no suggestion that these internalizations are further complicated by inner anxiety, pride or self-deception, such as Niebuhr would stress. Once these internalizations are recognized and renounced, our deeper authentic selves (Ruether) or innate humanizing tendency (Freire) can begin to flow forth. New social structures will emerge organismically. We do not find warnings, as we would among conflictivists, that any new state will also be flawed—though Ruether's denial of ideal eschatological resolution seems to acknowledge continuing imperfection.

Individual and social hope are understood historically, as concerning improved life in this world. Visions of better futures help people strive toward this. Little is said about spiritual or eternal reality or individual relationship with God. The humanization process itself can become theology's content, unaffected by scriptural or ethical norms or limits.

I affirmed that conflictive theologians, in emphasizing divine transcendence and the limitations that it, as well as sin, imposes on human life, may underemphasize God's activity in history and society. But I also wonder whether holistic theologians, in emphasizing God's activity in history and society, may underestimate sin and the limits that it and God impose on human life. Further, I have wondered whether our conflictive theologians, who represent privileged classes, may not take society's current imperfections seriously enough. But I also wonder whether our holists, who represent oppressed classes, may not focus so intensely on present injustices that they cannot adequately reckon with potential flaws in any alternative they might create.

Are the contrasts between these positions determined solely by their proponents' social location? Or can a generally satisfactory theology of society be devised that seriously considers their conflicting claims? I will attempt the task of devising a theology of society in chapter eleven.

PART THREE

A Constructive
Trinitarian Response

*T*his book's basic purpose is to make a positive Christian contribution to today's public conversation about issues of alienation. Part one identified some major issues raised in public discourse regarding psychological, ecological and social alienation. I sought to describe them as they emerge in public discourse apart from theological perspectives or comments. Part two examined ways in which current theological discourse is treating the same general themes. I showed that some new topics are being raised and that others prominent in public discourse are receiving relatively little attention. In part three I will develop my own constructive perspective on the major issues raised in both previous parts.

From the outset I rejected the notion that such Christian discourse must be validated by some general standard of rationality before it could be heard in public conversation (see introduction). No one rational standard can be identified and agreed upon today. Instead, arguments from many perspectives circulate in public conversation, including some distinctly religious ones. Contributions from Christian discourse influence millions in our culture.

But whereas I deny that Christian discourse must conform to one rational standard to be heard, I also reject the opposite mandate: that the

Christian outlook must simply be proclaimed in all its uniqueness and strangeness to the general public without regard for possible points of contact. I object to this orientation, first, because Christianity has always claimed that many of its foundational events occurred in the public arena—in the daily world of the first-century Roman Empire and for centuries before that among ancient Near Eastern nations. Since these events were public, connections can be drawn among them and other events and concerns of public life.

I have affirmed, further, that a Christian perspective, even if it cannot be proven true by one accepted rational standard (as can no other religion, worldview or social philosophy), can be shown to be plausible by articulating its internal consistency and by showing that it makes sense out of and contributes to some important issues in public conversation (see introduction).

In part three I will seek to make my Christian theology's inner consistency clear by outlining its orientation toward psychological, ecological and social issues. Then by providing my response to the issues raised in parts one and two, I hope to make significant contributions to public conversation (and further demonstrate the inner consistency of my perspective).

I understand Christianity to be based not on general reasoning or experience concerning the cosmos or human existence but chiefly on biblical claims concerning the life, death and resurrection of Jesus of Nazareth. These unusual claims account for Christianity's most distinctive features in relation to other religions and worldviews. To make Christianity's character clear, I believe, this Christocentric orientation must be kept in view. Yet since the events on which claims about Jesus are based occurred in the public realm, Christian theology will have difficulty dialoguing with public discourse if the nature of these events is widely disputed. Yet it is disputed today.

A "third quest for the historical Jesus" has begun. The claims of its most radical practitioners, often known as the "Jesus Seminar," have entered public conversation. This Seminar maintains that the real Jesus was very unlike the divine-human one who died and rose for the world's salvation, as Christians have traditionally believed.

Accordingly I need to begin my theological response by indicating, through discussion with the Jesus Seminar, what kind of a Jesus can serve as a foundation for my own theology. Such considerations, which will occupy the bulk of chapter eight, will clarify my positive understanding of Jesus and the general theological role I believe he can play. In a broad sense my theology will be trinitarian. Yet I will maintain that appropriate trinitarian claims, like all else, are based not on philosophic or scientific considerations but on Jesus' history.

Chapter nine will develop my theological anthropology and my response to the issues of psychological alienation raised in chapters two and five. Chapter ten will expand my trinitarian reflections and outline a theology of creation, helping me to articulate my perspective on the problems of ecological alienation raised in chapters three and six. Chapter eleven will sketch a theology of society and my perspective on the social alienation issues raised in chapters four and seven.

EIGHT

Theology: Christological & Trinitarian Foundations

*C*hristian theology, in my understanding, is based chiefly on what is most distinctive about it: the biblical claims made about Jesus of Nazareth, rooted in his life, death and resurrection. To articulate these claims, however, and to support them plausibly in public conversation, I must enter into dialogue with the widely publicized claims centering around today's "Jesus Seminar." This Seminar maintains that many affirmations about Jesus which Christians have traditionally believed have no foundation in his historical existence.

To prepare for this dialogue, it will be helpful to summarize, in the first part of this chapter, what the authors who are covered in part two of this book say about Jesus and his role in theology. Then I will examine the Jesus Seminar's methodology and major claims. Finally I will develop my own understanding of Jesus and some basic considerations regarding the Trinity. The major purpose of this chapter is to provide a basis for the theological understandings of the self, the environment and society which I will develop in chapters nine through eleven.

Roles of Jesus: Review
Most theologies and spiritualities covered in part two of this book operate

much as has "public theology" in the usual sense—that is, they seek to ground their central claims in some kind of knowledge generally accepted in the public world and not in distinctive Christian affirmations. However, since they all are Christian theologies or spiritualities, they all refer to Jesus in some way. To gain a grasp of what is involved in making Jesus normative for theology, let me review how our authors have grounded their approaches and what they have said about Jesus.

Bio-spirituality's chief concepts are taken from psychologist Eugene Gendlin. Its connecting of increasing body-awareness with a cosmic process conforms to familiar accounts of the evolutionary expansion of consciousness proposed by people such as Pierre Teilhard de Chardin. John Welch bases his theory of spiritual development almost entirely on the psychology of C. G. Jung.

Process theology is grounded in a rational philosophy (chiefly that of A. N. Whitehead) extrapolated largely from contemporary science. Rosemary Ruether seeks to derive her ecological norms from science and builds the rest of her theology largely on a feminist base. Michael Novak's theological points all seem consistent with capitalism. Reinhold Niebuhr's chief anthropological affirmations, he claims, can be confirmed by common human experience, whereas his social theology is rooted in "realistic" principles such as balance of power, justice and mutual love. For Juan Segundo, the historical movement of conscientization and liberation provides the chief norm.

When we consider Jesus more specifically, some of our theologies seem to interpret him as an illustration, or archetype, of a general principle which can be known apart from him. Bio-spirituality can cite some Scripture and speak of a Word wanting to become flesh among us, but here the written and living Words are adapted, without discussion, to signify consciousness's cosmic process. For Welch, Jesus provides the model for human development but almost wholly in the way that Jung's Christ-archetype symbolizes Jungian individuation.[1] Segundo selects the "ideologies" of evolution-becoming-self-conscious and a Freudian motif which he interprets as legitimating violence to express who Jesus is. Novak interprets certain theological principles connected with Jesus (incarnation, competition, separation of realms) in a way that facilitates capitalist appropriation. Ruether regards Jesus as an instantiation of the prophetic principle and as a partial expression of human fullness, though—as embodying a life free from desire for domination—in a rather radical, countercultural way.

When we turn to other theologies, however, Jesus appears to add something unique to them. In process theology, Jesus can embody the

Whiteheadian principle of creative transformation (Cobb). Yet the love expressed through him provides the chief reason for regarding the consciousness at the heart of an evolutionary cosmos, otherwise dark with suffering, as loving (Jay McDaniel).

Sallie McFague's remarks are difficult to synthesize. On one hand, she affirms that Christian theology should be grounded not on scientific views of creation but in experiences of salvation.[2] Jesus' destabilizing, inclusive, nonhierarchical vision plays a normative role in describing what salvation is. Yet on the other hand, this norm is derived as much from current social concerns as it is from Jesus. McFague says that Jesus is not qualitatively different from any other religious founder. Yet she also affirms that Jesus' self-sacrificing love for the least of creatures goes beyond anything evolutionary science can affirm. To some extent, Jesus, especially in his self-giving, seems to provide McFague's theology with a unique norm.

For Niebuhr, Jesus' self-sacrifice also makes him "the perfect norm of human nature" (1943:69), even though this norm cannot be followed in most public life. Especially through his cross, he establishes a unique redemptive relationship with God.

Finally, for some of our spiritual writers Jesus also has unique functions. For William McNamara, Jesus' death cry and resurrection are the source of all hope for overcoming suffering and fully relating to God. Jesus' lifestyle also calls us to challenge our commercial, individualistic civilization. For Alan Jones, Jesus not only exemplifies the spiritual journey toward God but is also the unique God reaching out in faithfulness toward us on our journeys.[3]

Jesus' theological function(s) appear more complex when we consider how our theologians handle scriptural material about him. Segundo claims that a historical reading of the Gospels discovers a Jesus mostly interested in interpersonal relationships, one who comes out socially conservative. Ruether, however, finds Jesus promoting a socially radical kind of servanthood. She also asserts that titles affirming his eschatological and supernatural character ("Son of Man") and his kingship ("Messiah") do not really come from him. Cobb affirms that stories of Jesus' wilderness temptation, struggle in Gethsemane and forsakenness on the cross are not reliable, though his call to God's kingdom is. McDaniel believes that Jesus did not manifest love or follow God's will as consistently as New Testament writers said he did. Finally, McFague, despite her emphasis on Jesus' destabilizing vision, is not interested in ascertaining its historical basis and finds New Testament texts so corrupted by ideologies of power that any such retrieval would be impossible. Yet she finds Jesus' vision communicated primarily through his parables, healings and common meals.

What impressions does this brief review yield of Jesus' role in contemporary theology? At first glance it might seem that he has no important function, for most theologians appear able to establish their basic principles without reference to him. At second glance, however, we begin wondering if some of the most basic emphases of certain theologians might be rooted in Jesus' unique features. Yet when we ask how anything about Jesus might be derived from our primary historical source, the New Testament, conflicting assessments and significant skepticism abound. Is it possible to possess reliable knowledge about Jesus? If so, can we conclude from it anything significant about current life's complexities? I can best answer through dialogue with a movement which, in an attempt to be current, pictures Jesus quite differently than traditional theology and spirituality have.

The "Jesus Seminar" on the Historical Jesus

Periodically New Testament scholars have asked what can be known about Jesus of Nazareth using the strictest historical methods of their day. The "first quest for the historical Jesus" covered much of the nineteenth century. It depicted Jesus as a prophet and ethical teacher, much like the theological liberalism of its time. This quest collapsed under arguments by Albert Schweitzer ([1906] 1968), Johannes Weiss ([1892] 1968) and others that Jesus was an apocalyptic fanatic little interested in ethics or history. A "second quest" stretching from the late 1940s to the early 1970s developed further an essentially apocalyptic portrait of Jesus.[4]

Then, beginning approximately 1980, scholars once again began seriously inquiring into what could be known about Jesus historically.[5] The "Jesus Seminar," a group of about seventy-five scholars who started meeting semiannually in the late 1980s, has produced the most radical results.[6] Since their conclusions have entered general public conversation, a theology which takes this arena seriously must dialogue with them.

Methodology. For many of the Seminar's proponents, the "first pillar" of their quest consists in sharply separating Jesus of Nazareth from classical theological affirmations about him. "The Christ of creed and dogma," it is claimed, "can no longer command the assent of those who have seen the heavens through Galileo's telescope" (Funk and Hoover 1993:2; compare Borg 1987:2-4).

The Jesus Seminar's major publication is dedicated to Galileo, Thomas Jefferson and David F. Strauss. In so doing, the Seminar self-consciously extends the Enlightenment project which proclaimed classical Christology incompatible with modern science and especially with its approach to historical truth. For these questers, such a Christology (by ascribing titles such as Son of God, Messiah and apocalyptic Son of Man to Jesus) had heavily infiltrated Mark's Gospel, composed, according to most scholars, by the late 60s C.E. (Meeks 1993).[7] The Gospels themselves, therefore, are thought to be so "embellished by mythic elements that express the church's faith in him" that "the burden of proof" falls on any claim that authentic historic elements are found there (Funk and Hoover 1993:5).

Even more so than in the first and second quests, the locus of the third has shifted toward secular universities and has been less connected with church concerns. In this setting, models from the history of religions, cultural anthropology and social sciences are often employed. Though Seminar participants claim that radical historical skepticism results if we focus on Jesus' words, they find that when he is interpreted in terms of crosscultural typologies (such as the sage, or teacher of wisdom) a plausible historical figure emerges. John Dominic Crossan frequently affirms that such studies, even those dealing with times and places far distant from first-century Palestine, provide "trans-temporal as well as trans-cultural" categories for interpreting Jesus (1991:73; compare pp. 104, 105, 127, 159, 210, 214, 264, 315, 319, 336, 341, 360, 384 and so on).

Much of the Jesus Seminar's work on the Gospels, however, consists in analyzing them into smaller and smaller basic units. This method must be employed, it is maintained, because the earliest recollections of Jesus were transmitted orally by functionally illiterate people. In such situations, it is claimed, some of Jesus' sayings would be remembered, but the contexts in which he uttered them would usually be forgotten. Moreover, only short, provocative, memorable sayings would be recalled and then be reworded through transmission. The critical task, then, consists essentially in digging beneath the larger, later narratives, discourses and theological affirmations which make up the Gospels to unearth brief aphorisms and parables that likely come from Jesus. In pursuing this task, the Seminar proposes that we have access to two fairly extensive documents predating Mark (fragments of several others also remain).

The existence of the first, "Q," is hypothetical; it would contain the material common to Matthew and Luke which is not found in Mark. Further speculative analysis has divided Q into an earlier sapiential layer, a second apocalyptic layer and a final introductory one (Kloppenborg 1987).

The second document, the Gospel of Thomas, was found in 1945, and contains numerous short sayings of Jesus minus any birth story, passion account or significant narrative connections. Some scholars further divide Thomas into two layers. While earlier consensus dated Thomas after the

four canonical Gospels (Grant and Freedman 1960), the Seminar proposes that the bulk of it was written by the 50s C.E. (Crossan 1991:427-28).[8]
About one-third of Thomas's sayings have parallels with the other Gospels,
and another one-third are gnostic.

In estimating whether a saying comes from Jesus, both the number of
independent sources attesting it and the historical strata where they are
found often carry great weight. Crossan, whose method is most rigorous of
all, finds 522 items (sayings, stories and so on) coming from 52 literary
sources prior to 150 C.E. which purport to tell of Jesus. However, he will
consider as possibly historical only those having more than one attestation.
Three hundred forty-two of the 522 items, or about two-thirds, fail this test.
Further, Crossan deals only with those which come from his first historical
stratum (30-60 C.E.), reducing the remaining 180 plurally attested com-
plexes to 131. (He acknowledges, however, that no absolute reason exists
why a singly attested item or one from a later stratum could not be historical.) Since both Q and Thomas are postulated in the first stratum (but
none of the Gospels is) a saying's appearance in both is counted as strong
evidence for historicity.

The Jesus Seminar thus supposes that the true reality of complex phenomena (the Gospels) can be found by analyzing them into their smallest
possible components (sayings) and distinguishing these from the links
(narratives, discourses, theological affirmations) which tie them together.
It proposes that truth found is greater the more closely that particular
statements mirror some original historical fact or saying. Earlier chapters
of this book, however, have repeatedly shown how this method of finding
truth by analyzing a complex whole into its parts characterized the mechanistic Newtonian paradigm.

Yet this paradigm's critics claim that the more organic, connective features of a whole also belong to its essential reality. As we proceed, then, we
will need to ask whether the Gospels' connective features (their narratives,
discourses and theological affirmations) might belong more directly to
their essential historical reality. For though the Jesus Seminar's privileging
of short, isolated sayings purportedly arises from considerations of oral
transmission, I shall have to ask how much it also stems from a preference
for isolating small, analytic, basic units. I suspect that this predilection
plays a strong role in the emphasis on Q, the early dating of Thomas and
the division of both into layers.

If short sayings are about all that come from Jesus, the narrative contexts
in which they appear must have been mostly created by the Gospel writers.
Further, Jesus' discourses themselves, which appear in these contexts, must

have been composed by the evangelists out of numerous briefer sayings. Seminar participants, then, analyze these discourses into many units judged to emanate from different sources and to carry diverging degrees of historical authenticity. (For an example of such analysis, see note 9.)

Not only are most historical episodes thought to have been created by later writers but also many links among them—that is, most of the Gospels' narrative structures themselves, as Cobb intimates. Crossan, who is most radical, thinks that of all the events reported in the passion narratives, Jesus' followers only knew that he was crucified. Apart from this fact, these narratives, including the events and persons they contain (Peter's denial, trial before Pilate and so on), were imaginatively composed from quotations from the Hebrew Scriptures interwoven with conjectures as to what might have occurred (1991:354-94).[10]

Many Seminar members regard most stories of conflict, whether among the disciples or between Jesus and opponents, as reflecting later struggles within and without the early church.[11] Many also think that Jesus had no distinct consciousness of mission, so stories of his calling and training disciples are later fictions. Quotations from the Hebrew Scriptures attributed to Jesus are often supposed to reflect the church's search for legitimacy,[12] and references by Jesus to the cross are usually thought to reflect a standpoint subsequent to this event.

Furthermore, sayings which sound like contemporary Jewish or general folk wisdom are usually subtracted from Jesus' repertoire, along with all affirmations characteristic of the early church, especially (as I previously stressed) those regarding his person or saving work. The product of this *criterion of dissimilarity* (which accepts only what is dissimilar from Jesus' environment as being from him) is an exceedingly idiosyncratic Jesus, having little or nothing in common with either current Judaism or the early church, and about whose actual history almost nothing was recalled. Later writers are supposed to have frequently revised, edited, interpreted and added a great deal to all that remains of him: a rather modest inventory of brief, memorable remarks.

Nonetheless, Seminar members insist that when all these subtractions have been performed the *distinctive language of Jesus* emerges. Like McFague, they stress that his aphorisms and parables cut against the contemporary religious and social grain. They surprise and shock, for they call for reversal of roles or frustrate ordinary expectations. They are characterized by exaggeration, humor, paradox and concrete, vivid images (Funk and Hoover 1993:31-32). They are given without interpretation, to invite hearers to think for themselves. Jesus, it is held, seldom initiated dialogue or cures; and since he counseled humility, he could have made no claims about himself (p. 33).

The criteria of shock, surprise and countering the religious/social grain have proven "exceptionally durable" (p. 31) and have often overridden the emphasis on multiple attestation. These characteristics, for instance, are found preeminently in the parables of the Good Samaritan (Lk 10:30-35), the Prodigal Son (Lk 15:11-23), the Unjust Steward (Lk 16:1-8) and the Vineyard Laborers (Mt 20:1-15), although each is found in only one source (Matthew's special material or Luke's). Despite this, the Jesus Seminar grants all these a "red" rating (for sayings it deems authentic).[13]

Jesus as sage. The Jesus Seminar seeks, on one hand, to be rigorously scientific by basing its Jesus-portrait on historically reliable atoms of information (chiefly sayings). Yet I have noted that it fills in this portrait by assuming that Jesus fits typologies of religious leaders furnished by cross-cultural studies. This "fit" cannot be measured by criteria as precise as those for sayings. Nonetheless most Seminar participants find that Jesus well fits the type of sage, or wisdom teacher. It is possible that this characterization as sage plays a greater role than the crucial parables just mentioned in deciding what composes the general portrait and the distinctive language of Jesus.

Marcus Borg stresses that Jesus was keenly aware of Spirit, by which he means a nonmaterial, numinous realm charged with energy and power. This realm, which has been experienced across cultures in what Huston Smith calls the *primordial tradition,* conflicts with the modern mechanistic worldview (1994b:127-31). Borg acknowledges that this tradition had to be overthrown at the Enlightenment for the modern world to begin (1987:26).[14] Yet he claims that the Spirit realm is still known, chiefly in individual experience, and that Jesus' main significance for today consists in making it real again.

When Jesus is interpreted through this typology, as bearer of a universal primordial tradition, his uniqueness in the sense of being the only savior is undermined (1994a:37). For although Borg finds that religions differ in their cultural components, he regards the experiences behind them as universal (p. 43 note 29).[15] And culture, he claims, is an obscuring net that people cast over a more basic "is-ness" of reality (pp. 68, 77).

Jesus' teaching, rooted in his experience of Spirit, purportedly appealed to neither tradition nor authority (since references to the Hebrew Scriptures are subtracted from what Jesus really said) but to his hearers' own experience (1984:237). Jesus appealed to their imaginations, inviting them to see reality in a new way—to see God not as "out there" but as the heart of a reality in love with us—as both immanent and yet transcendent (not identical with the sum total of things [1987:115, 28]). Crossan adds that Jesus' kingdom "is, was, and always will be available to any who want it" (1991:xii), which is the unifying theology of the Gospel of Thomas (pp. 267, 295-302). "Jesus' serene assertion of open and unmediated access to God" was derived not from "hidden mysteries of past or present but from watching nature's rhythms of here and now" (pp. 350, 295; compare Borg 1987:101).

Evidence for such affirmations is found largely in Jesus' statements about God's sending rain on just and unjust alike and caring for lilies of the field and birds of the air (Mt 5:45-46; 6:25-30; 10:29-31). All three are rated pink (deemed as probably authentic sayings) by the Jesus Seminar. They indeed indicate Jesus' deep sensitivity to nature, as some ecological theologians stress. But notice also the strongly panentheistic flavor of the awareness attributed to Jesus, who is supposed to have experienced God directly in the organismic rhythms of the present, rather than in the past or future.

According to Crossan, Jesus proclaimed a "brokerless Kingdom," where God could be experienced without mediation of religious authorities (1991:422-24).[16] As proclaimer of such a kingdom, Jesus could hardly regard himself as the necessary mediator between humanity and God. According to Borg, Jesus' chief emphasis was on God's compassion or mercy, as stated in Luke 6:36, though the Jesus Seminar ranked this verse only as gray (as resembling something Jesus likely said). Borg further stresses that the word for "merciful" *(oiktirmōn)*, though it occurs only here in the Gospels, translates a Hebrew word derived from "womb." He concludes, and Matthew Fox concurs, that God's mercy is womblike, nourishing and embracing (1984:133-34; 1987:102; 1994a:47-48; see Fox 1988:31-33).

Borg notes that the "heart" forms the center of the person in Scripture and claims that Jesus' wisdom teaching stressed dying to self at this level. Jesus' emphasis is well expressed in the challenge to deny ourselves, take up our cross, and follow him (Mk 8:34 and parallels). Yet although this passage is triply attested (Q, Thomas and Mark), the Jesus Seminar denies it to Jesus since it involves church language (about the cross, Funk and Hoover 1993:78-79). Borg apparently skirts this issue, claiming that the text refers to an internal process of dying to self and the world known to mystics in many cultures (1987:112, esp. note 65; compare 1984:242-43).[17] It can be paraphrased in general religious terms as dying to the finite and centering ourselves in the infinite (1984:246; 1987:111).

A nonapocalyptic Jesus. A sage who imparts wisdom about the everyday world would seem to differ significantly from an apocalyptic seer who announces that world's end altogether. Not surprisingly, when scholars, as in the second quest, emphasize Jesus' apocalyptic role, they reduce his teaching to an *interim ethic,* valid only for a brief interval before the End. Correspondingly the Jesus Seminar in stressing Jesus as sage has often denied him any apocalyptic function.

The second quest portrayed Jesus apocalyptically for perhaps three main reasons. First, Jesus apparently identified himself with the "Son of Man," a supernatural figure who would descend with the clouds to judge all nations. Second, Jesus often proclaimed the coming of God's kingdom with great urgency. And, third, scholars assumed that when the Judge or the kingdom arrived the space-time world would literally end.

Seminar members note that "Son of Man" as used in first-century Aramaic (Jesus' daily language) could simply mean "a human being." Yet the Gospels often apply this phrase to the apocalyptic judge figure. No clear evidence exists, however, that such a figure was known in Judaism at Jesus' time (Borg 1984:223-25).[18] Affirming that Jesus' hearers would have found apocalyptic connotations of "Son of Man" unintelligible and that the phrase's two meanings are very different, most Seminar participants conclude that when Jesus used it he simply meant "a human being." Only when the early church came to believe that Jesus had been raised into heaven, from whence he would shortly return, did it begin designating him "Son of Man" in an apocalyptic sense. Then, as Ruether affirms, it read affirmations about this figure back into Jesus' historical sayings (Perrin 1974:57-60; Borg 1994b:58).

Once the apocalyptic "Son of Man" sayings are subtracted from the historical Jesus, it can be seen that although he spoke with great urgency about the coming of God's kingdom, he did not expect it to arrive as a wholly transcendent reality which would abolish space and time. Indeed, scholars have increasingly acknowledged that though Jews in Jesus' time expected God to intervene in historical events, they supposed that the resulting order would be earthly, with much the same general features as the present (1994b:70-71). Indeed, most second-quest scholars did not strictly identify the kingdom's arrival with the world's end. They argued that Jesus saw God's kingdom as at least partially present, already affecting current spatio-temporal realities.

Yet whereas most second questers discerned some paradoxical, already-not-yet tension in Jesus' kingdom message, many Seminar members focus exclusively on its present character. The Jesus Seminar, in fact, designates all sayings about a present kingdom pink and all depicting it as future black (not an authentic saying). Jesus, it affirms, found God so real "that he could not distinguish God's present activity from any future activity. He had a poetic sense of time in which the future and the present merged" (Funk and Hoover 1993:137).

According to Borg the kingdom of God is "a symbol for the presence and power of God known in mystical experience." To enter it is to enter "the realm outside of time and history" (1984:254). However, Jesus' sense of God's presence "was almost lost on his followers," and an expectation of a future kingdom different from the present worked itself into the Gospels' composition (Funk and Hoover 1993:137).

To what extent are these affirmations about Jesus' time-consciousness derived from crosscultural notions about sages? They blend well claims that the kingdom of Jesus the sage "is, was, and always will be available to any who want it" and that his message emphasized neither historical events nor authoritative teaching but emerged "from watching nature's rhythms of here and now" (Crossan 1991:xii, 295).

A political Jesus. Though the Jesus Seminar virtually erases the eschatological and transhistorical dimensions of the Gospels' Jesus, it underlines his political features in bold relief. By "political," however, its proponents mean not formal governmental processes (for Jesus was clearly not involved in these) but the general realm of corporate human life.

Marcus Borg sketches a clear picture of how Jesus' message affected this arena. In Jesus' time, the tiny Jewish nation was in danger of being swallowed, socially and culturally, by far larger Gentile forces. To avoid this, many Jews decided to emphasize their own distinctiveness by pursuing an ideal, or "politics," of holiness. Holiness was especially defined by their law, which, as they understood it, involved numerous food regulations and tithes.

Socioeconomic studies have shown, however, that Judean peasants were heavily oppressed by the Roman agricultural system. Roman taxes devoured 15-20 percent of their produce. Yet Torah taxes required 20 percent more (Borg 1984:32-33, 59). Clearly many peasants could avoid destitution only by withholding much or all of the latter and forgoing expenses necessary to follow many food regulations. Jewish laws were enforceable only by social ostracism, meaning that many of the poor were socially rejected by those with the greatest passion for nation and law. Consequently, the latters' policy divided not only Jews from Gentiles, but many Jews from each other. Borg argues that the common wisdom of all societies involves setting similar social boundaries and deciding what—and therefore who—is right or wrong by such codes (1987:133).

In such a context, Jesus' acceptance of a wide variety of social outcasts appeared to those who were pursuing holiness to threaten national survival (1984:236). Jesus' attitude is largely inferred from parables such as the Good Samaritan, the Prodigal Son, the Vineyard Laborers and the Unforgiving Slave (although these, as previously mentioned, are only singly attested).

Very central was Jesus' practice of what Crossan calls *open commensality.* Crossan argues that Jesus and his disciples, in return for healings and exorcisms, normally received meals from peasants where everyone—outcasts, women, children—was included (1991:261-64, 303-53; Borg 1984:79-86; 1987:101-2). This open commensality was Jesus' foremost "strategy for building or rebuilding peasant community on radically different principles from those of honor and shame, patronage and clientage. It was based on an egalitarian sharing of spiritual and material power at the most grassroots level" (Crossan 1991:344). It not only cut across the grain of current Jewish society, which was largely divided by food regulations, but also sharply challenges fundamental divisions in all societies, as McFague and Ruether affirm (p. 263). Crossan, who depicts Jesus discerning God in nature's present organismic rhythms, is idealistic about peasant society as such, regarding it as inherently egalitarian and possessing strong utopian vision (pp. 263-64).

Crossan and Borg thus argue that Jesus sought to form a radically inclusive community contravening conventional ethical standards as to what, and who, is right and wrong. Jesus' ethics contradicted the common wisdom of all societies, which is based on rewards and punishments, and regards God basically as Judge (Borg 1994a:76-77). This is another reason Seminar members generally regard sayings about apocalyptic judgment, reward and punishment as unauthentic. They seem to clash with Jesus' open, accepting attitude. Seminar participants even regard calls to repentance as part of the apocalyptic mentality and inconsistent with God's forgiveness and eliminate them from Jesus' message (Funk and Hoover 1993:41).

Borg stresses that another dimension of Jesus' message—about turning the other cheek, surrendering one's shirt and loving enemies—carried significant political implications. The Jesus Seminar rates each of these exhortations red, as the statements first, second and fifth most likely (respectively) to come from Jesus, even though found only in Q. Borg argues that in a country under Roman occupation their meaning would have been obvious. Jesus was telling Jews not to join the resistance fighters (another form of the politics of holiness) but to exercise an overall social attitude, a politics of mercy or compassion, even toward their conquerors (1984:130-33; 1987:137-40). Borg and Crossan both show how some nonviolent Jewish protests against the Romans in the century preceding Jesus had been successful (Borg 1984:48; Crossan 1991:128-35). Crossan regards them mostly as spontaneous peasant actions.

Borg affirms that the experience of God's compassion which made Jesus a sage also led him to set a politics of compassion against a politics of holiness on the corporate level. As a true prophet, Jesus warned that the Romans would subjugate his people entirely and destroy their temple—the heart of their social, economic and religious life—if they kept following the politics of holiness path. By chasing out the money changers, he performed a symbolic prophetic act, not against the temple as such but against the way it was being used (Borg 1987:174-76; Funk and Hoover 1993:97-98; Crossan 1991:357, 359). So whereas Jesus was not an apocalyptic seer, he prophesied a genuine historical judgment, which he sometimes embellished with apocalyptic imagery.

When many Seminar members call Jesus political, they mean, in agreement with McFague and Ruether and in disagreement with Segundo, that he taught and lived out a radical social vision. This vision, however, was not "realistic" in the usual—Niebuhrian—sense, and Jesus was not involved in normal political processes. Yet Seminar members find that Jesus spoke seriously about an alternative way of communal life.

Trinitarian considerations. I am discussing the Jesus Seminar because it has entered public conversation recently but, above all, because dialogue with it will help me present my own approach to Christian theology. My approach, I have said, is basically trinitarian, but it is a trinitarianism whose roots must be found in Jesus' life, death and resurrection. Consequently our reading of these events is crucial. Having shown how the Jesus Seminar considers them, I am ready to explore what it might say about Jesus' relation to his Father and the Holy Spirit.

1. *Jesus and the Spirit.* The Jesus Seminar is congenial to the notion that Jesus mediates a realm of Spirit. For Borg this was Jesus' chief function. Borg does differentiate Jesus' "experiential" relationship to Spirit from a "doctrinal or trinitarian" one, but he does not explain further (1994b:27). The Gospels portray the Spirit's power as especially evident in exorcisms—the expulsion of evil *spirits.* For Borg, Jesus did this by "the Spirit of God" (1987:65). The Jesus Seminar affirms that "Jesus probably did exorcise what were thought to be demons" (Funk and Hoover 1993:52), and

Crossan takes seriously the central exorcism episode, the Beelzebul incident, which I will examine shortly (1991:318).

The impression that the Spirit was continuously active in Jesus' ministry comes largely from the Gospels' narrative framework, especially from Jesus' baptism (Mt 3:16 par. Mk 1:10 par. Lk 3:22), temptation (Mt 4:1 par. Mk 1:12 par. Lk 4:1) and return into Galilee (Lk 4:14, 18). Whereas the Jesus Seminar is dubious about this framework, Borg affirms that Jesus experienced a prophetic call at his baptism (1984:198), where he was called God's beloved son, though not in the unique sense that the church later believed (1987:41).[19] Borg finds some validity in the stories of Jesus' temptation (pp. 42-43) and return in the Spirit's power into Galilee (p. 66). He generally affirms that Jesus' "ministry began with an intense experience of the Spirit of God" (p. 42).

One group of Gospel sayings occurs at a crucial later point in this narrative framework. Jesus is accused of casting out demons by "Beelzebul, the ruler of demons." Jesus first replies that any power divided against itself will fall (Mt 12:25-26 par. Mk 3:23-25 par. Lk 11:17-18). The Jesus Seminar rates this saying pink in Luke and nearly pink in Matthew and Mark (Funk and Hoover 1993:330, 186, 52). Next, underlining what is involved in his entire exorcism ministry, Jesus affirms that "if it is by the Spirit of God that I cast out demons, then the kingdom of God has come to you." This Q saying (Mt 12:27-28) and its parallel (Lk 11:19-20) are again rated pink. So is the following remark about binding a strong man (Mt 12:29 par. Mk 3:27 par. Lk 11:21-22), which comes from Q, Thomas and Mark. But then a final saying about blasphemy against the Holy Spirit (Mt 12:31-32 par. Mk 3:28-29 par. Lk 12:10) is rated black, even though it also is triply attested by Q, Thomas and Mark.

Of interest in the Seminar's evaluation is, first, its rating this complex, which highlights the significance of Jesus' exorcisms through the Spirit, as quite authentic. Second, however, I note that it nonetheless regards the last saying, which again mentions the Spirit (and the "Son of Man" in Mt 12:32 and Lk 12:10) as unauthentic. Why? A chief reason is that the Gospel of Thomas, although generally supposed to be quite early, renders it this way: "Whoever blasphemes against the Father will be forgiven, and whoever blasphemes against the Son will be forgiven, but whoever blasphemes against the Holy Spirit will not be forgiven" (v. 44). Here, clearly, is a trinitarian formula. Yet according to the Jesus Seminar, the Trinity, like other classic church teachings, "did not arise until long after Jesus' death" (Funk and Hoover 1993:187). Much for this reason, this saying, along with its parallels which highlight the Spirit's work, is denied to Jesus' ministry, even though it meets criteria which the Seminar normally esteems very highly.[20]

2. *Jesus and his Father.* As with the Spirit, the impression of Jesus' continuing intimate relation with his Father is conveyed largely through the Gospels' narrative framework. Jesus' baptism, we have seen, includes his affirmation as the beloved Son. Then Satan tempts him to adopt false understandings of this Sonship with the challenge "If you are the Son of God . . ." (Mt 4:3, 6 par. Lk 4:3, 9). Borg finds some credibility not only in these stories but also in Jesus' transfiguration (1987:48-49), where the Father again affirms his Sonship (Mt 17:5 par. Mk 9:7 par. Lk 9:35). Yet the Jesus Seminar routinely regards all occurrences of "Son of God" and most occurrences of "Son" as church creations, leaving few sayings that evidence a Father-Son relation.

A major exception occurs with "Abba," an Aramaic term expressing intimate familiarity (somewhat like "Daddy"). Very few instances of others' employing this address are known. The Jesus Seminar (Funk and Hoover 1993:149), Crossan (1991:294) and Borg (1994a:35-36) concur that its use characterized Jesus. The intimacy and near uniqueness of this indicate something unusual about Jesus' filial relationship. (The Jesus Seminar, however, cannot regard Jesus' intense dialogue with his Father in Gethsemane as authentic, even though Mark depicts him using "Abba" [14:35], mainly on the grounds that no one overheard it and could thus verify it [Funk and Hoover 1993:120].)

Another text affirms this intimate relationship. Jesus exclaims that "no one knows the Son except the Father, and no one knows the Father except the Son" (Mt 11:27 par. Lk 10:22). But even though this verse comes from Q and is affirmed by the Gospel of Thomas, it sounds so like classical Christology that the Seminar designates it black.[21] Matthew follows with Jesus' saying about his easy yoke and light burden (11:28-29). Yet although this is again attested in Thomas, it also echoes the intertestamental wisdom work Ecclesiasticus (51:26-27), and the Seminar regards it as more or less borrowed from there. Thus the Seminar overlooks the possibility that the overall text (Mt 11:25-30) may express a wisdom Christology whose roots Crossan (1991:383) and Borg (1994a:109-110) regard as early, even though it eventually gives expression to some of the most classical christological themes. In this way also the Seminar denies authenticity to anything that could resemble church Christology.

In sum, the Jesus Seminar can regard Jesus as mediator of a Spirit realm, and it acknowledges an unusually close relationship between him and his Father. Yet its rejection of anything that sounds like classical theology leads it to deny the authenticity of several key texts which its principles of attestation would otherwise strongly affirm.

Jesus and the Trinity: Another View

I have affirmed that Christian theological discourse often belongs in public conversation, for it can present unique and fruitful perspectives on
numerous issues which affect many people today. Yet the Jesus Seminar has
also entered this realm, presenting a view of Jesus which, it claims, is based
on scholarly, objective grounds. This Jesus, however, is not characterized
by those transcendent titles which Christians have historically attributed to
him, nor are the accounts of his baptism and wilderness temptation, and
especially of his death and resurrection, regarded as historical. Must
Christian theology, if it is to respect scientific study, adopt a view of Jesus
quite different from the traditional one? Or can it offer reasons, plausible
in the public conversation, why a more classical view of Jesus should be
seriously considered?

An alternative methodology. The Jesus Seminar commences with a sharp
distinction between Jesus' actual history and classical christological confessions about him. It supposes, second, that Jesus' character can be illumined through crosscultural typologies taken from the history of religions,
cultural anthropology and social sciences. Third, it performs minute analy-
ses of the Gospels, dissolving their comprehensive interpretive frameworks
to retrieve discrete historical facts from beneath. Such a research program
is heavily indebted to the Enlightenment.

To orient itself rightly, I also believe, Christian theology must ask and
answer the question: Who was Jesus of Nazareth? Yet I begin with a more
organismic assumption—that no historical figure should be initially separated from that complex of interpretation and meaning through which
that figure has been perceived and has affected others. In Jesus' case, this
field of meaning far surpasses the way the early church experienced him
and extends down to the present. Accordingly I begin with a broad question (yet one which I believe has even set Enlightenment-style Jesus quests
in motion): what accounts for the fact that this man Jesus, and the institutions and social influences traceable to him, have wielded such extraordinary impact on the public world for more than nineteen centuries?

Part of the answer is surely that classical confessions about him—the very
ones which Enlightenment quests begin by rejecting—have been widely
believed. Consequently if we wish to gain an accurate picture of Jesus'
overall historical reality, we cannot initially posit a dogmatic disjunction
between his original historicity and the theological image that has accompanied many of his effects. For that image, or features of it, may reflect his

original reality. In general, we cannot start with the Enlightenment-inspired assumption (as our ecological theologians have; see chapter six) that most past tradition is distortive and incorrect.

This is hardly to advocate a general gullible reverence for traditional views. Many traditions and many claims within traditions have certainly been distortive, oppressive and false. I also will need to discern and reject unjustified claims about Jesus, for I also am accepting the validity of, and pursuing, a fundamental Enlightenment question: what really happened in history?[22] But I am also asking critically, what are the best framework and method for determining the answers?

Consequently I question the Jesus Seminar's "first pillar": its sharp disjunction between what was true of Jesus historically and what christological concepts affirm. This assumption leaves a major historical question without a convincing answer: if Jesus was entirely unlike what these concepts portray, how could they have possibly arisen, many within a generation? Is it plausible to assume that so rich, unique and influential a blend of perspectives emerged, rather haphazardly, from numerous discordant, anonymous and largely oral processes (though some might be traced to a single author, such as Mark)? Or are we more likely to discern historical truth by leaving open the possibility that the roots of at least some might be traced to a unique and creative person—the Jesus to whom these later figures refer as their source? I see no reason why it should be intrinsically more convincing to make anonymous sources or even specific authors the later Christology's origin.

Moreover, if these concepts are wholly unlike Jesus, why were they ever attributed to him in the first place? And if the early church put many of its own views in Jesus' mouth, why was this done so very seldom by the author from which we have the largest corpus—Paul? Further, if the early church invoked and mostly fabricated a Jesus-history to help handle its burning issues, why did Paul never do so in addressing many of his own issues: circumcision, justification, tongues speaking and so on (Wright 1992:421-22)?

I find similar problems with the Jesus Seminar's criterion of dissimilarity. By it, every expression resembling the early church, contemporary Judaism or general folk wisdom is subtracted from Jesus' sayings. The remainder composes the distinctive language of Jesus, consisting of aphorisms and parables that cut across the contemporary grain—marked by exaggeration, humor, paradox and concrete images which elicit surprise and shock.

Whereas Jesus certainly employed such language often, I wonder how complete a portrait of any historical figure can be composed simply from features that make that figure different. Will not anyone who makes an impact on contemporaries also share some important characteristics and expressions with them? And if anyone gives rise to a following, won't those adherents share some basic features with that person? A Jesus reduced to unique sayings alone appears truncated, shadowy and one-sided. I propose that a method allowing for some similarities between Jesus and his context will produce a more complete, flesh-and-blood historical figure.

I can certainly agree that Jesus' language was distinctively shocking, surprising and counter to the religious and social mainstream. However, other sayings attributed to Jesus—such as the veiled, paradoxical way he referred to himself as Son of Man or Son of God, or predictions of his death—are also shocking, surprising and countercultural. When such themes are expressed in this way, should they automatically be denied to Jesus because of their content? Or might the range even of Jesus' unique sayings be expanded, yielding a fuller portrait of this person?

I also discern some tension between the Jesus Seminar's ways of establishing Jesus' distinctiveness and its second major methodological feature—its use of crosscultural typologies. For having denied similarities and emphasized differences among Jesus and his immediate contemporaries and followers, this quest stresses that many similarities, but few differences, exist among Jesus and religious leaders in quite different times and cultures. (For example, it affirms that Jesus is a son of God like other religious figures but not the unique Son of God.)

Yet in both kinds of comparisons, should not historical inquiry be open to both similarities and differences? In employing crosscultural typologies, historical study must be open to what is different and even unique, for it is at least as concerned with the unusual and singular as with the repeated and common. I suspect, however, that the results that the Jesus Seminar obtains from typologies have as much to do with theological presuppositions as with actual comparisons. That is, significant distinctions between Jesus and others have already been ruled out by banning "church language" from the beginning. Similarities are found because it is presupposed to some extent that Jesus must be like other religious figures or must have expressed some universal religious awareness. (I have already suggested that such general presuppositions, such as that Jesus must have taught like sages in many religions, actually function as the deepest criteria for identifying his distinctive language.)

Perceiving the singular requires that study of any tradition begin with sympathetic efforts to view reality as its participants did, within their overall worldview. That is the best way of guarding against biases derived from our own era; it opens the possibility of having our perspective challenged and of discerning surprising things. This claim is consistent with my first methodological assumption, that a person cannot separate any historical figure or "fact" from a complex of meaning or "interpretation." I find this different from the Jesus Seminar's third feature: its initial dissolving of the overall framework of meaning presented by the sources and its search for atoms of factual truth among the pieces.

Yet this approach itself is part of an overarching framework of meaning, or worldview: essentially the mechanistic one crystallized at the Enlightenment. It construes the behavior of all phenomena as the sum of interactions among their parts, which can be subdivided almost indefinitely and which operate according to invariable mechanical laws. This worldview includes the claim that history is governed by such laws.[23] What is ultimately involved in conflicts among interpretive methods, then, are not simply procedural questions but differences in comprehensive interpretive frameworks, or worldviews (Wright 1992:137-39).

Such conflicts cannot be resolved by simple appeals to "facts," because different worldviews involve diverse notions of what count as facts. The mechanistic paradigm assumes that clear, discrete sayings or reportable events constitute the factual, or most real. The closer that reports are temporally to the events they represent and the closer that versions of sayings are to the time and form in which they were uttered, the more accurate they are generally considered to be and the most free from interpretation.

I, on the other hand, in line with the organismic paradigm, assume that some interpretive connections among events and sayings will be equally as "factual" and real—for interconnections are intrinsic dimensions of what things are. In some cases, reports of events and versions of sayings somewhat removed from the original occurrences or utterances, and thus involving a longer view, may better express their overall significance.

No study of history, therefore, can be divorced from overarching understandings of its nature and significance, for every historical inquiry presupposes some such perspective. Accordingly if we wish to attain as sympathetic and accurate a reading of an era as we can, our first question should not be "How can we eliminate distortions in its worldview?" (assuming that we approach it with a better worldview, or with none) but "What was the overall worldview within which its events were perceived as occurring?"

Having determined this as accurately as possible, historians who are open to learning something new will allow that worldview to dialogue with the one they bring, permitting the former to perhaps modify the latter. And insofar as they critique the former, they will recognize that they are revising it on the basis of another overarching understanding of historical truth.

The first-century Jewish worldview. The worldview within which Jesus and the first documents about him appeared was the first-century Jewish worldview. According to it one very distinct deity governed the cosmos. This God had long ago selected Israel as a special people, promising to deliver it from all enemies and establish it as a society experiencing God's presence, justice and peace. Through Israel, moreover, all nations would be blessed with the same presence, justice and peace. All history was understood as the story of that God's dealing with humankind and as directing it toward this end. This unique God brought forth the truly novel in history.

Yet Israel had often been oppressed by foreign powers, and now it languished under the harsh Roman yoke. Amid this oppression, it awaited that deliverance which God had promised in various forms, sometimes through an individual, one sometimes called the Messiah. When Jesus began his ministry, then, the chief question asked about him would have been, Are you the one who has come to fulfill God's promise? (Moltmann 1974:98-102). Jesus impacted history in his own time and continued to do so after his death because a significant group of people believed that he was the promised one. They continued to tell his story chiefly as the means by which God's promise to Israel and the nations was decisively fulfilled.

All who wrote about Jesus would have been deeply concerned about the meaning of his story and about how it fit into God's overall historical activity. All New Testament authors assume or allude to some version of this basic story; even Hebrews and Paul are best read, at least initially, with an eye to discerning theirs (Wright 1992:403-10). This means that when investigation approaches the Synoptic Gospels, their narrative frameworks can hardly be considered dispensable. True history, in these writings, would not be limited to glimpses gleaned from isolated sayings but would be embedded in the narrative connections integrating them into larger patterns of meaning.

Since the overall Gospels are intrinsically stories, it seems likely that many of the shortest units which compose them would also be. This seems likely in light of the fact that Jewish people constantly told stories—"of Israel's suffering and vindication; of exile and restoration; of Passover, exodus, wandering, and settlement" (p. 429). These were the grids through which they made sense of reality. They told stories of their rabbis and holy men, and when Jesus appeared, they would remember and tell stories of him. Understood in this light, several features of the Gospel stories hardly seem secondary.

Since questions as to whether Jesus fulfilled God's promises were constantly alive, references to the Hebrew Scriptures would often be pertinent to the point of the episodes recounted and not simply reflect the early church's search for legitimacy. Since, along with Jesus' messianic possibilities, his practices aroused intense opposition—as Borg clearly shows—it is highly likely that conflictive episodes marked his ministry and were hardly creations of later writers.[24] Then too to carry on a ministry in so volatile a climate, Jesus must have had some consciousness of mission, so this cannot be largely fabricated by later writers. Further, Jesus, as the Jesus Seminar generally agrees, took the social stance of a prophet and was historically perceived as such. But prophets were scrutinized not only regarding their words but also their deeds, which were often regarded as symbolic acts.

In general, it seems unconvincing to maintain that only Jesus' words would have been remembered and that his acts and features of their contexts would soon have been forgotten. Many episodes of his ministry were dramatic enough—especially those surrounding his crucifixion—that some details of who was there, what was done and especially of how Jesus carried himself would have vividly impressed those present. Finally being prophetically aware of the dangers of the time, Jesus could have plausibly foreseen his coming crucifixion (the common Roman punishment for those considered political rebels) and referred to it.

In light of these features of Jesus' context, it seems likely, as N. T. Wright proposes, that numerous memories of Jesus first circulated as stories with many features, which were only gradually reduced to bare essentials. The circulation of sayings without contexts (as found in Thomas, and hypothesized for Q) would mark a later stage, an extreme simplification of earlier tradition. The emphasis on sayings as the heart of religion suits the Greek mentality far better than the Jewish, which revels in story. The smoothing down of full narratives into short sayings would correspond with the expansion of Christianity from a Jewish milieu into a Greek one (and suggest a late date for Thomas[25]). To propose that sayings were expanded into stories hypothesizes a contrary "Judaizing" tendency, which would seem extremely unlikely after the destruction of Jerusalem in 70 C.E., subsequent to which Matthew and Luke were probably composed (Wright 1992:427-28; Wilkins and Moreland 1995:22).

I do not mean to suggest that the meaning of absolutely every Gospel saying is tightly interwoven with its context[26] or that sayings do not appear in a variety of forms and settings. Yet the claim that the evangelists' freely varied sayings and invented contexts seems to depend partly on an assumption that only a single precise, atomistic utterance can go back to Jesus and that all variations and settings are due to others.

In his historical ministry, however, as an itinerant teacher Jesus must have uttered the same basic sayings countless times, in various forms, with different interconnections and with varying applications. Accordingly those who wrote of Jesus may not have been faced simply with a few sayings in one or two forms without connections or settings, which they had to join, vary and contextualize. Instead, they may have been familiar with a welter of utterances, variations, connections and episodes from which they had to select (Wright 1992:423). That is not to say that they exercised no creativity. But it means that many ways of saying, interrelating and apply-ing things might be quite faithful to what Jesus said and did.[27]

Jesus as sage. The Synoptic Gospels certainly present Jesus as a wisdom teacher, as the Jesus Seminar stresses. Yet I must ask how accurate its por-trayals become when he is interpreted in light of crosscultural typologies such as the *primordial tradition*.[28] Borg writes that such holy men encounter "Reality-Itself," which transcends "all concepts of God" and the "sub-ject/object distinction" (1984:231). Though it would be foolish to place precise limits on Jesus' awareness of God, such descriptions are most appropriate for Eastern religions, whose ultimate experience is of a union where distinctions between God and the self vanish, rather than of com-munion with a God who is Other.[29] Yet Jesus clearly experienced his Father as an Other, a personal and volitional reality (see "Trinitarian Considerations" below) in line with his historic Jewish tradition.

Jesus therefore communed with God as transcendent, yet also encoun-tered God in nature (as immanent), as those parables stressed by the Jesus Seminar show (Mt 5:45-46; 6:25-30; 10:29-31). But although Crossan and others suggest that Jesus read off God's will directly from watching nature's organismic "rhythms of here and now" (1991:295), it would be good to examine these texts more carefully. The first two do encourage human activity modeled on nature's. The second, however, underlines God's glo-rious clothing of grass which quickly withers, whereas the third emphasizes God's notice of the lowliest creatures.[30] Both the second and third, that is, indicate that God regards and values natural creatures differently, and more highly, than direct human observations of it suggest. (I will discuss this further in chapter ten.)

In general, crosscultural typologies can turn Jesus into one who taught timeless wisdom—whose kingdom "is, was, and always will be available to any who want it" (Crossan 1991:xii). Yet this underestimates the extent to which Jesus, seen in his historical context, would have stressed the role of decisive historical events. The Jesus Seminar often handles Jesus' historical references inadequately, as seems evident in its treatment of Mark 8:34 ("Take up [your] cross and follow me").

Despite its triple attestation, this text is denied to Jesus by the inviolable principle that early church language could not have been uttered by him. This implies that Jesus could never have reflected seriously on the manner of his death or on any decisive significance it might carry (rather surprising for a daring prophet). Borg, however, seeks to rescue this saying by making it refer to a timeless inner truth: dying to the finite and centering in the infinite. Yet this not only removes this call from Jesus' history but abolishes its sociopolitical edge. For if Jesus said it, he was encouraging people to follow him in the kind of public witness which arouses social resistance (Yoder 1972:127-31).

Jesus' wisdom teaching undoubtedly employed vivid images and invited hearers to think for themselves. But is it correct to say that he appealed to their experience when the world that many parables present differed so radically from their ordinary one? Don't even his parables and aphorisms announce, with some authority, the coming of a quite different world? And how convincing is it to insist, as the Jesus Seminar does rigidly, that Jesus never quoted Scripture, never taught authoritatively, never used christological terms, almost never initiated discussion and was limited mostly to one-liners? Is it not more likely historically that a great teacher would be much more versatile and complex in his approach (as the Synoptics indeed present him)?

Finally Borg and Crossan discern that the Gospels not only treat Jesus as a wisdom teacher but contain elements of a wisdom Christology. Jesus occasionally appears as the incarnation, or child, of Wisdom, whom Hebrew tradition personifies as a woman (esp. Prov 8). Wisdom performs many of the same cosmic functions as John's Word (Jn 1:1-18) and is a chief source of this concept (Dunn 1980:163-73).[31]

With Jesus' Wisdom references, some Jesus Seminar adherents begin suggesting links between Jesus and the early church (Borg 1994a:96-118). Yet the Jesus Seminar, as usual, denies any such connection, for as I noted it regards the similarity between Jesus' saying about his easy yoke (Mt 11:28-29) and the wisdom book Ecclesiasticus as a mere routine quotation. When Jesus, apparently referring to himself, says, "Wisdom is vindicated by her deeds" (Mt 11:19), the Seminar concludes that this saying "about wisdom personified as a woman figure . . . could have been spoken by any sage. It does not exhibit any of the marks of Jesus' distinctive discourse"

(Funk and Hoover 1993:180). Yet despite this, many scholars would affirm not only that wisdom Christology occurs in the Synoptics but also that Jesus valued women highly (Ruether) and manifested many characteristics often regarded as "feminine" (even though Borg's emphasis on mercy's "womblike" character may stretch the linguistic evidence).

An eschatological Jesus. To picture Jesus as making no real distinction between present and future and as uninterested in approaching world-changing events, as the Jesus Seminar often does, is once again to remove him from his first-century Jewish context. It is to align him typologically with religions for which historical events are unimportant and which stress timeless experience and truth. Moreover, the Jesus Seminar's sharp distinction between future kingdom sayings (all rated black) and present ones (all voted pink) reflects its rather rigid, disjunctive use of categories and dissolves the already-not yet tension essential to the biblical awareness of temporality. For at least since Amos' time, Israelites had experienced that a prophesied event (for instance, "the Day of the Lord") could refer to both an impending situation and a far more distant one.[32]

Thus Seminar members are correct in recognizing that Jesus, in proclaiming the coming of God's kingdom with great urgency, did not expect history to cease immediately. Yet this need not have been incompatible with speaking of the eventual end of history as we know it, of a future universal judgment and of a coming Son of Man. The Synoptic Jesus, indeed, is better described as *eschatological* (as concerned with the present and future dimensions of God's most decisive and, in this sense, final) historical acts, rather than *apocalyptic* (as focused on a cataclysmic end).[33]

Seminar participants also sharply distinguish two uses of "Son of Man": one denotes generic humanity and is attributed to Jesus; the other, an apocalyptic use, is referred solely to the early church. Several problems exist with this division.

First, "Son of Man" appears sixty-two times in the Synoptics and thirteen times in John, all but once on Jesus' lips. But the remainder of the New Testament uses it only four times. Since third questers also hold that this figure was not common in contemporary Judaism, "Son of Man" seems to meet their criterion of dissimilarity quite well (Wilkins and Moreland 1995:91). That is, this title seems not to have been generally used in either Judaism or the early church, so we should conclude that it goes back to Jesus.[34]

That is what most scholars in the second quest held. But Seminar members will allow that only about a third of its uses, those which can clearly mean "a human being," might reflect Jesus' practice. Yet if the early church invented the apocalyptic usage, why does this hardly ever appear outside the Gospels, and why does hardly anyone but Jesus use it? If this use was not prevalent in Judaism, why is it more convincing to say that the church created it than that Jesus did?

Further, "Son of Man" is used in the New Testament in three ways, not just the two (generic and eschatological) identified by the Jesus Seminar. It appears in many passages where Jesus foretells his suffering. If Jesus used a term which often meant "a human being" to designate (1) himself, (2) someone who would come as judge and (3) one who would suffer, did it not function in the kind of indirect, enigmatic way that causes hearers to think for themselves—a style that characterizes the distinctive language of Jesus?

The generic vagueness of "Son of Man" allows it to be filled with a special content. This content is incredibly paradoxical and profound. The one who will come as Judge, who might be regarded as so exalted as to be removed from our situation and so fearful as to be oppressive—such a one not only has something in common with all humans but will undergo the worst kind of earthly rejection and suffering. Jesus' exaltation and his humility, his divine and his human side, are combined here in one polyvalent expression. This combination is often credited to Mark, who wanted to stress that communion with Jesus would also mean suffering with him. But why should Mark, rather than Jesus, have been first to realize that fellowship with him meant taking up his cross?

A political Jesus. In contrast to past studies which focused narrowly on apocalypticism or christological titles, the Jesus Seminar shows that Jesus, viewed in his historical context, had significant political concerns (with "political" meaning not direct participation in governmental affairs but involvement in life's corporate dimensions). The Seminar's sociological studies make Rome's oppression of Judea, especially of its peasants, vivid and concrete. They show how Jesus' concern for the poor and his acceptance of outcasts and sinners did not merely offend pious sensibilities but initiated a new kind of social reality which deeply threatened the old, as Ruether and McFague stress.

Yet acceptance of the rejected, inclusivity and a kind of preference for the poor are not inconsistent with calls to repent and with warnings of judgment for those who do not. For repentance and judgment are not uniquely apocalyptic phenomena (in the sense defined in "An eschatological Jesus" above); rather they are deeply ingrained in the prophetic tradition that Jesus—if one sees him in historical context—continued. I find no reason to think that Jesus did not proclaim to everyone the same mercy and judgment of the Father who "makes his sun rise on the evil and on the good, and sends rain on the righteous and on the unrighteous" (Mt 5:45).

Nonetheless, largely because this message included a call to repentance—to renounce everything which would block the coming kingdom—it often impacted people in diverse social groups differently. To those to whom wealth, ritual holiness, gender or social position gave a stake in the current system and a sense of superiority, the call to give up whatever hindered solidarity with all kinds of people usually came as very bad news. Yet to those who had little to lose and much to gain in a kingdom where all were equally valued, it could sound like very good news. In this sense—that the same message carried different implications for different groups, not that it favored some classes over others—Jesus exercised the "preferential option" for many of the socially disadvantaged that is stressed in Latin American theologies.

Perhaps some Seminar members affirm Jesus' sayings about forgiveness and acceptance but reject those about repentance and judgment because they believe that Jesus placed little emphasis on God's kingdom. If this kingdom were a wholly transcendent, world-ending reality, they might be right. But within Jesus' historical context, "kingdom" would be the most comprehensive way of designating the kind of social reality he was bringing.[35] Announcement of such a kingdom is not simply a message of acceptance but also a call to make the changes and adjustments involved in a new way of life. Jesus' teachings, as McFague and Ruether emphasize, call for sweeping reversals in relationships among rich and poor, men and women, and Jews and Gentiles.[36] In light of all this, although Seminar participants often regard Mark 1:15 as a Markan construction ("The time is fulfilled, and the kingdom of God has come near; repent, and believe in the good news"), this phrase seems to well summarize Jesus' message, as John Cobb affirms, whether or not Jesus uttered these exact words as a slogan.[37]

Finally, I agree with Borg that compassionate, nonviolent responses to enemies were essential to this new way. Uttered in the first-century colonial situation, turning the other cheek and going the second mile would unmistakably refer to relationships with Romans. Jesus intended to commend not merely inward attitudes but outward behaviors characterizing a social group. Such teachings may sound idealistic, but so did all those involving radical reversals among social groups. Jesus' main political contribution was to introduce an actual, even if radical, alternative social possibility.

Trinitarian considerations.[38] If we begin interpreting Jesus in light of his original historical context and its worldview, what can we say of his relations to his Father and the Spirit? Remember that the Jesus Seminar, despite its indebtedness to the Enlightenment, is very open to seeing Jesus constantly influenced by a Spirit-reality and by an unusual relationship with one he called Abba, or Father.

1. *Jesus and the Spirit.* I noted that a crucial role is assigned to the Spirit in the Gospels' narrative frameworks, especially in those events which initiate Jesus' ministry—his baptism, temptation and entrance into Galilee. The significance we grant to the Spirit in Jesus' ministry, then, will have much to do with the importance we ascribe to this narrative framework. Given the importance of story in Jesus' context and the urgency of questions as to whether he was fulfilling God's promises, narratives about a special outpouring of the Spirit at the beginning of his course would have had enormous significance for determining who he was, for a special outpouring of God's Spirit was expected at the last days (see, for example, Joel 2:28-32).

Since narrative "connections" convey inextricable dimensions of the meaning of such historical writings, we must conclude that Jesus' words and deeds were meant to be seen as interwoven with the Spirit's activity from the beginning. Matthew and Luke even trace the Spirit's influence, and thus the beginning of the fulfillment of God's promises, all the way back to Jesus' conception (Mt 1:20; Lk 1:35).

The Spirit's continuing activity, we have seen, is most evident in exorcisms, whose deepest significance is expressed in a saying that even the Jesus Seminar rates highly: "If it is by the Spirit of God that I cast out demons, then the kingdom of God has come to you" (Mt 12:28 par. Lk 11:20). I see no reason to deny the authenticity of a closely related, strongly attested saying about the Son of Man and the Spirit (Mt 12:32 par. Mk 3:28-29 par. Lk 12:10), which the Seminar rejects largely because it routinely dismisses any language resembling trinitarianism.

The Synoptics' overall narrative framework indicates that the significance of Jesus' life cannot be understood apart from his death and resurrection. Throughout his life Jesus makes some enormous claims—such as that he is bringing God's kingdom, integrally intertwined with the claim that he is empowered by God's true Spirit. But his opponents, we know, charge that he is guided by a demonic spirit. In such an oppositional drama,[39] Jesus' crucifixion functions not simply as a tragedy. It also appears to be a negative judgment on his claims and a vindication of his opponents' accusations. His resurrection, however, functions as a reversal of that verdict—as God's affirmation of Jesus' claims and condemnation of his opponents'.

Few references to the Spirit appear in the Synoptics' passion and resurrection accounts. Yet the overall Synoptic structure indicates that the resurrection confirmed its emphasis and Jesus' claims that the Spirit empowered his life. How? Other early sources affirm that in the resurrection the Spirit raised him to new life (Rom 1:4; 6:4; 8:11; 1 Pet 3:18; 1 Tim 3:16). Because these texts affirm and fittingly climax the developing pattern of the Synoptics' complex drama, I can regard them also as part of a broader historical narrative about Jesus and the Spirit.[40]

2. *Jesus and his Father.* A decisive, deep experience of his Father,[41] we have seen, marks the baptismal episode where the Spirit descends on Jesus. His Father's affirmation, "You are my Son, the Beloved; with you I am well pleased" (Mk 1:11), echoes Yahweh's words to his special Servant in Isaiah 42:1. It is widely agreed that Jesus is being bidden to exercise his calling as God's special Son according to the manner of the Servant who works through obedience, weakness and suffering (Is 42:2-4; 52:13—53:12).

After the Spirit drives Jesus into the wilderness, Satan challenges him with the taunt: "If you are God's Son . . ." (Mt 4:3, 6 par. Lk 4:3, 9). Satan tempts Jesus to prove this with miraculous displays of power (turning stones into bread, jumping off a high wall without injury). It is widely agreed that in refusing to perform these Jesus is resolving to exercise his role as "the Son of God" not in the exalted, marvelous manner that this title might well connote but after the humble Servant manner. This tension between Son of God and Servant, in fact, closely parallels that between the exalted and humble dimensions of "Son of Man."

This tension runs throughout the Synoptics' narrative framework. Those same demonic powers who must be exorcised by the Spirit often address Jesus as "Son of God" (Mk 3:11; Mk 5:7 par. Lk 4:41). His opponents tempt him to perform miraculous signs (Mt 16:1; Mk 8:11; Lk 11:16). When Peter confesses that Jesus is the Son of God (Mt 16:16), Jesus begins to foretell how he ("the Son of Man" according to Mk 8:31; Lk 9:22) will suffer. But Peter protests that this could never be the Son of God's role, prompting Jesus' harsh reply: "Get behind me, Satan!" (Mt 16:23 par. Mk 8:33). Here again Jesus strongly rejects the triumphal interpretation of Son of God and affirms the one involving the suffering of the Servant and the Son of Man. (It is precisely at this point, pivotal in the Synoptic narrative framework, that Jesus urges his followers to take up their cross and follow him.) Jesus again struggles with this temptation in Gethsemane where, in an intimate and painful dialogue, he cries, "Abba, Father, for you all things are possible; remove this cup from me; yet, not what I want, but what you want" (Mk

14:36 and parallels).

Then last, at his death, the agonizing temptation to assume the majestic Son of God role resounds in the cry: "If you are the Son of God, come down from the cross" (Mt 27:40). The painful dialogue between Jesus and his Father continues on the cross, and Jesus finally feels abandoned, crying out, "My God, my God, why have you forsaken me?" (Mk 15:34). Yet the Gospels and early New Testament writers proclaim that the Father—through the Spirit—raised Jesus from the dead (Rom 6:4; Gal 1:1; Phil 2:9-11; 1 Pet 1:3), vindicating his claim that he was following and rightly representing his Father throughout his life.

When the Gospels' overall narrative framework is seriously considered, it becomes difficult to routinely dismiss all mention of "Son of God" and "Son of Man" as early church creations. If we do, crucial features of the one about whom the writers are seeking to speak disappear. If the result is a Jesus who did not wrestle in this profound way with the dynamics of power and suffering—and urged his followers to take up this challenge—do themes such as Jesus' concern for the powerless, which the Jesus Seminar emphasizes, really carry the same depth of meaning? "Son of God" and "Son of Man" do not simply represent outmoded "dogmas" obscuring Jesus' true humanity. They are profound vehicles for articulating the subtle interplay between power and humility, success and suffering, the divine and the human.[42]

Once Jesus' special relation to his Father becomes foundational to much of what the Gospels say, it seems artificial to reject a triply attested saying such as "No one knows the Son except the Father, and no one knows the Father except the Son" (Mt 11:27 par. Lk 10:22)—especially when it appears in a wisdom Christology framework. Yet this very saying shows how intimate and personal this relationship was, and it makes plausible why Jesus himself (in contrast to the Gospels' narrative framework) would seldom openly call himself God's Son.[43] Moreover, since "Son of God" might well connote the kind of triumphalistic power that Jesus was concerned to avoid, it becomes plausible that he would characteristically employ a vaguer phrase for himself (Son of Man) which he could fill with new, paradoxical content (Cullmann 1959:279-81).

Summary and Conclusion

I have agreed with the Jesus Seminar when it regards Jesus as a sage, denies that he was an otherwordly apocalypticist, depicts his prophetic role against its socioeconomic background and acknowledges his deep relationship with his Father and a realm of Spirit. I have argued, however, that its sharp disjunction between Jesus and early church Christology cannot account for the latter's rise. I also find that its placement of Jesus in universal typologies can interpret him quite otherwise than his sayings and Jewish background warrant. (Oddly, while the Jesus Seminar's method is "Newtonian," its positive view of Jesus, at least as sage, has many organismic features.) Finally I have shown how its reductionistic approach often clashes with the worldview from which the Gospel stories arose. That worldview, in fact, coheres better with my own, which stresses the inseparability of fact and meaning.

If the Jesus Seminar cannot convincingly show how the notion of Jesus as a unique, divine but human figure arose—a notion which has deeply impacted the public world down to our day—can I offer an explanation? Let me begin by considering the first-century Jewish worldview. It provided a way of conceiving the uniqueness of a messianic figure: this person would accomplish those decisive acts which would bring God's salvation to the world. Various New Testament writers attribute just this kind of uniqueness to Jesus and thereby affirm many features of the current Jewish worldview. Yet they do not simply report that he straightforwardly fulfilled Jewish messianic expectations. Instead, the characterizations with which they describe him, though they were originally Hebraic notions, have undergone profound transformations. They have come to express highly nuanced, paradoxical intertwinings of majesty and humility, of power and suffering and of the divine and human. Indeed, the decisive saving acts at their root—crucifixion as a despised criminal followed by resurrection—involve such intertwining themselves. This way of salvation and the person who brought it were not constructed from straightforward applications of Hebrew concepts, however much they may correspond to features of these concepts in retrospect.

But neither, I maintain, could so profound an understanding of such a savior and his saving acts have been concocted rather haphazardly out of numerous anonymous notions circulating through the early church. The complexity and paradoxical character of such New Testament concepts as Son of Man and Son of God (I could name others if I had space) bear witness to unanticipated, highly unusual events and a highly unexpected, original person at their foundation. In other words, if what is at the core of these concepts[44] originated in neither first-century Judaism nor the early church, it must have arisen from the one possible remaining source: Jesus' historic activity and awareness themselves.[45]

If the best way to explain how the notion of Jesus as a unique, divine-human Savior arose is to affirm that its essential ingredients came from

Jesus himself, then it is plausible that he is indeed that Savior. It is also plausible that the first-century Jewish worldview, as transformed by Jesus and his saving acts, provides the best framework through which to perceive him. It is further plausible, since that framework involves claims about life's and the cosmos's ultimate meaning, that it is the best framework for perceiving the rest of reality as well. That does not mean that details of, say, scientific explanation should be deduced from this perspective but that it (rather than, say, the Enlightenment) provides an orientation through which the general nature and significance of science, and much else, can best be grasped.

Of course, there is no way of proving beyond all possible doubt, according to one absolute "public" standard, that the above proposals are true. Other explanations are possible. (For instance, perhaps claims about Jesus' uniqueness are traceable to him but he was deliberately deceiving people. Yet how consistent is such an affirmation with Jesus' overall character—with many other characteristics that most people regard as quite admirable?)

In dealing with other proposals, including the Jesus Seminar's, as to how belief in Jesus arose and with other general worldviews, my approach is to seek to show, through careful examination of the implications involved, that these others are less consistent than my own. However, if my overall perspective is at least as plausible as others, then I have every reason to present it in public conversation. In this conversation, as I have said, I can explain its character more fully and strengthen its plausibility in two ways: by exhibiting its internal consistency, and by showing how it makes meaningful contributions to current issues. That is exactly what I plan to do in the next three chapters.

I recognize, of course, that people will affirm this perspective most fully when they affirm it by faith. For it claims that Jesus brings a person into relationship with the one God of all reality, through the power of the true divine Spirit. This perspective will be embraced more fully the more deeply a person encounters the experiential realities at its heart and the more thoroughly it orients his or her daily life. Nonetheless I believe that it can also provide an insightful orientation toward the urgent issues of any time and place and therefore should be heard in public conversation.

Finally, my discussion of Jesus has shown that his saving acts and his notions about himself and his mission did not stem from him alone. Jesus understood himself to be carrying out his Father's will and to be living in deep communion with him (except for a break at Gethsemane and the cross to be explored in chapter ten). Jesus also experienced himself being empowered by God's Spirit. Jesus' saving work, that is, was not carried out by him alone but was the cooperative work of these three agencies. This trinitarian perspective on Jesus' work, in addition to what I said about him as sage and about his eschatological and "political" perspectives, will provide the foundation for the theologies of the self, creation and society developed in the next chapters.

N I N E

Psychology, Spirituality &
a Theological Anthropology

*I*n our contemporary world, is it possible—and if so, how is it possible—to develop a stable self? That is the main question I pursued in chapters two and five. Psychological alienation is the paradoxical condition of feeling distant from, at cross-purposes with or somehow blocking or submerging one's true self. In a certain puzzling sense, we are dimly aware of what that self might be— yet at the same time painfully ignorant of, exiled from, undermining or resisting that which is as close as breathing. Conflict rages among our inner drives, our various self-images and our outer social expectations. How can these all be brought into harmony in a relatively stable, abiding sense of self?

The basic organismic answer, we have seen, is that an underlying harmony, or at least strong tendencies toward harmony, among drives and between the drives and the self, already exist(s). Strictly speaking, there is only one drive, often called *self-actualization*. All other drives are simply aspects of it, and when we learn "to listen to [our] organism" (Rogers) and let this drive emerge undistortedly, its expressions will be those of our authentic self.

Some picture this underlying harmony rather simply as an *inner child*. Others, such as C. G. Jung, speak of a much more complex *individuation* process, intensifying during life's second half. But in any case, the only forces that can seriously split this actualizing drive are social expectations and structures which teach or force us to want or fear things other than those toward which it tends. Accordingly organismic therapists often assume that individuals can be greatly changed simply by learning to distinguish inner voices from outer social ones while social conditions remain the same. Yet many apparently assume that if everyone would follow their organisms' lead, profound social harmony would result (an assumption congruent with capitalism).

For organismic Christian spirituality this process acquires momentous proportions, for finding one's true self is closely linked to finding God. In *centering prayer,* the closer we come to the self's center, the more nearly we approach God. In *bio-spirituality,* much as for Matthew Fox and some ecological theologians (see chapter six), the more we allow our organismic processes to direct us, the more we participate in the cosmic unfolding of God's Word. In John Welch's Jungian interpretation of two great mystics (Teresa of Ávila and John of the Cross), the self and God are almost identical. The persona's shattering and the self's emergence become the inner meaning of Jesus' death and resurrection—that individuation which all humans undergo. Christ becomes an archetype of the self, the demonic symbolizes our hidden potential (the *shadow*), and Teresa and John become pioneers in humankind's evolution toward greater consciousness.

Though psychological alienation is a very real experience for all these approaches, it tends to exist somewhat on the surface, whereas harmony is the deeper way that things actually are. The spiritual task is to delve beneath the surface and participate directly in that harmony. Whereas centering prayer and Welch imply that individuals can attain this whatever their social situation, Fox insists (and bio-spirituality indicates) that new social and ecological attitudes are integral to overcoming psychological alienation.

The basic psychoanalytic response to alienation, however, expects tensions among drives—and between drives and social expectations—to exert continual pressure on a struggling self. In the extreme case (Jacques Lacan), the self is simply a societal fiction imposed on heterogeneous drives. For Sigmund Freud, the ego somehow emerges from the very differently directed energies of the id. Many object relations theorists, however, posit an incipient ego present from life's start. Yet in all cases the maturing self is constructed and reconstructed through continual struggle with drive demands and social codes. Moreover, the drives and the self are not so distinct from their social setting that they can attain harmony independent from that setting. Social structures are so deeply inscribed upon instincts that either selves cannot change much (Freud, Lacan) or, even though the drives possess some plasticity, selves will alter only when their social settings do (Marcuse).

Many psychoanalysts find contemporary social experience so fluid that people have difficulty finding objects around which to constellate a sense of self. Many people, accordingly, seek fusion with an omnipotent object guaranteeing either conquest of their environment *(grandiose narcissism)* or enveloping protection and affirmation *(regressive narcissism)*. Yet an object formed similarly—the ego ideal—can play a positive role if striven for as a goal through the challenging processes of self-formation and differentiation.

Whereas we cannot identify a psychoanalytic school of Christian spirituality, a few recent writers speak of finding ourselves and God in a conflictive way similar at points to psychoanalysis, to which they sometimes refer. Prayer involves not only increasing union with God but cries for help (McNamara), for within the self we sometimes encounter formlessness, emptiness and void (Jones). God is not nearly identical with our deepest selves but is a distinct Other, whose hiddenness is well represented by darkness.

Jesus' death is a real, historical event of cosmic anguish and abandonment. His life, death and resurrection, though they do compose the pattern for the deepest human journey, are not simply symbols for archetypal processes. For Christ is not merely a self-symbol; he is the divine-human person who undertook this journey first. This sort of spirituality seldom celebrates a historic evolution of human consciousness; more often it contrasts humanity's usual materialism, hedonism and egoism with Jesus' way. It tends to find alienation not just on the surface, but also in the depths, of how things are. It does not seek God on some other level but as a companion in the midst of the challenging journey.

Despite great differences between the two orientations just sketched, they both regard Jesus' way as the pattern for human life. In chapter eight I implied something similar when I argued that Christian theology should begin with God's saving acts through Jesus. For through him God's activity and character were revealed in a unique way. Yet more than God was revealed—so were God's saving intentions, or God's ultimate purpose, for humankind through the activities of One who was human. This means that Jesus did not simply tell us what humans were to be like. Through his life and character he showed us. Jesus, in other words, can serve as the norm for fulfilled selfhood and provide a theological standpoint for response to the issues raised by organicism and psychoanalysis.

This chapter will first show more fully how Jesus can function as this norm. Then I will expand on that by sketching some basic human capacities (for instance, conscience and the "soul") from a biblical perspective. Third, I will apply this vantage point to the main issues raised in chapters two and five. Finally, I will summarize my contribution to public conversation on psychological and spiritual alienation.

Jesus as the Key to Mature Selfhood

Within theological studies, psychology normally falls under the heading of theological anthropology. Here *anthropology* carries no special reference to primitive societies. It simply means study of human nature. Theological anthropology considers both humanity's positive potential (what it was intended to be) and its negative actuality (how it has fallen short). Most traditional anthropologies based their consideration of both aspects largely on Adam and Eve. Several problems exist, however, with this starting point.

One is that, aside from Genesis 2—5, Scripture says little about Eve and Adam.[1] Its portrait of them is exceedingly spare. This has made it easy for anthropology to read many kinds of notions into allegedly biblical pictures of normative human nature. Aristotelian theologians, such as Thomas Aquinas, could assert that "being in God's image refers solely to the mind" (*Summa Theologiae* 1.93.6). For Matthew Fox, in contrast, this image consists chiefly in imagination and creativity (1983:175).[2]

Against tendencies to derive biblical guidelines from more static images or definitions, I affirm that Scripture tells us what things are like mainly through narrating historical processes. Theologians generally agree, for instance, that the divine reality becomes known through a series of divine historic acts rather than through single events or precise definitions alone. Correspondingly I maintain that in Scripture human reality is revealed through a complex multitude of human acts—through numerous profound stories about human willing, yearning, loving, building, hating, sinning and destroying.[3]

Nevertheless, the sheer multiplicity and variety of such portraits prompts us to ask whether some vantage point might be found to provide focus, some perspective from which their significance for determining what humans are intended to be might become clear. Christians have generally considered Jesus to have fulfilled God's intentions for human nature. Although this common confession has seldom provided the chief orientation for theological anthropology,[4] I affirm that Jesus, rather than Adam and Eve, exemplifies the actualization of humankind's positive potential. Accordingly, the primary datum from which I will construct a theological anthropology is the biblical history of human willing, loving, sinning and so forth, considered as pointing to, fulfilled in and critiqued by the human activity of Jesus Christ.

Such an approach will not deduce everything more or less directly from Jesus. Its understanding of sin, for instance, will be drawn from episodes that conflict with Jesus' praxis and especially from concrete historical resistance to him (Finger 1989:146-54). Humanity's complex psychological character cannot be inferred from Jesus-stories alone but must be based on many other stories (including Adam and Eve's). Attention to biblical usages of anthropological terms (for instance, those translated "conscience" or "soul") will play a significant role. Nonetheless, in such an anthropology the historical portrait of Jesus will provide the ultimate vantage point or norm.

The call to selfhood. The Hebrew Scriptures regard human life as something bestowed by God's breath: God breathed into the Adam's nostrils the breath of life, and the Adam became a living being (Gen 2:7). In fact, all creation proceeds from God's breath, for "by the word of the LORD the heavens were made, and all their host by the breath of his mouth" (Ps 33:6). The word here for "breath" *(ruach)* is often translated "spirit" and sometimes approximates the New Testament meaning of God's Holy Spirit. Human life, then, is bestowed and maintained as a gift of God's out-breathing. In response, human breath is to be employed in praising God, thereby keeping humans in continual relation to their Creator and preserver (Wolff 1974:59-60).

In somewhat similar language, Hebrew Scripture pictures humans drawn into specific relationships and responsibilities through God's address, or call, and being summoned to give answer. In the wisdom writings, such responsible hearing is "the root of true humanity" (p. 74). Thus the Servant of Yahweh, whose role Christians believe Jesus to have fulfilled, stands "as prototype for humanity *per se*" in the following passage:

The Lord Yahweh has given me the tongue of a scholar;
So that I might know how to 'answer' him that is weary,
   he raised up a word.
Morning by morning God wakens my ear
   to hear as those who are taught.
The Lord Yahweh has opened my ear,
   and I was not rebellious, I did not shrink back. (Isaiah 50:4-5, Wolff's

translation; see p. 75)[5]

Through such calls, and in responses that they seek to make, persons begin truly to know themselves. "Self-knowledge does not come about through self-reflection"—not chiefly through introspection, centering or experiencing the felt meanings of feelings—"but through the call which opens up a new vista" (p. 76). Authentic self-awareness commences with initiatives and events which place individuals before new situations and thus bring to light their strengths and weaknesses, their wishes and fears, and call them to new kinds of action.

The foundational role of God's call is vividly illustrated in histories of many of Israel's great leaders. Their experiences should not be regarded as atypical, for they were the initial means through which God called an entire people. The history of Israel began with Abram and Sarai, who were called to leave their country and kin and travel toward a land which God would show them (Gen 12:1-3). In New Testament times, their response was still regarded as the chief instance of human faithfulness, or faith (Rom 4:16-22; Heb 11:8-12, 17-19).

When their descendants languished in Egyptian slavery, liberation began with God's well-known calling of Moses (Ex 3:1—4:17). Similarly the great prophets began their ministries in response to specific calls (Is 6:1-13; Jer 1:4-19; Ezek 1:1—3:12). These calls, however, challenged them to move quite counter to their contemporary societies and brought great conflict. Given this background (and much more could be given), we can appreciate how studies of Jesus which eliminate his calling (in his baptism), its testing (in the wilderness) and his controversies with opponents omit dimensions thought crucial to forming a person in Jesus' historical context (see chapter eight).

Such calls have at least two aspects. They involve risk—they call for courage, spontaneity and willingness to suffer in discerning God's direction into a dark, unknown future. However, they also demand obedience to whatever God reveals—so much so that our response can be summarized by this term. Jesus' response to God is epitomized as obedience in several key New Testament texts (Rom 5:19; Phil 2:8; Heb 5:8). However, we recall the vitality of his relationships to his Father and Spirit and his struggles with the character of his mission—in the wilderness, at Peter's confession, in Gethsemane, on the cross and in encounters with human and demonic foes. Indeed, Hebrews stresses that Jesus "learned obedience through what he suffered" (5:8; compare 5:7-9; 3:17-18).

Accordingly, if one summarizes Jesus' (and his Hebrew forerunners') response to God as obedience, one should notice that this is different from rigid, unimaginative conformity to legal precepts. Otherwise, however, *obedience* could be a good term for indicating that, in biblical perspective, the self's character is formed not chiefly through examining or experiencing our organism or deeper center but through active response to a call from beyond ourselves. (For a fuller discussion, see Finger 1989:94-96.)

Nevertheless, it seems that *faithfulness,* which expresses the personal, risky and spontaneous dimensions of this response yet includes the obedience aspect, is more adequate.[6] I propose therefore that in an anthropology grounded in biblical history as pointing to, fulfilled in and critiqued by Jesus' human activity, one major characteristic of mature humanity is *faithfulness.* However, most biblical characters, like most persons everywhere, do not develop very far in faithfulness and often move counter to it. Consequently another term is needed to describe humankind's more general relationship to God.

Recalling biblical affirmations about humans being dependent for breath on God's outbreathing, I propose *dependence* on God. I affirm, that is, from a biblical perspective, that all humans are dependent on God for their initial and continued existence and that however much they may oppose, ignore or be unaware of this, they can never fall out of this relationship. The mature, positive actualization of this relationship, however—grounded more in God's specific call than in God's general outbreathing—I name *faithfulness.*[7]

Though my description of faithfulness has been drawn largely from Jesus and those who anticipated him, trinitarian faith affirms that the one God is drawing all persons toward the maturity most fully revealed through them.[8] Let us see, then, what implications this notion of response to God's call would have for the general issue of becoming a self.

Selfhood would be formed through a process of encounter with different, sometimes unforseen and often difficult situations. Our full self would not be present at life's beginning as a far more real entity underlying a surface flux of diverse experiences and alienations. The self, rather, would attain form within this flux, by wrestling with these situations. This process, of course, would include increasing awareness of our drives and feelings, but not so much as stable rhythms underlying the self as energies which might take different forms in response to different situations. Our overall self, we might say, would have to be constructed and reconstructed in response to varying outward circumstances. So far, this process seems closer to the psychoanalytic than to the organismic perspective—though response would ultimately be to a guiding force rather than simply to conflicting drive and social demands.

Since biblical calls come to those with personalities somewhat formed, it is not immediately clear whether some incipient self is present from the beginning. Yet Jeremiah's call begins with the assurance that God knew him before he was conceived (Jer 1:5). Samuel (1 Sam 1:11-18), John the Baptist (Lk 1:13-17) and even all Christians (Eph 1:4-5) seem to be foreknown in this way too. Since God is said to be involved in the formation of the fetus (Ps 139:13-16), it seems that some incipient self exists from the start, as in much object relations, and that the self cannot merely be a social fiction (Lacan). Yet this does not conflict with the notion that the self keeps being formed and re-formed throughout life.

Selfhood and society. So far I have spoken mainly of the individual's formation. I have not asked whether our social matrix, except as an initial negative influence, need have relatively little impact on our basic self, as many organismic theorists imply, or whether personal formation is always deeply intertwined with this matrix and incapable of being significantly altered unless society is, as psychoanalysts who believe in the latter's possibility affirm.

Individuals in Scripture are called for the sake of groups. Abram and Sarai are called so that in them "all the families of the earth shall be blessed" (Gen 12:3). Moses is called in order to liberate Israel so that it will become God's "treasured possession," a "priestly kingdom," mediating God's presence to all nations (Ex 19:5-6). Ultimately it is groups of people, and through them all peoples, that are called to transformation in Scripture. Obedience is to be corporate, which is why Yahweh's covenant contains many social regulations. These regulations, if followed, will produce a social life manifesting God's character to the nations (Deut 4:6-8).

Moreover, personal identity is so intertwined with group structure in Hebrew Scripture that the former cannot exist without the latter (Robinson [1935] 1980). They are so interrelated that a figure such as the Servant can stand both for a great individual (whom Christians identified ultimately with Jesus) and for the whole nation (see Is 44:1, 21). Similarly the Son of Man is depicted as an individual (Dan 7:14) but also as "the holy ones of the Most High" (v. 18).

Even individuals called to separate from the crowd found adherents with whom they shared distinct lifestyles. Abram and Sarai had their own large household. Moses helped form new national legislation. Prophets normally had their own followings, or schools. All this indicates that in Israel personal development was deeply intertwined with some social matrix in all its phases.

If Jesus is the ultimate norm of authentic humanity, however, it would seem that this corporate element must vanish. For Jesus was, after all, an individual. Yet if we focus on the way Jesus acted toward others, our impression alters. Karl Barth has rightly said that what distinguishes Jesus

> as a true and natural man, is that in his existence He is referred to man, to other men, His fellows, and this not merely partially, incidentally or subsequently, but originally, exclusively, totally. When we think of the humanity of Jesus, humanity is to be described unequivocally as fellow humanity. In the light of this man Jesus, man is the cosmic being which exists absolutely for its fellows. (1960:208)

The behavior through which Jesus lived for others can perhaps best be designated as *servanthood*. It recalls how Jesus fulfilled the Servant role prophesied by Isaiah. Jesus emphasized servanthood, combining it with the Son of Man title, and explained its meaning for his followers shortly before his death:

> You know that among the Gentiles those whom they recognize as their rulers lord it over them, and their great ones are tyrants over them. But it is not so among you; but whoever wishes to become great among you must be your servant, and whoever wishes to be first among you must be slave of all. For the Son of Man came not to be served but to serve, and to give his life a ransom for many. (Mk 10:42-45)[9]

The ethical emphasis of this text recalls that the Servant's task involved calling all peoples to Yahweh (Is 49:5-6) and that Servant is also a corporate concept. This text thus indicates that Jesus' Servant mission was intended to gather a group of people living according to the servant way (Manson 1955:178-81, 227-32). This way surely has social dimensions, for it is part of Jesus' broader call to God's kingdom, where relationships among rich and poor, Jew and Gentile, male and female are reversed (see chapter eight). Jesus' call to personal repentance is always a call to God's kingdom. Since servanthood will be practiced by all who respond, I will call the second major characteristic of mature humanity *mutual servanthood*.

The adjective is important. By itself, emphasis on servanthood can encourage repeated submission to oppression and abuse. When that occurs, servanthood does not point toward healthy social relationships but legitimates the worst kinds of sinful ones, as Rosemary Ruether insists (see chapter seven). At other times, however, submission to oppression can be prophetic (as in nonviolent actions which exemplify servant behavior but expose the brutality of those who oppose it).

Mutual servanthood is a corporate behavior which often motivates and energizes participants to suffer for others. Nevertheless since individuals are dependent on God and interdependent with each other, no one should be expected to give repeatedly what they have not first received. Christians believe that the deepest kind of love originates from Jesus' unique self-giving servanthood and that mutual servanthood is a response to it and is energized by it. Throughout his life Jesus was strengthened by the giving of his Father and Spirit, to whom he also gave himself. Mutual servanthood, then, is ultimately a divine activity, flowing from the mutual self-giving of Son, Spirit and Father (as explained more fully in chapter ten).

Whereas mutual servanthood is the positive actualization of a fundamental structural feature of human nature, I will call this structure itself *cohumanity*. Just as *dependence* on God, considered as a basic anthropological structure, means that humans can never drop out of relationship with God, so *cohumanity* indicates that even if individuals try to ignore or oppose their fellows, they can never escape intrinsic interdependence with them (contrary to Nozick [see chapter four]).

Even rebellions against relationships or social structures are significantly shaped by that which is opposed. This again indicates that personal development is deeply impacted by our social circumstances and that personal transformation cannot go far unless the social circumstances are also altered. Marcuse's position, that social circumstances significantly imprint the most basic ways in which humans feel and think, seems basically accurate.

Finally, if humans are intrinsically cohuman, traditions (the means by which groups pass on their structures and wisdom) will be indispensable to human life. Although bad traditions surely exist, there is no warrant for automatically regarding traditions negatively and seeking to eliminate them, as Enlightenment individualism has dreamed. For healthy societies and individuals to exist, there must be healthy traditions.

Selfhood and nature. Human existence is shaped by broad structural relationships not only to God and with others but also with the rest of nature. This dimension, however, probably cannot be derived as clearly from Jesus, even though it is evident in his keen appreciation for natural creatures (Mt 6:25-33 and so on) and in his sharing ordinary human bodily needs.

Humankind's interdependence with nature is perhaps most evident in Genesis, where humans are made from the same "dust" as all other earthly creatures (Gen 2:7, 9, 19) and where many creatures suffer when humankind sins (3:17-19). Throughout Hebrew Scripture, moreover, the land's fate is deeply tied to Israel's obedience or disobedience (Deut 11:11-17; Jer 3:2-3; Amos 4:6-9). If Israelites, who do not absolutely own the land (only God does), fail to let it rest during sabbatical years, they will be removed so that this can happen (Lev 25:1-7; 26:34-35, 43; 2 Chron 36:21). Bad social, religious or ecological practices will cause the land to "vomit out" its violators (Lev 18:28; 20:22). On the other hand, faithfulness to God's religious and social regulations will bring blessings to the land.

Despite being interconnected with every creature, humans possess far greater capacity to affect the fate of all than does any other. Humanity's relationship with the rest of nature can be called *oversight.*[10] Oversight means that humans cannot avoid somehow shaping and directing the lives of many other species, even if they seek to avoid it (as some deep ecologists might), or whether they do so in a dominating, destructive fashion.

Oversight is positively actualized through *stewardship,* in which humans care for other creatures as God intends and avoid exploiting them for our own ends. As stewards, humans are under God's authority and are not now themselves evolution self-directing its own process (see chapters three, six). Since ecology shows that many ecosystems function best when following their own rhythms, stewardship would advocate that any interaction with them would be as well-informed about these rhythms as possible. Including oversight of nature among humanity's three fundamental anthropological structures indicates that the way people understand themselves and relate to God and other humans is inseparable from the way they shape nature.

Basic Anthropological Capacities
Though I am treating Jesus as the ultimate anthropological norm, I have indicated that not everything pertinent to human life can be derived directly from him. That is especially because, whereas Jesus wrestled with sin, he never shared our situation of captivity under it and our struggle to be liberated.[11] To best understand these dimensions, we must turn to biblical writings that express a more existential awareness of how sin disfigures us and of emerging potentialities for life in harmony with God.

It is sometimes said that Scripture presents no systematic anthropology. That is true in the sense that no comprehensive teaching is elucidated at any one place and that anthropological terms can be used in different ways. Nonetheless much as distinct understandings of God and history pervade the Bible, so its fairly fluid anthropological expressions will fall into significant patterns if we handle them neither too rigidly nor too loosely. We will even find that a somewhat systematic use of several anthropological terms was worked out by Paul.[12] Though some texts mentioned below express distinctly Christian experiences, trinitarian faith affirms that they articulate the destiny to which everyone is called.

Body. When traditional anthropologies considered biblical terms clustering around the word *body,* they assumed that the body of the individual, which separates one from others, was being designated. They usually discussed how this physical component was related to another, separable component called the *soul.* In Scripture, however, body words chiefly indicate that which unites creatures, rather than what distinguishes them. The Hebrew Scriptures have a single word *(basar)* for the whole mass of bones, blood and organs which make up the human and animal worlds. Bodies do not separate persons from each other and from other creatures; bodies place them in solidarity. Members of the same family or nation may be called each other's flesh, or bone and flesh (Gen 37:27; 2 Sam 5:1; Neh 5:5). *Basar* also refers to humankind from the perspective of its frailty and constant need for God (Job 34:14-15; 2 Chron 32:8; Is 40:6) and even its ethical vulnerability, although *basar* is not directly equated with sin.

In the New Testament, Paul uses the Greek word for body *(sōma)* to indicate what we think of as physical characteristics and also to indicate solidarity among persons. Sexual union is called becoming "one body," but one body can also indicate the unity of Christians in Christ (1 Cor 6:15-16; 12:12-31; Eph 5:28-31). Solidarity among humans and the rest of creation is indicated when Paul says that the Spirit who gives new life to our bodies (Rom 8:11) and groans within us as he hastens our renewal also groans in anticipation of a coming transformation throughout the entire creation (vv. 19-23).

Paul also uses body words to indicate the entire person—but seen from a particular standpoint, as is evident in the following parallels:

Let not sin therefore reign in your mortal *bodies [sōma]* . . . .

Do not yield your *members* to sin as instruments of wickedness,

but yield *yourselves* to God. (Rom 6:12-13 RSV)

To say "Yield your body" is a concrete, emphatic way of saying "Yield your entire self" (compare 12:1)! Note that in Romans 6 the body, understood in this sense, is the means of entering into solidarity with sin or God.

Flesh. The Hebrew Scriptures have but one word which is translated both as "body" and "flesh." Though the New Testament has two, "flesh" *(sarx)* can also be used in the same way as "body" *(sōma).* Flesh can indicate solidarities: racial ones (Paul calls Jews simply "my flesh" [Rom 11:14]), and both slavery (Eph 6:5) and freedom from slavery (Philem 16), which are social orders "according to the flesh." *Sarx,* like *sōma,* can also designate the entire person viewed from a particular standpoint.[13] However, when Paul speaks of human frailty, he uses flesh rather than body (1 Cor 15:50;

2 Cor 1:17; Gal 4:13).

This distinction develops into an important terminological difference when Paul uses *flesh* to denote sinful humanity, or humanity under sin's power.[14] For flesh involves being subject to "passions" *(epithymiai)* that frequently are contrary to God (Rom 13:14; Gal 5:16, 24). Following these, people become subject to spiritual forces that oppose God (Eph 2:2-3). Flesh itself, in fact, can denote a suprapersonal spiritual force which strongly opposes God (Rom 7:14; Gal 5:17). Flesh in this sense, then, indicates far more than human biology. It extends generally to placing our total reliance on things that are perceptible and measurable, such as Jewish law or customs (Rom 2:28; Gal 3:3; 6:13), pagan religious observances (Col 2:18-23) and human achievement or pedigree (2 Cor 11:18; Phil 3:3-7). What do the biblical uses of body and flesh tell us about human nature?

First, since they can describe the whole person seen from a particular angle, and since yielding or directing our body is a way of doing so with our entire self, they do not seem to denote a distinct human component separable from another, such as a soul. Body and flesh, in fact, seem to function not so much like nouns designating parts as like verbs indicating certain ways of being.[15]

Second, body terms do not refer to distinctions between humans but to solidarities among them, and among humans and other creatures. It is through bodily dispositions that we become connected with others. Paul's use of these terms indicates, in fact, that humans basically exist within one of two great solidarities: the flesh which opposes God, and the body of Christ. Body words confirm, from another angle, what was discovered in the notion of cohumanity—that the individual's character is essentially shaped by the solidarity of which he or she is a part.

Desires. Many New Testament writers use a common word—*epithymia* (and its verb form *epithymeō*)—to indicate desires of all kinds. In general Greek usage it carries no moral connotations. In Scripture it can refer to natural physical urges and even desire for God's revelation (Mt 13:17) or presence (Phil 1:23). Even the Spirit can be said to strive passionately *(epithymei)* against the flesh (Gal 5:17).

Yet in the overwhelming number of instances, this term indicates desires opposed to God, such as those that give birth to sin and then death (Jas 1:14-15). Sometimes it is best translated simply as "lust" (Rom 1:26), "covetousness" (7:7-8) or some other obviously negative term. Since New Testament authors regard human desires as generally perverted by a deeper orientation of persons against God, they would hardly recommend listening to them as a key to discovering our true selves. Yet "desires," in and of themselves, are neutral and can even be oriented toward the good.

Soul. The Hebrew word usually translated "soul" *(nephesh)* often designates the organs of the throat and neck. Since eating, drinking and breathing, which are essential to life, involve taking in things through these organs, *nephesh* can designate the entire person desiring or striving for life. It can even be translated "life." But while it can also indicate the source of our spiritual actions and emotions, *nephesh* never means a nonphysical, indestructible core of being. It always characterizes the person who can receive life only from God "but who is eager for God, spurred on by vital desire" (Wolff 1974:24).

The New Testament word for soul *(psychē)*, like those for body and flesh, can indicate the whole person. "Every soul" simply means "everyone" (Acts 2:43). *Psychē* can also indicate a person's "life." More precisely, like *nephesh*, *psychē* can mean "that specifically human state of being alive which adheres in man as a striving, willing, purposing self" (Bultmann 1951:205). As the human's intentional life, this soul can persist beyond death, but only if it is continually energized by God. For this word can also indicate perishable, even carnal, life apart from God (1 Cor 2:14; Jas 3:15; Jude 19).

In sum, words commonly translated "soul" no more denote a separable component than do body words. Soul, again like body, indicates the entire person viewed from a particular angle. Seen from this angle, human life involves continuously renewed purposive activity, such as we would expect from following God's call. Yet the connection of soul, or life, with breath suggests that it is sustained only by the repeated outbreathing of God.

Spirit. The Hebrew and Greek words rendered "spirit" often mean wind and are again connected with breathing. Moreover, they are the usual words for God's Spirit. Applied to humans, the Hebrew *ruach* comes closest to what we think of as the will. It can be patient or proud (Prov 16:18; Eccles 7:8), and can endure or be broken (Prov 18:14; Wolff 1974:37-39). But above all, it is that dimension of the person most open to being moved by God's Spirit.

The New Testament *pneuma*, like all Greek terms discussed so far, can refer to the whole person.[16] Phrases such as a "spirit of gentleness" (1 Cor 4:21; Gal 6:1) and the "spirit of faith" (2 Cor 4:13) refer not to components or entities but to overall human attitudes and orientations. Yet *pneuma*, like *ruach*, refers most distinctively to the whole person as open to God's Spirit.[17] And the Spirit, who raised Jesus from the dead, is, and bestows, divine life in the most direct sense (Jn 3:5-6; Rom 8:6, 10-12).

This divine Spirit does not repress the human spirit but, after delivering it from sin and death (Rom 8:2), opens it up to genuine freedom (2 Cor 3:17). Crying "Abba! Father!" within us, it testifies most intimately that we are God's children (Rom 8:14-16; Gal 4:6). The goal toward which the whole creation surges and groans is the freedom of God's children (Rom 8:21). Humans, then, are in solidarity with the rest of creation not only through their bodies but also insofar as they are energized by God's Spirit.

When human spirits are energized by God's Spirit, they often experience peace—yet not continual, undisturbed plateaus of peace, for the Spirit struggles mightily against the solidarity of the flesh working both within and outside us (Rom 8:5-8; Gal 5:17) and puts to death its sinful deeds (Rom 8:13). The Spirit's movement throughout creation, in which humans participate, is called a "groaning," for the Spirit wrestles against all that opposes freedom and life. Thus spirit/Spirit terminology expresses, from another angle, much of what I emphasized about human life as actualized through faithfulness to God's call.

Heart. Body, soul, and *spirit* do not denote some inner essence of the human being (rather, each indicates the whole person, but as seen from differing perspectives). One biblical term, though, does often designate our deepest interiority: *heart*. Like *nephesh* ("soul") the Hebrew *leb(ab)* can mean desire and longing (Ps 21:2; Prov 13:12). It can also indicate various emotions, especially courage and fear (2 Sam 17:10; Ps 40:12; Is 7:2). More self-reflective notions are conveyed by phrases such as our "heart smote" us, which expresses what we think of as conscience, and speaking in, or to, our heart, which means thinking something over (Gen 24:45; 1 Sam 27:1; 1 Kings 12:26-28). Whereas many current psychologies and spiritualities oppose reason ("the head") to the emotions ("the heart"), *leb(ab)* includes both.[18]

In the New Testament, the *kardia* (heart) is the person's true center, according to Jesus and others (Mt 12:34; Mk 7:18-23; 1 Pet 3:4). When people are truly united, they are united in heart (Acts 4:32; Phil 1:7; Col 2:2). Yet what we truly think or intend, or what is in our heart, is often deeply hidden under outward appearances (Mk 7:6; Rom 2:28-29; 2 Cor 5:12). Salvation occurs only when God transforms the heart in these depths (Mt 13:14-15; Jn 12:39-41; Acts 28:26-27; Heb 8:8-12; 10:16-17).[19] These last two features of biblical anthropology, perhaps more than any others, indicate that each human possesses a deep interiority which individuates one from another, as Niebuhr and Novak would affirm (see chapter seven)—in addition to our irrefragable corporate interrelations indicated by *body* and *flesh*.

Heart in the New Testament also refers to what we often think of as physical drives (Mt 5:28; Acts 14:17; Rom 1:24), emotions (Jn 16:6; Rom 10:1;

Jas 3:14), the will's intentions (Jn 13:2; Acts 8:22; 1 Cor 7:37) and thinking (Mt 24:48; Lk 2:51; Acts 7:23)—frequently on a subconscious level (Mk 11:23; 1 Cor 4:5; Heb 4:12). Heart again shows that biblical writers think of persons as units who cannot be subdivided into different faculties or components.

Conscience. The Hebrew Scriptures, we have noticed, can express the notion of conscience by the phrase, our "heart smote" us.[20] The New Testament has a precise word for conscience: *syneidēsis.* According to Romans 2:15, conscience witnesses to a divine law written on all hearts. Here, it seems, is a source of knowledge about God which everyone possesses. However, Paul's more detailed discussion shows that the matter is more complex.

In 1 Corinthians 8 and 10:23-30, Paul raises the problem of new Christians' eating meat which has been offered to idols (as most meat from Corinthian markets had been). Mature Christians, of course, know that "no idol in the world really exists" (8:4) and that meat sacrificed to one cannot hurt anyone. Yet the consciences of many new Christians still tell them that idols are real, so if they eat meat formerly offered to idols, they transgress what their conscience says. That is, Paul affirms that what conscience says may be false.[21] Nevertheless, it is extremely important that people's actions correspond with what their conscience tells them. Accordingly, Paul advises mature Christians initially to forgo eating meat offered to idols in order to avoid confusing or offending newer Christians.

The major point here is that conscience does not automatically affirm divine truth, or even truth about ourselves. It endorses whatever we believe to be true, as taught by our religion and culture. Conscience, we might say, is formed in accordance with some external source; it is religiously and socially constructed and conditioned. Only through a process of exposure to Christian truth does our conscience come to affirm it (1 Tim 1:5; Heb 9:9, 14).[22]

Reason. My discussion of *heart* showed that biblical writers, unlike many current psychologies and spiritualities, do not sharply contrast reason and feelings. Instead, both exercise significant functions of our deepest center. Reason plays an important role in human life, as is shown by the fact that the New Testament employs several nouns for "knowledge" and many verbs for "knowing," "thinking" and "considering."[23] Readers are continually urged to ponder, learn about and reflect upon life's meaning, especially that of God's saving activity.

Like conscience, reason focuses on something external to itself and does not ponder itself to find truth. Yet even though reason must play a significant role in discerning truth, and can know something about God, it is not sufficient to turn the whole person toward God (see Acts 14:15-17; 17:23-29; Rom 1:19-20; 2:14-16).[24] That can occur only when God, as Holy Spirit, touches and transforms the heart.

Psychological and Spiritual Dynamics

I began this chapter by outlining the main themes of a theological anthropology that takes Jesus as its norm. I then sketched some anthropological capacities as firmly as the somewhat fluid biblical materials allow. I can now devote the rest of this chapter to filling in my own theological perspective on psychological and spiritual alienation by discussing the basic issues raised in chapters two and five.

The role of drives. According to writers as different as Sigmund Freud and John of the Cross, the physical drives ("appetites" in John) pose great obstacles to unity in the self, for each drive is short-lived, blind and strives solely after its own gratification. Consequently drives militate against the unity of purposive activity necessary for there to be a self. The organismic perspective, on the other hand, regards diverse drives as aspects of one master drive and therefore not essentially conflicting with unity of purpose at all. Both Carl Rogers and bio-spirituality propose that in-touchness with our organismic feelings is enough to give coherent direction to our life. Matthew Fox affirms that our organisms are, and should be, motivated by pleasure and that unleashed desires need not spawn chaos but can be regulated by "a bridle of love."

My theological anthropology regards physical bodies as intrinsic aspects of what humans are, finding no indication that they are lower than some other component (such as a soul). Since all created capacities are at least potentially good, I can affirm that our drives, or desires, of themselves are potentially capable of indicating, or at least cooperating with, positive personal orientations. However, the strongly negative use of "desires" *(epithymiai)* in Scripture shows that, as actually operating, the drives often conflict with our optimum overall direction. Still this problem cannot be attributed to the drives themselves, as if the physical organism alone had become defective. For the passage which describes most vividly how sin operates in individuals emphasizes a stranger duality dividing the entire person.

"I do not understand my own actions," laments Paul, "for I do not do what I want, but I do the very thing I hate" (Rom 7:15). Yet even though the "I" does these things in one sense, there is another in which it does not. For "if I do what I do not want," Paul reasons, "it is no longer I that do it, but sin that dwells within me" (v. 20). And this "law of sin," which wars against the "I" that wants to do good, dwells especially "in my members" (v. 23), making "my flesh . . . a slave to the law of sin" (v. 25).

Paul, that is, recognizes a force, distinguishable from our inmost self (yet to which the "I" also paradoxically consents), which operates through our body, and yet is something greater than that body. For this force of sin, as the overall context shows, is a collective force which pervades the social world (5:12-13; 6:16-20). Its capacity to create such an internal division shows that it is capable of suffusing or capturing or imprinting the bodily desires at a very deep level (cf. 7:14).

Bodily desires *(epithymiai),* then, have the structural capacity of flowing in positive personal directions—but also of thoroughly opposing, and thereby dividing, our pursuit of such directions. That indicates that these drives are highly adaptable. It suggests that the physical human organism, rather than being automatically programmed toward either good or evil on a biological level, is quite flexible. It is capable of taking numerous directions under the influence of different forces. We cannot assume, then, that this organism, simply left to itself, would move in a God-ward direction.

Further, human actions always involve choice, and authentic choice is impossible unless organisms can be directed along other paths. Moreover, we cannot assume that individual organisms ever are left to themselves. For biblical affirmations about body, flesh and cohumanity indicate that these organisms are always shaped by corporate forces. I suspect, then, that simply "listening to one's organism," by itself, is an impossibility. I propose that no one really decides how to act unless this listening is also shaped, whether one is aware of it or not, by social expectations.[25]

I am not implying that every action is rigidly determined by some social code. For social expectations usually provide somewhat broad frameworks permitting a range of choices. I also do not mean that we cannot act contrary to given social expectations, only that even these actions are still shaped by such expectations negatively or by other expectations (in most societies, for instance, teenage rebellions fall into fairly standard patterns). However, since "following one's organism" involves congruence with some social patterns, many who experience significant self-actualization in this way, even if they reject certain corporate expectations, are probably fitting rather well into some culture or counterculture.

Indeed, listening to our organism, or to our inner child, can work well in societies which are (1) individualistic, allowing people to follow their inclinations, and (2) affluent and hedonistic, so that most desires can be satisfied without difficulty or reproach (see chapter two). However, if someone experiences self-actualization in such a society, this need not mean, theologically, that this person is moving in a Godward direction. For that society may be moving in opposition to God. If so, much of the actualization we experience could consist in conformity to that society and still be under the power of "the flesh."

Theology is unable to say precisely how blind, short-lived or narrowly focused each drive may be, for, contrary to Freud, it seems impossible to isolate pure biological drives (like separable Newtonian atoms) from the overall biosocial matrix through which they have been shaped. Yet theology also cannot, with organicism, assert that all drives are dimensions of one master drive. My major point is that the drives appear quite malleable and can be shaped in many ways. This should guard against biological pessimism, such as has sometimes infested Christianity, which assumes that organic processes automatically tend toward evil. It should also critique a biological romanticism which assumes that human organic processes, on their own, can inherently move toward good. For, as Reinhold Niebuhr maintained, human biological processes never operate autonomously but are always shaped by other factors (see chapter seven).

That does not mean, of course, that awareness of felt needs is unimportant in self-formation. We could hardly integrate drives with other factors if we were unaware of what they were saying. It only means that our organism cannot be regarded as a complete, fool-proof indicator of all that self-actualization involves. Further, given how extensively our desires are shaped by capitalism, it is naive to assert, as Fox does, that if we are motivated by pleasure, we will unfold toward God. It is also simplistic to assume that unleashed desires can be regulated by a "bridle of love" without indicating the radical change of perspective and ethical discipline that need to be involved.

Reason, imagination or feeling? For many current psychologies and spiritualities, alienation consists largely in being somehow distanced from our most intense and significant experiences and moods. Accordingly these approaches stress those capacities which connect us most directly to such phenomena: the emotions, or feelings, and that capacity through which these are often vividly symbolized—imagination. Reason, which remains more distant from particular experiences and classifies them into general categories, can be regarded as an alienating activity.

For bio-spirituality, feelings and images put us in touch with felt meanings, which are said to differ almost always from rational awareness. Fox often privileges "right-brain" activities (for example, art as meditation) over "left-brain" ones, though he sometimes speaks of balancing the two. Welch regards images as the basic route to psychological truth, though he acknowledges that they also give rise to thought. I argued, however, that he rates images more highly than did Teresa of Ávila or John of the Cross. Whereas Marcuse respects reason, he finds phantasy the key to visions, which can transcend personal and social alienation. Alan Jones, however, not only grants reason an important—though limited—role but warns that excessive reliance on experience can become a drug, requiring ever greater doses.

On such matters, Teresa, John and centering prayer are really on another wavelength. For although they find limited value in feeling, imagination and reason at certain stages, their real emphasis is on going beyond all three. John can speak drastically of the senses, imagination and reason being annihilated. If Teresa and John stress any human capacity, it is the will, for it is through love, which especially touches the will, that we finds deepest union with God.

What can be said about the roles and values of these various human capacities? I certainly agree that images are important. They form the vocabulary of dreams and frequently offer means of getting in touch with feelings. Vivid imagery runs all through Scripture, and its skillful use is a hallmark of the distinctive language of Jesus (see chapter eight). Imagination forms those visions of a better future that are essential for arousing individual and social hopes and releasing energy for transformation (see chapter seven).

I also grant that bio-spirituality's techniques can help people get in touch with felt meanings. But I find bio-spirituality inconsistent in sharply contrasting such techniques with all rational explanation and then placing the significance of these techniques within a vast and complex cosmogenesis, which it asks readers to simply accept. Bio-spirituality seems to be acknowledging that a spirituality needs a cosmic vision; yet it denies those processes of rational exploration and argumentation essential to authentically acquiring and affirming one.

Remembering the biblical understanding of the "heart," I am suspicious of privileging any human capacity above others. For if both reasoning and feelings emanate from the heart, both should be important means of apprehending psychological and spiritual reality. Moreover, if both are found in the heart, use of both would be appropriate when making the heart, or the self's center, our object of inquiry. But to exalt feeling or imagination because they more directly apprehend significant moods and experiences seems to imply that alienation and its overcoming have to do only with feelings—chiefly with how we feel about ourselves. It also seems to imply that comprehensive and sufficient awareness of ourselves (of our hearts) is available simply through feeling.

Without doubt, direct affective awareness of our experiences and moods is essential to overcoming psychological alienation. But I question whether all that needs to be apprehended about the self can be attained this way. I doubt, further, whether any self exists or can be adequately known simply by itself, apart from its social and natural relationships—any more than an organic drive can function apart from some social shaping. In other words, I question whether psychological alienation has to do simply with some isolable and directly known entity (the self) such that the more immediately this entity is apprehended, the more swiftly alienation can be overcome.

I affirm, on the contrary, that the self is also formed by various social and ecological relationships, so that overcoming even its self-alienation must involve some knowledge of these. But then the quest for adequate self-awareness will need to employ that capacity—reason—which steps back from immediate experiences and places them into broader categories and relationships.

Scripture, we have seen, employs many words for knowing, and these words urge people to ponder, learn about and reflect on life's meaning. That is partly because it regards people as concrete individuals existing in particular interpersonal and social relationships. To know who they are, they need to ponder themselves and those relationships. Even that capacity which might seem to enjoy most direct access to the self—conscience—is formed by such relationships. Scripture also employs many words for knowing because people need to know of God's saving historical action and how they are called into it if they are to become fully aware of who they are and what they can become.

In the biblical perspective, then, real self-understanding cannot be only direct, affective awareness of self; it will always involve some understanding of our world, other people and God. At the same time, of course, mere understanding of these things is never enough. We also need to embrace relationships with God and others and gain deeper insights about ourselves on an affective level, and we need to serve God and others in practical, ethical ways.

How does my perspective jibe with claims that the highest self- and God-awareness transcends all sensations, images and thoughts? Since God transcends all events, activities, symbols and concepts, God may indeed be encountered in ways which surpass space-time categories and our usual modes of apprehending them. Yet such *experiences* do not warrant the *metaphysical* conclusion often drawn from them—that space, time, sensation, imagination and reason are irrelevant to the self's deepest nature. Such a conclusion clashes with the biblical emphasis that humans are intrinsically bodily and that their life/soul, even though it may be extended beyond death, is perishable, existing at any time only through continually receiving from God.

From a biblical perspective, the claim that we essentially transcend space-time can be an attempt to deny our finitude and essential dependence on God. It may be a narcissistic attempt to identify ourselves with an omnipotent object. It may be an escape, as Ruether points out in chapter six, from a world riddled with uncertainty, death and decay, and from the risky venture of following God's call, fashioning and refashioning a fragile self out of changing experiences, drives and social pressures.

Still, experiences of union with God that transcend ordinary space-time awareness undoubtedly occur. But when they do, they should be gratefully received as gifts, making us even more aware of our finitude and dependence on God's awesome mystery. They are not to be taken, explicitly or implicitly, as evidence that we essentially transcend physical and social relationships.

Mystics such as Teresa and John describe their experiences much more than they teach metaphysics. Recall especially Teresa's insistence that we never outgrow our need for Jesus in his sacred humanity, who reappears in the last dwellings of her journey. In addition, whereas Teresa and John sometimes image the soul and God as almost indistinguishable, these images are balanced by those of God at great distances and heights.

I have argued that Welch assimilates the self more closely with God and the Christ-symbol than John and Teresa did (see chapter five). Moreover, centering prayer was originally prefaced by careful Scripture reading, which placed it within a biblical worldview. Only recently, responding "to the contemporary attraction for how-to methods" (Keating 1986:34), have these first steps been omitted, leading to an emphasis on experiential union which may be separated from this interpretive context.

Finally, what of Teresa's and John's emphasis on the will as the point of union with God? Though I resist privileging any human capacity above others, I appreciate their insistence that communion with God involves actions as well as experiences and thoughts. As Teresa said, all efforts at union with God are vain if they do not lead us to love and serve our neighbors. Yet she and John stress that following God's will demands a crucifixion of our will and of those pleasures which, in Fox's view, guide the organism.

The path of growth. Having discussed the drives and capacities that humans bring to life's tasks, what more can be said about the path along which God's call draws them? Should we expect healthy human activity to be regulated by some process of organismic self-balancing, or *equalization* (Goldstein), so that conflict would result only from breakdowns of natural functions? Or might conflict be more basic to human activity, even considered apart from sin?

Scripture is pervaded by visions of peaceful, harmonious societies, where everything operates in balance. These include imagery of nature's abundance and rhythmic processes. In a few cases, innocent children are highlighted (for example, Is 11:6-9). Such visions express the importance of organismic balance as an eschatological goal. If this balance is a meaningful goal, tendencies toward it must surely exist in the present. Human organisms must at least strive toward it, and it must be compatible with, and in some sense perfect, their structures.

However, in critiquing Matthew Fox, Thomas Berry and Brian Swimme, Sallie McFague argues that their celebratory view of nature well expresses an eschatological vision but not the dire reality of evolutionary conflict and struggle (1993:70-83). My perspective on organismic psychology and spirituality is similar: they accurately intuit dimensions of humanity's future goal, but they assume that present reality is, at bottom, much more like this than it is.

The centrality of God's call toward an unknown future and the adaptability of our drives indicate that even in a sinless world human activity might not always follow inner rhythmic patterns; it might involve uncertainties, mistaken choices and tensions.[26] In a world where our organisms are always shaped by distorted social patterns, we can expect such things to mark our paths, even when we function as well as possible. I agree with Alan Jones that in undertaking life's journey we must forgo desires for "a secure if cheap equilibrium" (1992:18), be ready to encounter a void at the heart of consciousness and realize that the wound of transcendence which draws us on can also drive us mad.

According to Jones and other spiritual writers I have discussed, the Jesus-story provides the key to the human journey. The *faithfulness* and *servant-hood* exercised in Jesus' life, death and resurrection form the foundation of my anthropology. Notice, however, that these require that we give ourselves, or dedicate ourselves, to others. Becoming a self, then, paradoxically requires a certain losing of ourselves even apart from sin (and thus a theoretical possibility of alienation from self).

Notice further that Jesus' self-giving in our sinful world was prompted and strengthened by the Holy Spirit, the breather of divine life, who groans with longing for newness and freedom throughout creation (Rom 8). By allowing himself to be guided by the Spirit and to be a channel for the Spirit's energy, Jesus let himself be drawn into situations where people were alienated from this source of life and hope—and often alienated socially and from any meaningful sense of self. Servanthood, then, meant that Jesus entered into the alienated situations of others and confronted the social, psychological and spiritual forces that oppressed them.

This orientation of servanthood toward his fellow humans was at the same time the expression of Jesus' complete faithfulness toward God: his trust in his Father's guidance and his openness to the Spirit's energy. In his humanity, Jesus entered into profound union with God—one of will, trust and love. Yet in this vulnerable humanity, Jesus was increasingly exposed to the violence of a society pervaded by conflict and alienation. His suffering increased, and at the end he could feel separated from and abandoned by his Father. As William McNamara says, on the cross Jesus suffered the radical loss of God and found himself helpless to achieve what he sought. Yet his final cries were answered by resurrection, through the Spirit's energy, back into the intimate divine life.

These paradoxes—of finding ourselves by losing ourselves, of gaining union with God by entering into conflict with society, of dying to our achievements and abilities but being resurrected by God's renewing life— are at the heart of the Christian understanding of how we find our true selves and overcome psychological alienation (especially 2 Cor 4:7-11; Phil 3:7-14). This seems different from a process of gradually penetrating our psychic interior until we find our deepest self organically intertwined with God.

On this path we do not so much focus on our depths as on others—not so much penetrate our interior resources as empty them out of concern for others until we are filled by the concerns and loves of others and, ultimately, by those of the divine Other. Moreover, those fillings are hardly automatic results of these emptying processes, so they might be interpreted simply as the abandoning of our persona and emergence of our deeper self (Welch). Instead, that emptying exposes our finite fragility directly to the harsh possibilities of despair and death, and those fillings occur by grace, and often unexpectedly, from the initiative of that Other.

How might such a dialectic operate today? It would begin when we were somehow called by the Spirit—not necessarily in a religious way, since God calls all people—who energizes hope for a new quality of life involving ourselves and others. Eventually we would realize the inadequacy of our own resources to attain this goal and acknowledge a deep need for strength beyond ourselves. Some such resources might emerge from a deeper self in Jung's and Welch's sense, surfacing with greater insight, sensitivity or other gifts as a superficial persona shattered.

But ultimately if finding ourselves is connected with increasing hope and concern for others, our confidence would have to be not just in our deeper self but also in some power guiding others. Trust would be not simply in the resources of a deeper center but in One who is creating a new future for many. Strength from this One might often be received through the *agapē* channeled through other persons. The stronger this hope, the more it would energize us to struggle against forces which block it and perhaps to suffer much as Jesus did in taking on similar opposition.

This hope would be partly social—it would envision ourselves and others living in some situation with transformed corporate features. Movement toward it would involve breaking in some way with old social patterns and beginning to exist in new forms of companionship. This would involve significant internal and external changes. In such a process much help could be gained from models of how to live differently, handed down through some tradition(s).

Although increasing union with God would usher us into this journey and would create significant communion with others, we might often feel alone, overwhelmed in attempts to forge a different kind of self and life direction. God's presence might be experienced not so much as a harmony that resolved all conflicts as through the call that created these conflicts—and yet as a companionship amid struggle. Self-identity would be found not by delving beneath this struggle to find peace on some deeper level but by discovering a purpose and direction in the midst of it and being known and loved by God precisely there. Paradoxically, when we felt most overwhelmed with the attempt and most fragmented in our sense of self and purpose—and thus "died" to our own efforts—we might well experience God's resurrecting and integrating presence.

Though much of this path can be traversed apart from specific awareness or confession of Christ, since God calls all people toward it, the spirituality involved is trinitarian. We are first drawn by God's Spirit to hope for a new situation energized by divine life. The Spirit leads us, as it did Jesus, to challenge situations in ourselves and others which oppose this life.[27]

Following the route of Jesus the Son, we encounter situations which exceed our abilities to resolve. Like Jesus, we must die to efforts to change things on our own and rely on the Father's love (however we may apprehend it) and guidance to raise us, again through the Spirit, to keep following this call. In this process, we are sustained by the Father's love, the Spirit's energy and the Son's companionship and example.

Yet this triune life is restless, constantly flowing out from itself to bring healing and liberation to the world. So even as we are filled with this life, it moves us to pour ourselves out to bring health and hope to others; and even as we are emptied and opposed in the process, we are brought up against our limitations and drawn to open ourselves for an even deeper filling. The triune life continually circles out from God into the world, drawing empty and oppressed creatures into its healing flow, filling them and sending them again into the world to bring love and liberation to even more.

People caught up in this flow will find themselves being repeatedly challenged, filled, emptied and again filled—and continually becoming and discovering who they are through these processes. Though these processes will tend, eschatologically, toward equalization of internal energies, points on the way may involve disruption and sacrifice of such balanced development.

The depths of the self. I have been critiquing the notion that our true self is some unchanging essence abiding at an interior depth, rather than an activity continually forged through encounters with others and God. Yet spirituality, Scripture and much current psychology agree that selves have significant depths, regions of which are unconscious.

Freud regarded the unconscious as a seething cauldron of desires, mostly unacceptable in society. For Marcuse, however, it also contained phantasies of positively functioning bodies and societies. For Jung the unconscious harbored many positive potentialities, some emanating from a collective, racial deposit. He regarded the *shadow,* or the person's apparently negative side, as "90% gold." Jung saw the *self* as something deeper than the *persona* or *ego,* a transcendent function initially hidden in the germ plasm which could integrate the conscious and unconscious.

Perhaps no approach emphasizes the psychic depths' positive potential more than the inner child movement. Earlier, transactional analysis had mentioned a Natural Child whose spontaneous feelings need to be channeled by the Adult. Yet this became John Bradshaw's Wonder Child, who is always aware of our real needs and desires; and it even became Charles Whitfield's transcendental self, an infinite awareness of cosmic harmony making itself known. A feeling of wholeness within ourselves and with the cosmos, wherein even evil and suffering have a perfect place, will arise if we let the inner child emerge. Fox also celebrates the naturalness of the child in everyone.

I have already alluded to notions of the deeper self in many spiritualities. Centering prayer, which aims at immediate, nondual experience of being, regards the true self as nearly identical with God.[28] Employing trinitarian conceptuality, Basil Pennington speaks of Christians proceeding from and returning to the Father in the Spirit and being in some way Christ. In somewhat similar language, Fox calls the Cosmic Christ everyone's true self and the creative activity birthing God's Son. For Fox, God "out there" is the ultimate dualistic notion.

Moreover, when Teresa speaks of God's watering the soul from the castle's innermost room, she may be imaging what John explicitly says—that God is the self's deepest center. Yet she implies an important distinction when she says that we can uproot the soul and plant it elsewhere. And both Carmelites balance merging imagery with that of God at great distances and heights. Further, when Teresa and John stress "self-knowledge," they do not mean awareness of harmony with God but are referring to sin and deep alienation from God. Finally, remember that Jones speaks of a void at consciousness's heart, and McNamara warns against longings for cosmic consciousness and oceanic feelings, because we are dependent on God as a distinct Other to sanctify us.

Does some dimension of the self transcend space and time, and is it identical with God? The biblical notion of the heart indicates an important depth dimension in every person. Romans 7 shows the individual wrestling with elements that are both "I" and "not I" in some paradoxical sense of which one is not fully conscious. Yet the words most often translated "soul" (*nephesh, pneuma*) indicate that selves receive life from God and are wholly dependent on it and thus perishable.

The body, moreover, cannot be separated from what the self is, and the body/self is inextricably shaped by social, and therefore finite, features. Conscience also, which some regard as the point where humans find unity with God, is structured by social forces. The self, then, in its deepest nature, is finite and dependent on God and therefore distinct from God— though God can, through grace, dwell intimately within it.[29]

The Spirit also wrestles and groans on these levels (Rom 8:26-27), showing that positive potential exists there for something more than any given structuring. This likely includes images of fulfilled selves and societies, as Jung and Marcuse claim. Moreover, some incipient self is present from the beginning, for God's call affirms that individuals have been foreknown. From this I conclude that, although no dimension of the self is entirely exempt from social shaping, its depths cannot be reduced entirely to structured forces either.

Given how the self develops through varied responses to historical relationships and tasks and recalling how even its drives are malleable, it is best to think of these depths not as unalterable givens but as flexible potentialities for developing in various ways. We may regard each individual, that is, as being significantly shaped and motivated by a bundle of preferences, inclinations and aptitudes originally deeper than conscious awareness. These are closely intertwined with our physical organism and vary among individuals, as physical characteristics do. Yet they do not rigidly determine specific actions; rather they provide a *range* within which we may respond to particular relationships and situations.

These potentialities and their ranges usually become better known through increasing experience. That is why it is helpful at times to reflect on our deeper self, or "listen to [our] organism," to hear what it is saying and the felt meanings it is experiencing. Yet we should not suppose that we are getting in touch with some fixed, perhaps even divine, entity. Instead, we are becoming more aware of a range of preferences and aptitudes which already have been actualized in certain ways and which can be further actualized in still others. What we "hear," then, is not so much a fixed self as certain potentialities for becoming a self.

Perhaps since this self is continually being forged, a term such as *transcendence* (Niebuhr, Friere [see chapter seven]) best expresses the character of this movement.[30] Though God's "breath" and call continually sustain this movement, they will never become the self's essence. Instead, our soul or life *(psychē)* will be won or lost in following, or not following, this call (see Mk 8:34-37). Given the uncertainties of existence and the challenges involved in God's call, individuals will often experience anxiety at deep, often unconscious, levels in making their choices (Niebuhr). This can distort their awareness both of reality and of their true potentialities.

Jung's language about a transcendent function hidden in the germ plasm could also be acceptable, provided that this function not be understood as wholly self-directing or as the unfolding of something entirely predetermined. Such a self would be deeper than the personalike reality indicated when Scripture emphasizes the difference between outward appearance and the heart (for example, 1 Sam 16:7) or when Paul talks about his pre-Christian identity "in the flesh" (Phil 3:4-7), and it might emerge more fully later in life.

However, despite occasional appearances of a child symbolizing renewal (for example, Is 11:6-9), Scripture gives no indication that the self develops simply by letting an inner child emerge. Instead, Scripture emphasizes growing up from childhood (1 Cor 13:11; Eph 4:14-15), which involves a discipline at times unpleasant (Prov 2:1-5; Heb 12:7-13). Such discipline involves following a tradition or authority. Nevertheless, such an emphasis hardly endorses every tradition, for the Bible stresses that false and distortive ones exist. And if such have shaped our identity, then recovering a more direct awareness of our potentialities, such as we may have experienced in childhood, could well contribute to forming a more authentic sense of self. This recovery, however, would be guided by a (tradition-shaped) Adult.

Further, though positive potential may well underlie some of a person's apparently negative sides, the intensity of struggle with sin, flesh and our desires precludes ascribing as much as "90% gold" to such a *shadow*. Moreover, since this struggle's corporate dimensions often involve the demonic (Mt 12:28; Eph 2:1-3), the latter cannot be reduced, as Welch does, to symbolism for a purely personal shadow.

Since the self receives life by inhaling, as it were, God's breath and can lose life by failing to do so, even its depths cannot be identical with God. Yet since its breath derives from God's breath, the two, while retaining their differences, can profoundly intermingle. To recall Teresa, God's life can be imaged as a stream constantly bubbling up at the center of our castle. At times this stream could so thoroughly water the self (as in Teresa's *consolations*) that the two could seem indistinguishable. In this sense God could be called, as John says, the soul's deepest center. However, this water, this life, is received in greater degree only through increased awareness of our utter dependence upon it. Thus the more we experience this, the more should we acknowledge our own "wretchedness and the very little we of ourselves can do if the Lord abandons us" (Teresa of Ávila [1577] 1980:6.1.10) and the less should we suppose that we are actually identical with God. Yet since we are genuinely renewed in such experiences by the direct touch of divine energies, we can appropriately say, as John did, that they convey divinization.[31]

The self in spiritual experience, then, is not best represented as actually being Christ, proceeding from and returning to the Father through the Spirit (Pennington), or as identical with the Cosmic Christ or as birthing God's Son (Fox). The Cosmic Christ and the trinitarian dynamic exist prior to us. People are indeed incorporated into Christ—but only because he first calls them and draws them to himself. He, through the Spirit, births us, not we him. Subsequently we do share, in some sense, his relationship to the Father and Spirit—but only because we become his sisters and brothers and are thereby caught up with him into the overall, dynamic trinitarian interchange of mutual love, obedience and adoration. (For fuller discussion, see chapter ten.)

Narcissism. Finally, what light might my theological perspective shed on those phenomena resembling narcissism, which characterize much contemporary alienation? Narcissism prevails in cultures where things alter so rapidly that many children are unable to internalize objects (in object relations' sense) stable enough to provide some core for an enduring sense of self (see chapter two). Frightened by an inner world of urges and impressions and an outer world of events and forces which it cannot clearly distinguish, and neither of which it can control, a young child identifies itself psychologically with an omnipotent object. This object promises it either control over its environment (grandiose narcissism) or protection (regressive narcissism) derived perhaps from early experiences of union with its mother.[32]

Yet narcissists continue to be threatened by the otherness of external events and persons, for they can neither control them nor, lacking genuine self-centers, creatively interact with them. Consequently, narcissists repeatedly build makeshift personalities in hopes of conforming to, yet manipulating, surrounding persons and events. But underneath the confidence and competence they project, they sense a hollowness at their personal core. Similarly in societies where everything changes rapidly, many persons not technically narcissistic repeatedly seek to construct some sense of selfhood or satisfaction from insubstantial impressions, images and relationships—yet they continually feel alienated from any personal center. Capitalistic society, according to Christopher Lasch, prizes and produces people who can contrive this kind of personality and will consume products promising pleasure and success.

According to many analysts, however, the primordial sense of oneness that can underlie regressive narcissism can also become the core of an ego ideal. People who can differentiate their imperfect, developing reality from this ideal and cope creatively with the otherness of different people and situations can strive positively toward it as a future goal.

Christian faith, with its emphasis on tradition, discipline and obedience, would agree that some stability in a child's surroundings is necessary for character formation. It would hardly affirm the modernist assumption that change, in and of itself, is positive. Yet its equal stress on risk and openness to the future indicates that parameters within which children are reared, as well as their caretakers, must also be flexible. Winnicott's "good enough mother" provides an attractive model for all caretakers—close enough to provide real warmth and affirmation, distinct enough to allow room for authentic choices and the often painful process of differentiation. These attributes, in fact, mark my characterization of God who, as Father, is often called parent of the Christian family—as one with whom we can sometimes seem to merge and yet one who calls us to strike out along individual, often difficult, life journeys.[33]

Closely related to its discussion of narcissism, the psychoanalytic critique of capitalism (Lasch, Marcuse) also helps clarify the contemporary significance of Christian teachings about pursuit of commercial satisfaction. Jesus clearly taught that making wealth our goal is incompatible with following God's direction.[34] In the New Testament in general, desire *(epithymia)* for riches is one of those forces which dominate our drives and actions and set them in opposition to God. But how, on a psychological level, might this chasing after material goods happen today?

Psychoanalytic critics argue that a society which makes its main goal ever-increasing production, consumption and profit breaks down most forms of stability, including objects for self-formation, and glorifies constant change. This process loosens the drives, or desires, from guiding structures or restraints. Yet since these desires, as Freud (and John of the Cross) noted, are short-lived, they must be multiplied and intensified to provide the motor for ever-increasing consumption and production. Advertising accomplishes this by bombarding people with images which promise satisfaction, followed by streams of other images which keep on promising happiness, popularity and success.

Yet none of these can really deliver such things, leaving a continual underlying sense of emptiness. Desire is "stimulated, perverted and given neither an adequate object upon which to satisfy itself nor coherent forms of control"; people's imaginations are thereby "exposed more directly than before to the tyranny of inner compulsions and anxieties" (Lasch 1979:90; 1984:32-33). Narcissists, and many who live in such a society, are particularly prone to patterning their self-images after such shifting commercial images which can never fill the void.

This process provides a plausible illustration of what Scripture means by coming under the corporate power of "the flesh." It is not that the desires *(epithymia)* and normal satisfactions of them are evil. Yet by themselves, I have said, desires do not automatically flow in any one direction but are always shaped by social forces. Moreover, the more social structures that capitalism dissolves, the more likely is it that the desires will be governed by capitalism's pursuit of profit and pleasure. In this way, these goals become supreme values, powers of the flesh which dominate personal and corporate life. They rob people of the true freedom which only arises, paradoxically, from obedience, or *faithfulness,* to God's call.

Christian faith, then, is incongruent with any social order based entirely on production, pleasure and profit.[35] And narcissist theory can help explain how, in such societies, persons can become inwardly enslaved. Of course, this bondage is frequently not obvious. People often seem to be making individual choices freely, and in a sense may be. The overall life patterns of many such persons, however, are dedicated to pursuits of pleasure, profit and consumption incompatible with true Christian freedom. Contrary to libertarianism (see chapter four), I must affirm that unrestrained consumer choices are not necessarily free. (It does not follow, however, that Christians ought to legislate more ideal choices into being.) And contrary to Rogers, I suspect that much of what our organism seems to be saying is shaped by capitalist forces.

Finally, narcissist theory suggests a possible origin for some spiritualities stressing unmediated union with God, especially with a panentheistic God through nature. A narcissist, lacking a self that is sufficiently stable to cope with the pain of differentiation from other humans and nonhumans, may long regressively for undifferentiated union with some cosmic sense of wholeness. Capitalist culture can arouse longing for a world where every desire flows forth unrestrainedly and is met by immediate satisfaction. Together these yearnings can produce the romanticized image of a highly sensuous, completely enveloping organismic totality where every action is spontaneous and reciprocated by a perfectly balanced response. The more such a totality is painted in glowing commercial-like colors and the more it minimizes the struggles involved in achieving actual social and ecological harmony, the more likely is it to be a projection of narcissistlike longing than a realistic portrayal of society and nature.

Whatever their psychological origins, we have found such effusive "Hollywood" imagery and minimizing of natural conflict in Swimme, Berry and Fox (see chapter six). Although Fox seeks to distinguish true pleasure from the sensory overloads of commercialized society, his language very often approximates the latter. I suspect that an overly romanticized vision of nature-society ultimately underlies Marcuse's work (see chapters two and four), possibly Ruether's (see chapters six and seven) and certainly Bookchin's (see chapters three and four) and deep ecology (see chapter three).[36]

Similar assumptions about harmony between our organismic tendencies and overall cosmic processes inform bio-spirituality (see chapter five) and even Rogers (see chapter two). Further, the inner child discussed in chapter two often appears as the kind of omnipotent true self that narcissists long for. All this is not to deny, however, that such visions may contain valid glimpses of the ultimate eschatological future. Some glimpses may function as an ego ideal toward which people may authentically strive *through* the pain of differentiation and conflict.

Summary

I have been developing the kind of public theology in which, I have claimed, specific Christian beliefs, not merely general ones that Christians hold in common with others, can make valuable contributions to public conversation. Having based my anthropology on the biblical history of human acts as pointing to, fulfilled in and critiqued by the human activity of Jesus Christ, let me summarize the chief contributions that it offers to public conversation concerning psychological and spiritual alienation. Though my description of mature human behavior was drawn largely from Jesus or from those who anticipated or confessed him, trinitarian faith declares that such persons reveal the goal that the one God desires for all humans and that God's Spirit, who always works in harmony with the Son, seeks in some way(s) to draw all of them toward it. (This will be more fully substantiated in chapter ten.) Here then is my summary, expressed in more public language.

To public discussion Christians can contribute the perspective that all persons have inherent worth, for even before birth they are selves in some incipient sense with great potentialities for development. At this point, each person possesses certain inherent preferences, inclinations and aptitudes which prescribe a range within which one will develop. Selfhood, however, is not complete in principle at this beginning, nor a latent fullness underlying all phases of development. It is gradually constructed as one interacts with different persons and situations. At the deepest level, selfhood is formed through responses to a drawing toward the future, which is often sensed only dimly (but which Christians understand as God's call).

The self is intrinsically shaped by social patterns and structures within which it emerges and by interactions with other persons. Consequently no substantial self exists separable from social and relational conditioning. This shaping extends to the biological drives, so that a purely physical, socially unformed component can never be identified. Yet developing selves are also marked by a freedom, in response to the drawing future, to transcend any biological or social state to some degree. Such shaping, then, does not determine all their acts; it only prescribes a range within which these will occur. This biological, social, relational and volitional construction continues throughout life.

Since the call toward our future is always somewhat unclear, involving unknown and risky situations, and since biological drives do not dictate developmental patterns but can be organized and altered in various ways, some conflict among aspirations and desires always accompanies construction of a self—and would even in a world without evil. Moreover, since no deep self center attains final form during this journey, even in an entirely good world individuals could sense that they were not, or did not know, what they ought to be—were distanced from their fuller selves. Finally, since becoming a self involves relationships, alienation from our authentic potential through excessive or inadequate commitment to persons or structures would always be possible.

In our far from perfect world, psychological alienation is often largely due to social patterns which are either too rigid, blocking expression of our drives, potentialities and choices, or too loose, providing insufficient structuring for them. The second is especially prevalent under capitalistic forces. These can dissolve traditional structures and encourage uninhibited expression of drives and preferences, spawning "selves" assembled from shifting surface impulses and images, lacking sufficient depth and center. But although alienation is prompted by such external forces, Christians can stress that even normal development involves possibilities for internal conflict and distance from what they truly are. Yet whereas this imbues life with uncertainty, it also underlies life's adventure, creativity and promise.

Moreover, since personal alienation is always intertwined with social malfunctions, increased self-awareness, necessary as this is, cannot sufficiently overcome it alone. Adequate personal transformation always involves some kind of social alteration and, since human individuals and groups are natural creatures, involvements with the rest of nature.

Since public conversation often ponders whether alienated selves can find themselves through some greater Reality, Christians can (and do) speak publicly about spirituality. Christians can assert that behind the unavoidable unsettledness of anyone's present and future lies the affirmation of One who knows and loves each person and wills to guide all toward greater self-realization in community with others and the rest of nature. Whereas people cannot expect that One to abolish all conflicts, they can experience that One's companionship along the way. At times this companionship can be close enough to be experienced as union; at other times it is distant enough to call forth our freedom and creativity.

Alienation from ourselves and being's Source will not be overcome simply by seeking experiences of its presence. Alienation must also be overcome through giving what (perhaps little) we have of love and sustenance to others. The way to self-fulfillment, paradoxically, involves self-empty-ing—though we cannot repeatedly empty ourselves if we do not also experience filling.

Christians cannot prove that self-emptying will be met eventually by increased infilling (any more than any other path to future fulfillment can prove that it will always work). They can only testify to their and the Christian tradition's experience of this—and their belief that God is faith-ful.[37]

This self-emptying also involves acknowledgment of our limitations and trust in forces greater than ourselves to attain our goals. Christians can point to Jesus as a historically plausible portrayal of living for others through dying to ourselves and our limited capacities. In any case, personal alienation is overcome, on the deeper spiritual level, not by sinking into some Source which separates us from the world of time and struggle but by giving ourselves as best we can to our call toward the future, to mutual relations with others, to harmony with the rest of nature and to One who promises unfailing companionship along the way.

T E N

Ecology, Spirituality & a Theology of Creation

*H*ow are the challenges of finding the self and healing the earth related? My discussion has highlighted two contrasting answers.

Organismic psychologies and spiritualities reply that selves and their organisms—and selves and God—are in essence more harmoniously related than may appear. Human consciousness and social structures, however, have introduced false divisions into these harmonies. But if these divisions can be apprehended and experientially transcended, the self will merge with its organism's self-actualizing process and its depths will merge into God. (It is sometimes implied that if this happens with enough individuals, social alienation will also disappear.)

Organismic ecologists add that harmonious rhythms pervade nonhuman nature and unite it also with selves. Yet human consciousness and the exploitative behavior issuing from it have disrupted these rhythms. However, if humans can discern these rhythms, resonate with them affectively (largely through their bodies, their point of contact with other creatures) and conform their actions to them, ecological alienation can be overcome. Ecological theologians add that our appreciation of and union with nonhuman creatures and their rhythms will deepen if we apprehend them as dimensions of an all-encompassing panentheistic God.

Psychoanalytic theorists, however, assert that antagonism is intrinsic among elements within the self. Darwinians add that competition rages among all natural creatures, humans included. Both finding the self and healing the earth, then, involve envisioning and superimposing some kind of order on these conflicts. Whereas some argue that a certain tendency discerned among the conflicting elements (for example, self-interest) can lead toward harmony, others believe that guidance for self-formation or environmental healing must come from somewhere else.

For spiritual writers appreciative of psychoanalysis, conflicts within selves, among selves and between selves and God stem not simply from faulty consciousness or social structures but are more intrinsic to the way things are. These can be overcome not by seeking a realm where harmony submerges them but by trust in a distinct, transcendent God who enters these conflicts and companions us through them. Current ecological theology, however, envisions a distinct, transcendent God only negatively. But might such a God help heal the earth? Determining this will be a major task of this chapter.

In chapter nine I agreed that experiences of self-organism and self-God unity do occur and that visions of increasing harmony among these validly express the Christian eschatological hope. Yet I maintained that organicism could not adequately account for the real distinctions among organismic drives and selves and among selves and God as affirmed in Christian faith. If such distinctions are real, potential for some kind of conflict and distance among them exists, even in the best of worlds. This I found more realistically affirmed by the psychoanalytic perspective, although it cannot explain how hope for increasing organismic unity is possible.

I have also wondered whether the Darwinian perspective, a cousin of the psychoanalytic, can provide adequate foundations for an environmental ethic. I have questioned whether the cooperative attitude required can really be derived from self-interest or sympathy, or whether a sufficiently holistic perspective can arise from an individualistic basis. I also have argued that the animal rights' principle of sentience cannot extend intrinsic value widely enough (see chapters three and six).

Chapter six considered a panentheistic ecological paradigm, which has much in common with organismic ecology. Like organicism, this panentheism convincingly based its holistic perspective on the interrelatedness of all creatures. I affirmed its extension of intrinsic value to all of them, along with its accompanying commitment to differences in instrumental value.

I found, however, that panentheistic ecology shared several weaknesses with organismic ecology. First, some panentheists derived cooperation, and also compassion, from self-interest. Second, others lauded both the balance found in stable ecosystems and evolutionary "progress" through disruptive episodes, yet they based cooperative ethics wholly on the former without adequate reason for preferring it over the latter. Third, whereas panentheists claimed that our interrelatedness with all other creatures should humble us, they placed guidance of the cosmos entirely in humankind's hands (as "evolution become self-conscious").

Further, I found that although our ecological theologians blame attitudes stemming from the Enlightenment for many environmental problems, they perpetuate some significant Enlightenment tendencies themselves. They privilege science, prize modern knowledge far above tradition, place humanity rather than God in charge of history and valorize the novel, the more complex and the more intensely experienced—values that guide capitalist expansion.

Moreover, I mentioned several problems with panentheism itself. Since it claims that all reality is part of God, this must include evil. Precisely in dealing with this issue, our theologians tend to push beyond panentheism's limits. Then too if humans are aspects of God, it is difficult to grant them genuine freedom.

If significant weaknesses can be found in Darwinism and in organismic and panentheistic ecologies, can I propose an alternative? My discussions of spirituality suggest that God is not best conceived as inseparably intertwined with selves or the world but as transcendent, or distinct from them in regard to being. Yet in current ecological theology this kind of transcendence is only critiqued—for distancing God from the world. But is another reading of transcendence possible? And might it affirm some or all of those six values in support of which panentheism is proposed (involvement, embodiment, cooperation, pluralism, compassion and responsibility)? (See chapter six under "Panentheism.") The major task of this chapter will be to find out.

First, I will develop the trinitarian character of my theology, showing how this leads to a theology of creation and comparing its implications to those of our ecological theologies (see chapter six). Then I will address issues of environmental ethics raised in chapters three and six and will again consider the six values ascribed to panentheism, asking whether my trinitarian approach can provide them conceptual and spiritual support. Finally I will briefly summarize the overall perspective developed, as was done in chapter nine.

A Trinitarian Theology of Creation

Traditionally Christian theology has handled creation toward the beginning of its systems, right after the doctrine of God, which was usually the initial topic.[1] The doctrine of God often commenced with arguments for God's existence, employing philosophical concepts and considerations relevant to intellectuals of the day. Much of this doctrine, in fact, including the Trinity, was frequently articulated philosophically, with little detailed input from Scripture. Following this, creation was discussed in relation to the scientific issues of the era, again with fairly little biblical reference, except to Genesis 1 and 2.[2] Theological anthropology usually came next, for its treatment of unfallen human nature, which focused on Adam and Eve, corresponded with the last item under creation—humankind's origin. Only when it began dealing with sinful human nature, after the Fall, did theology start incorporating greater amounts of biblical material.

In dealing with God and creation in this way, Christian theology made contact with the public world—at least with that of intellectuals and universities. Nevertheless, I have already mentioned a problem with beginning anthropology in a similar manner (see chapter nine). The Bible says so little about Eve and Adam that theologians of any age can read much contemporary philosophy and science into its teaching. Whatever is unique about the Christian view of human nature can be obscured. The same holds for the usual approach to creation. If creation is handled before specific biblical teachings about sin, Jesus, eschatology and other themes are considered, and discussed in terms of contemporary scientific issues and concepts, little more than slightly baptized versions of current scientific views may emerge.

Chapter six has shown that process theologians Ruether, Swimme, Berry and Fox follow the traditional pattern: they derive their theological perspective and environmental ethic chiefly from evolutionary science. Yet I maintain that much as the Christian perspective on human nature is unfolded by focusing on Jesus Christ, so the distinctive features of its understanding of the cosmos must begin with consideration of his life, death and resurrection. I concur with McFague that proper theological method begins with redemption and then moves to creation.

A retrospective approach. This route is followed in Hebrew Scripture. Scholars generally agree that Israel came to understand creation in light of its exodus experience of redemption (Anderson 1967:11-77; Young 1990:25-63; Reumann 1973:31-42; Finger 1989:408-11). Other ancient Near Eastern nations perceived creation in accordance with a cyclical view of history. In their creation festivals (such as the Babylonian new year), the primordial time of creation was not simply remembered but was believed to be recurring. Through such ritual reenactments, order once again triumphed over chaos, ensuring that the established natural rhythms and social structures would operate another year without change.

In the exodus, however, Israel experienced a power which broke through the natural and social orders, delivering it from the most powerful empire it knew. This convinced Israel that Yahweh governed the whole world (Ex 19:4-5). Moreover, since Israel's deliverance had set history on a new course, Yahweh's creating power could not be limited to establishing and maintaining fixed natural and social structures.

Israel's creation faith developed by tracing back this power which had established it almost "from nothing" to the origins of all things. The patriarchs' stories emphasize Yahweh's ability to accomplish universal purposes beginning from historically insignificant and biologically barren people. Whereas Mesopotamian creation accounts picture gods struggling to impose order on chaos, Genesis 1—2 depicts God calling things into being simply through a word: "Let there be . . . !" Genesis underscores this by placing the little-used word *bara'* at crucial points (Gen 1:1, 21, 27; 2:3-4; compare 5:1-2). In contrast to other Hebrew verbs of making, which imply use of preexistent materials, *bara'* indicates that something is created directly in its entirety (*TDOT* 2:242-49).

Creation language, however, also appears where Yahweh promises to do "new things" in history (Is 48:6-7; compare 43:19). Especially in Isaiah 40—66, it announces Israel's deliverance from Babylonian exile (51:9-11) and a coming new heavens and earth (65:17-18). That means that Yahweh's creative power (which acted, after all, in the exodus) cannot be restricted to primordial creation but can bring forth the genuinely novel in history. On the other hand, the relative infrequence of such language indicates that not all divine activity can be called "creative" in the specific biblical sense. (Even in Isaiah 40—66, *bara'* almost always refers to original creation; this verb appears only seven times outside this section and Genesis 1—6.[3]). Whereas Hebrew Scripture often extols the divine presence within life's natural rhythms (Gen 8:22; Ps 19:1-6; 104:10-30; and so on), theology will more appropriately call this God's *providence* rather than God's *creation*. For God's truly creative activity can break more sharply into the natural and social orders than this.

Many current theologies, including most ecological ones, emphasize the biblical element of novelty in God's creative action. Yet they tend to construe it as a general evolutionary feature. In this way they obscure the distinct character of truly creative acts in Scripture and interpret creation, as has most theological tradition, in line with a reigning scientific outlook (though sober readings of evolution—especially punctuated equilibria—do not find novelty everywhere [see chapter three]). But this overlooks the possibility that God's creative power could affect even evolutionary processes.

The distinctive biblical perspective on creation becomes sharpest, for Christians, in light of redemption through Christ. This redeeming activity is frequently identified as the culmination of the plan for which God designed creation.[4] Moreover, it itself is often called a new creation (for example, 2 Cor 4:6; 5:17; Gal 6:15; Eph 4:24; Jas 1:18).[5] Since Christ was so central to this fulfillment and ultimate expression of God's creative activity, he is frequently identified as the one through whom the original creation occurred (Jn 1:1-4; 1 Cor 8:6; Col 1:15-18; Heb 1:2).

However, to grasp what such affirmations mean for understanding creation, we must do more than simply accept them as dogma. To illumine their significance, we must ask how their foundations came to expression through Jesus' life, death and resurrection. My theological method, that is, must be largely retrospective: I must first examine how the new creation came about, then ask what light this sheds on the created world in general and the original creation.

The birth of the new creation. From chapter eight we recall that Jesus' relationship with one he called Father, even according to the Jesus Seminar's skeptical standards, involved unusual intimacy. The Hebrew Scriptures employ "Father" for God sparingly, for they emphasize Yahweh's awesome, exalted and righteous character. Thus when Jesus not only called God "Father" often and urged his followers to do so but also employed the more familiar "Abba," he was expressing an extremely close relationship with God. Although Father-Son language came to support patriarchy in the later church, its purpose in the New Testament is to express not gender but intimacy and mutual fidelity. To call God "Father" is to affirm that God is a loving, caring parent, such as many people associate more directly with their mothers.

Jesus' relationship to his Father was marked by faithfulness to his call (see chapter nine). This was tested in the wilderness through opposition by enemies and especially in Gethsemane and on the cross. Yet even though Jesus felt abandoned at the end, his Father's faithfulness manifested itself in raising him from the dead through the Spirit. Faithfulness, that is, characterized not only Jesus' relationship to his Father but also the Father's relationship to his Son. "The faithfulness of Jesus Christ" came to be understood as a revelation and actualization of God's faithfulness to humankind. Paul especially regarded "the faithfulness of Jesus Christ" (sometimes questionably translated as "faith in Jesus Christ"[6]) as the source of justification. Jesus' history shows, then, that faithfulness is not only a basic characteristic of mature human nature but also a chief attribute of the divine.[7]

Moreover, the faithfulness of Father and Son to one another, as actualized in Jesus' ministry, largely involved affirming and serving each other in a common mission, which the Spirit also energized. Thus something like mutual servanthood, another basic characteristic of mature humanity (see chapter nine), also has its source in God. Further glimpses into the inside of this relationship, so thoroughly affirmed in the Synoptics, appear in John's Gospel, especially in chapter 5. The oneness of Son and Father is described as that of working together, of a common task (5:17). Although this unity implies the Son's deity (v. 18), the Son does and decides nothing on his own. He acts only according to that will which the Father progressively reveals (vv. 19-20, 30). He even receives life from his Father (v. 26).

At the same time, however, the Father is causing events to bring divine honor to the Son (vv. 22-23). He has already granted eschatological judgment (v. 22) and raising the dead (vv. 21, 25) to the Son (vv. 22-23; compare vv. 32, 37).[8] The Father-Son relationship, then, is described as one of giving honor and fidelity to each other. It is also one of mutual love (v. 20; compare 14:31). Jesus' mission involves calling people to share in that loving, mutually affirming and responsive relationship between Father and Son (14:20-23; 15:9-10), which the Spirit energizes (14:26; 16:13-15).

Also recall from chapter eight that Jesus' ministry was continually empowered by the Holy Spirit. If we wonder how Jesus attained his confidence that God's kingdom was arriving through him, the answer could well be that it came from "an *awareness* of *otherly* power working through him. . . . In his action God acted. When he spoke or stretched out his hand, *something happened*—the sufferer was relieved, the prisoner freed, the evil departed. This could only be the power of God" (Dunn 1980:47).

Quite possibly, then, Jesus was aware of the kingdom's presence *"because the eschatological Spirit was present in and through him"* (p. 48). Accordingly, although the New Testament speaks of Jesus, after his resurrection, as sending the Spirit (Acts 2:33; Jn 15:26; 16:7), during his ministry the Spirit can be said to be the sender, whereas Jesus is the Spirit's agent, or servant (Moltmann 1981:74-75; Finger 1989:387-89). As the Spirit's instrument, Jesus exorcises evil spirits, heals and brings good news to the poor. His healings herald the kingdom of God's impact on the natural maladies that afflict humans. His healings and teaching are directed mainly at society's victims and insignificant ones, as proclaimed in a passage which he quotes from Isaiah's Servant:

The Spirit of the Lord is upon me,
  because he has anointed me
    to bring good news to the poor.
He has sent me to proclaim release to the captives
  and recovery of sight to the blind,
    to let the oppressed go free,
to proclaim the year of the Lord's favor. (Lk 4:18-19; compare Is 61:1-2)[9]

Jesus' concern for the apparently insignificant extended to nonhumans. He noticed that even the grass, which sprouts quickly but soon withers in the Palestinian heat, is clothed more beautifully than was Solomon (Mt 6:28-30). He also noticed sparrows, which were sold cheaply enough to provide peasants their only affordable meat source. He affirmed that even the death of the least of these is not "forgotten in God's sight" (Lk 12:6; see chapter eight, note 30). Here Jesus was not reading off God's character from nature (as Crossan says [see chapter eight]) but indicating that God observes nonhumans differently than humans normally do. Jesus' Spirit-empowered ministry was, as McFague says, strikingly inclusive, destabilizing, antihierarchical and included nonhuman creatures among the poorest of the poor.

Guided and affirmed by his Father and energized by the Spirit, Jesus approached Jerusalem, Gethsemane and Golgotha. But here his sense of relation to the Father, which had been so close, began changing.[10] In Gethsemane, Jesus pled in great agony for his fate to be altered. Yet he recommitted himself to faithfulness to his Father's will. Nevertheless the horrors of crucifixion proved to be such that Jesus came to feel wholly abandoned (Mk 15:34).[11] Jürgen Moltmann has proposed that such events push Christians toward trinitarian language (1974:200-207), for Christians have always found God present in the Jesus who suffers. Yet God is also the Father who apparently abandons him. The simple word *God* seems inadequate to express such a strange occurrence: we would have to say something like "God was abandoned by God." Instead, Moltmann claims, this concrete event in its saving significance—and not metaphysical speculation—drives us to make distinctions in what we mean by "God."

On one hand, Jesus the Son, who has identified wholly with our humanity, experiences the full reality of dying. And even more, he undergoes that experience of abandonment by God which is the fate of all who turn from God through sin. Yet it is hardly accurate to think of God the Father as aloof at that time or perhaps as pouring out vicarious anger on his Son.

The New Testament writers call this act the Father's giving, or giving up of, his Son—a profound act of love (Rom 5:8; 8:31-32; 1 Jn 4:9-10). God the Father, then, experiences the reality of death somewhat as does a human who watches a beloved one die. Such a person undergoes death not as actually dying but as an inexpressible grief, as one waits interminably and empathizes indescribably with the suffering—yet cannot mitigate it.

Why did God suffer so at the cross? Though the reasons are many, one reason surely is so that the whole history of human suffering, grief and abandonment might be borne vicariously, yet in concrete historical actuality, through God's gracious initiative. As the Son's arms are stretched out toward the sky and he cries out in his sense of abandonment, and as the Father gazes down, as it were, in anguish and compassion on his beloved Son, the whole history of human agony and ultimate desolation passes between them:

> All human history, however much it may be determined by guilt and death, is taken up into this "history of God." . . . There is no suffering which in this history of suffering is not God's suffering; no death which has not been God's death in the history upon Golgotha. There is no life, no fortune and no joy which have not been integrated by his history into the eternal joy of God. (Moltmann 1974:246)

Yet even more than human history is involved, for Jesus' sufferings are also regarded, biblically, as the apocalyptic sufferings of the end time, in which all creation groans and suffers with pangs of death and of new birth. The natural phenomena which accompany the crucifixion—the sun's darkening, the earthquake—are signs that all nonhuman nature's sufferings are also being caught up into, and experienced by, God (Moltmann 1990:151-59).

At the cross death, not simply as a physical occurrence but as a devastating force opposing the hope and joy and harmony built into creation, opposes God's life and love by threatening to break apart the mutual love and faithfulness of Son and Father. How does God—Son and Father—overcome this threat? By remaining inwardly one in their mutual surrender when they "are most deeply separated in forsakenness" (1974:244). The book of Hebrews gives a clue to the dynamic involved: Jesus "through the eternal Spirit offered himself without blemish to God" (9:14). The Spirit through which the Father sent the Son into his ministry and through which the Son accomplished the Father's will is also the "link" which bound them together through the agony of the cross.

Although death was actually entered into, and was borne by, the Godhead, the story did not end there. For though the Son truly died, the Father again sent the Spirit, who raised Jesus from the dead (Rom 1:4; 6:4; 8:11; 1 Pet 3:18; 1 Tim 3:16). To adequately articulate what occurred at the resurrection, we must again employ trinitarian terms. Through this event, the divine life, having tasted irretrievably of death, now surrounds it with its energy and joy. The resurrection, then, marks the beginning of the new creation.

It is Jesus' raising from destruction, abandonment and hell which most firmly undergirds the Christian affirmation that God's creation, including the original creation, emerges "from nothing *(ex nihilo)*." Paul, reflecting on the faithfulness that Abraham maintained despite his near-dead body and Sarah's barrenness (Rom 4:19), parallels it with Christian faith in Jesus' resurrection (vv. 23-25). In this context Paul calls the God in whom Abraham and Christians believe the one "who gives life to the dead and calls into existence the things that do not exist" (v. 17).

Elsewhere, pondering the utter powerlessness of Jesus crucified, Paul affirms that "God chose what is low and despised in the world, [even] things that are not, to reduce to nothing things that are" (1 Cor 1:28). Whereas *creatio ex nihilo* is affirmed in Hebrew Scripture (through use of *bara'*), it is grounded most fully in God's ability, actualized in Jesus' resurrection, to call forth a whole new creation. This resurrection, then, is not simply a novel event or possibility *within* the given world-system but an altogether new possibility *for* the entire cosmos (Moltmann 1967:179).

The new creation comes to life most directly through the Holy Spirit[12] in the form of a "first installment" (2 Cor 1:22; Eph 5:5) or "firstfruits" (Rom 8:23). This means that, whereas the new creation is truly here, it is present in an incipient way amid the old world, which is still subject to suffering and death. Therefore the Spirit works largely through a groaning which pulsates through redeemed persons and throughout the whole creation (vv. 19-27). The Spirit, that is, does not absorb persons into a timeless inner realm free from outer struggles. Instead, by bestowing authentic tastes of the new creation, the Spirit lures us to long and work for it and to struggle against death forces which still govern much of nature and history.

Important for my purposes is the directness with which the Spirit bestows divine life to us, just as to the dead Jesus (vv. 10-11). Johannine language speaks, in feminine imagery, of being born of the Spirit (Jn 3:3-8), which is the same as being born of God (1:13; 1 Jn 2:29; 3:9; 4:7; 5:1-4, 18). Salvation consists of God abiding in us and we in God, which includes the inward abiding of the Spirit (Jn 14:23-26; 1 Jn 3:24; 4:13). Or, to use Hebrews's language, it consists of being partakers of the Son and Spirit (2:14; 3:14; 6:4). Moreover, the individual believer's body (1 Cor 3:16-17;

6:17-20) and the church body (Eph 2:22; compare 1 Pet 2:5) are God's temple *because* the Holy Spirit dwells in them. Such expressions indicate that the Holy Spirit does not bestow divine life as an agent communicating something external to it. Instead, the Spirit bestows divine life so directly that it is bestowal of God's very self.

Further, the Spirit, by empowering and raising Jesus, was a direct agent (not a secondary one) of the salvation brought through Jesus' life, death and resurrection. Biblically, however, no power but God can directly bestow salvation (Is 43:10-11; 45:21-23). All this impels the conclusion that the Spirit cannot adequately be conceived as simply God's instrument or emissary but must be regarded, in the full sense, as divine (see Finger 1989:382-87 for a fuller discussion). Here again, examination of redemption's concrete, historical character pushes theology to make distinctions in God.

It is even clearer, if anything, that Jesus Christ is a direct agent of the salvation won through his life, death and resurrection. Many New Testament texts ascribe to him the kind of salvation that only God can bring (1 Cor 1:30; Eph 1:3-8; 2 Tim 1:10; and so on). In Johannine language, salvation consists of abiding in Christ (Jn 15:1-11) or, as we just saw, in Father, Son and Spirit. Many other kinds of texts could be used to show that for New Testament believers, Christ functions as fully divine. For instance, he is repeatedly called "Lord," a distinct title for God in Hebrew Scripture (1 Cor 16:22-23; Phil 2:9-11; compare Is 45:22-23). Moreover, in the foregoing passages and others Jesus is worshiped (Rev 5:12; Eph 5:19-20; Heb 1:6)—an activity that can be addressed only to God (see Finger 1989:389-405, 444-50 for a fuller discussion). Then too, several texts designate Jesus Christ as "God."[13]

My main point is that in Jesus' life, death and resurrection, which the New Testament regards as the climax of God's historical work intended since creation, divine reality involves three closely cooperating agencies: Son, Spirit and Father. Moreover, this work involves the incorporation of creation's suffering and death, and then of all creatures who respond to the Spirit, into God's life. But if creatures are incorporated into God's very life by these acts, then these acts are not simply external ones, leaving God untouched. In these unprecedented, unexpected acts, on the contrary, God opens up, reveals and gives God's self as God's self really is. God's climactic historical self-opening and self-giving involves the revelation of who God actually is. And since God acts and reveals God's self as triune in these events, I may conclude that this is how God always truly is.[14]

If creatures are incorporated into the divine life, then salvation involves divinization. Nonetheless, since salvation involves the drawing of creatures through the Holy Spirit toward ever-greater eschatological fullness, divinization cannot mean that they are equal with God. Divinization will consist not in becoming identical with the divine essence but, as chapter nine indicated, in being renewed through participation in divine energies. This participation involves a breathtaking closeness among creatures and God, yet one in which creatures still remain different.

From the new to the original creation. If, in the acts which birth the new creation, God appears as God always truly is, what implications can theology draw about the original creation?

1. *The God-world distinction.* I recently observed that from Jesus' resurrection out of abandonment and destruction, the New Testament affirms that God "calls into existence the things that do not exist" (Rom 4:17), or "things that are not" (1 Cor 1:28). This, I noticed, confirms Genesis's emphasis that God created *(bara')* simply through the divine energy, or word. Creatures, therefore, were not formed out of preexisting material, nor have they always existed alongside God. Consequently their being, as something derived from and dependent upon the divine being, cannot be the same as God's. This contradicts *panentheism's* assertion that God's being is necessarily interdependent and intertwined with that of the cosmos, or at least of some cosmos (see chapter six).[15]

This distinction between God and the cosmos appears at least highly plausible from another feature of God's redemptive activity. Jesus, along with his Father and Spirit, was especially concerned for, and bore the suffering of, the weakest and apparently least significant creatures. Christians have always perceived this as an astounding act of divine grace. However, if those creatures are part of God's being, or "body," then this suffering appears less astounding. For we inevitably feel concern and experience pain when a member of our body hurts, simply because it is part of ourselves. But if no natural interconnection between God and creatures exists, then God's concern and suffering for them appears much more as a voluntary act of love.

The scope of this love appears more surprising when we realize that it was exercised toward many humans who never asked for it and who resisted and even violently opposed it. For from the biblical standpoint, all humans resist God in some significant way and have become God's enemies (Rom 5:8-10). Yet Jesus bore not only the suffering which creatures already bore but the additional, undeserved suffering that humans inflicted on him. Even though these acts placed Jesus' murderers under God's judgment,[16] God's love toward them kept flowing forth. When we realize that Jesus' death was an act of love toward God's enemies, exercised precisely in the midst of the hatred they inflicted, the less it appears prompted by any natural connection between God and the world and the more it appears as a transcendent act of grace.[17]

The plausibility that God is different and distinct from the cosmos is heightened by tendencies I found in panentheistic theologians themselves to transcend the limitations of a God or goodness intertwined with evolution, especially when confronted with suffering and evil. Ruether acknowledges that the evolutionary life-force seeks to maximize each creature's existence without regard for others. Yet she defines the central notion "good" as something which transcends and counters this: "a balancing of our own drive for life with the life drives of all others" (1992:256).

Birch and Cobb's scientific approach indicates that death and evil might well extinguish life in the end. Yet we can trust and worship only a power that will finally overcome these forces. So they choose to trust life as God, even though science helps "but little" to assure life's triumph (1981:201). Moreover, process theologians claim that God's being is no different from that of actual occasions. Yet as *everlasting* and possessing a *primordial pole,* out of which lures toward overcoming evil are formed, this God is an exception to all other occasions involved in evolution in significant ways.

Finally, McFague self-consciously goes beyond evolutionary science when she affirms that Jesus' radical inclusiveness is incompatible with biological or cultural evolution and that a future resurrection will bring all suffering bodies a new day. She strains her panentheistic framework, however, when she speaks of God becoming "at risk" through embodiment, which seems to imply that God was not always embodied,[18] and when she exempts— arbitrarily, in my view—a dimension of God ("as Lover") from the evil inseparable from our world.

2. *Perichoresis.* My examination of Jesus' life, death and resurrection discovered a certain mutuality or reciprocity among the activities of Father, Son and Spirit. Whereas the Son yields himself to the Father's will, the Father brings glory to the Son. Whereas the Spirit sends the Son into earthly ministry, the Son sends the Spirit after his resurrection. Indeed, in the Trinity's saving activity, each person offers mutual fidelity and love to the others, and salvation involves incorporating humans into that mutually affirming and responsive relationship.

Now, if this reciprocity reflects the kind of relationships that always hold among these persons, then their eternal activity can be called a *perichōrēsis,* which means something like continually being and finding themselves in and through one another (Moltmann 1981:174-76; Finger 1989:446-50).

The eternal triune life, that is, cannot be conceived as static, for the reality of each Person consists, as it were, in repeatedly giving itself away to the others and in repeatedly receiving itself back from them. It involves a constant, dynamic exchange and interchange of energies—of life, love, goodness, honor, glory, joy, righteousness and purposefulness.

What happens in a *human* relationship where energies of this sort are interchanged? If love, goodness and joy are repeatedly exchanged, they tend to increase. Love exchanged between two or more healthy persons eventually expands until it overflows that relationship onto others. Similarly we may, following St. Bonaventure, image the divine love and goodness as a bright, sparkling fountain whose waters whirl around at greater and greater speeds, and in more and more complex patterns, until they overflow. That overflow we may picture as the creation of the universe (see Bonaventure 1978:24-27).[19] To guard this beautiful image from misunderstanding, however, I must make two qualifications.

First, we should not conceive the whirling as a necessary operation which love and goodness "must" perform, so that creation arises as an automatic, inevitable effect of the divine nature. For love and goodness are entirely voluntary, personal interchanges; if they produce anything, it is because the Persons exercising them freely choose to do so.[20] Still the overflow image helpfully expresses how love and goodness tend to freely operate.

Second, given the distinction between God and creatures, we must not suppose that the water represents a divine nature which directly becomes creaturely nature. It is better to imagine the water undergoing some kind of transformation (say, into mist) as it overflows so that its products are waterlike, as it were, but not directly water. Nevertheless water provides a good image for the way in which divine life can almost insensibly intermingle with the life it nourishes in creatures (as in Teresa of Ávila's castle [chapters five and nine]).

If the energies of the divine life are continually interweaving, we would surely expect the cosmos overflowing from them to manifest a high degree of complex, aesthetically stunning interrelatedness. Some degree of the celebrative wonder that Swimme and Berry express would be appropriate. We could well expect things to be connected through internal relations, as process theology emphasizes. We could also attribute much of this interrelatedness to the Son, or Cosmic Christ, as does Fox. It is consistent with texts which speak of creation occurring through *(dia)* Christ to regard him as giving shape and pattern to the Father's creative intentions (Jn 1:3; 1 Cor 8:6; Heb 1:2; and so on).

Still, I would affirm that the cosmos is ultimately patterned after the even more complex, multitwining dynamic of energies circulating among all three divine Persons. One could even speak of God being intertwined with such a cosmos, although in a different way than panentheism proposes, as the next theme will show.

3. *Self-limitation and incarnation.* In my perspective, creation could come into being only through God's self-limitation. For apart from the original creation, the only kind of reality that ever existed was, as it were, completely filled with God. Nothing existed "outside" divine reality. God did not create by setting creatures in some space removed from God (for no such space existed) but only by opening up, as it were, a space within the divine reality—by limiting Godself and making room for creatures to come to be (Moltmann 1985:86-93; the overflowing fountain image misleadingly suggests some exterior space into which the fountain flows; we might more appropriately imagine the whirling waters setting up a vortex within the fountain itself). The original creation, then, involved a divine self-limitation, or self-emptying *(kenosis)*.

Further, whereas the creative intention passed from the Father and was patterned by the Son, it actually communicated existence to creatures through God's Spirit (Gen 1:2; Ps 33:6; 104:30). And although we might think of the initial creation through the Word as something like the big bang, the Spirit, as the common images of breath and wind express, characteristically works in intimate, often imperceptible ways. We can infer, then, that the Spirit's original communication involved subtle, precisely nuanced energizing of the particular structure and activity of each new creature. The minute adaptations involved in acting in and among every creature, however, involve a further divine self-limitation, or humbling, on the Spirit's part. Today this movement in and among creatures involves a barely perceptible longing, a half-articulate "groaning" (Rom 8:22-27), for a fuller energizing by means of the life which emerged at Jesus' resurrection.

These reflections show that a transcendent paradigm of the God-world relationship—one which conceives of God's being as distinct from the cosmos's—need not portray God as distant from creatures, as panentheistic critics contend (see chapter six). For if that transcendent paradigm is trinitarian, God can indeed be present among creatures in a most profound way. That presence does not come about through possessing the same substance, as it does in panentheism, so that God and creatures are necessarily interlinked by the cosmos's given structure. Instead, that presence, and indeed the cosmos's very structure and existence, result from God's self-humbling, God's self-outpouring through love and grace.

This self-limitation, moreover, gives creatures a significant degree of freedom to act on their own. Since genuine freedom includes the possibility of contravening God's intentions and causing much evil, a God who wills to continue involvement with creatures is put "at risk," as McFague says. However, only agents who freely choose their circumstances, not a deity whose nature necessarily involves embodiment, can be said to take risks.

God's presence, or immanence, can be largely attributed to the Holy Spirit, who relates to creatures so intimately that God's difference from them (as expressed by images of breath and water, nourishing life) can sometimes be imperceptible. Consequently God can even be described as intertwined or interrelated with creatures, provided that the divine *kenosis* and their distinction in being is also clear. This intertwining, along with the image of creation as God's making room within God's self, legitimates maternal and feminine images for God. Creation can indeed be pictured as encircled by God as by a womb—as long as the distinction of mother and fetus is acknowledged as much as is their intertwining.

The original creation itself and the Spirit's movements among creatures are divine self-limitations, or self-emptyings. If such *kenosis* constitutes a primary pattern of God's interaction with the cosmos, there is nothing absurd in the possibility, astounding though it is, of God's self-emptying extending to the point of becoming personally identified with a single creature. Christians have long affirmed that such an identification occurred in the Son's incarnation, which was facilitated through the Spirit. However, in a cosmos patterned after the divine perichoresis, a human creature, like any other creature, is interrelated with all others. Accordingly when the Son became a particular human, the Son became interconnected with the cosmos in the way that all humans are.

McFague is far from correct when she complains that traditional incarnational teaching restricts God's intertwining with the world to a single person during a brief moment of the distant past (1987:54-56). In the incarnation, the Son through the Spirit began taking up the whole cosmos into union with himself.[21] As his humanity became increasingly vivified by the Spirit during his life, and especially at his resurrection, the potential for nonhuman nature to be transformed by the Spirit accordingly increased. Through Christ's incarnation, life, death and resurrection, nonhuman nature became as closely interrelated with the divine person (though it did not become identical with the divine nature) as it is with any human person.

4. *Eschatology, "progress" and evil.* Because Christ's work brought a new

creation whose possibilities exceed those of the old and because the Spirit's present activity surges toward ever fuller realization of those possibilities, theology may infer that the original creation was open toward a future goal. God, that is, did not originally create the fullness of what God intended; the original creation was preparatory and incomplete.[22] Since evil was able to emerge, the original creation must also have been fragile, liable to distortion and open to movement (through freedom) toward or away from God.

In the beginning, then, God created certain potentialities for the cosmos's development. God called into being certain spatio-temporal entities, their relationships and patterns of behavior. These provided a framework and ground plan within and from which the cosmos was to develop. Many potentialities may have been actualized sequentially when energy to release them became available, as Swimme and Berry say.

From a Christian perspective, God's guidance of the cosmos toward a goal provides the strongest basis for affirming some positive outcome from evolutionary trends. For although evolution is perceived as progressive in the popular mind, many scientists maintain that the overwhelming majority of its branches lead to dead ends (see chapter three). Moreover, criteria for measuring "progress," such as complexity and diversity, are extremely difficult to define and apply. Ability to master the environment is so much greater in humans than in other species that it is hard to designate this a general evolutionary trend. Further, punctuated equilibria asserts that directional change, rather than being generally characteristic of natural history, erupts in unusual episodes which counter its tendency toward stasis.

For these reasons I cannot claim, as Ruether does, that scientific evidence shows expansion of consciousness to be a general evolutionary principle. Nor, given evolution's many dead ends, mass destructions and general suffering, can I discern on evolutionary grounds alone, with Birch and Cobb or Margulis and Sagan, a life eagerly offering possibilities for richer experience every moment. To be sure, some scientific indications can be read these ways, but I find the overall scientific picture ambiguous enough that contrary readings are as plausible.

Another difficulty in grounding Christian interpretation of cosmic history in evolutionary science concerns the cosmos's goal. Christians believe that it will consist in full actualization of the new creation introduced through Jesus. This new creation was established by the outpouring of a self-giving, servantlike love which revealed God's inmost character and which provides the energy and pattern for a mutual servanthood that should characterize all human behavior (see chapter nine).

Yet this vulnerable, unlimited love expressed on the cross (McDaniel), with its radically inclusive thrust (McFague), conflicts with the drive, so widespread in evolution, toward maximizing our (or our species') benefit at others' expense. Therefore Christian hope which envisions this kenotic love enveloping the whole creation trusts that God will act, and already has acted, in ways that counter some basic patterns discernible in evolution. Much of the suffering that has already occurred will be overcome—as was Jesus'—by a resurrection, as McFague affirms. According to Christian theology, this will include the human body. Yet since human bodies are interdependent with other creatures (as I emphasized in discussing the incarnation), raising humans will involve raising much of the nonhuman creation.

Since this is the future that God desires for all humans, theology can infer, retrospectively, that humans were originally created with an openness toward it. Since the Holy Spirit has energized all creatures from the beginning, we can infer that the Spirit has always, in some way, called each person toward this future. That is my basic reason for affirming, as I did in chapter nine, that God's call toward faithfulness, mutual servanthood and stewardship, though made clear through biblical history, applies anthropologically to all humans.

Belief that God can and finally will overcome evil provides stronger grounds for affirming that the cosmos is ultimately governed by love and produces a greater spur to environmental action than does a consistent panentheism, which must include evil in God. (Indeed, it is precisely at this point that ecological theologians suggest considerations which transcend panentheism.) My transcendent, trinitarian paradigm affirms that since God called all creatures into existence from nothing, God has complete power (omnipotence) over them.

Yet understanding of any divine attribute must be shaped in light of Jesus' life, death and resurrection. This perspective has led me to stress God's self-limitation, which means that God voluntarily allows creatures to contravene the divine will and to affect God negatively. Omnipotence, then, cannot mean that cosmic history conforms exactly to God's ideal but that God can bring all the divine purposes to pass even when countless acts contradict that ideal.[23]

Theology cannot always say how God overcomes evil. If we suppose that we can explain or justify every evil occurrence, we fail to respect the depths, mystery and true horror of suffering and evil. I affirm, as I did in chapter nine, that struggle and conflict, and even pain and defeat, characterize the real world; they are not surface appearances that can be absorbed by and vanish into some deeper mystical realm. To be sure, God can use evil circumstances to bring forth good. Yet to suppose that massive social evils such as the Crusades (Swimme and Berry) or the industrial revolution (Birch and Cobb) or Hiroshima and Nagasaki (Margulis and Sagan) can regularly be justified by the "progress" they facilitate is to overlook the terrible suffering of many "little ones" involved—for whom Jesus was often most concerned.

Christians can address the mystery of evil most authentically by pointing to the cross. Where is God when inexpressible suffering occurs? At the cross the entire Godhead opened itself to experience all the evil that creation ever endured. We cannot know *why* much evil occurs, but when it does we can always affirm *where* God is and that God wills to be known. Much of evil's impact can be absorbed (though hardly rendered unreal) when we experience the deeply empathic, pervasive "fellowship of Christ's sufferings" (Phil 3:10; compare 2 Cor 4:8-11) in its midst. God is indeed, as Whitehead said, "the great companion, the fellow-sufferer who understands" (1929:406, 413). God, in classical, trinitarian theology, is "forever nailed to the cross" and not for a few brief hours, as McFague alleges (1987:75; compare p. 54).

Yet God is not present there for sufferers simply because parts of God's body are affected and God has no other choice. Instead God chooses to be there again and again, even when God has no direct connection with or responsibility for their pain. Ultimately that pain, though it can never be canceled or made unreal, can be suffused with resurrection life—both now and at the end of time. Both "the power of [Jesus'] resurrection and the fellowship of his sufferings" (Phil 3:10) can instill a confidence that evil will ultimately be overcome (and not, as in panentheism, always endure as part of God's body with creatures suffering under it). This kind of confidence, I believe, will far more likely motivate the truly oppressed to combat evil than will a God who cannot prevent much evil from occurring.

Environmental Implications

Chapters three and six stressed two values which must be encouraged in addressing today's environmental problems: cooperation and holistic vision. I asked whether contemporary public and theological paradigms grounded them adequately. This section addresses these two values and a third issue: the continuity of today's environmental challenge and of proposed solutions with the Enlightenment.

Cooperation. If current environmental devastation is going to cease, humans must seek to cooperate with natural processes rather than competing against them. Human groups interested in the same resources must also learn to cooperate. Although the Darwinian paradigm regards every creature as motivated by self-interest, it claims that cooperative behavior can arise when creatures recognize that their self-interests are bound up with others'. Humans, it is further argued, can cooperate with entire ecosystems, for they can learn that the latters' well-being is intertwined with theirs.

I believe that the extent to which self-regarding drives can be transformed into other-regarding attitudes is limited, for the energy of such drives is also directed against whatever thwarts fulfillment. Such cooperative attitudes are but the reverse of competitive ones. Accordingly, once individuals or groups recognize that fulfilling others' interests will help fulfill their own, they can become deeply committed to those others. Yet if those others develop interests conflicting with the drives on which these positive feelings are based, these attitudes will markedly alter.

In a world marked by conflict, the interests of at least some other individuals and groups will almost always seem to oppose, and sometimes deeply threaten, our own. Consequently the solidarity which arises from shared self-interest will nearly always see itself opposed, at some point, to others. In many such cases, commitment to our fellows will deepen only as hostility toward others hardens. Accordingly, whereas self-regarding drives can inspire amazing commitment and even self-sacrifice among comrades, they also motivate dislike, combativeness, and even atrocities toward outsiders. Many "isms" that generate social alienation today are energized by self-interest, which spawns both group solidarity and dualistic fear and hatred of "the other." Thus self-interest, though it can expand far beyond the individual, is particularly unsuited for motivating cooperation with *all* others.

We have seen that some organismic approaches also root cooperation in self-interest. For deep ecology, the cosmic Self involved in Self-realization is so directly connected with my and every other creature's self that to desire any other's enhancement is to desire my own. For Fox, compassion is based on the insight that "in loving others I am loving myself and indeed involved in my own best and biggest and fullest self-interest" (1990:33). McDaniel grounds love on the same basis (1990:29). Even panentheism, by making all creatures parts or aspects of God, finally roots divine love for them in God's love for God's own self.

I believe, however, that such appeals to cosmic oneness underestimate the real differences and conflicting interests between ourselves and other creatures. They inadequately recognize that in making almost any environmental choice, the interests of some creatures must suffer. And they appeal to a motive that cannot provide the radical other-directedness needed for the most difficult choices.

At the center of the transcendent, trinitarian paradigm is another kind of concern for others. The very existence of each trinitarian person consists in giving itself away to the others, and yet receiving itself back from them. This kind of self-giving love, which manifested itself most fully in God's outpouring for creatures at the cross, is called *agapē*. Agape can be contrasted with another form of love—*eros*.[24] Eros is based on, or motivated by, some lack, need or desire in the lover. Its beloved is desired *because* it will please, ennoble or complete the lover.

Agape, however, arises not in order to fulfill the lover's desire but to please, ennoble or complete the beloved. That does not mean that agape is a kind of bland, colorless will to bestow good, involving "no element of responsiveness to the qualities of the loved one," as Cobb and Griffin suppose (1976:46; see chapter six). It simply means that agape, which is deeply appreciative of the beloved, is not *based on* the lover's desire for such qualities.

I have claimed that mature human character involves giving ourselves to God (in faithfulness) and others (in mutual servanthood; see chapter nine). I have described how the Spirit draws us out of ourselves, into the concerns of others and toward the future. I have emphasized the paradoxes that by losing ourselves and dying to ourselves, we find ourselves and rise. It is not possible to do all this, however, unless we have first been found and energized by God's self-giving love. It is not possible to practice this consistently in social relationships unless we have been shaped by communities which endeavor to practice agape. Nonetheless I propose that this kind of love, which is concerned first of all to benefit the other and is not essentially rooted in self-interest, offers the most effective basis for environmental cooperation.

This love would be aroused by nonhuman creatures' intrinsic value, by their intricacy and beauty apart from any benefit they might bestow. This love would include appreciation for the fine balance of ecosystems and desire to disturb this as little as possible. Only such love of these creatures in and for themselves, I propose, can consistently counter the sometimes understandable desire to use them solely for our own ends. In response to other humans who contest our desires for the environment, agape would have us first seek to appreciate their perspective. In such conflicts, real needs and grievances often exist on both sides. Only an attitude that is open to truly hearing others, giving up something for their sake and even bearing some of the injustices involved, as Jesus did, can consistently counter the understandable desire to push our own cause.

I am not saying that the best environmental situation will result if some interests are wholly surrendered. For the optimum situation will involve balance among the needs of all, including those of nonhuman creatures. (To attain this, collectivities such as ecosystems and species may need to be given more weight than some individuals.) But I am saying that this perspective will most likely be attained through agapaic attitudes. For good environmental solutions will frequently require creative negotiations and will not simply emerge once the organismic rhythms governing the relevant situation are discerned.

Someone might object that an agapaic approach is far too idealistic to guide public policy, where only appeals to self-interest seem to work. Yet it could be practiced by smaller, more focused groups, such as deep ecology, Bookchin and Ruether recommend (see chapters seven and eleven).

Whereas Darwinians argue that self-interest can eventually be transformed into cooperation, organicists generally downplay self-interest and competition in nature and base environmental practice on examples of natural cooperation and ecosystemic balance. Organicists (here like Darwinians) generally seek to derive what we *ought* to do directly from what *is* the case in nature. I have pointed out, however, that organismic views presuppose that much competition occurs in nature and that competition which eliminates some species hastens the evolutionary "progress" they laud. Thus nature, by itself, can provide no clear preference for cooperation over competition.[25]

I find it preferable to disengage our admiration for natural cooperation and ecosystemic balance, of which ecology gives abundant current examples, from whatever role these played in evolution. For even if I believed that environmental values could be derived directly from evolutionary science (*ought* from *is*), the latter's portrait is too ambiguous to provide clear guidelines. For me, ecosystemic harmony chiefly functions not as a basis for ethics but as a beautiful, yet highly imperfect, mirror of trinitarian harmony—imperfect largely because the life that nourishes others is not always freely given, gratefully received and offered back to the givers; rather, it is often forcefully taken at the givers' total expense. Ecosystemic harmony functions, second, as a beautiful but imperfect image of creation's greater future harmony. Third, specific instances of ecosystemic balance can provide valuable input for particular environmental decisions.

In these roles, however, ecosystemic harmony does not provide the basis for ethical values. That basis, instead, is faith in God's creative intention and hope for creation's greater future harmony. Because we believe that God will someday pervade creation with agapaic love, we interact with it in ways which will express this agape as fully as possible now.[26]

Holistic vision. If current environmental devastation is going to cease, humans must develop more holistic vision, enabling them to appreciate how any one issue is interconnected with many others. The Darwinian paradigm, which focuses on individuals and their self-interest, seems inadequate for this. For even though individuals may recognize, intellectually, that their fate is tied up with that of much larger ecosystems, a focus on individual concerns makes it almost impossible to recognize as truly real the large range of factors which actually affect us. Some more immediate, probably affective, awareness of the whole and its interrelatedness is highly desirable.

Organismic approaches emphasize such an awareness, and I have found it generally helpful (chapters three and six). However, some organicisms stress unity among creatures so strongly that their diversities are not adequately emphasized. Oneness among creatures is probably affirmed nowhere more than in deep ecology. All creaturely selves are involved in the Self of the whole and its Self-realization. No ontological distinctions exist among creatures, who all share biocentric equality.

A similar mystic sense of oneness seems to characterize many ecofeminist celebrations of Gaia. Yet some ecofeminists identify shortcomings in such experiences of apparently undifferentiated unity. They point out, as do studies of narcissism (see chapters two and nine), that desires for such union may reflect an inability to cope with real distinctions and differences found in life. Those unable to cope (usually men, many feminists say) may long regressively for union with a larger Self, unconsciously desired as reunion with a safe, containing mother. These ecofeminists stress, however, as I do, that awareness of nature should involve deep appreciation for diversities and committed relationships with particular creatures (see chapter three). My emphases on distinctions between the divine Self and human selves (see chapter nine), and between God and creatures, underline this.[27]

I also find problematic Swimme and Berry's attempts to assert both each creature's utter uniqueness and its pervasive interconnections with all others.[28] It is not surprising that McFague affirms both overwhelming diversity and radical unity on the basis of their "Common Creation Story." Repeated affirmations that these two enhance each other appear to promote an ethical assumption, reminiscent of Newtonianism, that I question:

if individuals are simply allowed to be their unique selves, their differences will not clash but will automatically blend with and enhance each other.[29]

In reality, however, it is often true that the more diversities among individuals and groups are recognized and expressed, the greater does conflict among them become (witness, for example, today's ethnic struggles in the former communist world). Tendencies toward diversity and tendencies toward oneness often clash. That does not mean that diversities should be stifled, only that expectations about expressing them should not be governed by overly romanticized images of a nature where all things smoothly balance and conflict is never intense. Environmental decisions to increase diversity in an area (say, by introducing new species) may disrupt some of its previous stability, whereas efforts to increase stability may eliminate some diversity.

I also wonder how adequately diversity can be emphasized in a monistic worldview. Will not an authentic otherness of things—their deep mystery and capacity to surprise and shock us—be toned down if they all, including ultimate divine reality, are of the same stuff as we? I wonder, in fact, whether process theology, which offers the most articulated differentiation among ethical values, is really a consistent monism, for its differentiations arise from varying ways in which actual occasions are organized. These organizations, however, arise from the vast conceptual storehouse of eternal objects in God's primordial pole. But though process theology professes that God is an actual occasion like all others, God endures everlastingly while all others are momentary, and no occasion possesses anything like God's primordial pole. Is the diversity that marks a process world due to a God more different from it than monism really allows?

I do believe, however, that one reality does ideally balance diversity and unity : the divine three-in-oneness where each person's uniqueness is perfectly reciprocated by the others. Although creation is an image of this perichoresis, it is a rough one, which points more toward a hoped-for eschatological balance than any existing one. That means that work toward this future harmony cannot always be guided by eros—love motivated by hopes of satisfying, reciprocal responses from the people and situations it works with.[30] In a world where much discord still exists, attempts to overcome it may often be met with incomprehension, indifference or hostility.

The love motivating such activity, then, will have to be agape—love which aims at the good of other persons and situations, whether or not they respond positively.[31] It will need to work toward a future holistic vision of all creation interacting harmoniously through the struggles, breaks and tragedies of present creaturely existence and with a deep appreciation of difference.

Continuity with the Enlightenment. Ecological theologians blame the Enlightenment and its Newtonian paradigm for many of today's environmental problems. I argued in chapter six, however, that, whereas they repudiate Newtonianism, most of them retain many other Enlightenment tendencies. Specifically most make contemporary science the touchstone for all valid knowledge and articulate their viewpoints in terms as congruent with it as possible. Second, they regard current ways of knowing far superior to any from the past. Third, they eliminate divine intervention from the world and call upon humans, now regarded as evolution become conscious, to save civilization and creation. Finally their lauding of increased consciousness, richer experience and intensified human transformation of everything can subtly appeal to, rather than counter, those desires for constantly expanding consumption and production behind much of today's environmental crisis. What orientation might my perspective indicate toward these Enlightenment tendencies?

First (in response to the second point above), I affirm that history's most important events, and the decisive encounter between God and creation, occurred in Jesus' life, death and resurrection. Moreover, what happened then fulfilled far older purposes and trends. Consequently we cannot regard current ways of apprehending reality as far superior to anything from the past. On the contrary, I would expect some traditions, especially those clustering around Jesus, to contain insights vital for coping with any present. This does not entail a conservative preference for tradition per se, for Jesus himself was critical of many traditions. I focus on traditions around Jesus, on the contrary, because these announce the arrival of that radical future which can best illumine the significance of all presents.

Second (in response to the first point above), I find significant limitations in attempts to make science the touchstone for all valid knowledge and the preferred framework for articulating cosmic visions. Science by itself cannot answer questions about cosmic direction or ultimate purpose. Those who speak about the latter must introduce concepts and conjectures which science cannot really confirm, however similar to scientific ones they may sound (such as evolutionary "progress" toward increasing consciousness or complexity). Such constructs are almost always rooted, at least partially, in religious or metaphysical traditions (such as Hegel's).

These traditions actually do play normative roles in interpreting science, even though this often is not clearly acknowledged. I prefer to acknowledge that assumptions and values other than scientific ones always shape interpretations of the cosmos and to state my own as clearly as possible. This does not mean, of course, that reasons for the cogency of my position (such as I presented in chapter eight) cannot be given.

Third, despite affirmations that interdependence with other creatures should humble us, portrayals of humans as evolution become conscious exalt us to a cosmic status at least as prideful as the Enlightenment's, and far more so than that of any previous Christian era. Whereas traditional Christianity sometimes encouraged prideful behavior in practice (for example, by bishops, kings, supposedly favored nations), its teachings about utter dependence upon and faithfulness toward God, mutual servanthood toward other humans and stewardship toward nonhumans composed extremely strong strictures against this. But when the Enlightenment released humankind from any superior, historically acting force and placed total responsibility for the earth in human hands, it set in motion forces that recognize no limits to what they may do and that now devastate creation.

Affirmations that humans are evolution's consciousness continue to grant us, as a species, extraordinary responsibility and power and thereby encourage the illusion at the root of so many environmental problems. I believe that it can best be countered by a profound sense of humanity's limitations, not only through interdependence with other species but also through even more basic dependence on an active, loving and righteous transcendent God.

Finally, because organicism praises free expression of drives, it can join forces with other tendencies that have worked toward environmental devastation. Ruether finds expanding consciousness, and process theologians find urges for richer experience, at the heart of positive evolutionary trends. Fox lauds enjoyment of sensory desires, whereas Swimme and Berry popularize and glamorize cosmic history like a Hollywood spectacular. However, the rapid technological expansion which has scarred our environment has been fueled by, and keeps on fueling, desires for ever newer, richer experience, awareness and stimulation. This has produced a "narcissistic" culture devoid of stable values and models of personhood, where identities are increasingly formed around fleeting surface images (see chapters two and nine).

In a culture saturated by searching for the increasingly novel and stimulating, how well can environmental paradigms which promote these inculcate earth-friendly attitudes such as simplicity and restraint? How thoroughly can they counter those pervasive cultural proclivities which, I argued in chapter nine, are imprinted on our drives? I propose than an appropriate paradigm must stress our finitude and limitations as much as our thirst for the more complex, our organisms' and drives' capacities for sin as well as for wholeness and our need for traditions and roots as much as our thrust toward the new.

Panentheism and Spirituality

In introducing panentheism (see chapter six) I noted six criticisms that panentheists commonly make of God's transcendence as they perceive it in traditional Christianity. I also listed six contrasting alternatives that panentheists propose. To conclude my discussion of ecological alienation, I will show how my transcendent trinitarian paradigm would approach each of these themes. I will stress the significance of each for forming an environmental spirituality.

Distance and involvement. Panentheists often fault the traditional Christian emphasis on a God whose being is *distinct* from the world's for making God *distant* from the world. Of course this distinctness can be emphasized in ways that remove God almost entirely from creation.[32] But a trinitarian theology beginning from Jesus' life, death and resurrection starts at points where God connects most closely with creatures. On the cross God bears the apocalyptic sufferings of creation and opens God's self to all creatures' pain. With Jesus' resurrection, the Spirit begins renewing the whole creation, which has been taken up into increasing unity with Spirit and Son since his incarnation.

Moreover, the original creation began with God's making room within Godself, a space where creatures could come to be. Creation's intricate structure receives its design from the Son (or Word), and life is imparted to creatures by the intimate touch of the Spirit, who still surges among them. Creation is the product of God's overflowing, yet self-limiting love.

If God designed and created the cosmos intentionally, out of self-limiting love, why should someone suppose that God would be removed from and disinterested in it? If God carefully fashioned creatures, might not God have at least as much interest in them, and as much in common with them, as with beings by whom God was always inevitably conditioned, even if they composed God's "body?"

Further, if God chose to create, God does not absolutely need creatures. This, along with the distinct being God granted them, gives them genuine freedom. For if creatures exist because God needs them, or because they are features of God's very being, they must act in ways that meet those needs or conform to that being. But if those two conditions do not hold, creatures can explore more possibilities—sadly, even destructive ones. Such creative love is agape, which flows from concern for its beloved's good, whereas a panentheistic deity's love would have to be eros, based in some way on desire for the lover's own good.

Awareness of God's love and closeness, and yet of our distinct existence and true freedom, can arouse toward God the most authentic form of love: one that is freely given. And whereas love requires some similarity between lovers, love can also increase in proportion to their differences. The greater the gap, as it were, that love needs to span (the greater the variety of contrasts it has to harmonize), the richer, more profound and more powerful it needs to be. I propose that God's genuine distinctness from us can intensify extraordinarily the kind of love we have for God.

Spiritual nature and embodiment. Ecological panentheists fear that if God is entirely spiritual, and humans are encouraged to be like God, they will shun and fear the material world, especially its processes of change, decay and death. Due to such fears, Western humanity has indeed often ignored and also abused nonhuman nature, which exhibits these processes so clearly; men have often done the same with women, whom they have frequently identified with nonhuman nature.

Yet if at the incarnation the Son through the Spirit began taking up nonhuman creation into union with himself, and if it is as closely interrelated with his divine person as with any human person and if it will share in humanity's resurrection, then being material is certainly no obstacle to closeness to God. Moreover, if matter with its distinctions and interrelations was created to reflect the divine perichoresis and to express and communicate divine love, matter can certainly be loved. Further, if divine immanence, as McFague stresses, involves "radicality of love for the vulnerable and oppressed" (1993:162), did not God become profoundly immanent through Jesus' concern and suffering for fragile human and nonhuman creatures, among which the Spirit still moves?

McFague critiques traditional incarnationism for being a "metaphysics of presence," a desire to have God "present, fully and completely in one human being . . . to cover up the absence, emptiness, and uncertainty we sense . . . at the heart of things" (1987:24). But might not the body model, which images all things (and not just one person) as being, in some sense, God, be much more a metaphysics of presence—even when qualified by God as "breath" or "spirit"? Is not God close enough if God's self-emptying love is always available to, and desirous of surrounding, permeating and transforming, every creature? Might not such a presence be more appropriate for creatures with genuine freedom—more loving for creatures whose love involves mutual response—if God nevertheless remains distinct? Then God would remain the mysterious, elusive Other, who can only be known ever-anew through faith and love along our life journey and never through identity of substance (see chapter nine).

If God loves all creatures in ways consistent with this, is not that enough for us to love and respect them? Is it really necessary that they in some way be, or be parts of, God? Might not my paradigm, which stresses both God's ontological distinctness and his astounding closeness through love and grace, best satisfy McFague's criteria for God-world models, namely, radicalizing both immanence and transcendence (1993:137)?

If God's presence involves sharing creatures' sufferings, then we are not delivered from all encounter with decay and death but often experience God through them. Since God truly experienced suffering and death at the cross, relationship with this God will demand that we face them squarely. Authentic resurrection experience and hope arise not from avoiding death but out of deeply tasting its reality. We can discern in nature's decay and renewal cycle a parable of much Christian experience.

Individualism and cooperation. Panentheists fear that if God is represented as *a* distinct being and humans are encouraged to be like God, they will become increasingly individualistic and oppose the cooperative attitude necessary for overcoming environmental problems. Christian emphasis on God as uniquely personal has indeed led some to privatize their faith.

Yet the triune God is hardly an individual in the sense of being a wholly isolated, nonrelational monad; God is a perichoretic, multipersonal dynamism. It is misleading to say that the transcendent triune God has no "real" relationships with the cosmos (Cobb and Griffin 1976:21)[33] except in a technical, philosophical sense. In a religious sense, are relationships more "real" when grounded in the nature of things or in self-giving love and grace? Is the imperative to cooperation stronger when based on the essence of things or when undergirded by One who empties himself for others' sake, despite great unlikeness to others, lack of irrefragable connections with them and even hostility from them?

Of course, since my paradigm regards such relationships, and even creaturely existence itself, as gifts wholly dependent on God's grace, they might appear less stable and secure than something grounded in the nature of things. Perhaps panentheists emphasize evolutionary interconnections so often—even though eons of suffering and apparent purposelessness interlace them—because they can convey a sense of security. Especially if the "great Thou" with which all small selves "are finally one" is their center (Ruether 1992:253), then despite evolution's apparently overwhelming arbitrariness and impersonality, might they feel assured of inhering in its core?

Perhaps this seems more secure than accepting an inscrutable grace which we cannot control but for which we must continually trust the Giver.

In this sense all power is indeed on the transcendent God's side, and creation is suspended in an emptiness with nothing but God for support. Christians can only trust that God will continue to act as revealed in Jesus' life, death and resurrection. But trust in any ultimate force—Ruether's Matrix, Margulis and Sagan's or Birch and Cobb's "Life," or Lovelock's Gaia—also depends on some unprovable assumptions.

Since the triune God is a community, genuine openness to God involves openness to this mutually interacting dynamic and to all other creatures actually or potentially within this flow. To open ourselves to such a God is to renounce isolation for a life of cooperation. And since the triune flow is restless, surging outward to draw alienated creatures into its joy and life, we will find ourselves swept into this current and into the sufferings of creation (see chapter nine).

Absolutism and pluralism. Despotic human powers ignore reality's variety and divide people into opposing groups, legitimating violence toward all that is "other." Since they often solidify their hold by appeals to absolute values, our panentheists fear that presenting God as absolutely sovereign will sanction such efforts, as has often happened in Western history.

Yet the God revealed through Jesus' life, death and resurrection does not oppress God's enemies but gives himself for, and dies for, them. Moreover, these enemies are chiefly religious, political and demonic powers who claim absolute, ultimate allegiance for themselves.[34] Jesus overcomes them through a servantlike way that thoroughly critiques their modus operandi as well as their claims (see chapter eight) and is the most "destabilizing, inclusive, non-hierarchical" approach of all (McFague). Since even God's absoluteness, or ultimacy,[35] must be defined in light of these events, it must include the ultimacy of this kind of self-giving love. To affirm the triune God's ultimacy is to affirm the ultimacy of a self-giving love which critiques all other pretensions to absoluteness and thus can free people from such claims.

Given the frequent negative function of absolutes, it might seem best to attempt to live without any. Yet every comprehensive vision of the cosmos includes some ultimate value or reality (Ruether's "good" and her Matrix, Margulis and Sagan's "Life" and so on). Even efforts to live without ultimates are affirmations of ultimate values such as tolerance. Our most significant choice cannot be whether or not to live without some ultimate but to affirm that ultimate which best frees us from all partial and idolatrous claims upon our deepest allegiance. Such an ultimate will relativize all other claims to ultimacy and make possible genuine pluralism among the cultures and lifestyles that affirm them.[36]

Ecological panentheisms rightly emphasize the importance of valuing otherness, thereby undermining dualisms based on fear of it, which often lead to domination. Yet they often seem to attempt this by leveling down, rather than fully acknowledging, the mystery of otherness.[37] Their emphasis on interconnectedness can tone down evolution's unsettling strangeness—the ruptures between its periods, its mortal struggles among species, the gulfs between eons of apparently purposeless stasis and humanity's infinitesimal life span. Although our participation in this interconnected web is supposed to help us accept our finitude, it often seems mentioned to support our irrefragable intertwining with the infinite. And the body metaphor, however one emphasizes its feature of organic diversity, is still a monism portraying all creatures and God as of the same stuff.[38]

What if such toning down of otherness were rooted in a leveling of the most basic Otherness—God's? In that case, the intensity and richness of true love toward God would be diminished. The width of the gap between God and evil would be underestimated. Attempts to explain evil's persistence as inevitable and uncontrollable (if God is finite) or as justified for social progress or as somehow containable within God (alongside God as "Lover") might seem satisfying only because evil's strength had not been fully appreciated. We might also underestimate the wonder and grace of kenotic love, the significance of its decisive conquest of evil through Christ and the importance of participating as intentionally as possible in its source: the perichoretic life of the triune God.

Domination and compassion. Panentheists fear that if God is absolute and humans are encouraged to be like God, humans will strive to dominate others and the environment rather than developing the sort of compassion required to appreciate the importance of weaker creatures. Domination has indeed often been lauded in Western history.

Jesus, however, showed special compassion toward the most vulnerable human and nonhuman creatures. I find no suggestion that this flowed from the contribution such beings might make to his self-interest, the foundation for compassion for deep ecology and Fox. Instead, it seems that, as expressions of God's overflowing creative love, all creatures have intrinsic value. If the value of those most weak were based on their interconnection with me, their intrinsic value would be less, for it would depend partly on my self-interest. If their intrinsic value were derived entirely from evolution, or even ecology, it would likely be far less, for precisely the weakest (in the sense of least robust) must be sacrificed and consumed for the good of the whole.

The intrinsic value of other creatures can be learned far better from the

One who values those who are not intertwined with his being. This teaches us to value all creatures, even those who have no apparent connection with our well-being. Further, in actual practice the deepest challenge to valuing others arises not when common interests, or even enriching differences, exist but in becoming vulnerable to those who threaten us with harm. In such cases, God's valuing and even sacrificing himself for his enemies provides an extremely strong basis for compassion on those who not only seem unconnected to our self-interest but who oppose it.

Passivity and responsibility. Ecological panentheists fear that if God is regarded as omnipotent, people will avoid the difficult tasks of environmental involvement and simply leave everything up to God. Some people have indeed understood God's omnipotence in such a manner.

But if the omnipotent God limited the divine reality and ability to regulate every activity by creating creatures with genuine freedom, God expects humans to take initiative in every pressing circumstance. In contrast, panentheism, by making creatures part of God, does not distance them sufficiently from God's self-interest to render them truly free.

Moreover, the triune God asks for our receptivity, never our passivity. For if we truly open ourselves to the divine perichoresis, we will be energized and drawn, through its compassion for all creatures, into other lives far beyond ourselves. Nevertheless we will need to pour into this involvement only whatever strength and insight we have received. Though we will be called to strenuous tasks, they will be appropriate to finite creatures. We will be released from having to provide evolutionary history with a consciousness and from saving most species on earth.

Trust in a God who does not need the cosmos to exist but was able to create it will engender hope that our beautiful earth can be saved even if humankind in large measure disobeys. Yet this hope can never justify passivity for those who are receptive to the divine agape. Struggle against evil will less likely flag if it is believed that evil is neither inevitable and uncontrollable nor somehow part of God. Those who feel overwhelmingly crushed by evil will more likely be aroused if they believe that God can, and eventually will, abolish it. Those who find it difficult to trust God will likely act more confidently if assured that evil is not intermixed with God but that God opposes and abhors it and that at the cross God has already suffered evil's worst consequences and overcome them through a perichoretic love in which they can participate.

Summary

Since I intend my perspective to contribute to public conversations about ecological alienation, as well as to those among Christians, let me briefly summarize it in terms intelligible to the general public.

The natural world (which includes humans) is an expression of a love and beauty which ultimately govern the universe. Its creatures, with their intricacies and intertwined rhythms and harmonies, mirror the character of this love, even though somewhat imperfectly. Because each creature is an expression of this love, each is intrinsically valuable in itself. None is to be harmed unless careful considerations concerning relative instrumental values justify this, in which case no more harm than is necessary to attain these values is permissible.

Natural processes are self-maintaining and self-balancing to a very high degree. Yet these rhythms should not be regarded as ideals to which humans need only conform to attain perfect harmony with nonhuman nature (or among themselves). For humans are drawn toward a future which transcends any given state of affairs and in whose shaping they are to creatively participate through interaction with nonhuman nature. We also ought not to suppose that the type of future toward which we are drawn can be read off from past evolution. Significant trends, such as increases in diversity or complexity, are extremely difficult to define and measure (and general increases in consciousness or richer experience are harder to substantiate). Moreover, evolutionary history has abounded in dead ends, destruction and lengthy periods of stasis.

Whereas human hopes for the future, by their nature, are somewhat vague and without exact limits, human abilities and nature's carrying capacity are finite. The greatest current danger to the environment comes from the tendency, active since the Enlightenment, to disregard and transgress human and natural limits in pursuit of unlimited pleasure and profit. Emphases which encourage such transgression must be critiqued. These include denial of humanity's interdependence with other creatures, exaltation of humankind as evolution become conscious and inordinate emphasis on values such as expanded consciousness and richer experience.

Cooperation and holistic vision are values much needed for environmental challenges. Yet neither can be derived directly from nature. If cooperation is grounded in natural self-interest, it cannot expand widely enough to include all with whom cooperation is necessary. If it is grounded in instances of natural cooperation, no reason derived from study of nature can show why equal or greater weight should not be given to instances of competition or destruction. Cooperation must be based instead on the intrinsic value of all creatures, which calls us to preserve and promote their interests and to override those of any only when clearly indicated by their instrumental values for others. In many cases, interests of species and ecosystems will carry greater weight than individuals. Since interests of natural and human groups often clash, and we are normally prejudiced toward our own, we should initially seek to value others' interests more highly than our own.

Holistic perspective, likewise, cannot be consistently derived from an individualistic outlook, for that cannot expand enough to adequately envision the whole. Holism can sometimes be intuited through a mystical sense of harmony among all things. Such a vision, though, often fails to appreciate real diversities among them. Some proponents of this kind of vision assume that if each creature freely expresses its particular nature, unity among all creatures will emerge; but they too underestimate the extent of real diversity and its attendant conflict. Holistic vision is best attainable through a perspective which appreciates real diversity and conflict, yet regards greater harmony among creatures as a worthy future goal. In general, environmental values cannot be derived entirely from descriptions of what *is* (or has been) the case but must involve ethical choices as to what *ought* to be. Since such choices involve some vision or hope for the future, environmental values can be rationally based on an anticipated goal.

Since public conversations often ponder whether some planetwide or cosmic force may play a vital ecological role, Christians can (and do) speak publicly about such a reality. Whereas Christians should affirm that their God is *distinct* from the cosmos, they should refute the common assumption that such a deity need be *distant*. They should affirm that their God is especially close to and concerned about creatures in the most important ways—through love and grace. They should point out that if no essential distinction is made between the ultimate reality and the cosmos, evil must be part of that Reality and its continuing presence inevitable. Yet the vast scope of current human evil or of evolutionary sufferings cannot be justified by any general progress they may have facilitated. People are more likely to combat environmental evil if they believe that the cosmos's greatest force is not intermixed with it but abhors it, opposes it and will one day abolish it.

Moreover, Christians can question whether the great diversities and contrasts of the natural world, which elicit such awe and delight, are best accounted for by rooting them in a single divine substance, or whether they do not more likely reflect a Creator-creature distinction. Christians can testify that spiritual experience can be richer and more realistically related to the conflicts of earthly life if it is rooted not in absorption of all

things into the divine but in relationship to One who is wholly different—
and through that One to others who are relatively different. Such an ecological spirituality, like the more general spirituality presented in chapter
nine, must be able to cope realistically with a world of conflict and real difference.

ELEVEN

A Theology of Society

My last chapter stressed the importance of Christian belief in a transcendent God, whose being is distinct from the world's. It also affirmed that current environmental and social reality is scarred by significant conflicts. Might my social perspective, then, be similar to the conflictive ones presented in chapters four and seven?

According to libertarians Michael Novak and Reinhold Niebuhr, all people struggle for power or pleasure, and some amount of discord among them is inevitable. The solution, however, is not to grant a state greater power that it might guide behavior in preferable directions. For such a state will abuse power most of all, alienating people most drastically from their individual and social potential. Instead, according to libertarians, states should only prevent the worst crimes.

If individuals are left free to compete with each other, their desires for power will limit and balance each other, especially through a free market. Novak and Niebuhr, however, believe that free market institutions accumulate power too. Thus they add that the economic sector must be balanced and hence limited by political and cultural forces. Their basic conviction, phrased theologically, is that the sinful inclinations of all individuals and institutions are strong and will not change qualitatively; therefore the tendencies of each must be checked by all the others.

Accordingly social conflictivists are suspicious of idealistic visions of better future societies. If these are acted upon, they fear, the situations they will bring into being will likely be despotic. Therefore they interpret Christian visions of God's triumph at history's end as symbols of the individual's communion with a God who transcends time. God's transcendence is important, for it gives hope of ultimate fulfillment to individuals who will never find it on earth or in history.

Whereas this emphasis on God's transcendence resembles mine, many reasons for it do not. In chapter ten I interpreted eschatological visions as goals to be worked toward through concrete environmental action. Is my social perspective, therefore, more like that of holism, which stresses transformation of present reality?

Holists stress that if negative social institutions and forces are merely balanced by other negative ones, most situations which alienate people from their individual and social potential remain. Holists usually represent oppressed groups who are more severely affected by social malfunctions than are the privileged classes which conflictivists generally reflect. Therefore holists emphasize envisioning better futures (especially Freire), for this process gives oppressed peoples a sense of dignity and goals toward which to strive. Holists are optimistic, sometimes even romantic (especially Bookchin, Marcuse), about the qualitative personal and social changes possible if current sources of alienation can be removed. Yet holistic theologians, with their sights set on the historic earthly future, deemphasize or deny a God whose being transcends the world's.

It is interesting that the conflictivist-holist debate in public conversation has been paralleled historically by a similar division in Christian theology and social attitudes. Many Christians who have emphasized human sin *and* divine transcendence have been skeptical about possibilities of social transformation. Their social activity has been limited to conserving, or slightly bettering, whatever situation *is* the case. Other Christians, however, who have emphasized human transformation have taken sin and God's transcendence less seriously. They have been quite critical of their societies and emphasized and worked toward what *ought* to be. Chapter ten indicates that I am attempting to stress God's transcendence, human sin and the possibilities of social transformation. Can these apparent polarities coexist in a consistent social theology?

In this chapter I will first outline the foundations of my position. I will trace out the corporate implications of my claim in chapter nine that Jesus provides the norm for fulfilled humanity. Then I will reflect on a number of issues from chapters four and seven in light of this perspective. Finally, I will provide a brief summary of my view in the language of public conversation.

Foundations for a Theology of Society

My theology has taken Jesus Christ, as known chiefly through his life, death and resurrection and in trinitarian relation to his Father and Spirit, as the norm for anthropology and the starting point for understanding the creation. Somewhat like the Jesus Seminar, I emphasize his roles as prophet and sage (see chapter eight). I have noted that the teachings delivered in these roles often introduced, with drama, vividness and paradox, a surprising new world with novel kinds of relationships, attitudes and expectations. Moreover, Jesus' faithfulness toward God and servanthood toward fellow humans, while unsurpassed in their fullness, revealed the kind of human life to which all people are called (see chapter nine). Especially because Jesus' servanthood made clear that all people are created as cohuman, not as entirely separate individuals (Nozick), this same Jesus must provide the guidelines for my theology of society.

However, much as theological tradition has seldom made Jesus its starting point for anthropology or for understanding creation, its basic social teachings have not often been derived chiefly from him. As I proceed, I will consider some objections to making Jesus socially normative. First, how is Jesus' social role related to the social emphasis of the Hebrew Scriptures?

Social teachings and divine revelation. From its beginnings God chose Israel not simply for its own benefit but to be a channel through which God's blessings might spread to all peoples. Abram and Sarai were called not only so that their descendants might become a "great nation" but also that through them "all the families of the earth shall be blessed" (Gen 12:2-3). Israel was delivered from Egypt not simply to be Yahweh's "treasured possession out of all the peoples" but also to become a "priestly kingdom"— that is, a nation mediating God's reality to other peoples (Ex 19:5-6).

How were they to mediate this? One way was through the social statutes God gave them. Moses told the Israelites,

> You must observe them diligently, for this will show your wisdom and discernment to the peoples, who, when they hear all these statutes, will say, "Surely this great nation is a wise and discerning people!" For what other great nation has a god so near to it as the LORD our God is whenever we call to him? And what other great nation has statutes and ordinances as just as this entire law that I am setting before you today? (Deut 4:6-8)

Often during its history, Israel forgot this function of witnessing to the nations and supposed that God had called it solely for its own benefit. Yet Hebrew Scripture contains frequent reminders that God's distinct way of working through Israel was intended not to isolate it from other peoples but to manifest Yahweh's unique reality to them (Ruth 1—4; 1 Kings 8:41-43; Is 19:18-25). Centuries after the exodus, for instance, Yahweh declared to the special Servant,

> It is too light a thing that you should be my servant
>> to raise up the tribes of Jacob
>> and to restore the survivors of Israel;
> I will give you as a light to the nations,
>> that my salvation may reach to the end of the earth. (Is 49:6; compare
>> 42:4-6)

These emphases exemplify a feature of biblical revelation and salvation that extends into the New Testament: when God communicates a universal message, it is not sent out in a general form to all peoples at once; instead God focuses it, paradoxically, through a particular historical people.[1] Said more briefly, God communicates universal truth by means of the particular. That is because the most important knowledge about God cannot be conveyed adequately by general propositions, for it is knowledge of a divine person who calls us to know ourselves and others in relationship to that person.

A person can become known, however, only by our perceiving how that person acts in various situations. Thus the biblical God will come to be truly known through a series of acts in relationship to particular historical peoples. Other peoples will receive that knowledge only when the story of those acts reaches them. In many respects, that story will have greater impact, not less, the more vivid and specific it is.

The story of God's universal revelation and salvation through the particular has a specific trajectory in Scripture (Cullmann 1964:115-18). Beginning in earnest with one couple, Sarai and Abram, the human partnership expands until the exodus to include the entire nation of Israel. But as that nation becomes increasingly disobedient, God's special people narrows again to a faithful remnant within it. Eventually the human particularity shrinks to Jesus alone.[2] Yet after his crucifixion, resurrection and the day of Pentecost it begins expanding again as the church grows, through which the knowledge of God is destined to reach the whole world.

Viewed within this perspective, Jesus' life was not simply the career of an individual but a crucial phase in the revelation of God's universal will through the particular. In Israel's history, God's will and character were revealed, in part, through social phenomena. God's continuing revelation through the New Testament church, a corporate body, also included these. It therefore seems likely, at the least, that Jesus' life and teaching involved normative implications for social behavior which should not be interpreted simply as matters of individual ethics or be significantly readjusted to fit current circumstances. But let us look at that life and those teachings to determine which aspects might be called social, and in what sense.

Jesus' intention. Many of Jesus' teachings were uttered with a simplicity and directness that made their meaning unmistakable. Yet they sharply contravened the prevailing practices of his times and of all times.

This is especially true of many statements contained in his "Sermon on the Mount" (Mt 5—7). Perhaps two of Jesus' admonitions are most characteristic: "Love your enemies" (5:44), and "Do not resist an evildoer" but turn the other cheek, give up your cloak and go the second mile (vv. 8-42). The Jesus Seminar, recognizing these as supreme expressions of the distinctive language of Jesus, rates them as most likely of all to come directly from him.[3] Few scholars have ever doubted whether he said them. And in case Jesus' hearers were inclined to interpret them figuratively (as later Christians have often endeavored), the "Sermon" closes by comparing those who actually follow them with those who build houses on rock and those who do not follow them with those who build on sand (7:24-27).[4]

Given the directness of many such teachings, it seems difficult to conclude otherwise than that Jesus really intended people to follow them and that quite a different social order would result if they did. It also seems, as Marcus Borg maintains, that in their time they carried definite social implications. Yet many modern scholars (especially those in the "second quest" and Reinhold Niebuhr) have interpreted Jesus as a radical apocalypticist: as one who anticipated the space-time world's literal end in several years or decades. This provides a way of eliminating many of Jesus' more "strenuous" teachings from a person's theology of society.

These hard sayings are identified by Paul Ramsey as "all those vivid injunctions, so distinctive of Jesus, to nonresisting, unclaiming love, overflowing good even for an enemy, unlimited forgiveness for every offense, giving to every need, unconditional lending to him who would borrow." They can be eliminated because their "very *content* and *meaning* . . . show the effect of Jesus' kingdom expectation" (Ramsey 1950:34).[5]

In other words, Jesus allegedly taught such things because he believed that God would shortly intervene in history, eliminate the wicked and make it possible for the righteous to practice such behavior among themselves. If Jesus' historical expectations had been accurate, his "strenuous" teachings would soon have become feasible. But since his expectations were wrong, they need not be practiced in the world as we know it, where attempts to do so (it is assumed) obviously lead to intolerable suffering and victimization.[6]

If Jesus were seriously mistaken about subsequent history's course, however, it is not likely that the early church could simply have dismissed this without reconsidering his role in their faith. For in Jesus' own context, urgent questions about history's nature and future direction were arising on every hand (see chapter eight). His perspective on history was fundamental to the very character of his kingdom message and his messianic identity. Were he wrong about the first, the meaning of the latter two would be greatly altered.[7]

However, as the Jesus Seminar has rightly shown, Jesus did not anticipate history's radical apocalyptic end. In fact, few or no persons at the time seem to have really done so. The urgency of Jesus' kingdom expectation was fully compatible with history's lengthy continuance much as we know it and with the Son of Man's eventual future arrival. Jesus, then, apparently intended his direct, simple, but radical ethical injunctions to be practiced in a world marked by continuing injustice and oppression.

The New Testament intention. Many still argue that the New Testament as a whole does not endorse such a social ethics. It has long been held that the earliest church also expected history's imminent end and so devoted little reflection to how Christians should live in society. Only after it became evident that the Son of Man's *parousia* was being indefinitely delayed did Christians begin developing an ethic. But when so doing, they seldom referred to Jesus. Instead, they adopted ethical guidelines from the surrounding Greco-Roman world.

If the New Testament writers (apart from the Synoptic Gospels) derived social ethics largely from their current society—the argument concludes—should not a theology of society do so today? Even if this argument's dependence on the "delay of the parousia" theory is questionable, its claim that the New Testament as a whole does not derive social ethics from Jesus deserves serious consideration.

Outside the Synoptics, it is true, the New Testament does not often mention Jesus' particular teachings or details of his life. However, Jesus' life did not end accidentally with his cross. Instead, his death formed the consistent climax of his life-long Servant mission and its attendant conflict with religious, political and demonic enemies (see chapter eight). Is it possible, then, that when New Testament writers mention Jesus' death or cross, they are sometimes referring not simply to that specific event but recalling the

whole way of life which led to it and drawing ethical consequences from it
(somewhat as in Mk 8:34-37)? Let us see.

John writes, "We know love *[agapē]* by this, that he laid down his life for
us—and we ought to lay down our lives for one another. How does God's
love abide in anyone who has the world's goods and sees a brother or sister in need and yet refuses [to] help?" (1 Jn 3:16-17).[8] Here economic
implications and implications about radical, mutual self-giving are certainly drawn from Jesus' death. This passage sounds similar to another:

> God's love was revealed among us in this way: God sent his only Son into
> the world so that we might live through him. In this is love, not that we
> loved God but that he loved us and sent his Son to be the atoning sacri-
> fice for our sins. Beloved, since God loved us so much, we also ought to
> love one another. (1 Jn 4:9-11)

In this text, love is again especially evident in Jesus' death (his "atoning
sacrifice"). Yet this act is the consistent outcome of the Son's activity, beginning with his incarnation. Notice further that both texts stress the unique,
hitherto unknown quality of the love actualized and revealed through
Jesus' death.

This corresponds with John's account of Jesus' last night with his disciples. Here Jesus gives them a "new commandment": that they should love
each other just as he has loved them (Jn 13:34). How does he love them?
The paramount way is by laying down his life for his friends (15:12-13). On
this night, Jesus expressed that by washing his disciples' feet (13:1-11) to
indicate that they should also wash each others' feet (v. 14). Here again we
find emphasized the uniqueness of Jesus' kind of love, its expression in a
servanthood climaxed in his death and its foundational role for his followers' conduct. The meaning of these passages sounds quite similar to
another of Jesus' sayings:

> You know that among the Gentiles those whom they recognize as their
> rulers lord it over them, and their great ones are tyrants over them. But
> it is not so among you; but whoever wishes to become great among you
> must be your servant, and whoever wishes to be first among you must be
> slave of all. For the Son of Man came not to be served but to serve, and
> to give his life a ransom for many. (Mk 10:42-45)

Further, Paul encouraged the church at Philippi to act in unison: "Do
nothing from selfish ambition or conceit, but in humility regard others as
better than yourselves. Let each of you look not to your own interests, but
to the interests of others" (Phil 2:3-4; compare Gal 6:2). Not unlike 1 John
4:9-11, he urged them to have the same attitude as the one who "was in the
form of God" but "emptied himself," took on servant form and "became

obedient" even to "death on a cross" (Phil 2:5-8). Obedience also summarizes Jesus' behavior in Romans 5:12-21, and the attitude of faithfulness we are to have toward God is also modeled after Jesus (Rom 1:5; 6:16-17; 15:18; 16:19, 26; see chapter nine of this book).[9] Paul also appeals to Jesus' bearing of reproach in encouraging the Romans to be concerned for each other (15:1-3) and to "welcome one another . . . just as Christ has welcomed you" (v. 7). For Paul, Jesus' death for those who were sinners and God's enemies reveals, as it does for John, a love surpassing the highest love known among humans (5:7-10).

Paul also calls the Ephesians to "be imitators of God, as beloved children, and live in love, as Christ loved us and gave himself up for us, a fragrant offering and sacrifice to God" (Eph 5:1-2). Taking on the attitude that Jesus expressed at the cross makes people "kind to one another, tenderhearted, forgiving one another, as God in Christ has forgiven you" (4:32). In several other places, Paul calls his readers to imitate his behavior, just as he imitates Christ's (1 Thess 1:6; compare 2:14-15; 1 Cor 11:1; compare 4:16-17).

In encouraging the Gentile Corinthians to be economically generous, and thereby to express solidarity with Palestinian Jewish churches, Paul focuses on Jesus who, "though he was rich, yet for your sakes he became poor, so that by his poverty you might become rich" (2 Cor 8:9).[10] Paul, then, like John, draws significant ethical consequences from Jesus' way to and on the cross.

The book of Hebrews devotes a lengthy chapter to outstanding Israelite examples of faith, or faithfulness. The series climaxes with "Jesus the pioneer and perfecter of our faith[fullness], who . . . endured the cross" and whose steadfastness amid hostility should encourage readers in their own struggles (12:2-4). Hebrews elsewhere stresses that this pioneer of our salvation (2:10; compare Acts 3:15; 5:31) was wholly faithful to God (Heb 3:2, 6). Like Paul, Hebrews uses "obedience" to summarize Jesus' faithful human attitude. Hebrews stresses that he, like the letter's readers, learned obedience through suffering (5:8; compare 2:10) and likely recalls its climax at Gethsemane and the cross (5:7).

For Peter also, Jesus provides "an example, so that you should follow in his steps" (1 Pet 2:21). "When he was abused, he did not return abuse; when he suffered, he did not threaten; but he entrusted himself to the one who judges justly" (vv. 23-24). Accordingly when readers are persecuted, they should "not repay evil for evil or abuse for abuse; but, on the contrary, repay with a blessing" (3:9).

Finally, Revelation presents a Jesus "who loves us and freed us from our sins by his blood" as "the faithful witness" (Rev 1:5; compare 3:14). His followers keep "the faithfulness of Jesus" (14:12) and suffer for "the witness of Jesus" (1:2; 12:17; 20:4). This means maintaining a constant attitude in the face of an opposition often political and at bottom satanic. This witness can be sealed, as Jesus' was, by death (2:13; 6:9; 11:7; 17:6). Yet such faithful ones "have conquered [Satan] by the blood of the Lamb and by the word of their testimony, for they did not cling to life even in the face death" (12:11; compare 14:12).

Though my survey has been brief, it is enough to show that almost all New Testament writers outside the Synoptics in a number of significant places regard those attitudes and activities of Jesus which culminated in the cross as norms for Christian activity. The claim that most New Testament writers do not base their ethics on Jesus—and that contemporary theologies therefore need not—simply will not stand (see Yoder 1972:115-34). Further, John's and Paul's emphasis that the love revealed in Jesus' cross surpasses what humans had practiced or known provides a strong basis for regarding it as a distinct kind of love, which I have called *agapē* (see chapter ten).

All this raises strong reasons against dismissing Jesus' "strenuous" teachings as products of faulty historical perception and nonessential to his basic ministry. Precisely "nonresisting, unclaiming love, overflowing good even for an enemy, unlimited forgiveness for every offense, giving to every need, unconditional lending" (Ramsey 1950:34) are the outflow of *agapē*.[11]

Jesus' kingdom message. Having established that Jesus' life and teaching provide the basic guidelines for social ethics throughout the New Testament, let me return to the Synoptic Gospels. Here it will become obvious that his social teaching was far more detailed than a generalized message about love. And if the major emphases of this teaching can be found in many New Testament writers, we can conclude that Jesus' more detailed vision affected them, even if they do not always mention his specific words or acts.

Once "the kingdom of God" ceases being understood as wholly nonhistorical, it adequately expresses the major theme of Jesus' ministry, with its essential social dimensions (see chapter eight). I agree with Ruether that Jesus not only opposed all forms of social domination but critiqued the roots of desire for domination by modeling an alternate, servant way (see chapter seven). I also concur with McFague that this way was destabilizing, nonhierarchical and inclusive (see chapter six).

This involved, first, a critique of love of wealth. Borg and Crossan have vividly shown how most of Jesus' audience were oppressed by the rich of their time and how Jesus' practices, such as open commensality, radically challenged the social stratification marking that society and all societies. Jesus (Mt 8:20 par. Lk 9:58) and his disciples (Mt 10:8-11 par. Mk 6:8-10 par. Lk 9:3-4) lived inexpensively enough to identify with the poorest poor. Jesus never uttered a positive word about riches. He urged that our treasures be "in heaven" rather than invested on earth (Mt 6:19-21; compare Lk 12:33-34)[12] and that it is impossible to serve both God and wealth (Mt 6:24 par. Lk 16:13).

Yet rather than idealize poverty, Jesus' goal was a life free from anxieties about material needs (Mt 6:25-34 par. Lk 12:22-31), where we could give freely to any who asked and even give away our shirt and cloak (Mt 5:40, 42 par. Lk 6:29-30; compare Lk 3:11-14). It was a life in accord with nature (Mt 6:25-34 par. Lk 12:22-31)—yet not taught directly by nature, as Crossan and others claim (see chapters eight, ten). If Jesus was calling people to a corporate life to be actualized on earth, it would demand great changes in attitudes toward wealth. Rich or even modestly well-off people would need to make significant adjustments to join on equal terms (see Mk 10:17-22 and parallels). Jesus could even be said to be exercising a "preferential option for the poor," provided that this way was open to rich people who would make necessary changes.

The impact of this perspective on wealth surfaced in the earliest church's attempt to share material goods and in the fact that its first important divisions arose around this issue (Acts 2:44-45; 4:32-37; 5:1-11; 6:1-6). It took another important form, which united different cultures, in the collection which Paul, throughout most of his ministry, collected from Gentile churches to aid poorer Christians in Judea (Acts 11:27-30; 20:4; 24:17; Rom 15:25-27; 1 Cor 16:1-4; 2 Cor 8-9; Gal 2:7-10). Paul also critiqued differences among rich and poor which disrupted the Lord's Supper (1 Cor 11:20-22).[13]

John regarded sharing of goods with the needy as an exercise of *agapē* (1 Jn 3:16-17). James admonished the rich in a way reminiscent of Jesus and indicated that most recipients of his letter were poor (Jas 1:9-11; 2:1-5; 5:1-5). The pastoral epistles, by not condemning riches outright but encouraging the wealthy "to be rich in good works, generous, and ready to share" (1 Tim 6:18), express the most positive New Testament word on wealth. But even here readers are told to be content with food and clothing, for desire for wealth plunges "people into ruin and destruction," and "love of money is a root of all kinds of evil" (vv. 7-10).

The contrast between rich and poor often paralleled that between holy and unholy, as Borg shows, for many poor could not afford to maintain

Pharisaic purity standards. Jesus ate not only with the ritually unclean (Mt 15:1-9 par. Mk 7:1-13) but also with those considered "sinners" (Mk 2:15-17 and parallels) and constantly challenged current definitions of "righteous" and "sinners" (Lk 7:36-50; 15:1-7 par. Mt 18:12-14; Lk 18:9-14). His symbolically significant attack on the temple money changers challenged both economic and religio-cultic distortions (Mk 11:15-17 and parallels).

Removal of culturally divisive features of Jewish purity laws was essential to spreading the gospel to the Gentiles (Acts 10:9-29; 15:1-29). In this dimension, the law could be a "dividing wall" between them and Jews (Eph 2:13-16). Paul's crucial teaching on justification by faith denied that religio-cultic matters could make any basic difference in peoples' relationship to Christ (see especially Gal 2:11-21). The book of Hebrews, drawing deep symbolic meaning from the Israelite cultus, stresses its inability, by itself, to provide redemption.

This openness toward Gentiles, which potentially included people from all nations, tribes, peoples and tongues (Rev 5:9; 7:9), was rooted in Jesus' ministry. Though Jesus seems to have focused most of his ministry effort on Jews (Mt 10:5-6; 15:24), he frequently visited regions with large Gentile populations. More important, he rebuked negative attitudes toward foreigners (Lk 9:51-56) and used them as examples to reprove Israelites (Mt 8:5-10 and parallels; Lk 4:25-27; 10:25-37; 17:8; John 4:4-44). He expected Ninevites, the Queen of Sheba, inhabitants of Tyre and Sidon and even those of Sodom and Gomorrah to shame many Israelites at the final judgment (Mt 12:41-42 par. Lk 11:31-32; Mt 11:20-24 par. Lk 10:13-15; Mt 10:15 par. Lk 10:12).

Jesus also reversed the traditional eschatological hope even more explicitly: "Many will come from east and west and will eat with Abraham and Isaac and Jacob in the kingdom of heaven, while the heirs of the kingdom will be thrown into the outer darkness" (Mt 8:11-12). As Joachim Jeremias noted, "No Jewish scholar and no Jewish apocalypticist had ever dared to utter such a thing" (1982:43). If Jesus was calling people to a corporate life to be actualized on earth, it would demand great changes in attitudes toward cultic, racial and national differences.

Jesus' kingdom also reversed many customary perspectives on men and women. This underlines how thoroughgoing his inclusivity was, since, as Ruether emphasizes, women were usually the most oppressed in oppressed groups (the poor, the unholy, the Gentiles). Jesus had special concern for widows, who with no husband for financial support were often very poor (Mk 12:40 par. Lk 20:47; Mk 12:41-44 par. Lk 21:1-4; Lk 4:25-26 [Gentile widows]; 7:12-15; 18:1-8). Whereas rabbis would seldom talk to women and never teach them, Jesus commended Mary of Bethany, who was hearing his teaching, over her sister Martha, who was absorbed in domestic tasks (Lk 10:38-42; compare Jn 4; 11:1-37).

In perhaps the Synoptics' most profound dialogue (Mt 15:21-28), most extensive healing (Mk 5:25-34 and parallels) and most graphic reversal of "sinner" and "righteous" (Lk 7:36-50), a woman is the central character. When a woman exclaimed, "Blessed is the womb that bore you and the breasts that nursed you!" Jesus, rejecting the notion that a woman's chief value comes through childbirth, replied, "Blessed rather are those who hear the word of God and obey it!" (Lk 11:27-28).

In Israel, each person's identity was bound tightly to his or her family—especially a woman's, who was under her father's or husband's authority and usually wholly dependent on him financially. But whereas husbands could obtain a divorce far more easily than could wives (if wives could at all), Jesus said that the same considerations must apply to both (Mt 19:3-10 par. Mk 10:2-12). When Jesus was told that his mother and brothers sought him, he replied that his mother and brothers were all those who did God's will (Mk 3:31-35 and parallels). Jesus even said that he came to bring not peace but a sword, which would sharply divide families (Mt 10:34-36 par. Lk 12:51-53; compare Lk 14:26; Mt 8:22 par. Lk 9:59-60).

God's kingdom, then, called everyone to choose for something that could supersede his or her family and gave women an identity that transcended it. Various women left their homes to become Jesus' regular followers (Mt 27:55-56 par. Mk 15:40-41; Lk 8:1-3). In a day when a woman's testimony was seldom legally valid, Jesus' female followers became the first witnesses to his resurrection (Mk 16:1-8 and parallels).

Changes in women's roles were evident in the early church, where the Spirit descended on both daughters and sons, both male and female slaves (Acts 2:17-18; 21:8-9). Jesus' female followers participated from the start (1:14). In a culture where males alone counted in synagogue membership, frequent observations that "both men and women" were active are significant (5:14; 8:3, 12; 9:2; 22:4). Several women played prominent roles in establishing new churches: Lydia (16:11-15), Prisca (18:1-4, 18, 26; Rom 16:3; 1 Cor 16:19; 2 Tim 4:19), Damaris (Acts 17:34) and other unnamed ones (17:4, 12).

Phoebe was a church deacon, Paul's spokesperson and a patron of his and many others (Rom 16:1-2). Tryphaena, Tryphosa and Mary were deeply involved in mission work (vv. 6, 12). Junia, once Paul's fellow prisoner, was an apostle before he was (v. 7). Euodia and Syntyche, church leaders at Philippi, labored side by side with Paul (Phil 4:2-3).

God's kingdom, then, called everyone to a way of life that involved sweeping structural and attitudinal reorientations in the most significant socioeconomic relationships in life: between rich and poor, holy and unholy, Jew and Gentile, and men and women, with its implications for the most basic family dynamics.[14]

In addition, its approach of love toward enemies countered existing social practices (see chapter eight). This was a direct outworking of Jesus' agapaic way to the cross. It was reaffirmed in the most explicit later teachings on relations with the social order (Rom 12:14-21; 13:8; 1 Pet 2:21-23). Not only to renounce defending themselves against enemies, both local and international, but to actively seek to do them good involves enormous changes in the way people approach all conflict relationships. Since Jesus was and is calling people to a corporate life to be actualized on earth, it clearly demanded, and demands, great attitudinal and behavioral changes in all these areas.

Christian involvement in society. Early in this chapter, I noted that Christian views on society have often been divided in a manner similar to the conflictivist-holist debate. Many Christian groups, emphasizing the depth of evil in society, have sought either to maintain the status quo or to work for only slight improvements. I have argued, however, that Christians are to live by Jesus' radical teachings. Thus I cannot endorse this common "conservative" view. Other Christian groups, however, have emphasized human transformation and sought to restructure society. Since I have stressed transformation, am I advocating this "liberal," or holistic, orientation?

In chapter nine I noted that humans, according to Paul, belong to one of two great corporate solidarities: the flesh or the body of Christ. *Flesh (sarx),* on one hand, can indicate the bodies of all living creatures, which may be weak but were created as good; yet on the other, it denotes a corporate force which invades and enslaves humans (see chapter nine). This happens when realities that are perceptible and measurable take on ultimate value.

The biblical term *world (kosmos)* functions similarly. On one hand, it indicates that field of created potentialities, creatures and structures within which God designed human life to develop. The world, in this sense, is the object of God's special concern and love (for example, Jn 3:16-17). Yet closer examination shows that *world* more often appears as a whole system of social and moral life opposed to God (for instance, Jn 15:18-19; 1 Cor 1:20-30; 1 Jn 2:15-17).

Somewhat the same contrast pertains to the ultimate powers behind sociopolitical authorities, indicated by terms such as *thrones, dominions, rulers, powers* (Col 1:16).[15] They were created to order the lives of the nations. But they arrogated the role of gods, drawing ultimate worship to themselves. Insofar as they still exercise their created purposes, they carry on valuable functions which are worthy of compliance. Yet their disobedience turns whole societies against God.[16]

How can the same words be used for opposing realities?[17] God created various structures (and human capacities for developing them) through which the divine purposes were to be attained, so that these were at least potentially good. Such structures, however, could also become opposed to God and be corrupted in most of their functions. Thus they came to have a dual character. On one hand, the social forces which structure the "world" maintain a degree of social order and promote some positive features of culture and civilization. But at a deeper level, they channel all human experience and activity in directions which oppose God's kingdom. Although the church has broken the grip of these forces in various times and places, Scripture does not indicate that any kind of general historical progress will gradually diminish their universal social impact. The conflict between the way of God's kingdom and the way of the world is essentially as sharp as it was in Jesus' day.[18]

The world, therefore, conditions the overall way people perceive and respond to social reality, even though this reality has some positive features. This is extremely important if, as I have maintained, people's basic awareness of what they, their fellow creatures and society really are is inextricably structured by social factors (see chapter nine). It means that their unconscious and conscious convictions about reality are shaped by forces which, in their overall intention (even if not in every detail), oppose God. Every society, then, will be characterized by "standing forms of sin"[19]: by institutions and activities, such as slavery, racial discrimination or war, which seem perfectly normal features of the way things are but which strongly oppose God's will.

Given that all peoples will assume, in some important ways, that social life is different from what God wills, what should be the church's major social function? Not simply giving aid or maintaining or strengthening institutions here and there, though this may be important at times. For the unique thing Christians can contribute is to make an alternative way of life—God's kingdom—visible and actual. To show that ways of behaving and relating which differ from, and sometimes contradict, a current society's are actually possible—this is the most important task that Christians can perform. Yet such a vision cannot be communicated through words alone. To become visible and open to participation, it must be concretely lived. The church, then, must be a social unit in which the kingdom vision and reality are shaping new structures and behaviors and which is open for others to join.

This notion of Christian involvement in society affirms the biblical principle that God's universal will becomes known and active, paradoxically, through its actualization in particular, concrete situations. It also affirms that depths of evil exist in society, as do many traditionally conservative theologies. It does not aim directly at transformation of the whole, as do many liberal or holistic ones. Yet unlike conservative but like liberal approaches, it stresses transformation of social life—though in particular mostly local settings. It affirms that the most significant social changes are likely to occur through concrete impacts of Jesus' kingdom way. Those who follow it seek to live according to God's kingdom in their own situation and wait for the eschaton for God to transform and judge society as a whole.

Social Dynamics

The social reality for which Christians ought to strive, I have argued, should accord with Jesus' radical kingdom way, governed by *agapē*. Is this standpoint too idealistic to contribute to current public conversations about social alienation?

The "is," the "ought" and the future. Chapters four and seven frequently asked whether social theorists should simply observe how people *do* behave and what they actually desire, and then recommend arrangements that satisfy and balance these tendencies as much as possible; or should they elaborate some vision of what humans *ought* to be and desire and champion a better society based on it? (Environmentalists, remember, similarly discuss whether ethics should be derived from evolutionary tendencies or from other notions of how humans ought to interact with nonhumans.)

From a Christian perspective, we should be as realistic as possible about the way society *is* functioning. To suppose that people and institutions are better than their actual behavior is a romanticized escape from reality's darker side. (It is also unrealistic, however, to interpret things so negatively as to overlook positive social behavior.) Yet for several reasons, I cannot agree that the best social situations will emerge if "natural" desires and activities are as little regulated as possible.

First, I acknowledged in chapter ten that self-love, or self-interest, which libertarians regard as our strongest basic impulse, can expand to include other persons. Novak rightly adds that for most people it includes their families. Yet I also maintained that as it creates solidarity and justice within some circles, such as family, social class, or nation, it intensifies our sense of conflict with other circles. Self-interest is too limited in its original range to expand indefinitely and too rooted in gaining benefit for the self (that is, it is essentially *eros*) to inspire the self-giving *(agapē)* necessary for true social harmony. Although unregulated interplay among self-interests sometimes checks, balances or enhances them, it requires a great leap of faith to conclude that this would always produce optimum social harmony. Those who insist, like F. A. Hayek, that epistemological limitations should keep governments from adjusting the economy should acknowledge that they themselves have no real evidence that the opposite course would produce something far better.[20]

Second, those who extol lack of regulation usually claim that the lengthy, unregulated wisdom of social exchange has already produced some excellent arrangements. Yet those who maintain this (such as Hume) write from social settings which give certain classes great advantages over others. It can be argued that such arrangements disadvantage some groups greatly and hardly provide the greatest possible benefit for the greatest number. We should be suspicious of how many persons such arrangements help when Hayek attributes their selection to evolutionary struggle.

Third, even when "natural" tendencies of social forces are curbed by political arrangements to produce power balances among them, forces which are already dominant tend to retain greater power. That is quite evident when Niebuhr acknowledges that any social field must have an organizing center which possesses certain coercive powers over other forces. In international relations, we saw, this led to praising British colonialism and advocating American hegemony. Like social exchange's "unregulated wisdom," such power balances often leave groups which have long been subordinated in accustomed positions. This happens when Niebuhr largely excludes women from participation in relationships of power.

The deepest reason, however, that Christian theology cannot make social reality as it generally *is* its criterion is its conviction that a new and very different kind of reality already exists and will become more fully realized in the future. In the new creation inaugurated by Jesus' resurrection (see chapter nine), the kingdom that he brought with its "reversed" social relationships is already active. In this sense, Christian social theology is based on something which already is and not simply on hopes of what will be or ideals of what ought to be.

For this reason, I cannot interpret the incarnation, as does Novak, chiefly as God's acceptance of history's limits and evils (of what generally *is*).[21] For whereas God—Father, Son and Spirit—indeed bore these evils in the most profound way, God also opposed them uncompromisingly and triumphed over them in Jesus' resurrection. We should regard Jesus' non-violent response to evil and the New Testament's advocacy of the same agape not as putting up with evil but as opposing it in a radical way. God not only bears with evildoers patiently and lovingly; God also opposes the evil they do prophetically and opens up the contrasting kingdom way. Through this combination, God makes available the most meaningful means of countering evil.

Though Christian theology of society is based on the kingdom's presence, this kingdom, energized by the Holy Spirit, presses toward ever fuller manifestation. Its dynamism arises largely from the hope it arouses. Thus I agree with Bookchin, Marcuse, Jameson, Ruether and Freire that visions of a better future can point to very real social potentialities and can arouse life-transforming energy and passion for bringing them into being. I cannot, like Milton Friedman, accept a positivism that limits all valid statements to assertions about empirically verifiable facts. For such positivism, as Marcuse protests, identifies reality with the status quo.

I understand visions of a more idyllic human past, such as found in Bookchin and much ecofeminism, to be largely retrojections of this kind of future hope back into history. (I concluded in chapter ten that organismic evolutionary theories picturing a more benign past, like those of Swimme, Berry and Fox, are similarly retrojecting a vision of nature's eschatological future.) There is simply not enough evidence to show that before the rise of large civilizations, humans in general found nature either benign or hostile (as Marxists claim) or that their social units were egalitarian (Bookchin). There is also insufficient evidence for or against hypotheses of an early worldwide matricentric culture, its egalitarianism and its overthrow by militaristic, male, sky-god civilizations.[22]

Why, then, are such hypotheses attractive to many people? In my view it is because God calls everyone not only toward personal maturity (see chapter nine) but toward actualizing this in a social context, so that some longing for an ideal society becomes deeply embedded in most people. Marcuse, Bookchin, Ruether and Freire stress this transcendence toward a social future.

Although the Christian agapaic vision of the consummated kingdom may seem to flicker only occasionally in history and to be incarnated even less often, I maintain, as even Reinhold Niebuhr does, that it has elicited striking new trends in actual history and exerts a powerful impact on most social movements today. Moreover, since trinitarian faith affirms that one God is calling all individuals and societies toward the same final goal, I believe that various features in visions of ultimate social harmony found in many cultures (whether understood as future or past) can indicate the same basic hope.[23] Accordingly Christian faith will have significant points of contact with some current social movements.

If visions of a better society give some indication of what lies ahead, then history does have a goal and direction. I cannot agree fully that the age of metanarratives is past and that we live in a postmodern era where no over-all perspectives on history are possible. I disagree partly because this claim itself involves a sweeping interpretation of history—is itself a metanarra-tive, as Jameson says. Nonetheless postmodern skepticism can help guard against subordinating too many events too easily to overall schemes of meaning. For instance, whereas Milton and Rose Friedman's praise of nineteenth-century capitalism cites many advances in British and American life, it overlooks too many negative effects of this system on non-Western countries. In so doing their metanarrative functions, as postmod-ernists claim, as an ideology for a system of economic power.

Since I affirm that all history will one day be summed up in Jesus Christ, I disagree when Ruether maintains that history has no one goal. Yet I find it extremely difficult to identify trends leading directly toward it. For only events which manifest the agape of Jesus' kingdom truly herald that king-dom's consummation. In actual history, such events are usually intermixed with quite different ones or seem to be countered quickly by their oppo-sites. Further, to insist that events in which we participate point directly toward the *eschaton* can arouse unChristlike triumphalism and pride. However, groups that take up Jesus' challenging way, insofar as they truly live this out, participate in history's fulfillment—yet without attempting to determine exactly how well they may be doing so or how their efforts will interact with other salvific trends.

Jesus' way differs so sharply from current history, dominated by power strivings, that it will most likely be followed without compromise by those who believe, as did Jesus and most Jews of his day, that God will someday overcome evil entirely and consummate the kingdom in historical circum-stances of some kind (see chapter eight). For I doubt, as argued in chap-ter ten, that those who are truly oppressed by evil will struggle against it unless they believe that it can someday be abolished. And if they do not believe that God will someday accomplish this in a special way, those hopes for good's complete victory, which seem essential to their effective social involvement, will likely be identified with some flawed social movement, as critics of liberation efforts complain.

Yet to avoid idolization of imperfect social movements, I cannot endorse

Niebuhr's view that eschatological fulfillment occurs only in some eternal realm, divorced from history's course. That separates Christian hope so far from society that it seldom arouses efforts for more than slight social improvement, let alone transformation. Thus whereas contemporary holism emphasizes a historical hope but may idealize social movements falling far short of God's kingdom, Niebuhr's conflictualism has some place for kingdom ideals but denies their historical realization.

A more biblical approach, it seems, would affirm both these ideals and their historical actualization. Yet given evil's current impact on everything historical, it seems extremely improbable that any current historical movement could lead directly to this actualization. We must instead assume, as did Jesus and most Jews of his day, that God will act in some unusual way(s) to eliminate the worst effects of historical evil. Such acts are consistent with a fully transcendent God, who created natural and historical processes and is able to work beyond their usual operations—even if God does not often do so.[24]

Such acts, however, will transform neither history into eternity nor humans into angels. They will simply open the way for humans and non-humans, as created (though transformed in some way), to live in fully just, loving, peaceful relationships. This has great practical relevance: if we believe that these will someday be practiced among actual, finite creatures, we can work toward significant approximations of them now. Belief in this real possibility, even if initial efforts fall far short, energizes serious efforts to live this way and creates effective social alternatives to current conditions.

Hope for this final victory of good need not encourage escapism, as Ruether claims. Yet given its anticipation of some unusual future divine act(s), it may not entirely convince some. I find it preferable, however, to a hope that expects historical fulfillment but denies full actualization of justice, peace and love or one that affirms perfect justice, peace and love but denies their historical fulfillment.

The shape of new social structures. Whereas God's kingdom, and along with it human social hopes, will attain final fulfillment only at the eschaton, that kingdom is nonetheless truly present now. The new creation has already begun. Divinizing powers are presently transforming human lives (see chapter nine). Thus current corporate efforts at realizing God's kingdom actually participate in the final realities. This participation, however, is only evident with some clarity where Jesus' way of agape is practiced. This will often be the way of a minority, which cuts against the social grain. Violent retaliation against or overthrow of its opponents is incompatible with this.

Jesus' way, accordingly, will often be marked by suffering. In experiencing rejection or persecution, such communities will share in Jesus' cross. Yet precisely in such experiences they will open themselves to new filling by resurrection life, much as happens on the individual spiritual path (see chapter nine). God will be experienced amid conflicts with such a community's society and amid its internal conflicts as it wrestles with them in ways that parallel the individual journey.

Yet even if structures opposing God's kingdom can be overcome, it is misleading to imply that a new social order will flow forth rather effortlessly and naturally, as Ruether and Freire sometimes do. Freire seems to assume that those involved in liberation, once released from binding social structures, will rather swiftly and automatically discern how to humanize themselves, their oppressors and new societies. Freire and Ruether seem to visualize the structuring of new societies as flowing forth analogously to a productive natural process, once it has been freed from crippling human restraints. (Marcuse and Bookchin's heavy emphasis on constructive phantasy conveys the same organismic emphasis.) They seem to regard those involved as no longer importantly affected by former social restraints, however deeply these once bound them.

I maintain, however, that original social conditioning goes much deeper and will only with difficulty be reshaped (see chapter nine). I also affirm, with Niebuhr (in his critique of romanticism), that no naturelike human capacity untouched by sin and self-deception exists to provide an unobscured guide to restructuring social life. I do not mean, of course, that people should not be guided by organismic visions of social and natural harmony. I only caution that constructing social units approximating them will involve more uncertainty, disagreement and partial failure than holistic approaches often imply.

Segundo makes the liberating and humanizing process, freed from any intrinsic shaping or limits from Scripture or tradition, the substance of Christian faith. Yet this reliance on recent experiences and ways of thought as almost sole sources of truth and as far superior to any wisdom from the past recalls the Enlightenment attitude found in ecological theologians (see chapters six, ten). This attitude, however sharply it verbally castigates the historical Enlightenment, valorizes, like that Enlightenment, unlimited reconfiguration of reality according to human purposes. However accurately it may critique forms of oppression, human awareness and intentionality provide its norms.

Such social transformation is different from one where Jesus and his way provide foundational norms and where participants must accept a keen sense of their limits, over against other humans and nonhumans and especially over against God.[25] I realize, of course, that people who have been oppressed do not want their social visions censored by what others tell them. I am speaking, however, of the limits which shape the good news about Jesus and God's kingdom.

I also find, with Novak, that liberation movements tend to speak too naively of governments they will establish as being fully dedicated to public good. I expect all governments before the eschaton to be self-serving in some degree. With Niebuhr, I find governments' claims to be total public servants expressions of those pretentions to righteousness by which they seek to deceive their constituencies. Bookchin and Freire warn that if revolutionaries are not free from desires for domination, they will duplicate what they overthrow. I would add that no revolutionary group will ever be entirely free from these. This, of course, does not excuse those who have opportunity from constructing the most publicly responsive governments they can.

More positively, what might one expect transformed social units to look like? I expect that the new creation will more often emerge in groups dedicated to distinctive ways of living than it will pervade larger political units. These will include church groups and some others concerned about particular causes or lifestyles.[26] They will not always be radical or far "left." Many practices they recommend (such as traditional farming techniques by deep ecologists) might be quite conservative. Given the New Testament stress on marital fidelity, on moderation in food, drink, entertainment and so on, behaviors of some groups approximating the kingdom will appear quite conventional (though actually living by such values is, in many current contexts, quite radical). Given the difficulty of living in alternative ways, each group may do well only several of the things I now mention.

Ideally such groups will work toward overcoming the separation of domestic and productive spheres in modern life. All persons should engage in child-rearing and household tasks. All should have opportunity to pursue a vocation. If some involve themselves primarily in domestic tasks or those relating to the group's life, this will be based on choice, not gender. Sharing of possessions (cars, lawn mowers and so on) and wealth, as modeled in the early church, will lessen economic differences and each person's dependence on relatively large salaries. Ruether's suggestion for groups to own many things jointly but preserve private space for each person—for humans are individuals as well as communal—is attractive. Each such group would encourage creativity of various kinds, including artistic expression.

Such groups would make decisions in face-to-face settings often. However, for efficiency's sake, certain tasks and the decisions connected with them need to be delegated to individuals. I am not sure what Bookchin intends by affirming that "all mature individuals can be expected to manage their social affairs directly" (1982:336). If he means that they can understand all data relevant to these affairs and decide concerning each step in their management, I disagree. For in some matters almost everyone must trust leaders who exercise different functions. Such communities would in a sense model ecological ones, where all members are vital to the life of the whole. Yet to emphasize that no one is "intrinsically 'higher' or 'lower,'" as Ruether does, may obscure the fact that in some activities certain people will be entrusted with leadership over others—and that the organic metaphor itself involves a hierarchy of functions (1983b:67).[27]

It is conceivable that social renewal might spread somewhat as Bookchin envisions, originating with numerous grassroots organizations in a city or region and expanding until an entire area was in effect governed by alternative, face-to-face assemblies. I find it unlikely, however, that such grassroots movements would keep spreading, reforming the entire economic system and replacing national governments and international alliances with municipal federations. At some point the world's dominant economic and political systems, which oppose God's kingdom, will restrict or assimilate such forces, seriously curtailing their capacity to express and actualize alternative realities.

Such groups, then, should avoid pinning all hopes on global revolution, for if macroforces begin defeating or coopting them, they may give up altogether. It is better to create and maintain the best alternatives they can, largely in local situations, for the vision and energy that these inspire may well outlast particular successes or failures. Influence on large political structures is most likely to occur through "a minority tradition of direct action" (deep ecology) that seeks to influence particular decisions rather than to restructure the whole.

Deep ecology's emphasis on people adapting to bioregions and living as much as possible off what is produced there is appealing. Yet to do this consistently they will sometimes need to reject the latest developments of "technological rationality," which Ruether regards as "the highest gift of nature" (1975:205). Keeping up with recent changes often necessitates reshaping an economy in line with larger forces, depending on supplies and financing from elsewhere and eliminating local operations that are less profitable. Emphasizing regional development often means forgoing the advantages of the latest international developments and vice versa. Moreover, those involved in bioregional development cannot usually expect a benevolent larger government to be enforcing those patterns of production, distribution and technological development that Ruether finds desirable.

Novak rightly affirms that the Trinity's individuality-in-community provides the model for human communities. Yet given the strong individualism in Western societies, free expressions of individual inclinations will less often be compatible with true community than he supposes. I expect that most who endeavor to operate communally will often feel restricted by group constraints. In real life, maximum diversity and maximum unity do not always balance each other smoothly, contrary to Swimme, Berry and McFague (see chapter ten).

Capitalism. Is social freedom best attained through a free market or through structures which limit, or perhaps liberate, people from such a market? My response will consider capitalism in a "pure" form—as a consistent system of principles and structures. My conclusions therefore will not always apply directly to every situation where capitalism operates in a modified form (such as "democratic" capitalism).

Capitalist economies at their beginnings may make economic opportunities available to many. Yet their tendency, when unmodified by laws counteracting it, is to concentrate great wealth in relatively few hands. Capitalism's organization, as Daniel Bell says, is hierarchical and geared toward maximum efficiency. It does promote values such as discipline in those who run things and in workers insofar as they are workers. Teamwork is often valued, as Novak points out, insofar as it leads to efficiency and profit—but not in and of itself. Capitalism probably does encourage creative, practical reason and risk-taking (Novak) more than its critics acknowledge.

Historically capitalism has helped break down all social, cultural and moral forces that hindered maximum production, exchange and profit. For this reason it is difficult—though not always impossible—to balance capitalism by these other forces. Capitalism's main aim is not to provide services but to make a profit. Consequently this economic system seeks to go beyond meeting existing needs to create new wants and desires. The more that preproduction costs and times increase, the more advantageous is it to induce desire for products before they even appear. Thus capitalism, especially through advertising, seeks to shape psychic structures throughout a society. My evaluation is as much concerned with this aspect as with any economic one, although capitalism is not the sole cause of every trend I now mention.

Capitalism encourages in everyone, including its workers, insofar as they are consumers, what Bell calls *self-realization*—desire to explore ourselves and expand our desires and experiences without limit. (Chapter ten noted how Berry, Swimme, Fox, Ruether and process theologies can encourage this trend.) It seeks to stimulate the desires (*epithymiai* [chapter nine]) with promises of quick fulfillment and, since these are generally short-lived, to keep on intensifying desires and magnifying their hoped-for fulfillments. This *commodification* of desire penetrates to the unconscious (Jameson).

Caught up in streams of such sensations in surroundings which otherwise tend to be unstable, people lack objects around which to form centered selves (Lasch). Such selves as are formed are often depthless (Marcuse, Jameson). Possibilities for grappling with life's larger issues (Bell) and transcending the present tend to vanish. Life is increasingly reduced to one dimension (Marcuse). Ruether complains that women are pressured to be the chief purchasers and advertised objects propelling the process. Though this atmosphere does not affect everyone equally, I cannot agree that a free market which operates this way leaves everyone free to choose or to form selves which can make meaningful choices—even though, in a formal sense, they have many choices.

Capitalism, whose main goal is profit, also regards nonhuman creatures as potential sources of profit. Nature has (instrumental) value as used or transformed by humans but not (intrinsically) in itself. It is true, as libertarians maintain, that owners of natural resources often want to use them in the future and make some effort to preserve them. But capitalistic motives do not lead to preservation of features unconnected with profit (for example, logging companies are not usually concerned about purity of streams). And the further away that future is, the less important does it often seem to preserve anything for it.

Whereas the economic condition of Western workers has improved greatly over the last century, giving them a stake in the system's continuance, many Third World countries now function as sources of cheap labor and raw materials. This dependency on developed nations which, I argued in chapter seven, exists in Latin America is found in many other countries too. Though local rulers can be partly blamed for this, as Novak and Niebuhr charge, they could not function as they do without support from wealthy nations or corporations whose interests, at least in the long run, they serve. Here capitalism's concentration of wealth in relatively few hands hardly gives these countries or their workers access to employment or markets where they are "free."

I am arguing that capitalism leads to these kinds of situations when its principles operate without hindrance. Possibly some of these principles might not produce all these consequences when limited by other social and moral factors. Nonetheless, mutual servanthood, the primary social value of Christian faith, regards making the accumulation of wealth a person's major aim as incompatible with faithfulness toward God. Consequently Christian faith is incompatible with "pure" capitalism, a system based chiefly on profit. For Christians, life and work must be based on other aims.

How should Christians respond to capitalism? They can engage in pursuits that limit pure capitalism, as Novak indicates. However, since capitalism tends to penetrate personal and social formation at the deepest levels, the most helpful Christian response is the establishment of social groups where other values are instilled, from infancy if possible. Here values found in relationships with human and nonhuman others will especially be stressed. Creating things will be valued over possessing things. Satisfaction of appetites will not be denied, but it will be subordinated to the formation of centered selves and the pursuit of more meaningful purposes.

Since capitalism has global effects, it is valuable for even relatively small groups to practice cognitive mapping (Jameson)—efforts to trace its systemic effects on themselves and on the world's more disadvantaged people. These effects will be better understood if, as Jameson also recommends, different groups that are marginalized by them form social and political alliances.

How limited should government be? To solve the problems created by free markets I have recommended the construction of more ideal societies. But to what extent should governments be involved in promoting them, and who will decide what ideals are to be accepted?

Greatly expanded government will not reduce social alienation but will likely increase it, as both libertarians and holists affirm (see chapter four). Hayek's emphasis on government's limited knowledge also provides reasons for restricting it, even though our knowledge of what would happen with greatly reduced government is also limited.

From a Christian perspective we can add that government should be restricted because it, like every other reality before the eschaton, is affected by sin. With Niebuhr, Novak and libertarians, I do not expect any government before that time to be entirely benevolent. Like Niebuhr, I regard any government's claims to be so as pretentions to righteousness by which it seeks to deceive its constituents. Limitations on government in areas of personal freedom also guard the transcendence of individuals. Though divine transcendence and eschatology should not be separated from history as Niebuhr does, the God who draws history forward transcends finite reality much more vastly than holistic social theologies usually affirm. Intentional participation in the trinitarian fullness is rooted in personal encounter with this God in our *heart.*

Yet sharply curtailing government, as libertarians recommend, will hardly reduce social alienation, for other socioeconomic forces are oppressive and will simply fill the vacuum. Because capitalism tends to concentrate economic power in few hands, government activities which make economic opportunity available to many are appropriate. These include, among others, restrictions on monopolistic practices, provision of job training and making loans available to small businesses, especially in disadvantaged areas. Many social tasks are most ideally left to smaller groups energized by God's kingdom. Yet due to the size and complexity of most modern societies, they cannot address every need. It is appropriate for government programs, even if they are much less effective, to pick up some of the slack.

Government functions best when its own powers (for example, legislative and judicial) internally check each other and are checked by outside social forces. We should not expect, however, that a smooth balance will result. Some degree of conflict is inevitable in sociopolitical life, as in the psychological and ecological spheres. Hegemony of any one power is to be avoided as far as possible, in domestic as well as in international settings. A society should be open to the impact of new groups to avoid any balance from favoring the status quo. New interest groups will indeed clamor for increased power, much as Hayek and others dislike this. But hopefully this clamoring will be chiefly for greater freedoms, means of public expression and economic opportunities, not simply for government funds. Christians can usefully support moral and cultural forces which check the dominance of political and economic ones.

However, the main Christian social task is neither to promote balance of powers nor to support general moral and cultural forces. The main task is to provide something much more specific and concrete: forms of social life that express the presence of God's kingdom and provide significant alternatives to the ways life is usually lived. In this way, ideals and visions stressed by holists can be articulated and even realized—yet, as conflictivists demand, without being imposed on anyone by force. Government power should be limited to allow as many alternatives as possible to flourish and to permit such groups to take over some tasks usually allotted to government (education, job training, feeding and housing the poor, for example).

Summary

Human beings are intrinsically social and natural beings. They cannot avoid being essentially structured by interrelations with other humans, even if they try. Accordingly, social theories cannot begin their considerations with the isolated individual.

Human society is also intrinsically shaped by nonhuman nature and cannot be accurately considered apart from its relationships with nature. At the same time, being human involves having an irreducibly personal dimension of awareness and volition. All adequate societies must allow room for expression of this dimension, especially in relation to values and realities which transcend spatiotemporal phenomena.

As all individuals are dimly drawn toward a fuller future (see chapter nine), so are all societies. Physical and cultural changes (such as advances in science) demand that they alter their shape. To remain entirely the same is to deny capacities for greater wholeness. Yet societies are also rooted in the past, and meaningful change must incorporate many of its features. To stress production and experience of as many new things as possible and to abandon parameters from the past increases the risk that nature will be exploited and life be based on desires and fears that overwhelm construction of stable selves and relationships.

The basic dynamics of all large social units resist and subvert the emergence of the healthiest relationships toward which societies are drawn (this is a "realistic" view of social perfectibility). Clinging to past structures is not the only form of this dynamic. Efforts to replace these with entirely new structures also bring unhealthy dynamics into play and often do not appreciably improve things.

Substantial change is possible, however, through some smaller groups who attempt to live by visions of what *ought* to be—visions including radical but also traditional elements. Such groups can initiate real social change because they actualize new possibilities in perceptible, reproducible form. Yet since they go against cultural norms, they normally encounter opposition. Their tasks are difficult and usually only partially successful. They demand enough exploration and creativity that these social forms would probably not emerge easily and smoothly even in a world without evil.

The most preferable forms of present government make expression of such social alternatives possible and allow new voices to be heard in the public sphere. These governments' tendencies toward inordinate power and other evils are limited by balances among their own powers and between them and other social powers. An unregulated market does not achieve this, since it concentrates economic power in few hands. It enthrones the profit motive, which often leads to ecological damage and pursuit of pleasure, which undermine formation of stable selves and relationships. Social alienation, however, is not most effectively challenged by attaining balance among powers (which involves accepting what generally *is* the case) but by creating alternative structures that bridge conflicts among them (introducing what *ought* to be).

Christians believe that the kind of social life that ought to be already is real, even if in partial and imperfect ways, and that some day it will be fully actualized. These beliefs provide strong motives for actualizing this kind of life more fully. This social life overcomes exploitative relationships among genders, economic classes, ethnic groups and between humans and non-human nature. In such relationships, however, those involved retain their distinctive characteristics, enjoying a diversity-in-unity rather than becoming homogeneous. These communal relationships are ultimately rooted in close fellowship with God, who does not absorb humanity and nature but whose distinctness from them grounds their relative diversity.

TWELVE

A Christian Response to Psychological, Ecological & Social Alienation

Throughout this work I have discussed three phenomena that are evident to anyone who is well aware of today's world and have asked whether they might be related. First, many contemporary people feel distant from or at odds with or unsure of their real selves. Second, today's technological civilization seems estranged from and in the process of destroying its own biological base. Third, numerous individuals and social groups feel cut off from and oppressed by those very governmental and economic systems in which they participate. All three realms display a common pattern. The main entity—the self, the industrialized ecosphere, human society—is deeply and paradoxically divided against itself. Elements that should be supporting and sustaining one another are somehow estranged from and working against each other.

Noticing this common pattern of alienation in all three realms, I have asked whether they might be related. My main questions have been these: What causes psychological, ecological and social alienation? How might they be connected? How might they be overcome? I have sought answers from the standpoint of Christian theology. Under postmodernism's influence, some current theologians are no longer addressing such broad themes. Nonetheless theology, which deals with topics such as God and the meaning of human existence, is one of the few disciplines which can approach such comprehensive issues today. In a world where all facets of life are becoming increasingly interrelated, it is important to seek to understand their connections.

Risks are certainly involved in doing so. Modern knowledge is complex and specialized enough that no one can know as much as they might like about even one discipline. Much more could be said, and probably better said, about the three areas I have sought to survey. Moreover, any schema for organizing issues across several fields is bound to be somewhat imprecise. By dividing viewpoints into conflictive and organismic/holistic perspectives, I have doubtless missed some important issues and thinkers and perhaps overplayed others. Nonetheless I believe that an attempt to find some points of commonality among these three realms is well worth the effort. Each person today participates in all three. The complexity of any one can easily baffle us. Yet awareness of their interconnections can yield insight into, and suggest avenues for handling, a wide range of seemingly disconnected issues.

To summarize my overall findings, I will briefly outline my response to the major question: how are psychological, ecological and social alienation, and Christian responses to each of them, interrelated? In my summaries of chapters nine, ten and eleven, perspectives on each of these three areas were presented in the language of public conversation. In articulating this final conclusion, I will employ theological discourse more often.

Psychological and Spiritual Formation

Psychological alienation, from a Christian perspective, stems from two general kinds of causes. First, considered apart from the presence of evil, becoming a self is a process, extending throughout a lifetime, into which God calls everyone. Successful participation in this process involves, first of all, a basic faithfulness to God and to God's call. This call always includes walking along a certain path. This path may be shaped by a specific vocation. It always involves living a particular style of life in obedience to God. Becoming a self is also characterized by entering into relationships of mutual servanthood with other people. In addition, self-formation includes stewardship—care for and wise use of nonhuman creatures in companionship with them.

The self that develops is actually constituted, becomes what it is, through these three kinds of relationships.[1] All three involve a commitment to other partners—a giving of ourselves in relationship, which involves trust—and some degree of knowledge of what they are like. Becoming a self, that is, is not primarily a process of intensifying experience, expanding consciousness or increasing pleasure, though these will often occur within the framework of the three primary commitments. This path of self-development would be challenging even in a world unmarked by evil. Because we would always be in process and be giving ourselves to other partners, we would occasionally sense some difference, or distance, between what we were at given points and our complete self.

Psychological alienation arises, second, because all people have turned aside in some degree from God's call. To some extent everyone works against it and no longer hears it rightly. (For this reason, many today do not recognize the One who calls.) This turning negatively affects our relationships with human and nonhuman others. People may turn aside from God through pride, choosing some other path that seems to promise greater benefit to the self than the one along which God calls. More people probably turn back through fear over the path's uncertainty and the risks involved in relationships with others. For each one who resists God's direction out of a strong sense of self, probably several shrink back, fearing that their selves are too weak and unstable for the journey.[2]

Today many people flounder on the journey because they do not experience enough relationships that genuinely affirm them, provide them positive role models and yet challenge them to become distinct selves.[3] Experiencing others, both human and nonhuman, as sources of communion and support, and yet also as intrinsically different beings, is essential to self-formation rooted in development of trusting relationships. Individuals who are deprived of affirmation and self-assurance are often not in touch with their basic organismic wants. However, whereas awareness of these is necessary to self-formation, it is not sufficient. For selves are not formed simply through expression of inner dynamisms but chiefly through development of relationships with others.[4]

In today's society, where authentic relationships are difficult to form, many people seek meaning through intense personal experiences. These can be of physical pleasure, comfort, aesthetic satisfaction or merger with some spiritual force. They can be experiences of success or esteem from others. They can be fantasies of these things, chased through myriad relationships, activities and commercial purchases. They can be detailed journeys through our inner landscape or moments of expanded conscious awareness. Such experiences, however, are usually brief, leaving behind a void craving to be filled by others of greater intensity. The self becomes increasingly a product of its desires *(epithymiai)* and surface experiences, lacking depths formed by relationships and by commitments to values and projects with enduring meaning.

Many such individuals chase such satisfaction as they can hope for through increasing consumption of commercial products, which fuels today's economic system. Others paper over the hollow center with grandiose personas of themselves as attractive, successful or powerful—usually patterned after commercial images. Still others compensate for that lacking sense of self by identifying regressively with some source—a person, a group, a romanticized sense of nature, a god—which promises safety and containment but is no true other. Yet such persons are alienated from any true self-center, for when authentic development does not occur, such a center exists as a mere potential, in rudimentary form.[5]

How is psychological alienation overcome? We must be able to hear our organism and to know what we truly want. Yet these wants do not compose a direct path to true selfhood, for they are significantly shaped by our social context. The most important step is commitment to God and to what we understand of God's call, including the lifestyle it involves. This is chiefly a relationship of faith, or trust, though it involves some knowledge of who God is and what that call is about.[6]

God is experienced as an Other who companions us through those experiences of fellowship with and differentiation from others by which the self is constructed. Jesus' earthly journey provides the chief pattern for this. We participate in Jesus' crucifixion when he becomes known through experiences of our limits, sorrows and sins, and we take part in his resurrection when we are filled, through his Spirit, with his divine life, energy and joy. Many people experience union with God at times along this path, which is more than experience of their deeper selves. For it is because God is transcendent that this journey is so mysterious, unpredictable and characterized at times by both God's seeming absence and God's presence.

The path of self-development also includes relationships where we receive strength and models of formation from others. Growth especially involves the capacity to give ourselves to others (*agapē*), trusting that they, God or some others will give back what we need to be sustained.[7] In these relationships of mutual servanthood some legitimate experiences of pleasure, intensifying experience, expanding consciousness or general self-enhancement may need to be sacrificed. Self-formation also involves increasingly responsible use of nonhuman nature, combined with a deepening sense of appreciation for it and companionship with it. Through increasing awareness of our own natural bodily rhythms, which may well differ from the physical cravings induced by commercial society, we can increasingly enjoy nature, and through appreciation of nature we can increasingly become attuned to our natural bodily rhythms.

Ecological Formation

How are psychological and spiritual alienation and formation connected with ecological alienation and formation? Humans have been called to care for the earth and to use it wisely. Yet ecological alienation occurs, first, because nonhuman nature can resist human designs, compete with them and appear as the enemy. Despite nature's many harmonious rhythms, much about it is difficult to discover. The best means for avoiding its threats and harnessing its potential often take long to learn. And nonhuman creatures are frequently in conflict with each other. Even in a world without evil, humans would always sense some distance and some significant conflict between their own needs and natural processes.

Ecological alienation occurs, second, because humans seek to aggrandize themselves at the expense of nonhuman nature and in violation of its processes. They take competition and conquest as their main patterns of relationship to it and war against it. But eventually nonhuman nature, which provides humanity its biological foundations, breaks down and wars against us.

How are psychological and ecological alienation connected? Most humans today crave continual new experiences, satisfactions, profits and successes (real or imaginary) to fill personal emptiness. We seek to obtain most of these in the form of commercial products. To acquire these, we exploit nature in ways which exceed its limits, or carrying capacity. We lose that proper balance of appreciation and careful use that is essential to stewardship. Dependent on excessive commercial stimulation and out of tune with what we really need, we become estranged from our own bodily rhythms and also those of nature. Being more distanced from nature in this way, we can more easily regard it as an object to be mastered and an enemy to be conquered.

How can ecological alienation be overcome? Increasing knowledge about natural processes is important but will seldom be enough, for in most decisions humans make regarding nonhuman nature, several reasonable options will be available. The best response is seldom dictated by nature's laws, so room will be left for human choice. Stewardship often involves nature's transformation—within limits, of course, yet also in accord with human values.

We can also appreciate nature's creatures and rhythms as expressions of trinitarian beauty and harmony. Yet although God the Spirit breathes energy into all creatures, God is not substantially present in nature, and the best environmental response cannot be read from it. In environmental activities, as in personal growth, God can be experienced as the One who calls and companions us through the challenges and complexities involved.

In environmental matters, as in personal growth, we must also learn to serve other humans. In conflicts we must seek especially to care for those who oppose our efforts and to understand their perspectives. The more that stable selves can be formed, and inner emptiness and dispersion be overcome, the less will people crave intense pleasure and experience, which fuel the motor of environmental exploitation. Though humans will always be transforming nature in some ways, they can also learn to appreciate and enjoy much of it as it is, without ceaselessly converting it into consumable products. Appreciation of each creature can be enhanced by experiencing it as an expression of the overflowing agape which created the world and which enlivens each creature, including us, through the indwelling Spirit.

Social Formation
In what ways are the foregoing kinds of alienation and formation connected to the social sphere? Social alienation occurs, first, because humans have been given the task of devising economic, political and cultural systems which meet the needs and desires of numerous individuals at the same time. Yet the needs and desires of some persons always exist in tension with those of some others. As environmental and historical changes impact societies, the task of meeting different demands and expectations constantly changes. Even in a world without evil, some discrepancy and potential conflict among demands and expectations, and between them and the social systems designed to meet them, would exist.

Social alienation occurs, second, because at least some persons seek to better their situations at others' expense. Hierarchy or competition, rather than mutual servanthood, becomes their pattern of social relationships. Many persons seek wealth, prestige or power beyond the limits of fair distribution. Governments, even those professedly dedicated to evening matters out, grasp for these things themselves. Economic systems, even if they are recommended for promoting balance, advantage some to others' disadvantage. Meanwhile those oppressed by the social order seek to retaliate, and all its structures are troubled by revolution, war or the threat of them. In these ways, many individuals and groups feel estranged from, and victimized by, those very social structures within which they participate.

How is this alienation related to psychological and ecological alienation? The connection is largely circular. The psychological desires of people energize social systems while social systems shape and channel those desires. Today our main economic system, considered in and of itself (as unmodified by other forces), aims to produce as much profit as possible. Thus it seeks to break down all social and cultural forces which hinder its production, marketing and exchange activities. It regards nonhuman nature chiefly as raw material to be turned into wealth and thus as an object or obstacle to be mastered. To increase profits, it seeks to stimulate and expand individual desires for its products as much as possible. Governments seek to moderate some of these tendencies, usually with some success. Yet in the process they often become distant, bureaucratic and aggrandizing, manipulating the very people they profess to serve.

Shaped by these social processes, many individuals lack stable structures and models to help them form mature selves. With their desires stimulated by economic forces, and feeling insignificant and powerless due to governmental structures, they strive for consumable products to attain some degree of enjoyment and significance. Yet these strivings in turn fuel the economy's production of even greater profit and stimulation. Nature is further exploited, and people are more cut off from natural rhythms, intensifying their desires for pleasures produced by the economy. Government may attempt to curb the natural exploitation, but it can become larger and more overbearing in the process.

How can social alienation be overcome? The overall norm and model is God's kingdom, a society governed and indwelt by divine agape. In God's kingdom exploitative relationships are overcome among ethnic groups and between rich and poor, men and women, the governors and the governed, and humans and nonhuman nature. Since Jesus' ministry, this kingdom has been present among humans, authentically but only partially realized. Since God's kingdom is real now, people can seek to further actualize it in the present. Yet since it will be fully actual only in the future, any present realization will be imperfect and must be worked toward with patience and humility.

Even if negative social structures were destroyed (through a revolution), God's kingdom would not spring forth fully unless God should intervene. For the psychological and ecological effects of these structures would remain and would only gradually be overcome. Apart from divine intervention, the best hopes for significant social transformation rest with dedicated groups who seek to live out the kingdom in concrete, mostly local ways.

Such groups actualize new social possibilities in which others can share. Yet these are not likely to transform society as a whole, due to the depth to which negative structures have shaped people.[8] God is present in such communities as the Spirit who guides and fills them with agape. Since they usually go against society's grain, however, such groups often experience opposition and suffering. Thus they participate in Jesus' crucifixion, and in the Spirit's filling and joy they experience Jesus' resurrection.

Groups who seek to actualize God's kingdom can provide healthy structures and models for personal formation. Desires for pleasure, power or safety can be subordinated to the development of significant relationships and the pursuit of meaningful goals. Persons so formed can contribute to further development of social structures which reflect God's kingdom. Such communities will practice sustainable use of nonhuman nature along with enjoyment of it and companionship with it. These practices will renew nature and facilitate further wise stewardship of it.

Notes

Introduction

[1] An exception is Roszak 1992. Howard Clinebell's Ecotherapy (Minneapolis: Augsburg Fortress, 1996) appeared too recently to be considered in this book.

[2] Process theologian Jay McDaniel, however, gives his *Earth, Sky, Gods and Mortals* the subtitle *Developing an Ecological Spirituality*. Matthew Fox (1983, 1990 and 1988) has endeavored to create an ecological spirituality more directly than anyone else.

[3] See David Tracy, *Blessed Rage for Order* (New York: Seabury, 1979), pp. 3-14; for Tracy's own method, see pp. 43-56. Also see Gordon Kaufman, *An Essay on Theological Method* (Chico, Calif.: Scholars Press, 1975). I generally affirm the kind of "public theology" outlined by Ronald Thiemann (*Constructing a Public Theology* [Louisville, Ky.: Westminster/Knox, 1991]), esp. pp. 19-25. Thiemann, however, apparently grants the church a greater "responsibility" for supporting and enhancing public life than I do (see chapter eleven). (Compare also Tracy, "Defending the Public Character of Theology," *The Christian Century*, April 1, 1981, pp. 350-56.)

[4] Though there are various ways I could have attempted to do this, my general procedure has been to start mostly by perusing books that have sold widely in relatively sophisticated paperback bookstores and to ask what kinds of theoretical foundations seemed to undergird them. In some cases the authors I discuss have appeared recently in such bookstores. In other cases, the authors seem to have supplied foundations for these recent authors.

Chapter 1: The Roots of Contemporary Alienation

[1] For Aristotle, a scientific explanation of something must describe its four causes: (1) the immediately preceding or concurrent force that set it in motion *(efficient cause)*; (2) the form or structure according to which it develops *(formal cause)*; (3) the matter of which it is composed *(material cause)*; and (4) the goal or purpose toward which it tends *(final cause)*. For modern science, explanation must refer only to the efficient cause.

[2] Newton's three laws: (1) Every body continues in a state of rest, or of uniform motion in a straight line, unless it is compelled to change that state by forces impressed upon it. (2) The change of motion is proportional to the motive force impressed and is made in the direction of the straight line in which that force is impressed. (3) To every action there is always opposed an equal reaction.

[3] The force operating between any two masses is equal to the product of those masses divided by the square of the distance between them.

[4] Newton himself believed that God occasionally intervened to correct imbalances which slowly built up. But Newton's successors removed God entirely from the operation of the universe, and it is this latter view which usually goes by the name "Newtonianism."

[5] Mendel had actually made his discoveries in the 1860s, but his work remained unknown

until 1900.

[6]For the following, see Locke's *Second Treatise of Government* (1690; reprint Indianapolis: Bobbs-Merrill, 1952). On the State of Nature (pp. 4-10), it is not entirely clear whether Locke thought that it had ever existed or whether he was searching for a way to make vivid his theory of the basic structure of the state.

[7]Hume insisted, however, that passions are subjective dispositions, not "matters of fact" of the sort with which reason (as it operates in science) deals. Hume, then, made an important distinction between this kind of "reason" (with its realm of "fact") and "morals" (which deals with "oughts"). In this sense he denied that ethics can be based on what *is* the case ([1739] 1888:468-69). Yet he still based ethics on what *is* directly experienced, over against any *ought* considered as an ideal not directly experienced. It is in this sense that I say that Hume based ethics on the *is*, not the *ought*.

[8]Hume rejected the position that altruistic passions are ultimately derived from, or are merely disguised forms of, self-love ([1751] 1957:113-19).

[9]The differences in length and time, of course, would be hardly discernible if the train moved at a normal speed. A person needs to imagine the train moving at something like half the speed of light.

[10]In one famous experiment electrons were propelled through two parallel slits in a metal screen, after which they struck a photographic plate. Each electron made a tiny dot on the plate, which would seem to indicate that it was a particle and had come through one of the slits. However, the dots as a whole formed parallel bands with interference patterns characteristic of waves—which was apparently possible only if each had come through both slits.

[11]Some have proposed that our present universe will eventually contract (in a "Big Crunch") back to a point where matter is infinitely compressed and space infinitely shrunk, that this will explode in another "Big Bang" and that the universe moves through endless cycles of this kind rather than in one linear direction. Yet any evidence of previous cycles would be obliterated by each Big Bang. So no empirical support can be offered for this theory. It has also been proposed that ours is just one of many universes, with its own particular laws, and that other universes are eternal. It has been further proposed that new matter is continually being created, so the universe is not headed toward final equilibrium. But no evidence supports these hypotheses either (see Barbour 1990:136-38; Davies 1992:44-72).

Chapter 2: Psychological Alienation

[1]The laboratory where Freud worked was supervised by Ernst Bruecke (1819-1892), who had signed this "oath" along with Emil du Bois-Reymond, Hermann Helmholtz and Carl Ludwig.

[2]Freud never published this "Project for a Scientific Psychology." For a more detailed description, see Fancher 1973:63-97.

[3]In the girl's Oedipal struggle, she recognizes that she lacks a penis and desires her father to supply her with one. She is angry with her mother because she blames the mother for depriving her of a penis. Still, despite this breach between mother and daughter, a daughter remains closer to the initial experience of oneness with her than does a son.

[4]Marcuse thus praises art for its ability to "sustain the image of freedom. . . . There is no genuine work of art that does not reveal the archetypal content: the negation of unfreedom" (1964:144). This is quite unlike Freud, who argued that whereas art is an attempt to sublimate instinctual cravings, it is mostly a neurotic effort that has little impact on reality.

[5]Marcuse adds that even hierarchical relationships "are not unfree *per se;* civilization rests to a great extent on rational authority, based on knowledge and necessity" (1964:224).

[6]According to Fairbairn, however, modern physics shows that mass and energy are "one and the same," so the ego should not be conceived of as an inert mass needing to be activated by energy but as itself inherently energetic (Greenberg and Mitchell 1983:155).

[7]Fairbairn claimed that not a primitive ego but a "unitary, integral ego with its own libidinal

energy, seeking relations with real external objects" existed from the beginning (Greenberg and Mitchell 1983:163).

[8]Splitting and buried rage are stressed more by Melanie Kline, for whom the infant's original situation involved more unsettledness and paranoia than it did for Winnicott (see Greenberg and Mitchell 1983:119-50).

[9]See also Jessica Benjamin's critique of the paternal orientation of the Oedipus conflict (Benjamin 1978) and her critique of Lasch (Benjamin 1988:137-39, 156-59). The positive role of the ego ideal has been influentially presented by Janine Chasseguet-Smirgel in *The Ego Ideal* (London: Free Association, 1985). For discussion of her view, see Frosh 1991:83-88; Lasch 1984:178-82; and (finding it too steeped in the classical psychoanalytic tradition) Benjamin 1988:147-58.

[10]Lasch notes that criticism of psychoanalysis for elevating the paternal and rejecting the maternal is common, but he denies that psychoanalysis need always do this (1984:175; cf. p. 242). He argues that the superego by itself cannot produce authentic socialization (pp. 202-3). He insists "that a satisfactory resolution of the Oedipus complex accepts the father without betraying the mother." He affirms a positive role for the ego ideal, though he resists calling it "feminine" and the superego "masculine."

Benjamin, on the other hand, insists that a person can critique "masculine" emphases on separation and conquering the world without falling into regressive "fantasies of maternal utopia." Whereas she admits that this "reversal is undeniably present in some feminist thought," she affirms that Engel's "balance between separation and relatedness . . . avoids that pitfall" (1988:159). Benjamin believes that the Oedipus conflict does confront the child "with difference and limits" (p. 151; cf. p. 140). Her objection is not to these emphases but to the traditional Oedipal devaluation of the feminine. For if the Oedipus degrades the feminine, it fails to produce the very sort of differentiation it is supposed to achieve (pp. 159, 165).

[11]Benjamin bases such claims particularly on the research of Daniel Stern; see esp. his *Interpersonal World of the Infant* (New York: Basic Books, 1985).

[12]For a classic critique of the isolation of stimuli and responses from organic behavior in both Freud and behavioral psychologists, see Goldstein 1940:120-45, 165-70.

[13]Even though the group is "secondary to the individual, the 'we' should by no means be thought of simply as an extraneous and secondary connection between individuals" (Goldstein 1940:211).

[14]Cf. pp. 105-6: When such a person "is his complete organism . . . then he is to be trusted, then his behavior is constructive. . . . It will be individualized. But it will also be socialized." For additional argument that Rogers assumes a preestablished harmony among human tendencies, see Browning 1987:79-80.

[15]See Green 1945-1946:34-35 and Browning 1987:90-93. Browning also suggests that Rogers's kind of psychology is "most compatible with the values and world view of capitalism" (p. 84).

[16]The Natural Child, however, is often "manifested by autonomous forms of behavior such as rebelliousness or self-indulgence" (p. 69). In fact, "an *active psychosis* exists when the Child has the executive power and is also experienced as the 'real Self'" (p. 143).

[17]Berne included "OK" and "not OK" attitudes toward the world in general, yielding twelve possible positions toward self, others and world (1972:90-96).

[18]Some children, however, adopt others by the third year. If they experience continued neglect, they may conclude, "I'm not OK—you're not OK," spawning a despairing sense of self and world. If they are repeatedly abused, children may conclude, "I'm OK—you're not OK," a position that often underlies extreme antisocial behavior.

[19]This understanding of being OK "is not bound to our personal experiences, because we can transcend them into an abstraction of ultimate purpose for all men" (p. 50).

[20]In fact, a person without a functioning Adult is psychotic; "he is out of touch with reality. His

Parent and Child come on straight, frequently in a jumbled mixture of archaic data" (p. 104).

[21]He is quoting A. J. Deikman, *The Observing Self* (Boston: Beacon, 1982).

[22]For Bradshaw, Jesus' affirmations, "I am the truth" (Jn 14:6) and "before Abraham was, I am" (8:58), indicate not his unique divinity, as has been traditionally understood but the sense of special human worth each child naturally has (1990:178, 274).

[23]The Adult must tell the inner child "There are no fairy godmothers" (Bradshaw 1990:230; cf. pp. 15-17, 236); Whitfield opposes the notion of "quick fixes" (p. 64).

[24]Cf. p. xii: "It is possible to change the core beliefs *directly* and *quickly*. . . . This almost-immediate effect continues to amaze me."

[25]This "method of changing your personal history" (p. 178) consists of substituting new, vividly imagined scenes for painful historical ones, and "anchoring" the former by neuro-linguistic techniques.

[26]The anthropologist George Boas ([1965] 1990) noticed that ever since the scientific revolution, Western people have often searched for some primitive natural realm, unspoiled by human culture. They sought this successively among rural people, primitive peoples, women, the irrational and the collective unconscious. But as all these realms proved, upon closer investigation, to be tainted with evil, many have turned, as a last refuge, to "the cult of the child." Unlike earlier ages, which have almost universally regarded childhood as a state to be transcended, such persons have hoped to find purity and innocence, "the poetry, innate, untold," through reawakening the awareness of "being only four years old." Boas's investigation suggests, however, that this basic longing may now be focusing on childhood not because of new scientific evidence but because it seems to be the last remaining refuge.

[27]Jung thought of it as a more biological kind of life-energy (though he often called it *libido*). Although he regarded it as convertible in some measure to physio-chemical forces, he was little concerned about whether it was fully reducible to them.

[28]To support his theory of archetypes, Jung pointed to similarities among symbols occurring in many patients' dreams and those found in widely scattered religions, myths and cultures. Whereas his approach was often criticized as unscientific, recent psychobiology suggests that releasing mechanisms responsible for specific behaviors may be quite similar to what Jung called archetypes. They may help give a biological grounding for the tendencies of children to internalize the kind of *objects* that the object relations school has described (see Anthony Stevens, *Archetypes: A Natural History of the Self* [New York: William Morrow, 1982]).

[29]Cf. p. 69: "Are not Jesus and Paul prototypes of those who, trusting their inner experience, have gone their own individual ways, disregarding public opinion?"

Chapter 3: Ecological Alienation

[1]I am using the word *ecology* in a general sense to refer to the environment and recent concerns about it, not to the formal science of ecology.

[2]This very old notion, arising in ancient Greece, originally regarded humanity as halfway up the Chain, which was pictured as vertical and extending up through celestial hierarchies to God (Lovejoy 1936). By Darwin's time geologists were beginning to believe that the earth was many millions of years old. The Great Chain, however, was accommodated by laying it, as it were, on its side and disregarding the upper half. Then the links leading to humanity could be thought of as a historical progression.

[3]Lyell also taught *uniformity of state:* that the earth never really changes fundamentally over time. Alterations in one direction (e.g., emergence of seas) would eventually be balanced by those in the other (e.g., disappearance of seas). Some day, creatures such as dinosaurs would reappear. Though earth's time-frame was greatly extended by Lyell, its processes balanced each other rhythmically, cyclically and gradually in patterns of equal action and reaction befitting a Newtonian universe. Gould regards *uniformitarianism* as a methodological principle: to explain past changes in terms of presently observable processes. He insists,

though, that uniformities of rate and state are not methodological principles but "proposals that may be judged true or false on empirical grounds" (p. 120). It is possible, for instance, that the same processes might have operated and interacted differently (and perhaps somewhat catastrophically) in the past.

[4]Malthus, however, did not prophesy that surplus humans would die but hoped that his writing would encourage people to limit their families. Yet Malthus advised government not to provide social welfare, since this would simply increase the numbers of those who would eventually have to die.

[5]For instance, why are similar structures *(homologies)* found in distantly related creatures (such as the order of bones in humans, bats and moles)? Answer: Because they share common evolutionary descent. Why do some animals have *rudimentary organs,* such as adumbrated legs in snakes? Answer: They are relics of what was valuable in previous evolution (Ruse 1982:36-44, 53-57).

[6]For Darwin, chance mutations, which occurred very rarely, provided variation's main source. Yet he also supposed that each parent contributed half the material composing a new organism. Thus a novel trait in one parent would have half as much strength in each member of the succeeding generation, one quarter as much in those of the next, and would eventually be diluted out of existence.

[7]For Kropotkin's social-ecological views, see Pepper 1984:188-96. Social ecology will be discussed at the end of this chapter.

[8]During the 1880s and 1890s, August Weismann showed that reproductive cells are entirely distinct from the body's other cells. So those an organism receives from its parents are passed on, entirely unchanged, to its own offspring. Thus events during a parent's lifetime cannot alter the characteristics its offspring acquire. Mendel showed that each "factor" passed on to offspring (e.g., for green color in a pea) would be retained by them and passed on unblended to future generations even if its presence were not visible in some generations (e.g., when green "factors" were recessive and yellow ones dominant). Mutations would be passed on in the same way and not be diluted in successive generations, as Darwin thought (see note 6 above).

[9]Its initial expression was by the geneticist Theodosius Dobzhansky (1937). George Gaylord Simpson (1944) sought to correlate it with paleontology. Its three leading exponents were Dobzhansky, Simpson and Julian Huxley. For Simpson's critique of Huxley, see note 18 below.

[10]Fitness can provide no absolute measure of progress, for organisms can be fit only with respect to particular environments. When environments change, those who had been most "fit" often perish (Levins and Lewontin 1985:15-16). These authors assert that evolutionary theories do not merely describe changes that once occurred but connect them into "an ordered scale of states" tending in a certain direction and that such an effort is necessarily ideological (p. 12).

[11]This is the scale most often appealed to, yet there are many different kinds. In terms of the numerous biosynthetic reactions that bacteria carry out, they can be regarded as more complex than mammals (Levins and Lewontin 1985:17; cf. Oliwenstein 1993:22-23).

[12]Darwin assumed that intraspecies differences, given enough time, add up to differences among species, even though he could identify no mechanism underlying this transition from quantitative to qualitative change (Levins and Lewontin 1985:35-38). Like proponents of punctuated equilibria, these authors find the notion that "change, given enough time, produces *progress*" is still deeply embedded in most evolutionary theory (p. 24).

[13]Such societies involve very complex divisions of labor held together by mutual interaction among component parts. Levins and Lewontin find both population genetics (so basic to the neo-Darwinian synthesis) and current ecology dominated by elaborate statistical procedures which assume an equilibrium state among populations and disregard their past histories. They find it ironic that many environmentalists seek to oppose capitalist expansion by

extolling the notion of dynamic stability, developed in capitalism, as the model for nature.

[14]Ernst Mayr (1942) has been credited with this emphasis on the "founder principle." Most neo-Darwinists thought that subgroups within large species could gradually become separate species while remaining in contiguous locations. Darwin's notion of slow, incremental change dominated this approach (Stanley 1981:68-70).

[15]See Hsu 1986, who concludes that "perhaps God does play dice" (p. 285); Rampino 1991; Eldredge 1991; and Lovelock and Allaby 1983.

[16]Ayala defines progress as "systematic change in a feature belonging to all members of a sequence in such a way that the posterior members of the sequence exhibit an improvement of that feature." More briefly, progress is "directional change towards the better."

[17]Raup and Stephen Jay Gould argue that decreases in diversity after initial spurts of speciation are as plausible as continuing increases (Nitecki 1988:300, 335).

[18]Ayala rejects "independence from the environment" since creatures cannot be independent of the environment as a whole but can only exchange one environment for another. He agrees that humans exercise "control over the environment," but he denies that other organisms have anything like it (Nitecki 1988:91) Simpson further rejects Huxley's effort to draw conclusions from dominant types (pp. 6-7). He argues four things: that these types did not succeed each other either in time or descent; that their success was not due to the same factors; that their characteristics were not passed on to the next types; and that other dominant types could be mentioned, though they would less suit Huxley's scheme (Barlow 1994:36).

[19]For expressions of this view at the beginning of the environmental movement, see Blackstone (1974) and Passmore (1974).

[20]In "American liberalism, 'oppression' is among the cardinal sins. 'Liberty' and 'freedom' are sacred. Identify a minority that is oppressed by denial of its rights and you immediately create a strong argument for its liberation" (Nash 1989:162).

[21]Huxley believed that personal transformation, following the associationist psychology of David Hartley, involved a perpetual "destroying of the self" and its egoistic impulses, not an increasing sense of pleasure in altruistic ones, as Spencer claimed (Huxley 1989:15).

[22]Although affirming that "ethical nature may count upon having to reckon with a tenacious and powerful enemy as long as the world lasts," he refused to set a priori limits to "the extent to which intelligence and will, guided by sound principles of investigation, and organized in common effort, may modify the conditions of existence" (Huxley 1989:143). He concluded *Evolution and Ethics* with the appeal to all to "strive in one faith towards one hope" (1989:144). For the general social situation which Huxley addressed, see pp. 3-8, 22-24, 42-52.

[23]Despite Huxley's concern for social benevolence, he remained convinced that humanity and nature must always be in unremitting conflict. He proposed that in colonizing a new territory (such as Australia), an administrator should first "put a stop to the influence on external competition by thoroughly extirpating and excluding the native rivals, whether men, beasts or plants" (1989:75-76).

[24]Lovelock tends to regard the entire earth as an organism, since even rocks have been formed from creatures once alive. Lynn Margulis, as we shall see, affirms only that "the Earth's surface conditions are regulated by the activities of life" (1989:11).

[25]If all the atoms constituting our present earth were randomly mixed, "the probability that those atoms would combine into the molecules that make up our living Earth is zero." For life involves an "improbability that would make winning a sweepstake every day for a year seem trivial" (Lovelock 1988:24, 23).

[26]Lovelock finds this explanation much more convincing than usual geochemical theories, such as the one that states that carbon dioxide is emitted primarily by volcanoes and absorbed by calcium silicate rocks (1988:81 and Williams 1991:167-73).

[27]However, Lovelock has preached several times in the Cathedral Church of St. John the

Divine in New York. He reports that two-thirds of the letters he receives about Gaia concern religious issues (1988:203-4).

[28]Yet Lovelock also insists that "in Gaia we are just another species, neither the owners nor the stewards of this planet" (p. 14).

[29]Margulis and Sagan admit that they may have "overcompensated" a bit by inverting the usual hierarchy. Moreover, their ultimate aim is not to invert the hierarchy (by placing humans at the bottom) so much as to destroy all hierarchies by picturing "humanity as one among other microbial phenomena," for "there is no absolute dichotomy between humans and bacteria" (pp. 30-31).

[30]Lovelock surveys evolutionary history in a similar manner (1988:65-151), focusing largely on the composition of the atmosphere, the seas and so on.

[31]The authors claim that genetic information can be "distributed in the microcosm with an ease and speed approaching that of modern telecommunications—if the complexity and biological value of the information is factored in" (p. 82).

[32]"With the exception of a few exotic compounds . . . prokaryotic microbes can assemble and disassemble all the molecules of modern life" (p. 113). In fact, "all organisms today are equally evolved" (p. 16).

[33]Bacteria are *prokaryotes,* cells without nuclei. All other cells are *eukaryotes,* and all other living creatures are composed of them. Eukaryotes are surrounded by a membrane, have a nucleus containing most of their DNA and have oxygen-using parts called *mitochondria* (cf. pp. 115, 127). Margulis regards the division between prokaryotes and eukaryotes as the most fundamental in all earthly life (pp. 17, 113).

[34]Traditional Darwinists would reply that all such "cooperation" is really based on self-interest (pp. 47-48).

[35]"The biosphere . . . recovers from tragedies with renewed vigor. Nuclear conflagration . . . might prepare the biosphere for less centered forms of life" (p. 238).

[36]Technology is a product and triumph of the whole biosphere (pp. 24, 153, 195).

[37]Further problems exist in discerning whether Gaia is active or not. For instance, "Does Gaia ever overcompensate, or is the regulatory system perfect every time? If it is not perfect, what reasons are there to believe, for example, that a 100,000 year ice age is Gaia overcompensating for a hot spell . . . ? Who needs all this oscillating back and forth, all the overshooting? Isn't this whole theory unnecessary?" (Joseph 1990:76-77). Such imprecision gives Gaia an "almost religious, chameleonic ability to be applied to conflicting explanations of natural phenomena" (Penelope Boston, quoted in Joseph 1990:212).

[38]Since present and future worlds consist of rearrangements of elements that have always existed, Sagan sometimes implies that evolutionary change is unreal. "There is no history, evolutionary or otherwise, nor future, science fiction or otherwise, but only the language-filled present" (p. 182).

[39]Precisely speaking, deep ecology is a movement united by a platform of environmental principles (pp. 69-73) on which people adhering to different "ultimate premises" might agree (Drengson and Inoue 1995:10-12). Since I am concerned with the most ultimate perspectives underlying environmental approaches, I will focus on those developed by the founders of deep ecology, even though not everyone in the movement adheres to them.

[40]Rogers, you may recall, felt that people have direct access to their deeper, organic selves, at least in situations where they experience "unconditional positive regard," and denied that much of this awareness was hidden and distorted in the unconscious. Theodore Roszak (1992:282-305) proposes that a deeper wisdom of Gaia, passed down through evolution, is hidden in the id and contains the potential for personal and ecological liberation.

[41]In America, the naturalist Aldo Leopold is often credited with being the first to emphasize the intrinsic value, or "biotic right," of nonhumans and especially of ecosystems. For Leopold, "anything indivisible is a living being," and the earth itself is alive in some sense (quoting the Russian philosopher Peter Ouspensky [1878-1947] in Nash 1989:66). An envi-

ronmental decision "is right when it tends to preserve the integrity, stability, and beauty of the biotic community. It is wrong when it tends otherwise" (Leopold 1949:224-25).

[42]For the issue, see Bookchin and Foreman 1991:20. For Dave Foreman's response, see pp. 107-11, 125 (cf. pp. 41-42).

[43]Holmes Rolston carries this principle further. He finds value wherever there is positive creativity. Accordingly the earth, as "originating matrix" or "parental environment" of all terrestrial matter, has greater value than any particular ecosystem; but the universe as a whole has greater value than the earth, as its "generating matrix" (1988:197-99). Although J. Baird Callicott grounds his ethics (following Hume, Smith and Darwin) in sympathy, he extends this, following Aldo Leopold, to the entire ecosystem, so that the good of the whole is his standard for assessing the relative value of each of its parts (1980:324-25).

[44]Some early expressions of this viewpoint sounded misanthropic. Paul Taylor supposed that if humankind should annihilate itself, the rest of the biotic community would respond "with a hearty 'good riddance!'" ("An Ethics of Respect for Nature," *Environmental Ethics* 3, no. 3 [Fall 1981]: 209; see also his "In Defense of Biocentrism," *Environmental Ethics* 5, no. 3 [Fall 1983]: 241-43; see also "Are Humans Superior to Animals and Plants?" *Environmental Ethics* 6, no. 2 [Summer 1984], pp. 149-60). Callicott asserted that the "preciousness" of any individual was proportionate to that of its species and that today's human population is so disastrous for the whole eco-community that "the extent of misanthropy in modern environmental ethics may be taken as a measure of the degree to which it is biocentric" (1980:326). Though such sentiments were later qualified by their authors, they continued to be perceived as typical of radical environmentalism by some of its opponents and proponents.

[45]Foreman urges respect for today's natural creatures because they have traveled "that same three-and-a-half-billion-year evolutionary course we have" (p. 116). He affirms the inherent value of all creatures and habitats (pp. 53, 116).

[46]For Val Plumwood (1993), the chief flaw in both androcentrism and current environmental depredation is dualism, the treating of pairs such as male-female and reason-nature as opposed and the second as hierarchically inferior. Yet she argues that a feminism that simply reverses these pairs commits the same underlying error. Plumwood also challenges deep ecology's attempt to overcome dualism in a monistic way and stresses the importance of real appreciation of difference.

[47]However, deep ecologist Warwick Fox finds anthropocentric the oversimplified assumption that once an oppressive social structure is overcome, environmental problems will disappear, for it places human affairs at the center of everything (1989:16). He fears that ecofeminism makes this assumption in its focus on androcentrism. This allows nonandrocentric groups to overlook their present complicity in environmental destruction. Fox also finds at the heart of most forms of anthropocentrism the claim that one group constitutes humanity's essence and implies that radical ecofeminism may manifest this (pp. 22-25).

[48]Bookchin and Foreman 1991 is a major attempt at reconciliation which expresses the differing sensitivities of the two movements well.

[49]However, "discussions about whether the presence of this tendency is evidence of a predetermined 'goal,' a 'guiding hand,' or a 'God' are simply irrelevant for the purposes of this discussion. The fact is that such a tendency can be shown to exist in the fossil record, in the elaboration of existing life-forms from previous ones, and in the existence of humanity itself" (p. 42).

[50]Bookchin critiques postmodernism for diluting historical knowledge and mystifying the origins of our problems (p. 73). He affirms the Enlightenment for destroying religious superstition and political despotism and for emphasizing the notion of a shared humanity (p. 166; cf. Bookchin and Foreman 1991:59-60).

[51]This, of course, does not mean, as Bookchin emphasizes, that the moral ought is derived from whatever is the social praxis at any given time.

Chapter 4: Social Alienation

[1]Hopes for rapid yet "natural" and largely peaceful social transformation are not wholly absent from public discourse. New Age writer Marilyn Ferguson announces that the recent emphasis on transformation of personal consciousness has spawned a "leaderless but powerful network" of countless small, local groups working for "radical change" in all walks of American life (1980:23). Through holistic understandings of mind and nature, "for the first time in history, humankind has come upon the control panel of change" so that "we can intentionally align ourselves with nature for the rapid remaking of ourselves and our collapsing institutions" (p. 29). Though these countless innovators everywhere eschew formal organization and political or religious doctrine, their spontaneous energy arouses the hope that "after a dark, violent age, the Piscean, we are entering a millennium of love and light . . . 'The Age of Aquarius,' the time of 'the mind's true liberation'" (p. 19).

Similarly Fritjof Capra prefaces a rather thorough treatment of holistic approaches to physical science, psychology, medicine and economics with the *I Ching*'s assurance that "after a time of decay comes the turning point. . . . The movement is natural, arising spontaneously. For this reason the transformation of the old becomes easy. The old is discarded and the new is introduced. . . . No harm results" (1982:7). Yet even though similar hopes concerning social transformation may energize some of the perspectives I shall examine, few which are taken seriously envision so rapid and effortlessly "natural" a transition as do Ferguson and Capra.

[2]Current libertarianism is undergirded by a number of philosophical approaches, not all of which are compatible (see Barry 1986).

[3]Hayek argued that modern social science errs through *objectivism* (treating everything as abstract mathematical quantities), *collectivism* (treating entities such as "society" as wholes describable by behavioral laws) and *historicism* (supposing that forms of such wholes succeed each other in deterministic fashion (1953: chap. 7). In this, he opposes expansion of the Newtonian epistemological paradigm.

[4]For differences among what libertarians consider public good, see Barry 1987:64-69.

[5]Nozick acknowledges that a separate individual may choose to sacrifice something for the welfare of another. But he is arguing that the state cannot require this.

[6]Nozick does not mean that states actually emerged in this way. His point is that since a state *could* so originate without violating anyone's freedom, the existence of a minimal state is compatible with freedom. The details of his argument are too complex to sketch for my purposes.

[7]Hayek concedes that when a natural resource is rare, exploitation by a monopoly will conserve it longer. He declines to favor any monopoly, however, because of its social (as distinguished from economic) effects (1960:372).

[8]"Healthy landscapes and free markets are two sides of the same coin; one is the biological and the other is the human face of self-regulating ecological systems. . . . The economic power of free markets, like the ecological strength of natural communities comes from the profusion of diversity that emanates from both" (Hess 1992:225).

[9]His one reference to Bookchin seems negative, though it is not easy to be certain about this (p. 202).

[10]Many of the following remarks are in tune with the perspective of psychiatrist Thomas Szasz, a libertarian. It is difficult to derive a full-blown positive theory of self-formation from Szasz because so much of his writing is in critique of psychotherapy and society.

[11]Although Marcuse does not believe that early societies experienced material abundance, he grants that the more egalitarian structure of matriarchal societies may have facilitated "a non-oppressive distribution of scarcity" (1966:151).

[12]Marcuse stresses that not only imagination but reason also is energized by the memory of gratification (p. 31) and points toward and is receptive to ideals of human fulfillment (1964:167). He regards reason's universal concepts as "instruments for understanding the

particular condition of things in the light of their potentialities," and he feels that this function of thought is well articulated by Whitehead's notion of *eternal objects* (1964:215; cf. chapter six). At the scientific revolution, scientific reason was disconnected from notions of purpose and value (pp. 146-47, 232) and became the instrument by which the world was subjected to total administration (p. 169).

[14]For postmodern presentations of the all-encompassing role of commodification, see Debord (1983) and Baudrillard (1975).

[15]Jameson likes Lacan's analysis of schizophrenia. For Lacan, events and words do not gain meaning by signifying some reality beyond themselves but only by occupying a specific place in a "signifying chain" of many events or words. The chain itself, moreover, does not represent anything beyond itself. Schizophrenia occurs when that signifying chain snaps, disintegrating into "a rubble of distinct and unrelated signifiers" (1991:26).

[16]Bookchin occasionally indicates, however, that nature's severity plays a role in this. For instance, tribal elders desired more power in part because "in a world that is often harsh and insecure, a world ruled by natural necessity, the old are the most dispensable members of the community. Under conditions where food may be in short supply and the life of the community occasionally endangered, they are the first to be disposed of. The anthropological literature is replete with examples in which the old are killed or expelled during periods of hunger" (1982:81).

[17]He does caution, however, that his revolution will take time: "Sensibility, ethics, ways of viewing reality, and selfhood have to be changed" (1990:189).

Part 2: Contemporary Theological Discourse

[1]By *religious discourse* I indicate all kinds of speech commonly used in specific religious traditions. By *theological discourse* I mean the more particular, formal kind of language employed in discussing the beliefs of specific religions.

Chapter 5: Spirituality & Psychological Alienation

[1]Some of the spirituality that we will investigate in chapter five might be called *religious discourse*, but I will be searching for its theological foundations and asking of it theological questions.

[2]This is a main overarching theme of Brooks Hollifield, *A History of Pastoral Care in America: From Salvation to Self-Realization* (Nashville: Abingdon, 1983), as his subtitle indicates.

[3]Keating's full statement, which is fairly typical, runs as follows: "God and our true Self are not separate. Though we are not God, God and our true Self are the same thing" (p. 127).

[4]In the foreword to Campbell and McMahon 1985, however, Robert Sears notes that the authors' larger interpretive framework is not self-evident and requires further discussion (pp. viii-xi).

[5]McNamara is quoting a talk given by Herbert McCabe, O.P., but he gives no other source (1983:20).

[6]See Teresa's somewhat different but far more detailed discussion in [1562-1565] 1960:125-209.

[7]Teresa continues to discuss the influences of demons in succeeding chapters, however. Their activities are one of the chief obstacles on the journey to the center. See, e.g., 1.2.12, 15, 18; 2.1.5; 3.2.12; 4.3.10; 5.1.1; 5.2.9; 5.3.10; 5.4.4, 6, 8; 6.1.3, 9; 6.3.7; 6.6.2, 6, 7; 6.7.14.

[8]"All means must be proportionate to their end" (John of the Cross *Ascent* 2.8.2). But "among all creatures . . . none bears a likeness to God's being." ("Although . . . all creatures carry with them a certain relation to God and a trace of him . . . yet God has no relation or essential likeness to them. Rather the difference that lies between his divine being and their being is infinite" [2.8.3].) Therefore, since the intellect must work through the senses, "everything the intellect can understand . . . is most unlike and disproportionate to God" (2.8.5).

[9]When the memory is purged, however, it is not lost but becomes directly activated by God rather than through images (3.2.8). John is undecided, though, about the extent to which those who complete this night might still remember through natural forms (3.2.9, 12, 16; 3.13.8).

[10]John, like Teresa, regards the devil as an active agent seeking to subvert the pilgrim in numerous deceptive, subtle ways (e.g. 2.11.3-12; 2.16.3-4; 2.21.4-14; 2.26.14-27.6; 3.10).

[11]For the frequent references to the demonic in their works, see notes 7 and 10.

Chapter 6: Theology, Spirituality & Ecological Alienation

[1]Berry's foreword to this book, along with the citation of Berry that prefaces McDaniel's discussion (p. 109), leave little doubt of McDaniel's appreciation for Swimme and Berry's articulation of this theme.

[2]The universe "holds all things together and is the primary activating power in every activity"—even though, they add, it "is not a thing, but a mode of being of everything" (p. 27).

[3]"To get atoms in the universe to bounce together haphazardly to form a single molecule of an amino acid would require more time than has existed since the beginning, even a hundred times more than fifteen billion years" (p. 70). Considerations of this kind are often raised under the anthropic principle.

[4]Some examples are the following: "A pervasive desire among early animals is to increase in size" (p. 113); "The first heros to venture onto land were plants" (p. 116); Early cenozoic mammals' "movement into the future began with commitment to a vision," even though they could not, of course, "conceive of future forms of their descendants" (p. 138).

[5]For a readable introduction to the theme, see Cummings 1991. For the gradual blending of ecological themes into spiritualities stressing social justice, compare especially the first chapters of Dorr 1984 with Dorr 1990. For efforts to blend spirituality with science and the New Age outlook, see Capra and Steindl-Rast 1991 and Mahoney 1991.

[6]McFague critiques Fox's work for "glossing over the profound pessimism . . . in evolutionary history as well as the deep reservoirs of evil in the human heart." Yet she affirms that "its cosmological perspective, advocacy for the earth and all its life-forms, its poetic power and celebrative posture, are important aspects of planetary health" (1993:72). Ruether thinks that "Fox is basically on target," though "his chief defect is a certain superficiality" (1992:242). The inclusion of Fox's essay "A Mystical Cosmology: Towards a Postmodern Spirituality" in Griffin 1990 (see also Griffin's introductory remarks on pp. 1-13) indicates that he is regarded as resonating in a general way with the emphases of the process school. Fox attempts more intentionally than our other authors to retrieve premodern Christian tradition, even though he may be interpreting it unduly through his own lenses (see esp. Fox 1992).

[7]Although Fox affirms that humans are divine, he qualifies this by acknowledging that "ours is a created divinity, while God's is an uncreated divinity" (1983:235). Our unity with God "is not a loss of self or a dissolution of differences, but a unity of creativity, a coming together of different existences. Eckhart says that 'the soul becomes God but God does not become the soul.' There is a unity in diversity, a diversity in the union of love" (1988:50). Still, he can say that our cocreative activity with God is a "revelation of the divine essence" (p. 202).

[8]Fox also parallels the sacred phallos (the male phallus) with the Cosmic Christ (1988:176). Even the *Via Negativa* process of letting go of all images (see next paragraph) can be facilitated by "sexual sharing" (1983:137).

[9]The spiritual paths that compose Fox's *Original Blessing* (1983), along with the pages devoted to each, are the *Via Positiva* (pp. 35-131), *Via Negativa* (pp. 132-77), *Via Creativa* (pp. 178-249) and *Via Transformativa* (pp. 250-305). For these same four paths, see Fox 1992:57-187, 189-243, 245-382, 383-515 and 1994:92-112, 1-57, 113-29, 131-247, respectively.

[10]Fox does, however, approach this in his *Via Negativa*. Fox's overly optimistic view of unin-

hibited pleasure's potential appears in a remark such as "When the human race learns—if it learns soon enough—that it is our pleasure to outlaw war, then war will be outlawed" (1983:55). Fox's underestimation of the grip that socially channeled evil has on us is often evident in comments about war—for example, "Today it is more and more evident that the time has come for humanity to let go of war, to admit that it has outgrown war, and to move beyond war as a way of settling differences" (p. 13; cf. pp. 14, 80, 166, 252).

[11]Whereas the coconstitution of God by our present cosmos is the main emphasis of the theologies I am discussing, careful searching yields a few qualifying remarks. Birch and Cobb affirm that "God can exist without *this* world." Yet even if this cosmos should disappear, God's life would still depend "on there being some world to include" (p. 197). McFague writes that if God's present body were blown up, "another could be formed; hence God need not be seen to be as dependent on any particular body as we are on our own bodies" (1987:72; cf. p. 76). McFague speaks at times of God's embodiment resulting from choice (e.g., "God becomes dependent through being bodily" [1987:72; cf. pp. 73, 171, 185; 1993:102, 132, 156). She also calls God's interdependence with the cosmos "asymmetrical," affirming that panentheism "suggests that God is embodied, but not necessarily" (1993:149, 150). Perhaps, then, McFague does not precisely fit the panentheistic model as I have defined it, though she leans strongly in this direction. Perhaps she would reply that she neither fits nor does not fit this definition, since her models are not descriptions of God (1987:31-40). Yet a major point of the body model consists in the intrinsic connection it makes between God and some universe, even if we are simply being asked to imagine this.

[12]Such a comparison assumes, as most panentheistic theologians do, that humans are not essentially "souls" that are separable from their bodies.

[13]Yet one occasionally finds acknowledgment that other models need to be explored (e.g., McDaniel 1990:7-8).

[14]Influential, more popular expressions of these themes are Walter Rauschenbusch's *Christianity and the Social Crisis* (1907; reprint New York: Harper, 1964) and *A Theology for the Social Gospel* (New York: Abingdon, 1917). See also Ernst Troeltsch, *Protestantism and Progress* (1912; reprint Philadelphia: Fortress, 1986).

[15]McDaniel, another process theologian, does not "begin with the assumption that authentic Christian thinking is necessarily repetitious of, or revisionary of, traditional Christian views, biblical or post-biblical" (1990:11).

[16]Birch and Cobb admit that their criterion gives less-rich human experiences and some humans with less-rich experience lower worth. Yet since anyone's *potential* for rich experience must be considered, they support liberation from structures that deny fulfillment of this potential to many. They also acknowledge the danger of making one person's own notion of rich experience a criterion for others (pp. 163-65).

[17]These words from C. H. Waddington's *The Ethical Animal* (London: Allen & Unwin, 1960), p. 204, appear often in Birch and Cobb (1981:145, 146, 170, 189 and so on) despite their acknowledgment that Thomas Huxley warned "that we should not too easily derive an ethic from an account of evolution!" (Birch and Cobb 1981:142). For Waddington, who affirms evolutionary progress somewhat as Julian Huxley did (cf. chapter three), *anagenesis* meant an evolutionary improvement over a previously existing type (p. 126); applied to evolution as a whole, it indicated an overall tendency toward some kind of improvement.

[18]However, the authors cannot define *life* precisely because they cannot be sure where the line between living organisms and inorganic matter should be drawn. (On which side, for instance, should viruses be placed?) Yet they seem to regard life most often, like Lovelock, as a reversal of entropy (p. 93), as a spreading center of order in a less well-ordered universe (p. 42). "Indeed every power other than Life erodes order. Only Life creates it" (p. 192). Even if evolution per se has no goal, "Life" is credited, in language reminiscent of Swimme and Berry, with a high degree of purposeful agency: "It brought forth living forms upon this planet and multiplied them until it transformed the whole surface of the earth. It brought

forth human intelligence and through that transformed the earth once more" (p. 189).

[19]See note 15. Birch and Cobb caution, however, that "Life's" novelty is not simply "change in general" but a specific kind "which runs counter to the vast movements of change in the universe" (p. 184). It is not "the fundamental energy of the universe as such. It is instead an aim at the realisation of novel forms and richness of experience" (p. 189).

[20]Though they are paraphrasing Henry Nelson Wieman (*Methods of Private Religious Living* [New York: Macmillan, 1929], pp. 213ff.), they do not differentiate their views from his.

[21]The price paid for civilization "was enormous." It was "built on the destruction of the environment, the enslavement of masses of people, the reduced status of women, the hierarchical and exploitative organisation of society and the institution of war. Nevertheless, their achievements are impressive, the great increase in the human population which they made possible should not be simply deplored. The industrial revolution and the recent revolution in communications were falls upward as well. In each case the new has brought with it suffering and evil that has not occurred before. But the new also brought with it new stimuli, new hopes, new intensities of experience and new possibilities" (p. 121).

[22]"If this were a lifeless universe, there would be no pain, no sickness, no suffering, no sin, no injustice, no oppression, no death" (p. 193). "Until animal life came there was no suffering, but also there was little value. Animal life greatly increased instability into an otherwise regular world. But the instability was transcendence" (pp. 120-21).

[23]The question is "whether evil has the last word. If there is One who overcomes evil, then there is One who we can trust and worship unreservedly. That One is God" (p. 195). To "trust life" means to "live in the expectation that death's word is not the last" (p. 201). Cf. McDaniel 1990:50, 99; McDaniel adds that in his process view, "God is *a* reality rather than *ultimate* reality. God would be the supreme instance of actuality-in-process," for "worldly actualities embody . . . a creativity that transcends even God" (pp. 49-50).

[24]Still, the authors insist that "responsible speculation . . . requires firm grounding in personal experience and scientific knowledge and theory" (p. 200). For Whitehead, they claim, belief in life's final triumph was "reasonable and warranted, although the warrants cannot be fully reproduced here" (p. 201).

[25]This does not mean, of course, that ethics "can be reduced to a description of physical and biological processes." As we will now see, it has more to do with her view that "human conscience and consciousness arise from natural evolution." For a helpful overview of Ruether's ecofeminism, see Bouma-Prediger 1995:23-60, 135-73.

[26]Despite Ruether's attempts to retrieve elements from Christian tradition, *Gaia and God*, so far as I can see, describes her perspective only as "ecofeminist." I find no clear affirmation that it is normatively Christian.

[27]Such an assertion is commonly used by feminists to challenge "masculine" claims to "objectivity." It further entails "that the world not only appears differently . . . but itself will be constituted differently by the stance assumed towards it" (p. 39). Cf. Ruether's fuller discussion in 1983a:12-20.

[28]As we will see in chapter seven, Ruether believes that a transcendent God is created through projection of (largely male) fears of dissolution and death. She seems to believe that emphasis on ontological differences will lead to social and ecological dualism and domination. Bouma-Prediger affirms that "Ruether tends to engage in an *unargued* historicist reductionism in which God's action is reduced to action explainable entirely in terms of the world" (1995:153).

[29]"Resting in an interpretation of God's salvific love from some bygone time . . . will invariably be escapist, and finally destructive" (p. 45). McFague acknowledges the impact on her of Gordon Kaufman's *Theology for a Nuclear Age*, which insists that "humankind has moved into a thoroughly new and radically unique situation" (1985:ix).

[30]McFague is quoting Stephen Jay Gould's *Wonderful Life* (New York: W. W. Norton, 1989), p. 25.

[31]She also argues, as Murray Bookchin does, that blaming humanity in general for environmental problems, as deep ecology does, overlooks great differences in responsibility among different groups (p. 117).

[32]In *The Body of God*, however, McFague is not developing a Christian theology of creation derived largely from biblical sources but a Christian *theology of nature*. This theology of nature does not seek to establish Christian claims either by reason *(natural theology)* or revelation *(revealed theology)* but apparently assumes them and seeks "to reconceive belief in terms of contemporary views of the natural world" (pp. 66-67). It uses the contemporary scientific world picture "as a resource to reconstruct and express the faith" (p. 66). It seems to me, however, that such reconceptions or reconstructions might significantly critique and revise revealed theology. In any case, this *theology of nature* can also "enrich" contemporary scientific paradigms (p. 83). Although it does not seek support for Christian faith from science, it can interpret science in a "retrospective" way that shows a Christian reading to be plausible, even though others are possible (p. 76). Such a reading, for a Christian, can justify "the ways of the creator" (p. 75) and corroborate faith "in spite of evidence to the contrary" (p. 78; cf. p. 181).

[33]McFague acknowledges her indebtedness to Theissen for this emphasis (1985:257); also see Hefner (1993).

[34]Yet McFague finds in this new "countercultural and counterbiological" emphasis "hints and clues of a new stage of evolution" (p. 189).

[35]McFague observes that evil becomes more relative in an evolutionary system, where what is evil for some is good for others. She also notes that evil for some creatures can be regarded as necessary for the good of the whole and that evil can have educative value. (These seem compatible with Birch and Cobb's "fall upward.") Yet in the face of massive twentieth-century evils, McFague finds these qualifications somewhat hollow (pp. 141-42).

[36]Rudolf Bultmann's *Jesus and the Word* (1934), Ernest Colwell's *Jesus and the Gospel* (1963), Norman Perrin's *Rediscovering the Teachings of Jesus* (1967) and Milan Machovec's *Jesus für Atheisten* (1972); see Cobb 1975:97-110, 136-46.

[37]For the possible separability between God and the present universe as God's body in McFague and Cobb, see note 11 above.

[38]But what if human subjectivity and cultural evolution are simply products of a single evolutionary branch, jutting off sharply from others, and by no means slowly emerging components or overarching results of the whole? I also wonder whether claims about the gradual emergence of human characteristics seem plausible because these authors read them into the entire process from the start—whether through the process model of experience or Ruether's claim that consciousness is matter's interiority or McFague's decision to model the cosmos on the human body.

[39]"The entire insight upon which compassion is based is that the other is *not* other; and that I am *not* I. . . . In loving others I am loving myself and indeed involved in my own best and biggest and fullest self-interest" (1990:33).

[40]"We need to learn to feel the presence of other living beings and of the natural world as if they are part of us. We must feel their presence as if their destinies and our own are intertwined, as if their interests and our own are identified. . . . We must learn to love our neighbors as ourselves, realizing that our neighbors are part of ourselves" (1990:29).

[41]"If we are parts of God's body—if the model is totally organic—are we not then totally immersed, along with all other creatures, in the evolutionary process, with no transcendence or freedom?" (1987:76).

Chapter 7: Theology & Social Alienation

[1]Niebuhr's impact on American social theology, including on those who disagree with him, can hardly be overestimated. Studies of two movements I consider in this chapter take Niebuhr as their point of comparison: Judith Vaughan on Rosemary Ruether (1983) and

Dennis McCann on liberation theology (1981).

[2]The capitalist economy's principle of *efficiency,* which spawns a bureaucratic and hierarchical structure, contradicts the polity's principle of *equality* and culture's principle of *self-actualization* (or self-gratification; see chapter four).

[3]He can even say that "capitalism is also and above all a *social* system." Making credit universally available is one of its "institutional presuppositions" (1986:123-24).

[4]In *Will It Liberate?* Novak insists that commerce can flourish only where "a common universal morality" is observed whose "source lies in the human spirit" (1986:81). He also affirms that human rights "are endowed in individuals by their Creator, and are rooted in the liberties of the human spirit" and that the "shortest route toward understanding" that is "to see that these rights come directly from the Creator and reside in man's spiritual nature" (p. 63). Though he may be paraphrasing Cardinal Ratzinger in the latter reference, Novak still seems to relate elements of the "moral-cultural" system more directly to the "economic" system than he does in *The Spirit of Democratic Capitalism* (1982).

[5]When it is claimed that democratic socialist regimes in countries such as Sweden are morally superior to the U.S. model, Novak replies that the former are variants of *democratic capitalism* (1986:45-46; cf. 1982:144, 334).

[6]Novak 1970 is prefaced by part of John's poem "The Dark Night," but he refers to it and John only briefly in the text (p. 116).

[7]The six mentioned in this section are Trinity, incarnation, competition, original sin, separation of realms, caritas. *Caritas* is love for another person *as* other. That means, on the one hand, that a person should call others toward their highest possible self-realization (1982:354). In economics, however, it chiefly means letting each person choose according to his or her own self-interest, without imposing our standards on them. Novak does not ask whether these two approaches might sometimes be inconsistent.

Though he clearly favors "democratic capitalism," Novak affirms that the "Word of God . . . judges each and every system, and finds each gravely wanting" (1982:335). He believes that neither Christianity nor Judaism are uniquely tied to capitalism but that they have flourished and can flourish in all social settings (p. 336). Though Novak formulates his six doctrines in Christian terms, he mentions an analogue for each in Judaism. Very often, when mentioning the ideal religious base for democratic capitalism, Novak names Christianity and Judaism together.

[8]However, he finds this incompatible with the notion of class struggle. When Marxists affirm both class struggle and justice's final victory, he finds this contradictory (1986:109).

[9]Novak also finds competition legitimated because God, in the contest of life, does not seem committed to equality of results—as in parables where some are rewarded more than others. Novak notices—and handles somewhat unconvincingly—other teachings that contrast Christian virtue with worldly success and condemn desire for wealth (1982:345-46).

[10]See Galbraith 1952:13-17. Novak also argues, contrary to Galbraith, that "Merchandising is the *last* step of capitalism, not its first and defining difference" (1986:124).

[11]The *dependency* critique of capitalism finds minorities in Western countries in much the same situation as "underdeveloped" nations. Novak tries to deal with the income discrepancies between American whites and African-Americans. By showing that these are significantly related to differences in region, education, age and family structure, he apparently thinks he has defused criticisms that they are deeply linked to race. Novak also finds that certain black cultural habits deter the pursuit of wealth (1982:220, 223). He does, however, recognize some psychological barriers caused by discrimination. He favors some government measures to encourage establishment of small businesses in largely black areas.

[12]"Genuine individuality, embodying both distinctness and uniqueness, is a characteristic of human life. . . . Nature supplies the particularity, but the freedom of the spirit is the cause of true individuality. Man, unlike animal existence, not only has a centre but he has a centre beyond himself. . . . This capacity for self-transcendence which distinguished spirit in

man from soul (which he shares with animal existence), is the basis of discrete individuality, for this self-consciousness involves consciousness of the world as 'the other.' . . . Human
consciousness involves the sharp distinction between the self and the totality of the world"
(p. 55). For Niebuhr, the problems of self-formation and the possibility of psychological
alienation are ultimately rooted in this transcendence and not simply in the process of
structuring the self around objects from our surroundings (cf. chapter two).

[13]He argues that rational (in my terms, "public") discourse about each can uncover its limitations and bring humans to awareness of that finite-infinite tension which governs their
existence, yet without being able to provide the religious answer (which only revelation can
give [1941:15]).

[14]However, like Marcuse, Niebuhr speaks of eros in a positive sense, as "the natural vitalities
sublimated rather than repressed by reason" (p. 31).

[15]Niebuhr claims that this becomes evident precisely "in the highest reaches of the freedom
of the spirit" (p. 258). Precisely when one's self-transcending movement enables one to contemplate the loftiest aims and to review past actions in light of them, one will discover, if
one is honest, that one's will has always been inclined toward evil. One discovers that one's
will is still free in the sense of striving toward transcendence but consistently inclined
toward evil in its particular choices.

[16]More specifically, in political affairs Niebuhr felt that sacrificial love can do four things: (1)
check tendencies to conceive national interest too narrowly, (2) encourage politicians to
emphasize not only values that serve their own interests but also those that transcend them,
(3) keep "realists" from falling into moral cynicism and (4) undercut self-righteous pretensions by which all governments seek to glorify their own causes and blame all evil on
their enemies (Harland 1960:193-95).

[17]"The contradictions of history are not resolved in history; but they are only ultimately
resolved on the level of the eternal and the divine" (Niebuhr 1943:46).

[18]For Niebuhr, balance and tension also exist among social virtues. We have already seen how
mutual love, though its practice may be enhanced and positively critiqued by sacrificial love,
involves a reciprocal self-interest incompatible with the latter. Similarly, laws of justice (concerned with establishment of liberty, equality and order) aspire toward the ideals of love
(1943:246-47); yet as their operation in adjudicating competing claims shows, they involve
both approximations and contradictions to the latter (p. 251). Further, concrete structures
of justice aspire toward, yet only imperfectly embody, these laws of justice.

[19]This analysis is found in Niebuhr and Sigmund 1969, the Latin American section of which
was written by Paul Sigmund. Its overall perspective, however, is surely congruent with
Niebuhr's views.

[20]The "underside of this transcendent male ego is the conquest of nature" (1983a:47).
Whereas Ruether, unlike some radical ecofeminists, denies that an ideal matrifocal culture
existed in hunter-gatherer times (cf. chapter three), she believes that humans originally
worshiped a Great Mother. She finds the Hebrew imaging of God through one gender "a
sharp departure from all previous human consciousness" (1983a:53). Though Ruether
stresses that the Hebrews saw nature as God's good creation and did not seek to escape
death, she finds Christianity heavily influenced by world- and death-denying Jewish apocalypticism and Greek Platonism. Thus she often connects the Hebrew emphasis on a transcendent God rather directly with Greek depreciation of nature.

[21]Ruether regards Freudian psychology "as the chief tool for reinforcing patriarchal culture"
today (1975:151). That is because it defines women's nature as lack (specifically, of a penis)
which can only be fulfilled through a male (through sexual union with a male and bearing
a male child). Within the psychoanalytic tradition, however, Karen Horney strongly challenged this reading (pp. 143-44). Ruether recognizes that Jung's psychology attributes higher qualities—such as empathy and artistic creativity—to the feminine. Yet these, she argues,
function mainly to enhance the one-sided male ego (as when a man's *anima* makes him a

more rounded person) so that they still basically serve the masculine (pp. 151-59).

[22]Social and ecological change are always a "return to harmony with the covenant of creation," even though their specific outworkings will be different in different situations (p. 255).

[23]Ruether explicitly says that this is the case with women (1983a:63, 173, 183).

[24]References to Bookchin are on p. 185 (note 23) and p. 213 (note 17). Like Bookchin, Ruether occasionally uses "libertarian" to describe a view she favors (e.g., 1972:149; 1983b:66).

[25]Ruether notes that the appearance of capitalism's productive-domestic distinction in the nineteenth century coincided with a new attitude toward middle-class women. Rather than symbolizing characteristics inferior to men, they were now treated as exhibiting superior virtues (empathy, gentleness, deeper religious nature and so on). In this *romantic feminism*, later elaborated by Jung in his own way, women, as guardians of the domestic sphere, appeared able to save men from the harsh egoism stressed in the business world. Ruether insists, however, that romantic feminism still consigns women to a restricted sphere subordinated to men. And since qualities which allegedly belong to one sex (such as empathy) are really available to both, it, like all other traditional views of women, splits the human race dualistically into two halves and alienates individuals of one sex from traits which supposedly belong to the other. Moreover, like Niebuhr, it splits society into a domestic realm where higher virtues (such as sacrificial love) can be practiced and a public sphere where they cannot (1975:23, 199).

[26]"The development of eschatological and ascetic religion represents the final stage in the suppression of maternal genesis and the elevation of the male self to supernatural status" (1975:16).

[27]However, since the interiority of our organism is personal, the interiority of the Matrix must also be, so that in death our achievements and failures will somehow be gathered into the "great collective personhood" of "Holy Being" (1983a:258).

[28]The Jubilee theme seems especially prominent in Luke 4:18-21. For the proposal that Jesus proclaimed a Jubilee, see Yoder 1972:64-77.

[29]Yet perhaps this emphasis stands in tension with more dramatic expectations in her earlier work: e.g., "revolution entails nothing less than a transformation of all the social structures of civilization . . . literally a global struggle to overthrow and transform the character of power structures and points forward to a new messianic epiphany that will as far transcend the world-rejecting salvation myths of apocalypticism and Platonism as these myths transcended the old nature myths of the neolithic village" (1972:125). We seek to "reclaim spirit for body and body for spirit in a messianic appearing of the body of God" (p. 126). Ruether often expressed hopes for the birth of a "new man" (pp. 179, 180, 183, 190).

[30]Though Ruether appears to be representing Latin American liberation Christology in enunciating the themes paraphrased in my last three sentences, these themes sound more like hers than those of the three authors she mentions (Leonardo Boff, Jon Sobrino and José Miranda). She adds that the cross symbolizes God's victory "only if we deny this victory of evil by continuing Jesus' struggle against it" (p. 29).

[31]Cf. Matthew Fox's claim that Jesus came not to be king but to distribute a royal personhood to everyone (see chapter six).

[32]This emphasis seems to contradict Ruether's assertion that "all power and domination relations in society are overcome by overcoming the root metaphor of relationship to God modeled on king-servant relations" (1983a:30).

[33]The first two propositions in this paragraph are ones that Michael Francis, in his presentation for Novak's American Enterprise Institute, calls "easily defensible." The next two are among his more "controversial" propositions ("Dependency: Ideology, Fad, and Fact" in Novak and Jackson 1985:88-105). Whereas I generally agree with all four propositions, I note that government has become a bit more democratic in Latin America in general dur-

ing the last decade. While Novak generally disagrees with these points, he finds some plausibility in them, especially about uneven distribution of wealth (1986:127-31).

[34]Freire could have been included under public discourse (part one), but he has become
part of North American discussion as much through being appropriated in theological discourse as in any other way.

[35]Continuing the organismic conceptuality, Freire finds that the suffering that oppressed
people experience in being unable to act responsibly "is rooted in the very fact that the
human equilibrium has been disturbed" (p. 65, quoting Erich Fromm).

[36]*Ideology* indicates "all systems of means, be they natural or artificial, that are used to attain
some end or goal" (1982:16).

Chapter 8: Theology: Christological & Trinitarian Foundations

[1]Welch perhaps goes most clearly beyond Jung when he affirms "the impossibility of life, no
matter what the human development, to finally and fully satisfy life's promise" (1990:167),
and that we must finally, like Jesus, "bear the suffering trusting in the dark, incomprehensible love of God" (p. 164). By building so extensively on Jung without questioning his theories, however, Welch can hardly gain the approval of those many psychologists who question the scientific credibility of Jung's work.

[2]Her *theology of nature* seeks not to base Christian understanding of nature on contemporary
scientific models but to reconceive the Christian doctrine of creation by means of them
(1993:65-66). While this formulation apparently makes a Christian teaching not based on
science prior, McFague does not say how it is arrived at. It is always possible that allotting a
major place to current paradigms (e.g., "The Common Creation Story") could in fact alter
the content of what is believed.

[3]Centering prayer, in what I have covered, says little about Jesus, except that when those who
have been baptized into Christ pray, they are in some way the Son proceeding from the
Father and returning to him in the Holy Spirit's love. It is difficult to tell whether the Son
here is something greater than us or another name for our deeper selves.

[4]A representative effort is Gunther Bornkamm, *Jesus of Nazareth* (New York: Harper, 1960).

[5]Some examples of third quest work, apart from and more moderate than the Jesus Seminar,
are E. P. Sanders, *Jesus and Judaism* (Philadelphia: Fortress, 1985) and *The Historical Figure of
Jesus* (London: Penguin, 1993); Geza Vermes, *The Religion of Jesus the Jew* (London: SCM,
1993); and John Meier, *A Marginal Jew* (New York: Doubleday, 1991).

[6]I will consider as sources for the Seminar's views their collective publication *The Five Gospels*,
edited by Robert Funk and Roy Hoover (New York: Macmillan, 1993), and the works of
Marcus Borg and John Dominic Crossan. I will refer to their collective views as "the Jesus
Seminar's." On occasions where Borg or Crossan is distinguished from the Jesus Seminar,
his disagreement with specific conclusions in *The Five Gospels* is in view.

[7]Crossan, however, places Mark in the late 70s (1991:430).

[8]Crossan divides Thomas into two layers. In addition, he proposes that there also existed by
60 C.E. a Miracles Collection, containing episodes now found in Mark 2—8 and John 2—9,
and a Cross Gospel, a linked passion narrative now embedded in the Gospel of Peter (which
he dates in the mid-second century).

[9]According to Mark 12:38-39, Jesus warned his followers: "Beware of the scribes, who like to
walk around in long robes, and to be greeted with respect in the marketplaces, and to have
the best seats in the synagogues and places of honor at banquets!" Mark pictures Jesus proclaiming this in the Jerusalem temple. Luke 11:43, however, depicts Jesus saying, "Woe to
you Pharisees! For you love to have the seat of honor in the synagogues and to be greeted
with respect in the marketplaces." Luke places this in a series of criticisms pronounced during a meal in a Pharisee's house (vv. 37-53). Despite the similarities between these sayings,
the Jesus Seminar regards them as reflecting two originally distinct ones, with Luke's coming from Q and Mark's from his own source. This multiple attestation increases the likeli-

hood that some such saying came from Jesus and earned both sayings a "pink" rating (see note 13).

The chief reason for postulating different sources is that Luke's mentions "Pharisees," whereas Mark's refers to "scribes." Many Seminar scholars doubt that Pharisees were active in Galilee in Jesus' day. But they affirm that a general class of scribes was. They therefore suppose that reference to conflict with Pharisees reflects the church's struggle at a later time. Accordingly, they judge that Luke's context, a meal in a Pharisee's home where Jesus uttered various other criticisms, was invented by Luke. (Many would also judge that the Marcan saying was placed in the temple by Mark.) In fact, many Seminar participants would regard all references to conflict with Pharisees as creations of later writers (see note 11). In this particular case, however, Mark's saying, which does not mention Pharisees, would be earlier than Luke's, though Luke's is judged to come from the earlier source Q (Funk and Hoover 1993:106). This complication shows how multiple considerations enter into assessing any one saying and that in some cases a general principle (here, Q's historical priority) is overridden by other factors. Such complexities mean that Jesus' discourses are analyzed into many units thought to derive from different sources with diverse degrees of historical authenticity. For instance, in Luke's overall discourse (11:37-53), only verse 43 receives a "pink" rating; verses 39-41, 44 and 52 are "gray," whereas verses 42 and 46-50 are "black" (see note 13).

[10]For the more common scholarly view that the passion narratives contain much historical material, see Johnson 1996:110-11.

[11]Marcus Borg, as we shall see, emphasizes Jesus' conflict with Pharisees. For his rejection of such stories as creations of the evangelists, see 1994a:123 note 50.

[12]According to the Jesus Seminar, Jesus' earlier followers were functionally illiterate (Funk and Hoover 1993:27). According to Crossan, Jesus did not know the Hebrew scriptures as texts and would not have quoted them, which would have been too heady for peasants (Borg 1994b:34). Borg, in contrast, thinks that Jesus was very familiar with the Old Testament and perhaps knew it all from memory (1987:40).

[13]The Jesus Seminar ranked sayings attributed to Jesus into four categories and printed them in different colors in *The Five Gospels*. A saying printed in red means that in its estimation Jesus undoubtedly said it, or something very like it. Pink means that Jesus *probably* said something like it. Gray indicates that he did not say it but that the ideas involved are close to his. Black means that he did not say it and that it represents a different tradition (Funk and Hoover 1993:36).

[14]Borg notes that recent science is challenging the mechanistic view at micro- and macrolevels and is thus undermining the chief objection to the primordial tradition (p. 34).

[15]We are separated from the realm evident in these experiences "only by filmy screens of consciousness" (p. 34).

[16]A key text for this unmediated access to God is Matthew 7:7-11 ("Ask, and it will be given you; search, and you will find . . ."), rated pink by the Jesus Seminar.

[17]Borg does acknowledge that this emphasis had continuing impact because of the continuity between what Jesus taught and the way his life actually ended (1987:113-14). Borg finds Jesus' saying about servanthood (Mk 10:42-45) making the same point (1984:243-44). The Jesus Seminar, however, rates it only as gray since it seems to reflect leadership struggles in the early church and because of its theological interpretation of Jesus' death as a "ransom for many" (Funk and Hoover 1993:95-96).

[18]For detail on this, see Dunn 1980:67-82. For an opposing view, see Witherington 1990:233-43.

[19]Borg strongly implies that Jesus also had a vision of the Spirit descending as a dove at his baptism. He reports that at a 1992 meeting the Jesus Seminar was evenly divided on whether Jesus had visions (p. 44 note 36).

[20]For other reasons involved in rejecting this saying, see Funk and Hoover 1993:52, 187, 337.

Borg, however, defends an early date for Matthew 11:25-27 (1984:232, esp. note 9). He allows that some church titles for Jesus may have roots in his experience (1987:50).

[21]The Jesus Seminar also grants some plausibility to Father-Son language, where Jesus asserts that only the Father, but not the Son, knows the exact timing of the End (Mt 24:36 par. Mk 13:22). It seems unlikely that the early church, which was allegedly seeking to exalt Jesus, would invent such a saying. Some participants voted it pink or red, though its overall designation came out gray (Funk and Hoover 1993:251).

Finally, the parable of the Leased Vineyard (Mk 12:1-11), which Mark has Jesus telling soon after his entry into Jerusalem, mentions the murder of the landlord's son. The Seminar designates it gray and its parallel in Thomas pink but argues that Jesus told it as a disturbing story without clear application and without intending the son as himself (Funk and Hoover 1993:510-11). However, in both Mark and Thomas, Jesus immediately quotes Psalm 118:22, which clearly applies the parable to himself, indicating that he may have called himself "Son" in another way that the Jesus Seminar denies.

[22]I believe, however, that this question was not posed only by the Enlightenment but that it is implied by the historical claims made in Scripture.

[23]In critiquing Enlightenment historical methodology, I do not mean that all Seminar members follow it consistently. Some, like Borg, find in Jesus a Spirit-dimension which transcends such laws. This is a major reason Borg affirms the plausibility of some episodes, such as Jesus' temptation, which most Jesus Seminar participants reject because they apparently escape all means of factual verification (Funk and Hoover 1993:133-34). Although I find Borg closer than many others to a broader historical perspective, I also find that his claims for historicity sometimes transgress the limits of the strict historical method he often tries to follow.

[24]It is "extremely probable that such opposition . . . did not take the form of a single question or challenge, answered by a single remark. . . . Debate is likely to have raged to and fro, more like the protracted and frankly rambling discussion in John 6 than like . . . in Mark 2 and 3. It is, further, highly probable that a group around Jesus, regarding itself as the nucleus of . . . some sort of spearhead of renewal, would instantly 'read' any opposition in terms of the battle, with clear scriptural precedent. . . . As they retold the story . . . they would naturally . . . shrink the scene to its bare essentials" (Wright 1992:431).

[25]For Wright's comments on Q and Thomas, see pp. 435-43.

[26]Nor in stressing narrative connections among sayings do I mean that the evangelists arranged everything into strict chronological sequences. Some episodes appear in a different order in different Gospels. Moreover, narrative contexts are sometimes fairly loose (as often in Luke's "travel narrative" [9:51-19:44]). I mean, instead, that the Gospel writers arranged events and sayings into patterns, which are sometimes historically sequential, and that the meaning of most events and sayings is intimately interrelated with the significance of these broader patterns.

[27]The Gospels give us not so much Jesus' *ipsissima verba* (his very words) as much as his *ipsissima vox* (his authentic voice; Wilkins and Moreland 1995:77). When stories and sayings are in basic agreement but differ in details, this is usually a strong indication of historical authenticity. Exact agreement among sources raises the suspicion that their coincidence has been fabricated (p. 34).

[28]For the *primordial tradition*, see "Jesus as Sage" under "The 'Jesus Seminar' on the Historical Jesus" in this chapter. Jesus is also often likened to wandering Cynics, who devoted themselves mainly to ironic, humorous and often scathing critique of society, especially of the wealthy and cultured. Though Jesus made numerous biting criticisms of these things, he emphasized a positive alternative social vision far more than Cynics did (see "A political Jesus" later in the text).

[29]Borg articulates this union-communion differentiation precisely, but he seems to regard it of little real importance, acknowledging only in a lengthy footnote that early Jewish mysti-

cism was of the latter kind (1984:231, 373 note 4; cf. 1987:43-44, 53 note 21).

[30]Sparrows were sold so cheaply that they were the one meat source Palestinian peasants could afford. Matthew 10:29 reflects this: "What do sparrows cost? A penny apiece? Yet not one of them will fall to earth without the consent of your Father" (as quoted in Funk and Hoover 1993:172-73). The Lukan parallel (also rated pink by the Jesus Seminar) asks, "Are not five sparrows sold for two pennies?" (12:6), probably indicating that if a person spent this amount, a fifth was thrown in free. Here Jesus is saying that even this free one is not "forgotten in God's sight."

[31]For further work on wisdom Christology, see Schüssler Fiorenza 1983:130-40 and 1994:131-62.

[32]For instance, the "Day of the Lord" in Joel refers at least to a contemporary locust plague (chapter 1), a coming military invasion (2:1-11) and a future cataclysm involving all nations (2:30-32).

[33]The apocalyptic mentality, in distinction to a prophetic or generally eschatological one, is often characterized in four ways: (1) focusing chiefly on history's final, cataclysmic events; (2) regarding the present as largely devoid of God's presence; (3) withdrawal from contemporary society; and (4) stressing fantastic images of cosmic conflagration and renovation (cf. Finger 1985:111-12).

[34]I object to using the criterion of dissimilarity to exclude from Jesus' own use all titles used by other people—to say, "If anyone else used a title, Jesus could not have used it." However, if good evidence exists that almost no one but Jesus used a title, this dissimilarity between Jesus' usage and other peoples' is good evidence that the title came from him.

[35]Yet since the kingdom involved the living presence of God among people, it cannot be reduced to social dimensions alone.

[36]For details on this, see Finger 1985:277-91. Following Borg, the ritually holy and unholy should be added to this summary. Borg, however, despite his political emphasis, ends up describing "kingdom of God," consistent with the rest of his theology, as "a symbol for the presence and power of God as known in mystical experience . . . Jesus' name for what is experienced in the primordial religious experience" (1984:254).

[37]The argument that Mark created this summary of Jesus' gospel is weakened by the observation that both Matthew and Luke epitomized it in the same way, yet clearly distinguished it from the early church's basic message (Mt 28:19-20; Lk 24:46-47), whereas Mark seems to regard the church's gospel as "the good news of Jesus Christ, the Son of God" (Mk 1:1; cf. Wilkins and Moreland 1995:34).

[38]For much fuller consideration of these themes, see Finger 1989:379-405, 433-55.

[39]When we read the Synoptics in light of Jesus' original context and worldview, we cannot regard Jesus' conflicts with his opponents as simply read back into his life from early church struggles, as the Seminar members propose. These conflicts are absolutely essential to the dramatic structure of the Synoptics' narrative framework.

[40]Although the resurrection experience provided the standpoint from which the Synoptics were written, I do not find it plausible that convictions about the Spirit's agency in this event were simply extrapolated back into Jesus' life. Seminar members find this agency active there, even though they discount the Synoptics' narrative framework. I do not believe that affirmations about the Spirit would have been connected with Jesus' life unless something about that life made this attribution plausible. Another connection between the Gospels and the resurrection accounts is found in Acts 2:33, where Jesus poured out the Spirit after his resurrection (cf. Jn 16:7), and in the Gospels' assertion at Jesus' baptism that Jesus would baptize with the Holy Spirit (Mt 3:11 par. Mk 1:8 par. Lk 3:16 par. Jn 1:33).

[41]I use the name *Father* here because the Synoptics employ it to indicate that relationship of intimacy and fidelity that I trace in this section, and not gender. I believe that this understanding of *Father* critiques the patriarchal use of the term that later grew up in the church and which many feminists rightly criticize. (For further discussion, see Finger 1989:485-90.)

[42]Mark, it is commonly held, expresses this tension by calling Jesus the Son of God at the beginning and end of his Gospel (1:1; 15:39), but interpreting the content of that phrase as the suffering Son of Man (e.g., Perrin 1974:78). I find it more convincing to attribute the discovery of this dialectic to Jesus than to Mark. For an argument that the Gospels as well as the rest of the New Testament emphasize this sort of paradox and that it is most plausibly traced to Jesus, see Johnson 1996:151-66.

[43]In addition to Matthew 11:27 par. Luke 22, Jesus calls himself "Son" in the sense implying "Son of God" when he says that he does not know the time of the final eschatological hour (Mt 24:36 par. Mk 13:32), when he affirms his Messiahship at his trial (Mt 26:63 par. Mk 14:61 par. Lk 22:70) and in his postresurrection commission to his disciples (Mt 28:19). Two parables also imply that Jesus is God's special son: the vineyard (Mt 21:37-38 par. Mk 12:6 par. Lk 20:13 par. Gospel of Thomas 65:6) and the wedding celebration (Mt 22:2). Jesus clearly uses this term much less than he does "Son of Man."

[44]Since the Gospels present Jesus' authentic voice and not always his very words (note 27), not every occurrence of, say, "Son of Man" need indicate that Jesus used exactly that term on that precise occasion but only that such a title adequately reflects the substance of what he said. Decisions about specific texts are matters for historical study and exegesis.

[45]If a person argues, as do Norman Perrin (1974:57-60) and Marcus Borg (1994b:58), that such titles were applied to Jesus as a result of his resurrection, I reply that this event was understood as a vindication of Jesus, as affirming what he had historically claimed to be (Wright 1992:399-400). He would not have begun to be acclaimed as Son of Man or Son of God if these titles did not accurately represent something evidenced by his life. In other words, the church began attributing these titles to Jesus after the resurrection, but they were not invented at that time.

Chapter 9: Psychology, Spirituality & a Theological Anthropology

[1]The rest of the Old Testament refers to Adam only in Deuteronomy 32:8;1 Chronicles 1:1; and Job 31:33. It refers to Eve not at all. Apart from the important New Testament references to Adam in Romans 5:12-21 and 1 Corinthians 15:45-50, Adam and/or Eve appear only in Luke 3:38; 1 Corinthians 15:22; 2 Corinthians 11:3; 1 Timothy 2:11-15; and Jude 4.

[2]The suitability of humanity's first pair is further lessened if, as Irenaeus suggested, they are best regarded as childlike, just beginning on life's path. Then they could hardly serve as models of mature humanity, or even of more complex forms of sin.

[3]For this and much of what follows, see Finger 1989:65-114. In the space available, I cannot indicate in detail why or in what sense I find the biblical records valid (for this see 1985:177-256). I have shown in chapter eight why I regard the Synoptics' Jesus-stories and the Hebrew-Christian worldview within which they occur as the framework for viewing all reality. This worldview is found chiefly in the canonical Scriptures. The biblical themes mentioned in this chapter are general features of this worldview, not highly debated details. Specific scriptures cited are not intended to be proof-texts but clear expressions of the themes I mention (see also note 12).

[4]It has, however, been central in anthropologies as diverse as Friedrich Schleiermacher's and Karl Barth's.

[5]The next verse, which to early Christians seemed to express Jesus' experience, reads, "I gave my back to those who struck me, and my cheeks to those who pulled out the beard; I did not hide my face from insult and spitting" (Is 50:6). In fact, the rest of the chapter can be read as prophetic of Jesus.

[6]Hebrews 11, which celebrates the Old Testament heroes of faithfulness, points toward Jesus as "the pioneer and perfecter of our faith[fulness]" (12:2; cf. 2:10). Several crucial Pauline texts on justification by faith, which are usually translated as dealing with "faith in Jesus Christ," are better translated as "the faithfulness of Jesus Christ" (Rom 3:22, 26; Gal 2:16; 3:22; cf. Gal 3:2, 5, 11, 23-26; Phil 3:9; see Hays 1983; Finger 1989:174-79, 186-89).

[7]Using the terminology of John Macquarrie and Rudolf Bultmann, taken from Martin Heidegger, I call dependence an "ontological" characteristic, having to do with humankind's most fundamental "structure," while faithfulness is an "ontic" one, resulting from human activities (Macquarrie 1965:29-37).

[8]Full affirmation of this point is developed in a doctrine of creation, which is the subject of my next chapter.

[9]The Jesus Seminar recognizes that this passage climaxes Jesus' journey to Jerusalem, which began with confession of his Messiahship and his emphasis on his followers taking up their crosses (Mk 8:27—9:1). Although this structural placement, the use of Son of Man and the "theological" statement about a ransom are, for the Seminar, signs of heavy editorial activity, they still rate the statement gray, as resembling the sort of thing Jesus likely said (Funk and Hoover 1993:95-96). We, however, find this statement's placement and its combination of servanthood with Son of Man significant indications of authenticity.

[10]Genesis 1:28-30, apparently describing a feature of the "image" of God in humanity, grants humans "dominion" over other creatures. If understood in the general Hebrew sense, this word could perhaps describe what I mean by *oversight*. But this text has been so often used to justify exploitation of nature that I avoid this word.

[11]Christians believe that Jesus lived in a world disfigured by sin. In this sense he experienced the bondage it brings and was tempted by it in the same basic ways that all humans are. Yet since he never gave in to sin, he never experienced this bondage inwardly (cf. Heb 4:15).

[12]I cannot possibly, in the space available, argue that Paul (and Hebrews and John and so on) presents a valid understanding of Jesus' activity. I have limited this kind of argumentation to showing, in some detail, why I believe that the Jesus story found in the Synoptic Gospels is worthy of serious consideration (see chapter eight). Though I am well aware that different biblical authors write with differing terminology and from various perspectives, I can only ask readers to entertain the possibility that this diversity enriches what we know about humans and is fundamentally consistent with the basic story of God-with-humanity. Throughout the present chapter, the themes I raise can be found in many authors or, at a minimum, in many places in one author. The cogency of my exposition will depend significantly on the overall internal consistency of these themes with others developed in chapters nine through eleven and in their relevance to contemporary issues (see also note 3).

[13]"Our bodies [flesh] had no rest" (2 Cor 7:5) and "my mind [spirit] could not rest" (2:13) both seem to mean "I or we could not rest."

[14]Paul can speak of "the body of sin" (Rom 6:6) and "this body of death" (7:24) and of putting "the deeds of the body" to death (8:13). But in each case it is not the body as such that is sinful but the body as under the dominion of another force.

[15]Martin Heidegger called such ways of being *existentialia*. Rudolf Bultmann understood some central anthropological terms along these lines (Macquarrie 1965:3-37).

[16]As indicated by the parallelism between "flesh" and "spirit" mentioned in note 13. Further, Paul could close his letters with "The grace of our Lord Jesus Christ be with you [all]" (Rom 16:20; 1 Cor 16:23; 2 Cor 13:13) just as he could with "The grace of our Lord Jesus Christ be with your spirit" (Gal 6:18; Phil 4:23; Philem 25).

[17]This is most evident in contrasts where "soul," or *psychē*, words denote humans who lack God's transforming Spirit, whereas "spirit," or *pneuma*, words indicate those who do not (1 Cor 2:14-15; 15:44-46; Jude 19; cf. Jas 3:15).

[18]*Leb(ab)* indicates "everything that we ascribe to the head and brain—power of perception, reason, understanding, judgment, sense of direction, discernment" (Wolff 1974:51). In fact, "these things circumscribe the real core meaning of the word," and it "least of all means the emotions" (p. 55).

[19]The first three texts quote Isaiah 6:9-10. The last two quote Jeremiah 31:31-34 (cf. also Mk 11:12; Lk 24:25; Acts 7:51; Rom 10:6-10).

[20]The Hebrew Scriptures developed no more precise concept of conscience because self-

knowledge comes only from "the God who speaks and who reveals himself . . . and makes possible responsible action. . . . The I is a single person confronting God who speaks. Conscience is hearing in the sense of willing adherence" (*TDNT* 7:908).

[21]This is affirmed by texts which say that conscience can be corrupt (Tit 1:15), seared (1 Tim 4:2), evil (Heb 10:22) and productive of dead works (Heb 9:14). Even Paul, who had great confidence in the witness of his conscience, insisted that not conscience, but God, is the final judge (1 Cor 4:4-5).

[22]A correspondence between what conscience says and what a person does is always extremely important, even for the mature (Acts 23:1, 24:16; 2 Cor 5:11; Heb 13:18; 1 Pet 3:16). If a person disregards his or her conscience, faith can be destroyed (1 Tim 1:19).

[23]The most common noun for *mind* or *reason* is *nous*, which appears twenty-three times. Common verbs for mental activities, not counting those for hearing and seeing, are *ginōskō* (about 200 occurrences), *krinō* (about 140), *epiginōskō* (about 40), *hēgeomai* (28), *syniēmi* (25), *manthanō* (24) and *phroneō* (22). The most common words for knowledge are *sophia* (49), *gnōsis* (28) and *epignōsis* (20).

[24]For a discussion, see Finger 1985:247-56.

[25]Cf. those studies which suggest that people profiting from Rogers's therapy do not really reject their social upbringing but, after having questioned it, readopt many of its values (chapter two, note 15).

[26]This would fit with Irenaeus's view that Adam and Eve were not created as adults who basically knew how to act but more like children who had to learn through trial and error (cf. note 2).

[27]The difference between us and Jesus is that he did not experience sin and alienation within himself and did not have to oppose these on that level (cf. note 11). Nevertheless, he had to struggle against forces that sought to fragment and alienate him internally. He also had to acknowledge the limits of his human efforts, "die" to exaggerated expectations of what he might do (chiefly as an all-conquering Messiah) and continually rely for strength on divine resurrecting power.

[28]I recall Thomas Keating's statement, mentioned in chapter five of this book: "God and our true self are not separate. Though we are not God, God and our true self are the same thing" (1986:127).

[29]The fact that even its "soul" and "spirit" words (like its body words) indicate ways of being, or the entire person viewed from a certain angle, provides another indication that the Bible does not speak of a deepest self which is a complete, spiritual, though hidden, entity from the start.

[30]Transcendence, as Niebuhr used it, affirms that persons strive toward (and/or fear) some possibility not present in the material world. I, however, would say "not yet present" to indicate that people are not simply directed toward a spiritual realm, as Niebuhr often stressed, but more toward the future. I would also stress that this transcending self is rooted in and inextricably shaped by finite situations that it can never fully transcend.

[31]Centering prayer, Fox, Teresa and John all regard spirituality's goal as *divinization*, which John defines as becoming by grace what God is by nature. To emphasize the distinction between humans and God more clearly, I prefer to stress Eastern Orthodoxy's denial that any creature can become identical with (or even know) the divine *essence*. Yet Orthodoxy strongly affirms divinization in the sense of transformation by divine *energies*. (The clear distinction between God's essence and energies derives from Gregory Palamas [1296-1359].) I affirm divinization in the latter sense.

[32]Theorists so diverse as Freud, Marcuse, Winnicott, Jung and Chodorow have postulated that infants experience an undifferentiated oneness with their mothers in which they seem to be omnipotent and reality seems to form a coherent whole. Jessica Benjamin, however, utilizing recent observations on infant behavior, argues that responsive mutuality between infant and mother is more common, although this can degenerate into fusion (see chapter two,

note 11). Whatever the original mother-infant relationship, however, longing for some primordial state of union seems to underlie many narcissistic phenomena.

[33]The notion of the church as a mother who nourishes Christians and holds them within her body, yet also helps them grow in different ways so that they may serve within the world, also fits well with this general concept. Moreover, God as parent could equally well be called Mother. I use Father because it is the biblical term, which indicates intimacy and fidelity, not gender (see Finger 1989:485-90).

[34]E.g., you cannot serve God and wealth (Mt 6:24 par. Lk 16:13 par. *Gospel of Thomas* 47:1-2); do not be anxious about food and clothing (Mt 6:25-34 par. Lk 12:22-31 par. *Gospel of Thomas* 36); the parable of the rich farmer (Lk 12:16-21 par. *Gospel of Thomas* 63:1-2); do not lay up treasures on earth (Mt 6:19-21 par. Lk 12:33-34 par. *Gospel of Thomas* 76:3). The first three are rated pink by the Jesus Seminar. Almost all scholars agree that Jesus regarded dedication to wealth as incompatible with dedication to God. For a fuller treatment of this theme, see chapter eleven.

Of course the Hebrew Scriptures sometimes promise wealth as a reward for obedience. Yet it is promised to those who live within a society that follows Yahweh. When society as a whole departs from Yahweh, unjust pursuit of wealth is one of its major sins, and those who remain faithful often become "poor and needy." The New Testament never speaks positively about wealth. For further discussion, see Finger 1985:284-88.

[35]This does not mean that production and profit can play no role at all in a society congruent with Christian faith. Even in Michael Novak's "democratic capitalism" these forces are balanced by moral and social-cultural ones. See chapter eleven for fuller discussion.

[36]Though centering prayer lacks the sensory dimensions of union with God-nature, to the extent that it emphasizes rather swift attainment of union unaffected by deep psychic conflicts it may appeal to narcissistlike longings. In Teresa of Ávila and John of the Cross, however, experiences of union are preceded by profound experiences of struggle and differentiation. To the extent that Welch regards the self as identical with God and Christ, a narcissistlike sense of fusion may be operating, although his account of individuation involves considerable struggle.

[37]If participation in public conversation consists largely in clarifying a person's position and explicating its internal consistency, and less in seeking to prove its cogency by commonly accepted standards, discussion will likely involve, on the part of many parties, much "testimony" to how their perspectives work out in practice.

Chapter 10: Ecology, Spirituality & a Theology of Creation

[1]Many systematic theologies, however, prefaced the doctrine of God with an epistemological section on how God and other theological matters can be known—say, through revelation or reason, or some combination of the two. This section on the sources of theological knowledge and the kinds of evidence and degrees of certainty that characterized theological affirmation was often called *prolegomena*. For further discussion, see Finger 1985:18-29.

[2]I am describing how the theology of creation has been handled in traditional systematic theologies. McFague understands "theology of nature" differently, as starting from redemption (as does my own theology of creation). Yet she conceptualizes, or "remythologizes," it in terms of the contemporary scientific picture of reality to a far greater extent than I do (1993:65-66).

[3]Deuteronomy 4:32; Psalms 51:10; 89:12; Isaiah 4:15; Jeremiah 32:22; Amos 4:13; Malachi 2:10. Only in Psalm 51:10, Isaiah 4:15 and Jeremiah 32:22 does *bara'* refer to something other than the original creation.

[4]Affirmations regarded as part of the earliest Christian kerygma (see Finger 1985:36-40) present Jesus' work as the fulfillment of God's historical plan (Acts 2:23; cf. 13:27; Rom 1:2; 1 Cor 15:3-4). Later texts call it the mystery hidden throughout previous generations (Rom 16:25-26; Eph 1:9-10; 3:4-6; Col 1:26-27; 2:2). Others refer to it as destined from before the

beginning of the world (2 Tim 1:9-10; Tit 1:2-3;1 Pet 1:20; cf. Heb 9:26).

[5]These fairly obvious texts, however, only begin to express this theme. According to Paul Minear, "the new creation" is one of the three main images of God's people, or the church, in the New Testament (1960:105-35).

[6]The Greek *pistis Iēsou Christou* can be translated both as "*faith* in Jesus Christ" and "the *faithfulness* of Jesus Christ." Although modern translators, influenced by Martin Luther, have almost always chosen the former rendering, strong arguments exist for selecting the latter at least in Romans 3:22, 25, 27; Galatians 2:16; 3:22; and possibly in Philippians 3:19; Ephesians 3:12; 4:13; 1 Timothy 3:15. Translating these texts in this way still leaves untouched others which affirm that justification is also appropriated, from the human side, by faith in Jesus Christ. For fuller discussion, see Hays 1983, Hays and Dunn 1991, and Finger 1989:174-90.

[7]For its centrality in the Hebrew Scriptures, see Finger 1989:177-79.

[8]Cf. Jesus' affirmation in the Synoptics: "All things have been handed over to me by my Father" (which is followed by "and no one knows the Son except the Father, and no one knows the Father except the Son and anyone to whom the Son chooses to reveal him" [Mt 11:27 par. Lk 10:22]). This verse comes from Q and is supported by the Gospel of Thomas, providing strong grounds for accepting it as authentic. Yet the Jesus Seminar rejects it, largely because it contains "church" language (see chapter eight).

[9]In Luke this quotation sums up the purpose of Jesus' ministry, which Mark and Matthew summarize as "Repent, for the kingdom of heaven has come near" (Mt 4:17; compare Mk 1:15).

[10]Perhaps his awareness of the Spirit also faded, for the Spirit is hardly mentioned in the passion narratives.

[11]There is, however, a psychological paradox in this cry: "My God, my God, why have you forsaken me?" It does express the feeling of being totally abandoned. Yet the very address, to "my God," indicates that the sufferer has not ceased believing in, or clinging to, God in an even deeper sense. Such a paradox occurs every time believers reproach God for being unjust, unresponsive or unloving—for no matter how ill-treated, unheard or unloved such persons may feel, such cries are appeals to the One who is still considered, perhaps at some unconscious level, just, responsive and loving.

[12]In fact, were I to begin trinitarian reflection from a Christian experience of redemption (instead of through its historical foundation), I would begin with the Spirit. Moltmann points out that two orders in trinitarian reflection are possible (1979:80-96). The *protological*, which Christian theology has almost always followed, reasons from eternity before creation to the present. Thus it speaks (first) of the Father, whose creative work is exercised (second) through the Son, and then is actualized (third) through the Spirit. But trinitarian theology can also work *eschatologically*. In this case it begins with the Spirit who actualizes divine life in the present, then moves to the Son, whom the Spirit glorifies, and finally to the Father, in whom all things will finally be summed up (cf. 1 Cor 24—28). In my earlier work, I have followed the eschatological order (Finger 1989:380-90).

[13]John 1:1 and 20:28 clearly do, and probably also John 1:18 and 1 John 5:20. The book of Hebrews designates the Son as God (1:8-9) and briefly describes his divine character (1:2-3), while Colossians depicts him in similar terms (1:15-17, 2:9). In several other places Jesus is, in all likelihood, called "God" (Rom 9:5; Tit 2:13; 2 Pet 1:1).

[14]"The unity of the *nature* and the *revelation* of God is what is meant by the doctrine of the Trinity" (Brunner 1960:220). I am not affirming a mere *modalism*, according to which the three persons are simply modes, or appearances from the human perspective, of what God is like. Instead, I claim that part of the wonder of salvation is that God appears and gives Godself to us as God truly is. In claiming this, theology is not being presumptuous. For theology is not claiming to have discerned this by human powers but to be responding to what God has, through surprising and overwhelming grace, chosen to reveal.

[15]For the possibility that McFague does not regard God's being as always necessarily interdependent with the cosmos', see chapter six, note 11.

[16]The kerygmatic speeches in Acts regard Jesus' death as a judicial murder (2:23; 3:13-15; 5:30), yet one in which all peoples were implicated, not only Jews (4:24-27).

[17]I am well aware of the problems involved in the traditional distinction between nature and grace, especially of the Orthodox objection that it separates an autonomous humanity from God (see Finger 1994). My use of these terms here intends no systematic distinction between them.

[18]If McFague would cite references like those in chapter six, note 11 (cf. note 15), to affirm that "God is embodied, but not necessarily" (1993:150), I would reply that in them she is really affirming what I have called a transcendent God-world paradigm, where God's being is distinct from that of the cosmos.

[19]Bonaventure (1217-1274), following Francis of Assisi (1182-1286), frequently emphasized the divine goodness and emphasized the thesis, which he took from pseudo-Dionysius, that "goodness of itself is self-diffusive." I can accept this statement if it is not taken to mean that goodness expands by some strict inherent necessity but it is recognized that goodness is an entirely free, voluntary activity.

[20]Though I am using abstract nouns such as *love* and *goodness,* I do not mean to imply that they are somehow realities in themselves, superior to the trinitarian persons who exchange them. With Catherine LaCugna (1991), I believe that trinitarian thinking becomes distorted when general terms (such as "divine essence") are employed as if they designated realities distinct from and somehow more fully divine than the persons. Like Lacugna, I insist that divine reality is to be found nowhere but in the mutual activities of the divine persons.

[21]The Son's union with nonhuman nature was not personal, or hypostatic, as was his union with humanity in Jesus of Nazareth. If the latter were thought of as a "direct" union, the former might be called "indirect." Thus though I cannot affirm as McFague does that the universe is *the* incarnation of God (1987:62), I can affirm that the universe is taken up into and vivified by the incarnation of God.

[22]This, of course, corresponds with Genesis 1—2. (I see no need to limit the "days" of Genesis 1 to any particular time period, since [among other reasons] the word *day* can describe the entire process in Genesis 2:4. For a discussion of "scientific creationism," see Finger 1989:418-20, 424-26.)

[23]For a discussion of omnipotence and predestination, see Finger 1989:129-32, 504-5.

[24]For fuller discussion, see Finger 1989:77-79, 429-30, 491-93. The classic work on this subject is Nygren 1953. We have seen that for Niebuhr agape is the supreme form of love, but only eros is really practicable in history (see chapter seven). McFague finds agape to be the kind of love extended by God "as Mother" but eros to characterize God "as Lover" (1987:101-9, 130-36).

[25]Based on nature, in fact, as I pointed out in chapter six, we could often praise destruction as the route to progress. I found traces of this in the positive roles Margulis and Sagan attribute to Hiroshima and Nagasaki, Swimme and Berry to the Crusades and Birch and Cobb to the industrial revolution. Nature could also condone violence in pursuit of environmental aims, as I found Dave Foreman advocating (chapter three).

[26]This hope for what has "not yet" occurred is rooted in the faith that we have "already" experienced a foretaste of it. Christians believe that they have already experienced that agape of God in Christ communicated through the Holy Spirit, and it is precisely this that arouses hope and longing for the filling of all things with this love.

[27]We also saw that deep ecology's biocentric equality grants all creatures, including inanimate ones and collections such as species and ecosystems, *intrinsic value.* But although it claims that this perspective fosters appreciation of greater diversity, I have complained that, by itself, it gives no help in making environmental decisions. I have preferred Birch, Cobb and McFague's emphasis that differences in *instrumental value* must also be recognized and that

these form the basis for decisions. I have also generally agreed with Birch, Cobb and Ruether that granting greater value to species and ecosystems over individuals often better enhances diversity (chapter six).

[28]On uniqueness: "To be is to be different"; the universe "works to assure" each particle of its special role (Swimme and Berry 1992:74, 52). On interconnectedness: Each particle is instantaneously and "intimately present to every other particle"; "at the heart of the individual is everyone else" (pp. 29, 134). However, the significance of either individuality or connectedness seems undermined when Swimme and Berry claim that the universe recreates itself anew every instant and that trillions of creatures have often been destroyed to allow something new to arise. Such assertions also seem to trivialize conflict and destruction, and this, I will now argue, is often a shortcoming of the organismic paradigm.

[29]This emphasis seems to appeal to the desire of many people today to both express their individuality fully and be embedded in meaningful communal relationships—without acknowledging that attaining one of these often sharply conflicts with attaining the other. It is also reminiscent of the commercial emphasis on "having it all": on possessing the fullness of every pleasure without recognizing that choosing one entails excluding others.

[30]Though intratrinitarian love is reciprocated by appropriate responses, I do not believe that it is motivated by hope of these. Our clue to this love's character is the utterly self-giving displayed in Jesus' ministry. Eros and agape are distinguished not by any responses they may happen to receive but by the *motives* on which they are based. Agape is not motivated by hope of response, even though it may often get a response. The love motivating intratrinitarian activity, then, will have to be agape: love that aims at the good of other persons and situations, whether or not they respond positively.

[31]However, as stressed in chapter nine, no one can consistently do this without also being received and affirmed by significant others and, ultimately, by God. Receiving agape and giving it alternate, as dialectical moments, in self-formation. My main point is that as we truly mature in this kind of love, the intention to give ourselves without expecting positive response comes to predominate.

[32]Cf. John of the Cross: "All the being of creatures compared to the infinite being of God is nothing. . . . All the beauty of creatures compared to the infinite beauty of God is the height of ugliness. . . . All the grace and elegance of creatures compared to God's grace is utter coarseness and crudity" (*Ascent* 1.4.4). (Passages such as this make it difficult to affirm that God is as closely connected with the *self* [in Jung's sense] in John as John Welch claims it is [cf. chapters five and nine in this book].)

[33]For a discussion of this issue, see Johnson 1996:224-27.

[34]Chapters eight and nine showed that "the flesh" dominates human lives when its values become the ultimate ones to which people are committed. Biblical "principalities and powers" include forces that stand behind earthly rulers and systems. Insofar as these earthly representatives claim ultimate allegiance for themselves, they become demonic.

[35]"Absolute" can connote that all reality whatsoever is included in a being (as in Hegel's Absolute). Since the triune God grants genuine existence to a multifaceted cosmos, it is probably best to call this God the "ultimate" rather than the "absolute" reality.

[36]For further discussion, see my "A Mennonite Theology for InterFaith Relations," in *Grounds for Understanding*, ed. Mark Heim (Grand Rapids, Mich.: Eerdmans, 1997).

[37]According to Ruether, "compassion for all living things" will lead to "breaking down the illusion of otherness" and to encounter with the "ongoing Matrix of the whole" (1992:252-53).

[38]For this general line of criticism, especially with reference to Goddess and process theologies, see Plumwood 1993.

Chapter 11: A Theology of Society

[1]I affirm that God also communicates an awareness of divine reality through a "general revelation," but that it is very difficult to draw specific social or ecological consequences from

it (cf. Finger 1985:247-55).

[2]It is likely that a faithful remnant of Israel remained in Jesus' time. His mother Mary, in fact, can be regarded as a symbol of it—or indeed as the Remnant, given the close identification between a group and a person who represents it in Hebrew thought (Finger 1989:473-76; cf. my discussion of the individual and corporate character of God's Servant in chapter nine). Nevertheless, human obedience was not perfectly fulfilled in Mary as it was in Jesus, and in this sense he alone actualized human partnership with God.

[3]The sayings to turn the other cheek, give up your cloak, go the second mile and love your enemies are ranked as those first, second, fourth and fifth most likely, respectively, to come from Jesus (Funk and Hoover 1993:549).

[4]The Jesus Seminar rejects these as Jesus' words because they have parallels in later rabbinic teaching and because they allude to final judgment, whereas Jesus, it is claimed, did not (Funk and Hoover 1993:158-59). I find the first reason an inadequate ground and the second reason an incorrect ground for denying this saying to him.

[5]Instead of referring to Jesus' approach as "nonresisting love" or "nonresistance," I prefer "nonviolent resistance." For Jesus often resisted the opposition of his enemies—but did so in a nonviolent way. Even the counsels to turn the other cheek, give up your cloak and go the second mile are not simply nonresistant compliance but creative ways of responding to aggression and a refusal to be passively nonresistant in the face of it.

[6]Reinhold Niebuhr believes that Jesus made this historical mistake but seeks to give his strenuous teachings some validity by regarding them as indications of history's ultimate meaning *(agapē)*, even though they are not often directly practicable in history (1943:47-52).

[7]The standard theory of the "delay of the parousia" asserts that when Jesus failed to soon return as the supernatural Son of Man, the church hung on to their faith in him as Son of Man and Lord but postponed his return indefinitely. I suspect that had their faith been as strongly based on his early return as holders of this theory usually imply, the readjustment or even loss of faith would probably have been much greater.

[8]For my purposes it is sufficient to show that a certain perspective on Jesus' death was present in Johannine literature, without deciding whether the Johannine epistles were or were not written by the author of John's Gospel.

[9]Richard Hays argues that by using "obedience" in Romans 5, Paul recalls Jesus' history (1983:166-67). For the centrality of obedience in Romans, see Minear 1971.

[10]"Becoming poor" here refers to Jesus' overall self-giving, and commentators usually assume that Paul cannot also be referring to Jesus' earthly poverty as a consequence of this. Yet this conclusion seems to be based on the supposition that Paul was not interested in Jesus' earthly life. To me, given the whole discussion of literal wealth and poverty in 2 Corinthians 8—9, it seems likely that Paul was referring to both. In any case, important economic and social (interethnic) consequences are drawn from the overall form of Jesus' ministry.

[11]The argument that New Testament writers outside the Synoptics did not derive their social ethics from Jesus often appeals to major texts on Christians' relations to society. It claims that these emphasize Greco-Roman thought patterns. For an argument that Ephesians 5:18—6:9, 1 Peter 2:13—3:12 and Romans 12:14—13:14 are really rooted in the agapaic way of Jesus, see Finger 1989:79-88.

[12]This can be understood as investing our treasures in the kingdom of heaven (Matthew's usual phrase for "kingdom of God") rather than (or in addition to) these treasures being of a spiritual nature.

[13]Pauline churches apparently had a few wealthy members, who provided for many of the poorer ones (see Meeks 1983:51-73).

[14]Although conversions to the new movement often disrupted families and called persons to decide for Christ over their families, the early church was not antifamily but was very concerned to build and preserve stable families among its new members.

[15]In the majority of cases where Paul refers to "rulers" in the plural *(exousiai),* this term indi-

cates demonic powers which stand behind worldly governments (1 Cor 15:24; Eph 1:21; 3:10; 6:12; Col 1:16; 2:10, 15). These were ultimately responsible for Jesus' death, but he triumphed over them in his resurrection. Yet in Titus 3:1, and especially Romans 13:1-2, *exousiai* could mean human political rulers. (The word for "rulers" in Romans 13:3 [*archōn*] denotes supernatural powers in its only other Pauline uses [1 Cor 2:6, 8; Eph 2:2]). For a general discussion of this issue, see Morrison 1960. For the demonic interpretation of *exousiai* in Romans 13, see Cullmann 1956, esp. pp. 55-60, 95-114. For an opposing view, see Murray 1968:252-56. (In its only New Testament uses outside Paul, *exousiai* designates demonic powers in 1 Peter 3:22 and political governors in Luke 12:11.) For my view, which approximates Cullmann's, see Finger 1989:84-88.

[16]In my interpretation, the principalities and powers of the New Testament perform the same essential functions as the gods of the nations in Hebrew Scripture. For further discussion, see Finger 1989:84-88, 147-51, 154-58.

[17]This contrast also characterizes "the law," which on the one hand is "holy and just and good" (Rom 7:12) and, on the other, is the "dividing wall" that Jesus had to destroy (Eph 2:14-15; see Finger 1989:155-57).

[18]For fuller discussion of these issues, see Finger 1989:284-87. I am rejecting "postmillennial" interpretations of God's work in the world.

[19]The phrase is Albrecht Ritschl's ([1874] 1966:338).

[20]Though some studies show that comparatively greater or lesser government regulation in specific times and places produced certain results, these cannot directly indicate what significantly less regulation would produce throughout the range of rapidly changing modern societies. Milton and Rose Friedman (1980) argue that earlier American and British history provide evidence for unregulated capitalism's success. Yet they do not pay adequate attention to its negative effect on less developed countries.

[21]I also hold that competition cannot be supported theologically as Novak does. He maintains, correctly, that Christian faith regards life as a challenge where much depends on our decisions. Yet these decisions have mainly to do with developing attitudes of mutuality and agape toward others, which surely differs from intense competition against them. Novak correctly notices that in Jesus' parables, people are often rewarded unequally. Yet, while on occasion benefits may apparently accrue to the "haves" (Mt 25:14-30 par. Lk 19:12-17), they more often go to the "have nots" (Mt 20:1-15; 22:1-14 par. Lk 14:16-24) and reverse current notions that the wealthy are more favored. Jesus, we have seen, has no good word for the desire for riches or the rich themselves.

[22]For an interesting discussion that challenges some of these hypotheses, see Ruether 1992:143-55.

[23]I am not saying that such visions as wholes are simply alternative pictures of the Christian hope. I believe the radical kingdom vision of agape to be unique. But certain intimations of or longings for it may be mixed, along with elements of very different kinds, in other religious or social visions.

[24]It is much harder to conceive of a panentheistic God doing so, since such a God is usually thought of as coconditioned not only by natural creatures but also by the laws governing their activities. Even when these laws are understood as statistical and incompatible with rigid determinism, it is not usually thought that their normal operations can be contravened by events unusual enough to overcome much of the evil in history.

[25]Accordingly evangelistic proclamation of these new possibilities cannot simply communicate "awareness of being oppressed but nevertheless being masters of their own destiny" (Gutiérrez [1973] 1988:116) but must announce the shape of God's kingdom and the importance of responding to it through repentance and faith.

[26]It is impossible to judge how thoroughly the Spirit of Christ may pervade any such group. Though those which explicitly confess Christ may, in general, be more fully directed by his Spirit than others, some may be deeply resisting the Spirit. And since the one God calls all

people toward social wholeness, some groups which do not confess Christ, yet live in a fashion approximating his way, could be surprisingly in tune with the Spirit. Christians should not seek to judge how fully the Spirit may be present elsewhere but to reflect, by word and deed, who Jesus is and what he calls people to.

[27]For the argument that organicism, despite Ruether's "democratic" use of it, really involves hierarchy, see Bouma-Prediger 1995:154-58.

Chapter 12: A Christian Response to Psychological, Ecological & Social Alienation

[1]I have also argued, however, that some incipient self is present from before birth and that each one possesses differing inherent preferences, inclinations and aptitudes (see chapter nine). Thus whereas all selves are intrinsically shaped by their relationships, they are something more than the simple sum of those relationships.

[2]Perhaps a fear of weakness and instability also underlies some strong responses so that they are really attempts to cover up the former.

[3]Winnicott's "good-enough" mother, who provides the infant with warmth and positive regard, yet withdraws enough to let it experience its own distinctiveness and frustrations, is a good example of this (see chapter one). Jessica Benjamin outlines a theory of intersubjective development in the infant years which also points in this direction (1988: 11-50).

[4]Though organismic psychologists may conceive of these dynamics as including social drives, these exist in a self already conceived of as essentially complete (Rogers). In my view actual relationships with others, and not simply an inner desire for them, are integral to what should be called the self.

[5]Cf. what I said about the incipient self (note 1).

[6]Matthew Fox distorts this meaning of faith or trust when he makes it basically trust in our own organismic possibilities instead of in an Other, namely, God (1983:82-84). Fox replaces commitment with feeling and relationship to another with self-awareness.

[7]Our finitude and dependence on God mean that humans cannot consistently give love to others unless they have been loved. To try to love and serve others consistently without receiving love can be hurtful and is ultimately impossible.

[8]Many conservative social theologies, as we saw in chapter eleven, emphasize the pervasiveness of social evil and put little emphasis on social transformation. Many liberal theologies, in contrast, emphasize transformation but put little emphasis on evil. My approach, by stressing the possibility of significant local change, emphasizes both transformation and the pervasiveness of social evil.

References

Adorno, Theodor, and Max Horkheimer. 1972. *Dialectic of Enlightenment*. New York: Herder & Herder.

Ager, Derek. 1993. *The New Catastrophism*. Cambridge: Cambridge University Press.

Anderson, Bernhard. 1967. *Creation Versus Chaos*. New York: Association.

Barbour, Ian. 1990. *Religion in an Age of Science*. San Francisco: Harper.

Barlow, Connie, ed. 1994. *Evolution Extended*. Cambridge, Mass.: MIT Press.

Barlow, Nora, ed. 1958. *The Autobiography of Charles Darwin, 1809-1882*. New York: Norton.

Barry, Norman. 1986. *On Classical Liberalism and Libertarianism*. London: Macmillan.

———. 1987. *The New Right*. London: Croom Helm.

Barth, Karl. 1960. *Church Dogmatics 3/2*. Edinburgh: T & T Clark.

Barth, Markus. 1974. *Ephesians*. Garden City, N.Y.: Doubleday.

Baudrillard, Jean. 1975. *The Mirror of Production*. St. Louis: Telos.

Bell, Daniel. 1973. *The Coming of Post-Industrial Society*. New York: Basic Books.

———. 1976. *The Cultural Contradictions of Capitalism*. New York: Basic Books.

Benjamin, Jessica. 1978. "Authority and the Family Revisited: Or, A World Without Fathers?" *New German Critique* 13:35-58.

———. 1988. *The Bonds of Love*. New York: Pantheon.

Bentham, Jeremy. [1789] 1948. *An Introduction to the Principles of Morals and Legislation*. New York: Hafner.

Berne, Eric. 1961. *Transactional Analysis in Psychotherapy*. New York: Ballantine.

———. 1972. *What Do You Say After You Say Hello?* New York: Grove.

Bertalanffy, Ludwig von. 1968. *General Systems Theory*. New York: George Braziller.

Best, Steven, and Douglas Kellner. 1991. *Postmodern Theory*. New York: Guilford.

Birch, Charles, and John Cobb. 1981. *The Liberation of Life*. Cambridge: Cambridge University Press.

Blackstone, William, ed. 1974. *Philosophy and the Environmental Crisis*. Athens: University of Georgia Press.

Boas, George. [1965] 1990. *The Cult of the Child*. Wartburg Institute. Reprint Dallas: Spring.

Bonaventure. 1978. In *The Classics of Western Spirituality*. New York: Paulist.

Bookchin, Murray. 1982. *The Ecology of Freedom*. Palo Alto, Calif.: Cheshire.

———. 1971. *Post-scarcity Anarchism*. Berkeley, Calif.: Ramparts.

———. 1990. *Remaking Society*. Boston: South End.

Bookchin, Murray, and Dave Foreman. 1991. *Defending the Earth*. Boston: South End.

Borg, Marcus. 1984. *Conflict, Holiness and Politics in the Teaching of Jesus*. Lewiston, N.Y.: Mellen.

———. 1987. *Jesus: A New Vision*. San Francisco: Harper.

———. 1994a. *Meeting Jesus Again for the First Time*. San Francisco: Harper.

———. 1994b. *Jesus in Contemporary Scholarship*. Valley Forge, Pa.: Trinity.

Bosanquet, Nick. 1983. *After the New Right*. London: Heinemann.

Bouma-Prediger, Steven. 1995. *The Greening of Theology*. Atlanta: Scholars.

Bowler, Peter. 1983. *The Eclipse of Darwinism*. Baltimore: Johns Hopkins University Press.

———. 1984. *Evolution: The History of an Idea*. Berkeley: University of California Press.

———. 1988. *The Non-Darwinian Revolution*. Baltimore: Johns Hopkins University Press.

———. 1989. *Evolution: The History of an Idea*. Rev. ed. Berkeley: University of California Press.

Bradshaw, John. 1990. *Homecoming: Reclaiming and Championing Your Inner Child*. New York: Bantam.

Browning, Don. 1987. *Religious Thought and the Modern Psychotherapies*. Philadelphia: Fortress.

Brunner, Emil. 1960. *The Christian Doctrine of God*. Philadelphia: Westminster Press.

Buchanan, James, and Gordon Tullock. 1962. *The Calculus of Consent*. Ann Arbor: University of Michigan Press.

Bultmann, Rudolf. *Jesus and the Word*. 1934. New York: Scribner's.

———. 1951. *Theology of the New Testament*. Vol 1. New York: Scribner's.

Callicott, J. Baird. 1980. "Animal Liberation: A Triangular Affair." *Environmental Ethics* 2, no. 4:311-38.

———. 1991. "Can a Theory of Moral Sentiments Support a Genuinely Normative Environmental Ethic?" *Inquiry* 35, no. 2:183-98.

Campbell, Peter, and Edwin McMahon. 1985. *Bio-spirituality: Focusing as a Way to Grow*. Chicago: Loyola.

Capra, Fritjof. 1982. *The Turning Point*. New York: Bantam.

Capra, Fritjof, and David Steindl-Rast. 1991. *Belonging to the Universe*. San Francisco: Harper.

Chodorow, Nancy. 1978. *The Reproduction of Mothering*. Berkeley: University of California Press.

Cobb, John. 1975. *Christ in a Pluralistic Age*. Philadelphia: Westminster Press.

Cobb, John, and David Griffin. 1976. *Process Theology: An Introductory Exposition*. Philadelphia: Westminster Press.

Cobb, John, and W. Widick Schroeder, eds. 1981. *Process Philosophy and Social Thought*. Chicago: Center for the Scientific Study of Religion.

Colwell, Ernest. 1963. *Jesus and the Gospel*. New York: Oxford University Press.

Crick, Francis. 1966. *Of Molecules and Men*. Seattle: University of Washington Press.

Crossan, John Dominic. 1991. *The Historical Jesus: The Life of a Mediterranean Jewish Peasant*. San Francisco: Harper.

Culligan, Kevin. 1982. "Toward a Contemporary Model of Spiritual Direction: A Comparative Study of St. John of the Cross and Carl Rogers." In *Contemporary Psychology and Carmel*, pp. 95-166. Edited by John Sullivan. Washington, D.C.: Institute of Carmelite Studies.

Cullmann, Oscar. 1956. *The State in the New Testament*. New York: Scribner's.

———. 1959. *The Christology of the New Testament*. Philadelphia: Westminster Press.

———. 1964. *Christ and Time*. Philadelphia: Westminster Press.

Cummings, Charles. 1991. *Eco-spirituality*. New York: Paulist.

Darwin, Charles. 1859. *On the Origin of Species by Means of Natural Selection*. London: John Murray.

Davies, Paul. 1992. *The Mind of God*. New York: Simon & Schuster.

Dawkins, Richard. 1983. "Universal Darwinism." In *Evolution from Molecules to Men*, pp. 403-25. Edited by D. S. Bendall. Cambridge: Cambridge University Press.

———. 1989. *The Selfish Gene*. Oxford: Oxford University Press.

Debord, Guy. 1983. *The Society of the Spectacle*. Detroit: Black & Red.

Devall, Bill, and George Sessions. 1985. *Deep Ecology*. Salt Lake City: Peregrine Smith.

Diamond, Irene, and Gloria Orenstein. 1990. *Reweaving the World: The Emergence of Ecofeminism*. San Franscisco: Sierra Club.

Dorr, Donal. 1984. *Spirituality and Justice*. Maryknoll, N.Y.: Orbis.

———. 1990. *Integral Spirituality*. Maryknoll, N.Y.: Orbis.

Dowling, William. 1984. *Jameson, Althusser, Marx*. Ithaca, N.Y.: Cornell University Press.

Drengson, Alan, and Yuichi Inoue, eds. 1995. *The Deep Ecology Movement: An Introductory Anthology*. Berkeley, Calif.: North Atlantic.

Dunn, James D. G. 1975. *Jesus and the Spirit*. Philadelphia: Westminster Press.

———. 1980. *Christology in the Making*. Philadelphia: Westminster Press.

———. 1991. "Once More, *Pistis Christou*." In *Society of Biblical Literature 1991 Seminar Papers*. Atlanta: Scholars.

Durnbaugh, Donald. 1968. *The Believers' Church*. New York: Macmillan.

Dobzhansky, Theodosius. 1937. *Genetics and the Origin of Species*. New York: Columbia University Press.

———. 1955. *Evolution, Genetics and Man*. New York: Wiley & Sons.

———. 1962. *Mankind Evolving*. New Haven, Conn.: Yale University Press.

Egan, Harvey. 1982. *What Are They Saying About Mysticism?* Ramsey, N.J.: Paulist.

Ehrlich, Paul. 1991. "Coevolution and its Application to the Gaia Hypothesis." In *Scientists on Gaia*, pp. 19-22. Edited by Stephen Schneider and Penelope Boston. Cambridge, Mass.: MIT Press.

Eldredge, Niles. 1985. *Time Frames*. New York: Simon & Schuster.

———. 1989. *Macroevolutionary Dynamics*. New York: McGraw-Hill.

———. 1991. *The Miner's Canary: Unravelling the Mysteries of Extinction*. New York: Prentice-Hall.

Engel, Stephanie. 1980. "Femininity as Tragedy: Re-examining the New Narcissism." *Socialist Review* 53:77-104.

Fairbairn, W. R. D. 1952. *An Object-Relations Theory of the Personality*. New York: Basic Books.

Fancher, Raymond. 1973. *Psychoanalytic Psychology: The Development of Freud's Thought*. New York: W. W. Norton.

Ferguson, Marilyn. 1980. *The Aquarian Conspiracy*. Los Angeles: Jeremy P. Tarcher.

Finger, Thomas. 1985-1989. *Christian Theology: An Eschatological Approach*. 2 vols. Scottdale, Penn.: Herald.

———. 1994. "Anabaptism and Eastern Orthodoxy: Some Unexpected Similarities?" *Journal of Ecumenical Studies* 31, nos. 1 and 2 (Winter-Spring): 67-91.

Fox, Matthew. 1983. *Original Blessing*. Santa Fe, N.M.: Bear.

———. 1988. *The Coming of the Cosmic Christ*. New York: Harper & Row.

———. 1990. *A Spirituality Named Compassion*. New York: Harper & Row.

———. 1992. *Sheer Joy: Conversations with Thomas Aquinas on Creation Spirituality*. San Francisco: Harper.

———. 1994. *The Reinvention of Work*. San Francisco: Harper.

Fox, Warwick. 1984. "Deep Ecology: A New Philosophy of Our Time?" *The Ecologist* 14.

———. 1989. "The Deep Ecology-Ecofeminism Debate and Its Parallels." *Environmental Ethics* 11, no. 1 (Spring): 5-25.

Freire, Paulo. 1972. *The Pedagogy of the Oppressed*. New York: Herder & Herder.

Freud, Sigmund. [1920] 1955. *Beyond the Pleasure Principle*. Standard Edition of the Complete Psychological Works 8. London: Hogarth.

Friedman, Milton. 1953. *Essays in Positive Economics*. Chicago: University of Chicago Press.

———. 1962. *Capitalism and Freedom*. Chicago: University of Chicago Press.

———. 1975. *Unemployment Versus Inflation?* London: Institute of Economic Affairs.

Friedman, Milton, and Rose Friedman. 1980. *Free to Choose*. London: Seckler & Warburg.

Frosh, Stephen. 1987. *The Politics of Psychoanalysis*. New Haven, Conn.: Yale University Press.

———. 1991. *Identity Crisis: Modernity, Psychoanalysis and the Self*. New York: Routledge.

Funk, Robert, and Roy Hoover. 1993. *The Five Gospels*. New York: Macmillan.

Galbraith, John Kenneth. 1952. *American Capitalism*. Cambridge, Mass.: Riverside.

Gamow, George. 1961. *Biography of Physics*. New York: Harper & Row.

Gilder, George. 1981. *Wealth and Poverty*. New York: Basic Books.

Goldstein, Kurt. 1939. *The Organism*. New York: American Book.

———. 1940. *Human Nature in the Light of Psychopathology.* New York: Schocken.

Gould, Stephen Jay. 1987. *Time's Arrow, Time's Cycle.* Cambridge, Mass.: Harvard University Press.

———. 1992. "Punctuated Equilibrium in Fact and Theory." In *The Dynamics of Evolution: The Punctuated Equilibrium Debate in the Natural and Social Sciences,* pp. 54-84. Edited by Albert Somit and Steven Peterson. Ithaca, N.Y.: Cornell University Press.

Grant, Robert, and David Freedman. 1960. *The Secret Sayings of Jesus.* New York: Doubleday.

Green, Arnold. 1945-1946. "Social Values and Psychotherapy." *Journal of Personality* 14.

Greenberg, Jay, and Stephen Mitchell. 1983. *Object Relations in Psychoanalytic Theory.* Cambridge, Mass.: Harvard University Press.

Greene, John. 1981. *Science, Ideology and World View: Essays in the History of Evolutionary Ideas.* Berkeley: University of California Press.

Griffin, David, ed. 1988. *Spirituality and Society.* Albany, N.Y.: SUNY Press.

———. 1990. *Sacred Interconnections.* Albany, N.Y.: SUNY Press.

Gutiérrez, Gustavo. [1973] 1988. *A Theology of Liberation.* Maryknoll, N.Y.: Orbis.

Hardy, Alister. 1975. *The Biology of God.* London: Jonanthan Cape.

Harland, Gordon. 1960. *The Thought of Reinhold Niebuhr.* New York: Oxford University Press.

Harris, Thomas. 1967. *I'm OK—You're OK.* New York: Harper & Row.

Hayek, F. A. 1949. *The Road to Serfdom.* Chicago: University of Chicago Press.

———. 1954. *Individualism and the Economic Order.* London: Routledge & Kegan Paul.

———. 1955. *The Counter-Revolution of Science.* Glencoe, Ill.: Free Press.

———. 1960. *The Constitution of Liberty.* London: RKP.

———. 1979. *The Political Order of a Free People.* Vol. 3 of *Law, Legislation and Liberty.* London: Routledge & Kegan Paul.

Hays, Richard. 1983. *The Faith of Jesus Christ.* Chico, Calif.: Scholars.

———. 1991. "*Pistis* and Pauline Christology: What Is at Stake?" In *Society of Biblical Literature 1991 Seminar Papers.* Atlanta: Scholars.

Hefner, Philip. 1993. *The Human Factor: Evolution, Culture and Religion.* Minneapolis: Fortress.

Hegel, G. W. F. [1807] 1931. *The Phenomenology of the Mind.* New York: Harper.

Hess, Karl. 1992. *Visions upon the Land: Man and Nature on the Western Range.* Washington, D.C.: Island.

Hollifield, Brooks. 1983. *A History of Pastoral Care in America: From Salvation to Self-Realization.* Nashville: Abingdon.

Hsu, Kenneth. 1986. *The Great Dying.* San Diego: Harcourt Brace Jovanovich.

Hume, David. [1739] 1888. *A Treatise of Human Nature.* Edited by L. A. Selby-Bigge. Oxford: Clarendon.

———. [1751] 1957. *An Enquiry Concerning the Principles of Morals.* New York: Bobbs-Merrill.

Huxley, Julian. 1942. *Evolution: The Modern Synthesis.* New York: Harper.

Huxley, Thomas. 1989. *Evolution and Ethics: With New Essays on Its Victorian and Sociobiological Context.* Princeton, N.J.: Princeton University Press.

Jameson, Fredric. 1971. *Marxism and Form.* Princeton, N.J.: Princeton University Press.

———. 1981. *The Political Unconscious.* Ithaca, N.Y.: Cornell University Press.

———. 1991. *Postmodernism.* Durham, N.C.: Duke University Press.

Jeremias, Joachim. 1982. *Jesus' Promise to the Nations.* Philadelphia: Fortress.

John of the Cross. 1991a. *The Ascent of Mt. Carmel.* In *The Collected Works of St. John of the Cross.* Translated by Kieran Kavanaugh and Otilio Rodriguez. Rev. ed. Washington, D.C.: ICS.

———. 1991b. *The Dark Night.* In *The Collected Works of St. John of the Cross.* Translated by Kieran Kavanaugh and Otilio Rodriguez. Rev. ed. Washington, D.C.: ICS.

———. 1991c. *The Living Flame of Love.* In *The Collected Works of St. John of the Cross.* Translated by Kieran Kavanaugh and Otilio Rodriguez. Rev. ed. Washington, D.C.: ICS.

Johnson, Luke Timothy. 1996. *The Real Jesus.* San Francisco: Harper.

Jones, Alan. 1992. *Journey into Christ.* Cambridge, Mass.: Cowley.

Joseph, Lawrence. 1990. *Gaia: The Growth of an Idea.* New York: St. Martin's.

Jung, C. G. 1933. *Modern Man in Search of a Soul.* New York: Harcourt Brace.

———. 1957. *The Undiscovered Self.* New York: New American Library.

Käsemann, Ernst. 1969. *New Testament Questions of Today.* Philadelphia: Fortress.

Kaufman, Gordon. 1985. *Theology for a Nuclear Age.* Philadelphia: Westminster Press.

Keating, Thomas. 1986. *Open Mind, Open Heart: The Comtemplative Dimension of the Gospel.* Amity, N.Y.: Amity House.

Kirchner, James. 1991. "The Gaian Hypotheses: Are They Testable? Are They Useful?" In *Scientists on Gaia,* pp. 38-96. Edited by Stephen Schneider and Penelope Boston. Cambridge, Mass.: MIT Press.

Kloppenborg, John. 1987. *The Formation of Q.* Philadelphia: Fortress.

Kovel, Joel. 1976. *A Complete Guide to Therapy.* New York: Pantheon.

LaCugna, Catherine Mowry. 1991. *God for Us.* San Francisco: Harper.

Lasch, Christopher. 1979. *The Culture of Narcissism.* New York: W. W. Norton.

———. 1984. *The Minimal Self.* New York: W. W. Norton.

Laszlo, Ervin. 1972. *The Systems View of the World.* New York: George Braziller.

Lauer, Quentin. 1987. *A Reading of Hegel's "Phenomenology of Spirit."* New York: Fordham University Press.

Leopold, Aldo. 1949. *A Sand County Almanac.* New York: Oxford University Press.

Levins, Richard, and Richard Lewontin. 1985. *The Dialectical Biologist.* Cambridge, Mass.: Harvard University Press.

Lewontin, Richard. 1991. *Biology as Ideology: The Doctrine of DNA.* New York: HarperCollins.

Locke, John. [1689] 1965. *Essay Concerning Human Understanding.* New York: Collier.

Lovejoy, Arthur. 1936. *The Great Chain of Being.* Cambridge, Mass.: Harvard University Press.

Lovelock, James. 1987. *Gaia: A New Look at Life on Earth.* New York: Oxford University Press.

———. 1988. *The Ages of Gaia.* New York: W. W. Norton.

———. 1989. In *Abstracts of Chapman Conference on GAIA Hypothesis* (March).

Lovelock, James, and Michael Allaby. 1983. *The Great Extinction.* Garden City, N.Y.: Doubleday.

Lyell, Charles. 1830-1833. *Principles of Geology.* 3 vols. London: John Murray.

Lyotard, Jean-Francois. 1984. *The Postmodern Condition.* Minneapolis: University of Minnesota Press.

Machovec, Milan. 1972. *Jesus fur Atheisten.* Stuttgart: Kreuz-Verlag.

Macquarrie, John. 1965. *An Existentialist Theology.* New York: Harper.

Mahoney, George. 1991. *Mysticism and the New Age.* New York: Alba House.

Malte, Faber, and John Proops. 1993. *Evolution, Time, Production and the Environment.* 2nd ed., rev. and enl. Berlin: Springer-Verlag.

Mandel, Ernest. 1975. *Late Capitalism.* London: NLB.

Manson, T. W. 1955. *The Teaching of Jesus.* Cambridge, Mass.: Harvard University Press.

Marcuse, Herbert. 1964. *One-Dimensional Man.* Boston: Beacon.

———. 1966. *Eros and Civilization.* Boston: Beacon.

Margulis, Lynn, and Dorion Sagan. 1986. *Microcosmos.* New York: Touchstone.

Maslow, Abraham. 1954. *Motivation and Personality.* New York: Harper.

———. 1965. *Eupsychian Management.* Homewood, Ill.: Dorsey.

Mayr, Ernst. 1942. *Systematics and the Origin of the Species.* New York: Columbia University Press.

———. 1992. "Speciational Evolution or Punctuated Equilibria." In *The Dynamics of Evolution: The Punctuated Equilibrium Debate in the Natural and Social Sciences,* pp. 21-52. Edited by Albert Somit and Steven Peterson. Ithaca, N.Y.: Cornell University Press.

McCann, Dennis. 1981. *Christian Realism and Liberation Theology.* Maryknoll, N.Y.: Orbis.

McDaniel, Jay. 1990. *Earth, Sky, Gods and Mortals: Developing an Ecological Spirituality.* Mystic, Conn.: Twenty-third.

McFague, Sallie. 1987. *Models of God.* Philadelphia: Fortress.

———. 1993. *The Body of God.* Minneapolis: Fortress.

McNamara, William. 1983. *Earthy Mysticism.* New York: Crossroad.

———. [1977] 1991. *Mystical Passion.* New York: Paulist; Rockport, Maine: Element.

Meeks, Wayne. 1983. *The First Urban Christians.* New Haven, Conn.: Yale University Press.

———, ed. 1993. *The HarperCollins Study Bible.* New York: HarperCollins.

Merchant, Carolyn. 1992. *Radical Ecology.* New York: Routledge.

———. 1996. *Earthcare.* New York: Routledge.

Merton, Thomas. 1951. *The Ascent to Truth.* New York: Harcourt Brace.

———. 1968. *Zen and the Birds of Appetite.* New York: New Directions.

———. 1969. *Contemplative Prayer.* Garden City, N.Y.: Doubleday.

———. 1978. *The New Man.* New York: Farrar, Strauss & Giroux.

Miles, Margaret. 1990. *Practicing Christianity: Critical Perspectives for an Embodied Christianity.* New York: Crossroad.

Minear, Paul. 1960. *Images of the Church in the New Testament.* Philadelphia: Westminster Press.

———. 1971. *The Obedience of Faith.* Naperville, Ill.: Allenson.

Moltmann, Jürgen. 1967. *Theology of Hope.* New York: Harper & Row.

———. 1974. *The Crucified God.* New York: Harper & Row.

———. 1979. *The Future of Creation.* Philadelphia: Fortress.

———. 1981. *The Trinity and the Kingdom.* New York: Harper.

———. 1985. *God in Creation.* San Francisco: Harper.

———. 1990. *The Way of Jesus Christ.* San Francisco: Harper.

Morrison, Clinton. 1960. *The Powers That Be.* Naperville, Ill.: Allenson.

Murray, Charles. 1984. *Losing Ground: American Social Policy, 1950-1980.* New York: Basic Books.

Murray, John. 1968. *The Epistle to the Romans.* Grand Rapids, Mich.: Eerdmans.

Nash, Roderick. 1989. *The Rights of Nature.* Madison: University of Wisconsin Press.

Niebuhr, H. Richard. 1951. *Christ and Culture.* New York: Harper.

Niebuhr, Reinhold. 1934. "The Problem of Communist Religion." *The World Tomorrow* 17:378-79.

———. 1941. *The Nature and Destiny of Man.* Vol. 1. New York: Scribner's.

———. 1943. *The Nature and Destiny of Man.* Vol. 2. New York: Scribner's.

———. 1944. *The Children of Light and the Children of Darkness.* New York: Scribner's.

———. 1959. *The Structure of Nations and Empires.* New York: Scribner's.

Niebuhr, Reinhold, and Paul Sigmund. 1969. *The Democratic Experience: Past and Prospects.* New York: Praeger.

Nitecki, Matthew, ed. 1988. *Evolutionary Progress.* Chicago: University of Chicago Press.

Novak, Michael. 1969. *A Theology for Radical Politics.* New York: Herder and Herder.

———. 1970. *The Experience of Nothingness.* New York: Harper & Row.

———. 1982. *The Spirit of Democratic Capitalism.* New York: Simon & Schuster.

———. 1986. *Will It Liberate?* New York: Paulist.

———, ed. 1981. *Liberation South, Liberation North.* Washington, D.C.: American Enterprise Institute for Public Policy Research.

Novak, Michael, and Michael Jackson, eds. 1985. *Latin America: Dependency or Interdependence?* Washington, D.C.: American Enterprise Institute for Public Policy Research.

Nozick, Robert. 1974. *Anarchy, State and Utopia.* New York: Basic Books.

Nygren, Anders. 1949. *Commentary on Romans.* Philadelphia: Fortress.

———. 1953. *Agape and Eros.* Philadelphia: Westminster Press.

Oliwenstein, Lori. 1993. "Onward and Upward?" *Discover,* June, pp. 22-24.

Olson, Mancur. 1965. *The Logic of Collective Action.* New Haven, Conn.: Yale University Press.

———. 1982. *The Rise and Decline of Nations.* New Haven, Conn.: Yale University Press.

Passmore, John. 1974. *Man's Responsibility for Nature.* London: Duckworth.

Pennington, M. Basil. 1977. *Daily We Touch Him.* Garden City, N.Y.: Doubleday.

Pepper, Stephen. 1984. *The Roots of Modern Environmentalism.* London: Croon Helm.

Perrin, Norman. 1967. *Rediscovering the Teachings of Jesus.* New York: Harper & Row.

———. 1974. *A Modern Pilgrimage in New Testament Christology.* Philadelphia: Fortress.

Petrovič, Gajo. 1967. "Alienation." In *The Encyclopedia of Philosophy,* 1:76-81. New York: Macmillan/Free Press.

Plumwood, Val. 1993. *Feminism and the Mystery of Nature.* London: Routledge.

Rampino, Michael. 1991. "Gaia Versus Shiva." In *Scientists on Gaia,* pp. 382-90. Edited by Stephen Schneider and Penelope Boston. Cambridge, Mass.: MIT Press.

Ramsey, Paul. 1950. *Basic Christian Ethics.* Chicago: University of Chicago Press.

Reumann, John. 1973. *Creation and New Creation.* Minneapolis: Augsburg.

Ritschl, Albrecht. [1874] 1966. *The Christian Doctrine of Justification and Reconciliation.* Clifton, N.J.: Reference Book.

Robinson, H. Wheeler. [1935] 1980. *Corporate Personality in Ancient Israel.* Rev. ed. Philadelphia: Fortress.

Rodman, John. 1977. "Liberation of Nature?" *Inquiry* 20 (Spring): 94-101.

Rogers, Carl. 1951. *Client-Centered Therapy.* Boston: Houghton Mifflin.

———. 1961. *On Becoming a Person.* Boston: Houghton Mifflin.

Rolston, Holmes, III. 1987. *Science and Religion.* New York: Random House.

———. 1988. *Environmental Ethics.* Philadelphia: Temple University Press.

Roszak, Theodore. 1992. *The Voice of the Earth: An Exploration of Ecopsychology.* New York: Simon & Schuster.

Rothbard, Murray. 1973. *For a New Liberty.* New York: Macmillan.

Ruether, Rosemary Radford. 1970. *The Radical Kingdom.* New York: Paulist.

———. 1972. *Liberation Theology.* New York: Paulist.

———. 1975. *New Woman/New Earth.* New York: Seabury.

———. 1983a. *Sexism and God-Talk.* Boston: Beacon.

———. 1983b. *To Change the World.* New York: Crossroad.

———. 1992. *Gaia and God.* San Francisco: Harper.

———. 1993. *The Body of God.* Minneapolis: Fortress.

Ruse, Michael. 1982. *Darwinism Defended.* Reading, Mass.: Addison-Wesley.

———. 1988. *Philosophy of Biology Today.* Albany, N.Y.: SUNY Press.

———. 1989. *The Darwinian Paradigm.* New York: Routledge.

Sagan, Dorion. 1990. *Biospheres.* New York: McGraw-Hill.

Schneider, Stephen, and Penelope Boston, eds. 1991. *Scientists on Gaia.* Cambridge, Mass.: MIT Press.

Schumpeter, Joseph. 1979. *Capitalism, Socialism, and Democracy.* London: Allen & Unwin.

Schüssler Fiorenza, Elisabeth. 1983. *In Memory of Her.* New York: Crossroad.

———. 1984. *Bread Not Stone.* Boston: Beacon.

———. 1994. *Jesus: Miriam's Child, Sophia's Prophet.* New York: Continuum.

Schweitzer, Albert. [1906] 1968. *The Quest of the Historical Jesus.* New York: Macmillan.

Segundo, Juan Luis. 1976. *The Liberation of Theology.* Maryknoll, N.Y.: Orbis.

———. 1982. *An Evolutionary Approach to Jesus of Nazareth.* Maryknoll, N.Y.: Orbis.

———. 1984. *Faith and Ideologies.* Maryknoll, N.Y.: Orbis.

———. 1992. *The Liberation of Dogma.* Maryknoll, N.Y.: Orbis.

Simpson, George Gaylord. 1944. *Tempo and Mode in Evolution.* New York: Columbia.

———. 1949. *The Meaning of Evolution.* New Haven, Conn.: Yale University Press.

Singer, Peter. 1975. *Animal Liberation.* New York: Random House.

Smith, Adam. [1759, 1792] 1976. *The Theory of the Moral Sentiments.* Edited by D. D. Raphael and A. L. Macfie. Indianapolis: Liberty.

———. [1776] 1985. *The Wealth of the Nations.* Abriged ed. New York: Random House.

Sobrino, Jon. 1978. *Christology at the Crossroads.* Maryknoll, N.Y.: Orbis.

Somit, Albert, and Steven Peterson. 1992. *The Dynamics of Evolution: The Punctuated Equilibrium Debate in the Natural and Social Sciences.* Ithaca, N.Y.: Cornell University Press.

Stanley, Steven. 1981. *The New Evolutionary Timetable.* New York: Basic Books.

Stigler, George. 1975. *The Citizen and the State.* Chicago: University of Chicago Press.

Swan, Jim, and Thomas Hurley. 1985. "Questions Raised by the Symposium: Is the Earth a Living Organism?" In *Proceedings of "Is the Earth a Living Organism?"* Amherst, Mass. (August).

Swimme, Brian, and Thomas Berry. 1992. *The Universe Story.* San Francisco: Harper.

Szasz, Thomas. 1974. *The Myth of Mental Illness.* New York: Harper & Row.

———. 1977. *The Theology of Medicine.* Baton Rouge: Lousiana State University Press.

———. 1978. *The Myth of Psychotherapy.* Garden City, N.Y.: Anchor/Doubleday.

———. 1992. *Our Right to Drugs.* New York: Praeger.

Teresa of Ávila. [1562-1565] 1960. *The Life of Teresa of Ávila.* In *The Collected Works of St. Teresa of Ávila,* vol. 1. Translated by Kieran Kavanaugh and Otilio Rodriguez. Washington, D.C.: Institute of Carmelite Studies.

———. [1577] 1980. *The Interior Castle.* In *The Collected Works of St. Teresa of Ávila,* vol. 2. Translated by Kieran Kavanaugh and Otilio Rodriguez. Washington, D.C.: Institute of Carmelite Studies.

Theissen, Gerd. 1985. *Biblical Faith: An Evolutionary Approach.* Philadelphia: Fortress.

Thompson, William, ed. 1987. *Gaia, a Way of Knowing: Political Implications of the New Biology.* Great Barrington, Mass.: Lindisfarne.

Toulmin, Stephen, and June Goodfield. 1962. *The Architecture of Matter.* New York: Harper.

Vaughan, Judith. 1983. *Sociality, Ethics and Social Change: A Critical Appraisal of Reinhold Niebuhr's Ethics in the Light of Rosemary Radford Ruether's Works.* Lanham, Md.: University Press of America.

Visvader, John. 1991. "Gaia and the Myths of Harmony." In *Scientists on Gaia,* pp. 33-37. Edited by Stephen Schneider and Penelope Boston. Cambridge, Mass.: MIT Press.

Weiss, Johannes. [1892] 1968. *Jesus' Proclamation of the Kingdom.* Philadelphia: Fortress.

Welch, John. 1982. *Spiritual Pilgrims: Teresa of Ávila and Carl Jung.* New York: Paulist.

———. 1990. *When Gods Die.* New York: Paulist.

Whitehead, Alfred North. 1929. *Process and Reality.* New York: Free Press.

Whitfield, Charles. 1987. *Healing the Child Within.* Deerfield Beach, Fla.: Health Communications.

Wilkins, Michael, and J. P. Moreland, eds. 1995. *Jesus Under Fire.* Grand Rapids, Mich.: Zondervan.

Williams, G. R. 1991. "Gaian and Nongaian Explanations for the Contemporary Level of Atmospheric Oxygen." In *Scientists on Gaia,* pp. 167-73. Edited by Steven Schneider and Penelope Boston. Cambridge, Mass.: MIT Press.

Witherington, Ben, III. 1990. *The Christology of Jesus.* Minneapolis: Fortress.

Wolff, Hans Walter. 1974. *Anthropology of the Old Testament.* Philadelphia: Fortress.

Wright, N. T. 1992. *The New Testament and the People of God.* Minneapolis: Fortress.

Yoder, John Howard. 1972. *The Politics of Jesus.* Grand Rapids, Mich.: Eerdmans.

Young, Henry. 1990. *Hope in Process.* Minneapolis: Augsburg Fortress.

Young, Norman. 1976. *Creator, Creation and Faith.* Philadelphia: Westminster Press.

Author Index